Daily Readings from
Spiritual Classics

Daily Readings from Spiritual Classics

Edited by

Paul Ofstedal

Augsburg • Minneapolis

To
Anne, Daniel, Joseph, Ruth,
and my dear wife Dorothea

DAILY READINGS FROM SPIRITUAL CLASSICS

Copyright © 1990 Augsburg Fortress. All rights reserved. Except for brief quotations in critical articles and reviews, no part of this book may be reproduced in any manner without prior written permission from the publisher. Write to: Permissions, Augsburg Fortress, 426 S. Fifth Street, Box 1209, Minneapolis, MN 55440.

Scripture quotations unless otherwise noted are from the Revised Standard Version of the Bible, copyright 1946, 1952, and 1971 by the Division of Christian Education of the National Council of Churches.

Cover design: Jennifer Brommet

Library of Congress Cataloging-in-Publication Data

Daily readings from spiritual classics / edited by Paul Ofstedal.
    p.   cm.
   ISBN 0-8066-2424-8
   1. Devotional calendars.   I. Ofstedal, Paul, 1932–
BV4810.D257   1990
242'.2—dc19   89-30976
                                                CIP

The paper used in this publication meets the minimum requirements of American National Standard for Information Sciences—Permanence of Paper for Printed Library Materials. ANSI Z329.48-1984.

Manufactured in the U.S.A.   AF 9-2424

94   93   4   5   6   7   8   9   10

CONTENTS

ABOUT THE
CONTRIBUTORS

Susan Reese Carloss is a pastor of the Evangelical Lutheran Church in America (ELCA) serving a congregation in Storm Lake, Iowa.

Alvin Rogness is president emeritus of Luther Northwestern Theological Seminary, St. Paul, Minnesota, and the author of many books.

Mary Hull Mohr is professor of renaissance, medieval, and English literature at Luther College, Decorah, Iowa.

Allan Sager is professor of contextual education and director of internships at Trinity Lutheran Seminary in Columbus, Ohio, and author of *Gospel-Centered Spirituality*.

Mary Schramm formerly codirected the retreat program at Holden Village in Chelan, Washington, and now manages St. Martin's Table, a Christian education center in Minneapolis. She is author of *Gifts of Grace*.

Richard Koenig is an ELCA pastor serving a congregation in Woburn, Massachusetts, and has served as editor of *Lutheran Partners* magazine.

William Smith is professor of pastoral theology and ministry at Luther Northwestern Theological Seminary.

Robert Stackel is a retired ELCA pastor living in Charlotte, North Carolina.

Walter Wietzke is a retired ELCA pastor who served as director of the Division for Theological Education and Ministry of the American Lutheran Church.

Gracia Grindal is associate professor of pastoral theology and ministry at Luther Northwestern Theological Seminary.

James Limburg is professor of Old Testament at Luther Northwestern Theological Seminary and author of *Psalms for Sojourners*.

Jane Strohl is associate professor of church history at Luther Northwestern Theological Seminary.

Vernon Schreiber is an ELCA pastor serving a congregation in Yardley, Pennsylvania, and author of *Abba! Father!*

Herbert Brokering is a retired ELCA pastor living in Minneapolis, and editor of *Luther's Prayers*.

Wilfred Bockelman is a retired ELCA pastor living in Burnsville, Minnesota, author of *Finding the Right Words,* and creator of the board game "Life Stories."

Durwood Buchheim is professor of preaching at Wartburg Theological Seminary, Dubuque, Iowa.

Stephanie Frey is an ELCA pastor serving a congregation in St. James, Minnesota.

Arndt Halvorson is professor emeritus of pastoral theology and ministry at Luther Northwestern Theological Seminary.

Roy Hammerling is an ELCA pastor serving a congregation in South Bend, Indiana.

Edna Hong is author of numerous books and, with her husband Howard, is the coeditor of the critical edition of the works of Søren Kierkegaard in English.

Howard Hong is professor emeritus at St. Olaf College in Northfield, Minnesota.

Hubert Nelson is an ELCA pastor serving a congregation in Minneapolis.

Carroll and Mary Hinderlie live in Minneapolis. Carroll is a retired ELCA pastor and Carroll and Mary together directed the retreat program at Holden Village in Chelan, Washington.

Jeanette Strandjord is an ELCA pastor serving a congregation in Spring Green, Wisconsin.

Mark Gravrock is an ELCA pastor on the faculty of Lutheran Bible Institute in Seattle, Washington.

Marilyn Preus, writer and teacher, is on the staff at Victory Lutheran Church in Minneapolis.

Nelson Preus is a retired ELCA pastor and former district president of the American Lutheran Church, now living in Fridley, Minnesota.

Paul Ofstedal is an ELCA pastor serving a congregation in St. Paul, Minnesota.

PREFACE

C. S. Lewis argued for reading books of time-tested value. "A new book is still on its trial. . . . It has to be tested against the great body of Christian thought down the ages, and all its hidden implications (often unsuspected by the author himself) have to be brought to light. . . . The only safety is to have a standard of plain, central Christianity . . . which puts the controversies of the moment in their proper perspective. Such a standard can be acquired only from the old books. It is a good rule, after reading a new book, never to allow yourself another new one till you have read an old one in between" (*Letters of C. S. Lewis,* Harcourt Brace Jovanovich, 1975).

But how to get acquainted with the "old books"? The following pages introduce the reader to 26 of the finest writers from St. Augustine to the present. Two weeks of readings are devoted to each. These include a preface introducing each writer and accompanying devotions by a contemporary theologian, commenting on selected excerpts from the writer's work. We've also included a suggested bibliography. It's only a start, but we hope to whet your appetite for more from these and yet other Christian classics. The Hasidic unit, though not Christian, acquaints us with a kindred spirituality worth our knowing.

I regret that two noted contemporary theologians died before completing their contributions: Dr. Gerhard Frost and Dr. Joseph Sittler. Lacking Dr. Frost's unit, I've included 14 of Frost's own writings. The person to whom he refers in the first piece happens to be Joe Sittler, so we have something of the legacy of both of these men.

Now, put yourself in the shoes of the contributors who dared to publicly "gild the lily" by adding their own commentary to excerpts from recognized classics! Theirs has been a humbling task, a task requiring courage, entered into with trepidation. We are in their debt. This had to be a labor of love for them and for Augsburg. I also thank the staff and members of First Lutheran Church in Williston, North Dakota, for their encouragement in this protracted project.

I have dedicated this to my beloved family as a combined guilt and love offering. The love hardly needs comment, but the guilt does. My intentions ever since I took a "Christian Classics" course at Luther College

(Decorah, Iowa) were to acquaint my future family with these beacons of faith and wisdom. Too many years went by before I acted on those good intentions. Once more, it's "better late than never."

Throughout this volume, source references that relate directly to the classic author in question are keyed, using the author-date reference system, to the bibliography at the back of the book. As you read, you will note, following quoted material, both an author's last name and a year enclosed in parentheses. To find the source of a quote, refer to the bibliography at the back of the book. There the last name of the author in parentheses is listed alphabetically, followed by the year of publication and the rest of the source information.

May our reading herein be to the praise of his glory who made peace by the blood of his cross (Col. 1:20).

PAUL OFSTEDAL
Ash Wednesday, 1989

ACKNOWLEDGMENTS

"The Apologist's Evening Prayer" is from *Poems* by C. S. Lewis, copyright © 1964 by the Executors of the Estate of C. S. Lewis, and is reprinted by permission of Harcourt Brace Jovanovich, Inc. and William Collins Sons & Company, Ltd.

Excerpts from *The Pilgrim's Regress: An Allegorical Apology for Christianity* copyright © 1958 Eerdmans, Grand Rapids, MI, are used by permission of William Collins and Sons.

Excerpts from *Meditations with Meister Eckhart,* selections, translations, and adaptations by Matthew Fox, copyright © 1983 Bear & Company, Inc., P.O. Drawer 2860, Santa Fe, NM 87504-2860, are used by permission.

Excerpts from *Disciples and Other Strangers* by Edward J. Farrell, copyright © 1974 Dimension Books, Denville, NJ 07834, are used by permission.

Excerpts from *The Silent Life* by Thomas Merton copyright © 1957 by The Abbey of Our Lady of Gethsemani, renewal copyright © 1985 by the Trustees of the Thomas Merton Legacy Trust, are reprinted by permission of Farrar, Straus & Giroux, Inc. and the Merton Legacy Trust.

Excerpts from *Thoughts in Solitude* by Thomas Merton, copyright © 1956 New Directions Publishing Corporation, are used by permission.

Excerpts from *New Seeds of Contemplation* by Thomas Merton, copyright © 1961 by the Abbey of Gethsemani, Inc., are reprinted by permission of New Directions Publishing Corporation.

Excerpts from *The Imitation of Christ* by Thomas à Kempis copyright © 1986 Octagon Books, a division of Hippocrene Books, are used by permission.

Excerpts from *Pensees* by Blaise Pascal copyright © 1958 E. P. Dutton & Co. are used by permission of J. M. Dent & Sons and Everyman's Library.

Excerpts from *The Habit of Being* by Flannery O'Connor, copyright © 1979 by Regina O'Connor, are reprinted by permission of Farrar, Straus & Giroux, Inc.

Excerpts from *One Generation After* by Elie Wiesel, copyright © 1970 by Elie Wiesel, are reprinted by permission of Random House, Inc. and Georges Borchardt, Inc.

Excerpts from *The Practice of the Presence of God* by Brother Lawrence, translated by G. Symons, copyright © 1941 Forward Movement Publications, 412 Sycamore Street, Cincinnati, OH, are used by permission.

Excerpts from *The Practice of the Presence of God* by Brother Lawrence of the Resurrection, translation by John J. Delaney, translation copyright © 1977 by John J. Delaney, are used by permission of Doubleday, a division of Bantam Doubleday Dell Publishing Group, Inc.

Excerpt from "Lord of All Hopefulness" is reprinted by permission of Oxford University Press, London.

Excerpt from "Eternal Spirit of the Living Christ," copyright © 1974 by The Hymn Society, Texas Christian University, Fort Worth, TX 76129, all rights reserved, is used by permission.

Excerpts from *The Prayer of Cosa* by Jessey Cornelia, copyright © 1985 by Jessey Cornelia, are reprinted by permission of Harper & Row, Publishers, Inc.

Excerpt from "All Creatures of Our God and King," text copyright © J. Curwen and Sons, is used by permission.

Susan Reese Carloss

C. S. LEWIS

ACH year from 1950 to 1956, a new book was published in a captivating children's series: the Chronicles of Narnia. The author of the series had already established himself in the fields of medieval and 16th-century literature and Christian apologetics; his science fiction writings were popular, and he had captured the attention of a wide audience through his radio series for the British Broadcasting Corporation. But when the lively imagination of C. S. Lewis brought us from our world into the mythical world of Narnia, he may have given us the most enduring of his writings.

Clive Staples Lewis (1898–1963) was born in Belfast, Northern Ireland.

Lewis taught for 40 years, mostly at Magdalen College, Oxford, but at the last he held the chair in Medieval and Renaissance English literature at Cambridge University. His literary criticism is still required reading for students of English literature. His Christian writing, fairy tales, and science fiction revealed the reason and logic of the scholar that he was, and the creative imagination of the poet that he hoped to be.

He used fantasy and myth in the seven Chronicles of Narnia and in his science fiction: *Out of the Silent Planet, Perelandra,* and *That Hideous Strength.* Fantasy also was employed in *The Great Divorce,* in *Till We Have Faces,* his personal favorite, and in his popular *The Screwtape Letters.*

The strength of his logical thought was displayed in his letters, essays, sermons, and poetry, as well as his apologetics: *The Problem of Pain, Mere Christianity, The Abolition of Man, Miracles, The Four Loves,* and *Letters to Malcolm.* Although he was raised in a Christian home, Lewis's own journey to faith was a long and complicated one. Two of his books describe his spiritual quest: *The Pilgrim's Regress* and *Surprised by Joy.*

C. S. Lewis is a popular writer because he wrote to laypeople as a layperson; his style is straightforward, clear, and respectful of his readers. His brilliant imagery continues to communicate the gospel in fresh and powerful ways. He placed into the service of the gospel his learning, his logic, his imagination, and the strength of his conviction. His unique style bears a credible, relevant witness that will endure.

Lion Song

DAY 1 In *The Magician's Nephew* in the Chronicles of Narnia, the divine Lion, Aslan, sings the land of Narnia into being. The tale imagines Narnia's creation in these words:

"The Lion was pacing to and fro about that empty land singing his new song. . . . And as he walked and sang the valley grew green with grass. It spread out from the Lion like a pool. It ran up the sides of the little hills like a wave.

"Polly was . . . beginning to see the connection between the music and the things that were happening. . . . When you listened to his song you heard the things he was making up: when you looked round you, you saw them" (Lewis 1955a).

"The heavens are telling the glory of God . . ." (Ps. 19:1). Everywhere we look, there are signs of the Creator's almightiness, visible in each designer original.

The Maker of heaven and earth created all things by the commanding power of the Word. Word said, "Let there be." And there was! Where there was nothing, Word called into being a whole world, and people to inhabit it. Word made us, and a beautiful world to meet our creature-needs. "He spoke, and it came to be" (Ps. 33:9).

Our faith affirms that this Word of power became flesh in a person. In Jesus Christ, the Word broke into song: all of God's grace notes rang out in him, and the music of redemption was heard by the world that he had made. It was nothing less than a new creation. "He was in the beginning with God; all things were made through him, and without him was not anything made that was made" (John 1:2-3). "For in him all things were created, in heaven and on earth, visible and invisible, . . . all things were created through him and for him" (Col. 1:16).

The creation of a work of art, the writing of a work of literature, the birth of a child: each of these can be for the creator an occasion for great joy. What joy the Creator of all things must have had in making a world, as Word spoke into being each rock, every tree! "When he established the heavens, I was there, . . . then I was beside him, . . . and I was daily his delight, rejoicing before him always, rejoicing in his inhabited world . . ." (Prov. 8:27a, 30-31).

God's joy in creation continues as God's word sings "Life!" into barren, empty places today. What joy the Singer must have when this music brings life and salvation to those who hear!

Lord, let your Spirit sing the song of faith into our ears, that we may believe. Amen.

New Creation

"Did you ever think, when you were a child, what fun it would be if your toys could come to life? . . . Imagine turning a tin soldier into a real little man. It would involve turning the tin into flesh. And suppose the tin soldier did not like it. . . . All he sees is that the tin is being spoilt. . . . He will do everything he can to prevent you. He will not be made into a man if he can help it.

"What you would have done about that tin soldier I do not know. But what God did about us was this. . . . God, the Son, became human himself. . . . For the first time we saw a real man. One tin soldier—real tin, just like the rest—had come fully and splendidly alive" (Lewis 1971a).

Through centuries of time, children of a fallen race—the sons of Adam and the daughters of Eve—carried with them the memory of a garden and searched for a way to restore what had been lost there. They could find no way.

There was only one way.

In Jesus Christ, God took the initiative for a new creation. He became a human being so that humanity might be reconciled to God and be recreated in God's image. "[Jesus Christ] is the image of the invisible God" (Col. 1:15). In this Second Adam, a new creation in God's image was brought into being. "For the first time, we saw a real man."

Now, in the waters of Holy Baptism, the sons of Adam and the daughters of Eve exchange old for new, tin for real. They receive a gift: a new nature, the nature of Christ; and a new realness, a new reality. "For as many of you as were baptized into Christ have put on Christ" (Gal. 3:27). Those who are joined to Christ in Baptism have put on his nature: the recreated image of God in the face of humanity, humankind "fully and splendidly alive."

"Those whom he foreknew, he also predestined to be conformed to the image of his Son, in order that he might be the first-born among many brethren" (Rom. 8:29).

"Our real selves . . . are all waiting for us in him," Lewis contends. A new Adam, a new Eve wait to meet us in Christ. "Out of ourselves, into Christ, we must go," there to find our real selves when we find him. "Therefore, if any one is in Christ, he is a new creation; the old has passed away, behold the new has come" (2 Cor. 5:17).

O God, mold me into the image of your Son, forming his life in me. Amen.

The Prodigality of God

DAY 3

In *The Four Loves*, Lewis distinguishes between several kinds of love. Of these types of love: *"There was no doubt which was more like Love Himself. Divine Love is Gift-love. The Father gives all He is and has to the Son. The Son gives Himself back to the Father, and gives Himself to the world, and for the world to the Father, and thus gives the world (in Himself) back to the Father too"* (Lewis 1971b).

Every good and perfect gift is from above (James 1:17). Daily work, home and family, food and clothing—all we need from day to day are the gracious gifts of a heavenly Father.

Jesus' parable of two brothers in Luke 15 describes a father, also. The story tells of the repentance of a wasteful son who had engaged in excess, squandering the gift of his inheritance. The father, who welcomed him with open arms, is no less prodigal in the extravagance of his love, the reckless excess of his forgiveness, the lavishness in his "welcome home" party.

The prodigality of God is the theme of the New Testament; the heart of the gospel is that "God so loved . . . that he gave" (John 3:16). God gave the treasure of God's heart to the world in the child of Bethlehem.

"Thanks be to God for his inexpressible gift!" (2 Cor. 9:15). For us, this wondrous gift was given, as the Father came down the stairs of heaven with a baby in his arms. Heaven's greatest gift, wrapped in baby softness with all of God's great power and love, was demonstrated gently in Mary's little one.

In *The Last Battle* of the Chronicles of Narnia, Lucy confessed: "In our world, too, a stable once had something inside it that was bigger than our whole world." Such is the gift of our Father for us. And through this gift come all others: the forgiveness of sins, life, and salvation.

But the gift is Christ's, also. He reaches down to embrace our lostness, and restores us to his Father's house. He takes our "creaturely predicament" into himself, and presents his Father with the gift of redemption's handiwork. "In the Incarnation, God the Son takes the body and human soul of Jesus, and, through that . . . all the creaturely predicament, into his own being. . . . 'He came down from Heaven' can almost be transposed into 'Heaven drew earth up into it' " (Lewis 1973b).

"When all things are subjected to him, then the Son himself will also be subjected to him who put all things under him, that God may be everything to everyone" (1 Cor. 15:28).

Glory to God in highest heav'n,
Who unto us his Son has giv'n. Amen.
(*Lutheran Book of Worship* [LBW] 51)

Death Backwards

DAY 4

In one of the most moving narratives based on the Passion of Christ, the divine Lion of Narnia, Aslan, gave his life for a child. At dawn, on the following day: *"They looked round. There, shining in the sunrise, larger than they had seen him before, shaking his mane . . . stood Aslan himself.*

"Aren't you dead then, dear Aslan?" said Lucy.

"Not now," said Aslan. ". . . Though the Witch knew the Deep Magic, there is a magic deeper still which she did not know. . . . If she could have looked a little further back . . . she would have known that when a willing victim who had committed no treachery was killed in a traitor's stead, the Table would crack, and Death itself would start working backwards" (Lewis 1950).

The only Son of God, whose power was recognized by the wind and the waves and the unclean spirits who obeyed him, was himself obedient to the will of his Father. "For the joy" that was set before him, he chose the way of obedience that led to his suffering and death on the cross.

In *The Problem of Pain*, C. S. Lewis speaks of obedience to God in this way: "In obeying, a rational creature consciously enacts its creaturely role, reverses the act by which we fell, treads Adam's dance backward, and returns." The obedience of Christ was perfect, and fulfilled the Law's demands, turning back the terrible effects of Adam's dance.

"He humbled himself and became obedient unto death, even death on a cross" (Phil. 2:8). "So one man's act of righteousness leads to acquittal and life for all men. For as by one man's disobedience many were made sinners, so by one man's obedience many will be made righteous" (Rom. 5:18-19).

Because of that Man's obedience, death started its long journey backwards. For centuries it had claimed every son of Adam and each daughter of Eve, but it could not hold this one. His resurrection word had brought life to Lazarus, a little girl, a young man. And on Easter, resurrection power entered his own tomb, and death became obedient to Life.

Easter was the first day of a new age. There is more to come! At the last day when this age ends and the new age begins, death itself will "work backwards," returning all of its subjects to the Lord of Life. "In Christ shall all be made alive" (1 Cor. 15:22).

> *Oh, thou that art unwearying, that dost neither sleep*
> *Nor slumber, who didst take*
> *All care for Lazarus in the careless tomb, oh keep*
> *Watch for me till I wake.*

(Lewis 1958)

17

Meet Life

D A Y
5

"It is always shocking to meet life where we thought we were alone. . . . There comes a moment when the children who have been playing at burglars hush suddenly: was that a real footstep in the hall? There comes a moment when people who have been dabbling in religion . . . suddenly draw back. Supposing we really found him? We never meant it to come to that! Worse still, supposing He had found us?" (Lewis 1947).

The woman stood in a garden, bent with grief. She heard the man speaking to her, but tears blinded her eyes.

Mary Magdalene had come to the tomb of her Master, expecting to find death there. Instead, it was Life that greeted her. "Mary," he said.

Life called her by name, addressing her fears, her grief, her pain. But she was not ready for such a meeting. She was seeking her Master, but was not expecting him to greet her. She had thought she was alone.

The one she had thought was the gardener was, in truth, the Gardener's Son, fresh-risen in victory. Surprised by joy, Mary saw Easter in him, and she told his disciples, "I have seen the Lord" (John 20:18).

Along a country road, two friends were joined by an unknown traveler. The two were in despair, mourning the death of their Lord. "But we had hoped that he was the one to redeem Israel" (Luke 24:21).

They were expecting to share their sorrow as they walked along the way. Instead, it was Hope that met them on the road. Hope opened the Scriptures to them. Hope broke bread with them. They had not known that it was Easter. But Easter found them.

Confused by the events of the past few days, seven of Jesus' disciples went fishing. They returned to their old life, to the familiar feel of the nets. The next morning, a fisherman they did not know called to them from the shore and gave them advice for a catch.

They had been expecting nothing, and that was what they had caught. But at the fisherman's words, their nets overflowed. They were surprised by a Miracle, and John knew, "It is the Lord" (John 21:7).

We are often in places where we do not look for life. When we bury one whom we have loved, when we face illness or loss, we are not expecting life, or hope, or miracle. The surprise of grace meets us on the road, at our work, at the graveside. The Lord finds us, and we meet life.

Lord, sometimes we forget that it is Easter, and we do not expect to meet you on our road. Surprise us with the joy of your presence. Amen.

All Is Grace

If thou think for me what I cannot think, if thou
Desire for me what I
Cannot desire, my soul's interior Form, though now
Deep-buried, will not die,
No more than the insensible dropp'd seed which grows
Through winter ripe for birth
Because, while it forgets, the heaven remembering throws
Sweet influence still on earth,
Because the heaven, moved moth-like by thy beauty, goes.
Still turning round the earth.

(Lewis 1958)

The human race has shown remarkable resourcefulness in our attempts to provide a substitute for grace. We place our trust in things, in power, in reputation, and in our own intellect. But no matter how much we know or have, or who we are, we will always come up glory-short. The wisdom of this world is folly with God, the power of this world is weakness to God, the righteousness that we have to offer God is as filthy rags.

These words from *Pilgrim's Regress* are the song of one who is poor in spirit. This is a confession of spiritual poverty, of humility before God. In thought, in will, and even in his life itself, the singer is utterly dependent upon God. The singer knows that all is grace. "He is the source of your life in Christ Jesus, whom God made our wisdom, our righteousness and sanctification and redemption" (1 Cor. 1:27-30).

Jesus Christ is all we need. He is our life, our wisdom, our righteousness, our sanctification, our redemption—our grace. Our sufficiency is from him. The apostle Paul confesses, "Whatever gain I had, I counted as loss . . . because of the surpassing worth of knowing Christ Jesus my Lord" (Phil. 3:7-8).

"Let not the wise man glory in his wisdom, let not the mighty man glory in his might, let not the rich man glory in his riches; but let him who glories glory in this, that he understands and knows me" (Jer. 9:23-24).

Thoughts are but coins. Let me not trust, instead
Of Thee, their thin-worn image of Thy head.
From all my thoughts, even from my thoughts of Thee,
O thou fair Silence, fall, and set me free.
Lord of the narrow gate and the needle's eye,
Take from me all my trumpery lest I die.

(Lewis 1965b)

19

Joy

DAY 7 In *Surprised by Joy*, Lewis records his spiritual pilgrimage and describes his return to faith. At first "turning," his belief was theistic: *"This was a religion that cost nothing. We could talk religiously about the Absolute: but there was no danger of ITs doing anything about us. It was "there." . . . It would never come "here," never (to be blunt) make a nuisance of Itself"* (Lewis 1955b).

God's grace continued to work in his life, through his reading, through his friends: "Soon I could no longer cherish even the illusion that the initiative lay with me. My adversary began to make his final moves."

Although at the moment he felt himself to be "perhaps . . . the most dejected and reluctant convert in all England," he nevertheless experienced a freedom and joy at his return to Christianity that he described in these words: *"I became aware that I was holding something at bay, or shutting something out, . . . that I was wearing some stiff clothing, like corsets, or even a suit of armor, as if I were a lobster. . . . I could open the door or keep it shut; I could unbuckle the armor or keep it on. . . . I chose to open, to unbuckle, to loosen the reign. . . . I felt as if I were a man of snow at long last beginning to melt* (Lewis 1955).

Our spiritual journeys all differ. Some of us, like St. Paul, were traveling along our own road when God's grace surprised and "turned" us. Others of us stay on the path all of our lives, and never remember its start. But the joy of melting—the joy of salvation—is the same for us all.

"Create in me a clean heart, O God, and put a new and right spirit within me. Cast me not away from thy presence, and take not thy Holy Spirit from me. Restore to me the joy of thy salvation, and uphold me with a willing spirit" (Ps. 51:10-12).

The joy of salvation is a characteristic common to faith. It can be experienced in the quiet confidence of renewed faith, or in the exuberant praise of a heart "forgiven leaping," a spirit set free to sing. And the joy is not ours alone. Heaven, too, rejoices in the turning back to God.

Snowmen and snowwomen that we are, we need spring joy. Unfaithfulness has packed the snow and ice around the cold ball of our rejection of God so that we are snowbound, unable to melt of our own volition. The warmth of God's spirit and God's grace can melt us into life and set us free for joy!

God of hope, fill us with all joy and peace in believing. Amen (Rom. 15:13).

Sprouts

DAY 8 *"As [Christ] said, a thistle cannot produce figs. If I am a field that contains nothing but grass-seed, I cannot produce wheat. Cutting the grass may keep it short: but I shall still produce grass and no wheat. If I want to produce wheat, the change must go deeper than the surface. I must be ploughed up and resown"* (Lewis 1971a).

Seeds of doubt, seeds of worry, seeds of fear or anger: all yield their own sad harvest. No matter what efforts might be made to change the result, doubt-seeds sprout doubt, worry-seeds come up frowning. Fertilizer and cultivation may affect the yield, but it is the seed that determines the product.

We have been planted into the kingdom of God at our Baptism, and the field of our lives produces a harvest. But unless God has sown the seed, only one crop will come up: weeds. We might cut the weeds down, we might try to cover them up or disguise their weedy looks. But the only way to change the harvest is to pull the weeds out by the roots, plough them under, and reseed.

No matter how much we might wish to change our own nature, any attempt that we make to change the harvest of sin will fail. All attempts at self-improvement, even if successful, will result in just that and no more: an improved self. God offers us not an improved self, but a new self: alive to God, alive to righteousness.

As Lewis wrote in *Perelandra,* "It is not mere improvement, but Transformation." We cannot transform ourselves, but Christ can form himself in us, giving his gifts of a new heart, a new creation.

God's Word reveals to us our need for more than just a surface cure. God's Word is the plough that opens up the fields of our lives and lays them bare, exposing the roots of our sinful nature, removing the seeds of death, so that God may plant God's life in us. "For he who sows to his own flesh will from the flesh reap corruption; but he who sows to the Spirit will from the Spirit reap eternal life" (Gal. 6:8).

Our sinful nature has planted in us seeds of fear, self-centered greed, pride, anger, envy, hatred. The harvest of sin is death. But God's gift is a new crop of God's own planting. The harvest of that gift is transforming life. "The fruit of the Spirit is love, joy, peace, patience, kindness, goodness, faithfulness, gentleness, self-control" (Gal. 5:22-23).

Lord, make me new. Pull out the roots of sin within me, and sow in me the seeds for a harvest of life. Amen.

Ransom

DAY 9 Assigned a redemptive task by the heavenly powers in *Perelandra*, Ransom arrived in the unfallen Paradise, which had two inhabitants, a new Adam and Eve. Demonic Weston, the "Unman," tried to tempt the Lady of the planet into disobeying God, and Ransom presented reasons for her obedience, engaging the Unman in a debate to prevent the planet's fall.

When Ransom saw that he was losing the argument, he realized that in order to accomplish his mission, he must fight the Unman in direct combat. He struggled with that decision: *"He believed he could face the Unman with firearms . . . but to come to grips with it, to go voluntarily into those dead yet living arms, to grapple with it, naked chest to naked chest. . . . Perhaps he would fight and win, perhaps not even be badly mauled. But no faintest hint of a guarantee in that direction came to him from the darkness. The future was black as the night itself.*

'It is not for nothing that you are named Ransom,' said the Voice. . . . 'my name also is Ransom' " (Lewis 1965a).

Jesus entered into battle with the ancient enemy of humankind. Although he was tempted to exchange God's will and plans for the schemes of the Evil One, Jesus prevailed in his obedience to the Father. To each of the adversary's proposals, Jesus responded with the Word of God. Empowered by the Spirit, he emerged victorious—our Ransom.

"For we have not a high priest who is unable to sympathize with our weaknesses, but one who in every respect has been tempted as we are, yet without sin. Let us then with confidence draw near to the throne of grace, that we may receive mercy and find grace to help in time of need" (Heb. 4:15-16).

The New Testament often pictures the Christian life using the imagery of a struggle—a battle waged by the saints of God against the powers of darkness. "Fight the good fight of the faith" (1 Tim. 6:12), and "Be strong in the Lord and in the strength of his might. Put on the whole armor of God, that you may be able to stand against the wiles of the devil" (Eph. 6:10).

For the struggles and conflicts in which we are engaged, St. Paul urges our dependence upon the strength and power available to us by God's Spirit. The champion who came to fight for us invites us to celebrate his triumph and to participate in his victory. He fights in our place, and his victory is ours.

Support us in our final strife and lead us out of death to life.
(*LBW* 230)

Christic the Neighbor

DAY 10
"There are no ordinary people. You have never talked to a mere mortal. Nations, cultures, arts, civilization—these are mortal. . . . But it is immortals whom we joke with, work with, marry, snub, and exploit—this does not mean that we are to be perpetually solemn. . . . But our merriment must be of that kind. . . which exists between people . . . who have . . . taken each other seriously. . . . And our charity must be a real and costly love. . . .

"Next to the Blessed Sacrament itself, your neighbor is the holiest object presented to your senses. If he is your Christian neighbor, he is holy in almost the same way, for in him also Christ vere latitat—the glorifier and the glorified, Glory Himself, is truly hidden" (Lewis 1977).

"Who is my neighbor?" a lawyer wanted to know, seeking from Jesus a statute of limitations that would restrict his own obligations.

Jesus told the lawyer a story about a man who had been wronged. This man needed a neighbor. Robbed, beaten, left for dead, his pleas were ignored by those who took a wide detour around his human need.

The neighbor that he discovered was an unlikely one; his accent betrayed him as a foreigner. But this neighbor saw; he had compassion, he stopped, he healed, he saved. We know the Neighbor's name.

Jesus' story was more than just a legal opinion; it was a disclosure of God's truth. "Who is my neighbor?" He is the one who helps, who heals, who stoops, who bears our burdens, who saves. Christ is the Neighbor who offers his "real and costly love" to us and for us.

Jesus gives us the church as our neighborhood of faith. But we are also his body, his neighborhood for others. Our Christian "with-ness" calls us to a compassion that extends to the Christ in each neighbor, near or far. "And the King will answer them, 'As you did it to one of the least of these my brethren, you did it to me' " (Matt. 25:40).

If Jesus had answered the lawyer with a detailed list of who was neighbor and who was not, compassion might have been easier for us to measure out. If we knew the bounds of our neighborhood, we could know when we were finished with our compassion requirement.

But the neighborhood that Jesus describes is a much larger place. The assignment he leaves with us is greater than any commandment: to meet him in the face of each stranger, each neighbor.

Neighbor God, you came near to us in Jesus Christ, healing and saving. Meet us now in your Word, and in your people. Amen.

Night Comes

The residents of the "gray town" in Lewis's fantasy, *The Great Divorce*, live a twilight existence in which evening never advances into night. Although they are welcome to leave the gray town for the joy of heaven, most of them are unwilling to leave behind their favorite sins. They live with the haunting fear that night will come, bringing with it the utter darkness of hell.

> *I put my ear close to his mouth. "Speak up," I said.*
> *"It will be dark presently," he mouthed.*
> *"You mean the evening is really going to turn into a night in the end?"*
> *He nodded.* (Lewis 1973a)

Children are not the only ones who fear the darkness; night has often been depicted as a time of anxiety and dread. Jesus gave symbolic meaning to the night when he said, "We must work the works of him who sent me, while it is day; night comes, when no one can work" (John 9:4). Jesus' picture of night represents the end—of opportunity for work, of life.

Luke remembers that night was approaching for three travelers on a dusty road. Two of them were grieving the death of their Master, and their dreams were at an end. On the road, they had met a stranger, whose words had given them new hope as he opened the Scriptures to them. As they approached their destination, they pleaded with him: 'Stay with us, for it is toward evening and the day is now far spent.' So he went in to stay with them" (Luke 24:28-29).

It is "evening" for our world when hope is hard to find, evening in our families when troubles come, evening in our lives when we experience loss, illness, pain, or grief. And we know that night will come at our death, and at the end of this age. We, too, pray to the risen Master, "Stay with us, Lord, for it is toward evening." In Jesus Christ, God has come to God's people; in Jesus Christ is God's pledge to stay with us. Immanuel, God-With-Us, promises, "I am with you always" (Matt. 28:20), and "I will never fail you nor forsake you" (Heb. 13:5).

Jesus' presence sustains us in the evening times of life. His promise stretches past the darkness into the brightness of day, as Revelation pictures the new age: "And there shall be no night there" (Rev. 21:25).

> Abide with me, fast falls the eventide.
> The darkness deepens; Lord, with me abide.
> When other helpers fail and comforts flee,
> Help of the helpless, oh, abide with me. Amen.
> (LBW 272)

Knit to Christ

DAY 12 *"Prosperity knits a man to the World. He feels that he is 'finding his place in it,' while really it is finding its place in him. His increasing reputation, his widening circle of acquaintances, his sense of importance, the growing pressure of absorbing and agreeable work, build up in him a sense of being really at home on Earth"* (Lewis 1982).

"... Which is just what we want." This discourse on worldliness is really part of an advice column from *The Screwtape Letters*. It was written by an experienced devil to an apprentice devil, to guide the inexperienced devil in corrupting a human soul. "Just what they want" is the falling from grace, the turning away from God, "unravelling ... souls from Heaven and building up a firm attachment to the Earth."

Prosperity and success can enable the world to take up residence in the center of our being. An abundance of things, wealth, renown: these can provide a false sense of security. Soon the heart is tempted and begins to lean toward these things for support and meaning. Stitch by stitch, a "knitting" is done, joining the person to the world, until it is no longer clear which possesses which. The world "finds its place" in us. Jesus reminds us that "where your treasure is, there will your heart be also" (Luke 12:34).

An affluent farmer had a bumper crop and needed more space to store all of his grain and goods. He resolved to build bigger barns, reasoning "And I will say to my soul, Soul, you have ample goods laid up for many years; take your ease" (Luke 12:19). That rich man was the fool in Jesus' parable, for soon after saying this, he died. Careful to provide for his own prosperity, he had neglected to nurture a relationship with God.

Here on earth, we are "strangers and exiles" (Heb. 11:13). Lewis writes in *The Problem of Pain*, "Our Father refreshes us on the journey with some pleasant inns, but will not encourage us to mistake them for home."

Though he was the heir to all of heaven's treasures and the earth's sovereign Lord, Jesus Christ made himself poor for our sake that we might be made rich toward God. He desires to knit us to himself, giving us an abiding home: "Here we have no lasting city, but we seek the city which is to come" (Heb. 13:14), and "But our commonwealth is in heaven, and from it we await a Savior, the Lord Jesus Christ" (Phil. 3:20-21).

Lord, knit us to you with the threads of your sure promises, that no temptations may lead us from our life in you. Amen.

Fear Not

DAY 13 The world of Narnia rushes to its incredible conclusion in *The Last Battle: "As they came right up to Aslan, they all looked straight in his face; . . . when some looked, the expression of their faces changed terribly—it was fear and hatred. . . . But the others looked in the face of Aslan and loved him, though some of these were very frightened at the same time"* (Lewis 1956).

An awareness of "the holy" brings with it a mixture of feelings; the prospect of a divine encounter often evokes a deep and terrible fear.

Scripture records many visitations from the Almighty or his representatives, and the appearance of the divine messenger strikes fear into human hearts. The words "Fear not!" often introduce the message.

When God spoke through God's own Son, angels delivered the gracious words "Fear not!" to frightened shepherds. When Jesus was transfigured in unearthly splendor before his disciples, the Voice assured the awed men, "Fear not!" The greeting of the resurrection angel to the anxious women at the tomb began "Fear not!" The gospel's good news is that God is here in Jesus Christ, and that behind the mystery and inscrutableness of God is God's greatest secret, the face of love toward us in Jesus Christ.

"In this is love perfected with us, that we may have confidence for the day of judgment, because as he is so are we in this world. There is no fear in love, but perfect love casts out fear" (1 John 4:17-18).

Late Hebrew thought visualized a fearful "day of the Lord" with its coming judgment; some New Testament images point to the expectation of a final act of God that will separate the old and the new age, and bring judgment upon all humankind. The Christian church points to the future with hope, confessing that history will culminate with the glorious coming again of the Lord Christ.

Lewis's judgment scene in *The Last Battle* illustrates the confrontation with Christ, who reveals the secrets of hearts. He is the door, open to all who gaze into his face, where they see love.

> Jesus, thou art all compassion;
> Pure, unbounded love thou art;
> Visit us with thy salvation,
> Enter ev'ry trembling heart.
> (*LBW* 315)

26

Glory Be

DAY 14 *"These small and perishable bodies we now have were given to us as ponies are given to schoolboys. We must learn to manage: not that we may someday be free of horses altogether but that someday we may ride bareback, confident and rejoicing, those greater mounts, those winged, shining and world-shaking horses which perhaps even now expect us with impatience, pawing and snorting in the King's stables. Not that the gallop would be of any value unless it were a gallop with the King: but how else . . . should we accompany Him?"* (Lewis 1947).

"No eye has seen, nor ear heard, . . . what God has prepared for those who love him" (1 Cor. 2:9). Scripture hints at the wonderful future that God has prepared for God's people; more than these glimpses we cannot see. Viewing these truths in God's word, it is as if the curtain that obscures the future is lifted for brief moments, and we peek inside at the glory to be.

What we do know is that there will be a radical transformation of all that we know.

"Lo! I tell you a mystery. We shall not all sleep, but we shall all be changed, in a moment, in the twinkling of an eye, at the last trumpet. For the trumpet will sound, and the dead will be raised imperishable, and we shall be changed. For this perishable nature must put on the imperishable, and this mortal nature must put on immortality" (1 Cor. 15:15-53).

What is perishable will change clothing, putting on the imperishable instead. Mortal nature will be exchanged for immortality, death for life. Greater transformation could hardly be imagined.

"So is it with the resurrection of the dead. What is sown is perishable, what is raised is imperishable. . . . It is sown a physical body, it is raised a spiritual body" (1 Cor. 15:42).

Like all the King's horses in Lewis's imagination, waiting with impatience in the King's stables, we lean toward the future and wait for the glory that is to be. We have the Prince's own promise that one day we will gallop, "confident and rejoicing," with our King. All creation, too, waits with us, standing on tiptoe to catch a glimpse of that new day.

The future for God's people will be infinitely greater than anything we could ask or think or imagine. We have the promise of Christ: "I will come again and will take you to myself, that where I am you may be also" (John 14:3). And if that is all that we know of heaven, it is enough.

Lord, sustain us with your many and great promises as we wait for your future to unfold. Amen.

GEORGE MACDONALD

G EORGE MACDONALD had come to my attention through an anthology of his writings selected and published by C. S. Lewis in 1956 under the title *George Macdonald: an Anthology.* I also knew through Lewis's autobiography, *Surprised by Joy,* that Macdonald's writings had been a decisive factor in his return to the Christian faith.

Macdonald (1824–1905), a Scottish preacher and writer of fantasy, lived in poverty and in reiterated failure most of his life. He suffered from consumption, but he appears to have been "a sunny and playful" man, resting back in what he called "the holy present."

In August 1960 our son Paul, returning from two years at the University of Oxford, lost his life in a street accident before reaching home. Among his effects, in his billfold, we found several prayers carefully copied in his handwriting. The well-worn pages told me that he must have returned to these prayers again and again. Later, when his library arrived, we found the source of these prayers, *Diary of an Old Soul.* We wrote to the publisher in England and were able to get several copies, but were told that it was now out of print. Augsburg Publishing House in Minneapolis has since published it in several editions. In recent years there has been a resurgence of interest in Macdonald, and titles such as *Phantases,* the *Curdie* books, and the *Golden Key* are again available.

C. S. Lewis says of his works, "In Macdonald it is always the voice of conscience that speaks . . . in that very voice of conscience every other faculty somehow speaks as well—intelligence and imagination and humor and fancy and all the affections; and no man in modern times was perhaps more aware of the distinction between Law and Gospel, the inevitable failure of modern morality. The Divine-Sonship is the key concept which unites all the different elements of his thought . . . to speak plainly I know hardly any other writer who seems so close, or more continuously close, to the Spirit of Christ himself. Hence his Christ-like union of tenderness and severity. Nowhere else outside of the New Testament have I found terror and comfort so intertwined" (Lewis 1956).

My only regret in using these sonnets—all taken from *Diary of an Old Soul* (Augsburg Publishing House, 1975)—is that the meditations that follow may only weaken or diffuse the wealth of the sonnets themselves.

Our One Need: God

Not, Lord, because I have done well or ill;
Not that my mind looks up to thee clear-eyed;
Not that it struggles in fast cerements tied;
Not that I need thee daily sorer still;
Not that I, wretched, wander from thy will;
Not now for any cause to thee I cry,
But this, that you art thou, and here am I.

She was four, and her mother had died. She could not be consoled. Her father and her brother tried. They told her stories, they brought her toys. For a moment she was distracted. But then she began crying again, pushed the toys aside, and sobbed, "I don't want nothin', I want my momma."

Why did she want her momma? Because her mother made meals for her, tied her shoestrings, sang lullabies, or cradled her when she was sick?

Why do we need God? Deep down, why do we cry for him? Is it because we are afraid of losing our jobs, catching some dread disease, failing a test? Perhaps because the future looms with such dangers? Is it even because we are sinners and need salvation, forgiveness, and restoration?

These are legitimate needs. If on our own we have the good fortune to have met these needs, or to live in the illusion that we have met them, then we may pretend to have no need of God. If we do, we fail to understand both ourselves and God.

God wants to give us himself. If we have all good things, but we don't have him, deep down we will cry with the little girl, "I don't want nothin'." Nothing but God himself will do.

We are created by him and for him; we are destined to live with him. Without him we are fish out of water, birds without air. The profoundest autobiography for any of us is "I came from God and I return to God." Thou art thou, and here am I.

"My soul waits for the Lord more than watchmen for the morning" (Ps. 130:6).

Lord, Simply Come

Come to me, Lord, I will not speculate how,
Nor think at which door I would have thee appear,
Nor put off calling till my floors be swept,
But cry, "Come, Lord, come any way, come now."
Doors, windows, I throw wide, my head I bow,
And sit like some one who so long has slept
That he knows nothing till his life draws near.

God has not asked that we be perfect, or even religious. We need meet no standard of saintliness before he will come. He only asks that we let him come. At first thought, this seems too easy. Does he make no judgment between good and evil? Would he have come to a Nero, or a Genghis Khan, or a Hitler? He did come to a Paul while Paul was still hating Christians and stalking them to their deaths.

There is something preposterous about God wanting us at all. None of us is good through and through. We are a motley company for a holy God. We despoil his earth, and we often ignore or despise one another. The strange story of the Bible, which we call the gospel, is the good news that he is so greedy to have us that he sent his only Son to die in an effort to reclaim us.

No religion in all the world is quite as audacious as the Christian faith. All other religions imply that only by a good life does a person invite the presence of God. One's house had better be cleansed of sin before a God will deign to take up residence.

Whatever unsavory crowd we may be entertaining—greed, pride, lust—if we are in earnest about having the Lord as an honored guest and friend, he will help us evict the intruders. Once they begin to leave, we will know a peace that only the Lord can give.

"Behold, I stand at the door and knock; if any one hears my voice and opens the door, I will come in to him" (Rev. 3:20).

Rights and Gifts

D A Y
3

Lord, I have fallen again—a human clod!
Selfish I was, and heedless to offend;
Stood on my rights. Thy own child would not send
Away his shreds of nothing for the whole God!
Wretched, to thee who savest, now I bend;
Give me the power to let my rag-rights go
In the great wind that from thy gulf doth blow.

Under the law of the land I have rights. The Declaration of Independence uses the words, "Life, liberty, and the pursuit of happiness." I have the right to hold property, to be rewarded for labor, to appeal to the courts for justice.

God gives no rights. Life, liberty, and the pursuit of happiness are his gifts, privileges loaned us for a day. God retains ownership. If we have rights at all, we have but the right to give them in service to others.

When Job was stripped of all his wealth he said, "The LORD gave, and the LORD has taken away; blessed be the name of the LORD" (Job 1:21). He was affirming that before God he had never had a right to his wealth. It had been a gift, a trust. Now it was gone. It would have been absurd for him to appear before the high court to reclaim what had never been his.

Once we understand that over against God we have no right to ownership, only stewardship, we can stop our jealous protection of our "rag-tag" rights. No longer will my marriage be a grim 50-50 contract that I guard with care, no longer will my neighbor's barking dog send me to the police. My wife or husband or neighbor has been loaned to me for my care. I become an advocate for community and world justice, not to defend *my* rights but the rights of the poor and voiceless. Only as we have this turnabout will life be relaxing enough for us to have joy and peace.

"If any one forces you to go one mile, go with him two miles" (Matt. 5:41).

Deeds Are Doors

DAY

4

*I would go near thee—but I cannot press
Into thy presence—it helps not to presume.
Thy doors are deeds, the handles are their doing.
He whose day-life is obedient righteousness,
Who, after failure, or a poor success,
Rises up, stronger effort yet renewing—
He finds thee, Lord, at length, in his own common room.*

The Lord has invited us to come to him. But how do we come? Martin Luther, in his Small Catechism, admitted that he couldn't come to the Lord on his own. "I believe that I cannot by my own reason or strength believe in Jesus Christ my Lord, or come to him," he wrote, then added "but the Holy Spirit has called me through the Gospel."

Would the Lord really invite us, knowing that we are not able to come? Strangely enough, he does. He wants us to learn two things: first, that in our self-centeredness, we, like Adam and Eve, are really running away from him; and second, that he is ready to help us come. Most of all, he wants us to know that he has already come and is standing at our door knocking. He is calling us through the gospel, the wonderful story of God's love in Christ Jesus. In a profound sense we are *drawn* to him probably more than coming to him, if there is a difference.

We come by doing his will. Deeds open the door to him. By showing kindness to people in need, by working for good causes, by praying for others, by writing letters to lonely people or calling them—by doing these things we are in company with Jesus who is the servant of all.

"Come, O blessed of my Father, inherit the kingdom prepared for you from the foundation of the world" (Matt. 25:34).

We Claim Him

DAY
5

I am lost before thee, Father! I will
claim of thee my birthright ineffable.
Thou lay'st it on me, son, to claim thee, sire;
To that which thou hast made me, I aspire;
To thee, the sun, upflames thy kindled fire.
No man presumes in that to which he was born;
Less than the gift to claim, would be the giver to scorn.

God gives and gives and gives. He gives us himself, and with himself everything he has. However presumptuous this may seem, not to claim him and what he has is to rebuff him.

It is little wonder that it's very difficult for us to believe this. The hard fact of our daily lives is that we pay for what we get. We pay for our salaries by our work. We pay for an A in school by our study. If we overpark our cars, we pay a fine.

That which blocks us out from God and his gifts is not primarily the sins of violence and sex (sins of the flesh), but unbelief. To brush off God and his giving as fantasy or nonsense is to insulate ourselves from much of his grace. He still gives us gifts such as life, food, shelter, health, family, and friends. But the vast treasures of his kingdom—love and faith and hope—are closed to us. Most of all, unbelief cuts us off from fellowship with him. A daughter who in rebellion and rejection has turned from her mother may receive a check from the loving mother every month. But deep down, the daughter needs her mother more than she needs just a check.

Until we open ourselves to life with God, we will be impoverished. And until we see that everything good in our lives is a gift from him, the gifts themselves will lack the aura they should have.

"Every good endowment and every perfect gift is from above" (James 1:17).

We Trust Him

Too eager I must not be to understand.
How should the work the Master goes about
Fit the vague sketch my compasses have planned?
I am his house—for him to go in and out.
He builds me now—and if I cannot see
At any time what he is doing with me,
'Tis that he makes the house for me too grand.

Need we understand how the universe came into being? Or why human beings were created? Need we understand why a young woman dies of leukemia or why her grandfather, knowing no one, languishes in a nursing home?

Out from the mystery of existence it is as if God says, "Trust me." The mystery will remain, however much we try to penetrate it. Is it not presumptuous for any of us to become God's attorney for the defense and attempt to justify him? Our only options are to trust him or to let him go.

To trust him may not be easy. With so many things going wrong in the world and in our own lives, is it possible not to call him to account? Could he not prevent the disasters that plague us? Should we not demand that he ask our forgiveness for having made us as we are and for putting us in a world so full of trouble?

Any option other than to trust him will not satisfy. There is no joy in believing that there is no God and that the universe is a cold, impersonal machine; or in believing that he has forgotten all about us; or in fearing that he is a harsh judge always giving us what we deserve.

To trust him is after all the only option that gives peace. We start with a God who created us in love and who redeemed us in love. Life takes on meaning when we trust him to use every circumstance in life, pleasant or unpleasant, to give us courage and hope. Life opens up with new joys as we trust his way, the way of the servant.

"The Lord is my shepherd, I shall not want" (Ps. 23:1).

His Unchanging Love

Some say that thou their endless love hast won
By deeds for them which I may not believe
Thou ever didst, or every willedst done;
What matter, so they love thee? They receive
Eternal more than the poor loom and wheel
of their invention ever wove and spun.
I love thee, for I must, thine all from head to heel.

I have friends who believe that God finds them a place in the parking lot, that he recovers lost keys, or that he keeps them from flunking a course. They pray, and it is done.

God has put no limits on what we can pray for, it is true. And who am I not to bother God with such prayer—who am I to think my friends a bit naive? Maybe they are right? In any event, when they find their keys, they thank God. And that's enough.

He is after all the giver of all good. Recovering one's keys may not be a major good, compared with Christ dying on a cross to redeem the world. But even the so-called trivia of life are a part of his great package of blessings. If the keys are lost and never found, however hard one prays, the truly wonderful gift, the gift of forgiveness and life with him, is not lost.

We pray that our friend will arrive safely at his destination, but there is an accident and he is killed. We pray that the plant may not close, but it does, and we lose our jobs. We pray that our marriage will hold, but it falls apart and in pain we go our separate ways. These are bigger issues than the loss of keys, and prayer fails. It is then that we fall back on the one unchanging guarantee of God's love, the cross of Christ. He does love us, no matter what happens in the variables of life, because he died for us. We love him, not because of recovered keys, but because in the cross he has reclaimed us as his own. This is the measure of his love.

"See what love the Father has given us, that we should be called children of God; and so we are" (1 John 3:1).

Doubt, the Intruder

But why should it be possible to mistrust—
Nor possible only, but its opposite hard?
Why should not man believe because he must—
By sight's compulsion? Why should he be scarred
With conflict? worn with doubting fine and long?
No man is fit for heaven's musician throng
Who has not tuned an instrument all shook and jarred.

Sometimes we grow in trust in the very face of doubt. Our trust in God may grow to be so strong and untroubled that we leave doubt behind, but on the way we very likely may have done long battle with doubt. For many of us faith and doubt may continue side by side, and only by the Spirit's help are we able to rest confidently in the love of God.

Faith in God is not like faith in a new car, for instance. You see the car, you try it out, it works. But God we have never seen or touched or heard. You may have evidence of God's love in one way or another. But sometimes your prayers seem to reach deaf ears, and things go wrong. Where is God? Does he care? Doubts rear a wall, and mistrust takes over.

Jesus once indicated that God is reached by a narrow passage. We don't drift on a broad highway into the riches of the kingdom. There are struggles within ourselves and in our world. We may be wounded and scarred. We are caught in eddies of unworthy passions. The future may loom with perils. We lose our bearings and everything looks black. It is when faith finds its way through bewilderment and fear that it grows strong. In Macdonald's words, it is the only way our instrument can be tuned for heavenly melodies.

"The father of the child cried out, . . . 'I believe; help my unbelief' " (Mark 9:24).

The Grand Mood

In the low mood, the mere man acts alone,
Moved by impulses which, if from within,
Yet far outside the center man begin;
But in the grand mood, every softest tone
Comes from the living God at very heart—
From thee who infinite core of being art,
Thee who didst call our names ere ever we could sin.

We all have moods. Sometimes everything looks dark, and we hardly know why. We get up in the morning and wonder why we can't sing. Nothing really bad has happened to us, but we are gloomy.

Fortunately God has not commanded that we have one mood or another. He knows we have our ups and downs. "He knows our frame," says the psalmist, "he remembers that we are dust." We have fears and anxieties when at the moment there is nothing to be afraid of.

Of course, as the hymn writer says, "We walk in danger all the way." But we also walk with God all the way. If we let our minds imagine all the possible things that could go wrong, we will live constantly with fear.

But God wants to give us the grand mood. He doesn't want us to probe into our own minds and hearts to find it, nor into the world around us. He wants us to keep our eyes on him. Remember that Peter began to sink when, walking toward Jesus on the Sea of Galilee, he took his eyes off Jesus to look at the billowing waves around him.

And what do we see when we focus on Jesus? We see a Lord who loves us so much that he died on a cross for us. We see a God "who, from our mothers' arms, has blessed us on our way."

"Surely goodness and mercy shall follow me all the days of my life" (Ps. 23:6).

Accepted

DAY **10**

Law is our schoolmaster, Our Master, Christ
Lived under all our laws, yet always prayed—
So walked the water when the storm was highest.
Law is thy Father's; thou hast it obeyed,
And it thereby subject to thee hast made—
To rule it, Master, for thy brethren's sakes—
Well may he guide the law by whom law's maker makes.

Christ obeyed God's law perfectly. He was tried and tested, tempted as we are, but did not sin. And this he did for us. In some strange way he gives us his righteousness, so that in the sight of the Father we are perfect. It is almost as if God, like an indulgent father, has a blind spot and thinks his child is without fault.

Of course God knows. He knows all our sins and shame. But in Christ we are restored to him as if we had never sinned. He has promised not to remember our sins. They are washed away in the blood of the Lamb, as far as the east is from the west.

We can never know the wonder of this miraculous turnabout unless we have earnestly tried to obey his law and create our own righteousness. Paul said that for him the law only made his plight more desperate. "I do not do the good I want, but the evil I do not want is what I do. . . . Wretched man that I am," he wrote. "Woe is me! For I am lost," cried Isaiah. For them there was no hope in obedience to the law. Bankrupt, they were driven to God's mercy, to Christ's redemption. If there is no mercy, there is no hope. The law becomes a schoolmaster, directing us to find hope in some other way. And there is a way. By grace through faith we are saved.

Can we do other than walk in a daze to believe that we are accepted by God, not because we have obeyed the law, but simply because the Lord died for us and flings wide the door of his kingdom for us?

"There is therefore now no condemnation for those who are in Christ Jesus. For the law of the Spirit of life in Christ Jesus has set me free from the law of sin and death" (Rom. 8:1-2).

The Waiting God

I see a little child whose eager hands
Search the thick stream that drains the crowded street
For possible things hid in its current slow,
Near by, behind him, a great palace stands,
Where kings might welcome nobles to their feet,
Soft sounds, sweet scents, fair sights there only go—
There the child's father lives, but the child does not know.

Are we like the child who searches the muddy stream for things, when all the while his father sits in the palace waiting to give him all good?

Many of us do just that. We probe around for things that will give us satisfaction. It may be money. It may be prestige or power. It may be taking first in life's mad race. All the while we have a deep suspicion that somewhere a great treasure is hidden, if only we could find it. And God sits in the palace window waiting to give it to us.

The supreme treasure is God himself. The cross is the assurance that he wants us to claim him, now and forever. We live with him and get caught up in his ways. We learn that we are important simply because he loves us and makes us his children. No longer need we fight for a place in the sun. We learn that we become servants as he became the servant of all. To give, we discover, is more blessed than to receive.

Back in the palace, we have his ear at all times. He comforts us in our griefs, he gives us hope when we are discouraged. In the hour of death he is at our side ready to put us on our feet again in his everlasting kingdom.

"Fear not, little flock, for it is your Father's good pleasure to give you the kingdom" (Luke 12:32).

Blessing in Loss

So, Lord, if thou tak'st from me all the rest,
Thyself with each resumption drawing nigher,
It shall but hurt me as the thorn of the briar,
When I reach to the pale flower in its breast.
To have thee, Lord, is to have all thy best,
Holding it by its very life divine—
To let my friend's hand go, and take his heart in mine.

God wants us to have all good. That we know. But it is God who defines the good. And his thoughts are not always our thoughts, nor our ways his ways. It just could be that we become absorbed in all sorts of things that, if not in themselves harmful, still distract us from God and the good he wants us to have.

What would we include in an inventory of good things? Health, certainly. But there have been times when sickness has given us a whole new understanding of blessings we had failed to claim. For most of us, money seems good. Again, there are instances when money, not being used for good purposes, becomes the tyrant and insists on being accumulated and hoarded. People lose the joy of giving it away. Many people think it good to be winners. If that becomes a passion, a person can't enjoy anyone else who does better, or earns more, or looks better, or is praised more.

It may then be a blessing from God to lose some of the things we count dear. Their loss may even draw us nearer to God himself. We had been counting on these questionable goods for happiness, only to discover when they're gone that happiness was some other place. God waits in the wings to give us unsuspected comfort and joy. For him to draw nearer is the best blessing of all.

"But seek first his kingdom and his righteousness, and all these things shall be yours as well" (Matt. 6:33).

Ready for the Lord

My Lord, I have no clothes to come to thee;
My shoes are pierced and broken with the road;
I am torn and weathered, wounded with the goad,
And soiled with tugging at my weary load;
The more I need thee! A very prodigal
I stagger into thy presence, Lord of me:
one look, my Christ, and at thy feet I fall!

His doctor told him he had but six months to live. He told his pastor that he was afraid to meet God, and added, "I know I have to be cleaned up before he will let me in."

Aren't we all inclined to be like that? Dare we think that God will receive us as we are—with the dust and grime of our lives? We have disappointed and hurt so many people by what we have done and, even more, by neglecting the many things we might have done. If we were to list them, they would fill page after page.

The glorious news from God is that we need not get cleaned up at all to be ready for him. He comes, accepts us as we are in faith, then goes to work to clean us up *after* we are with him. Our hearts are filled with unworthy guests—pride, envy, greed, defensiveness. When the Lord enters, these low visitors become uncomfortable, and one by one will be on the way out.

They do not leave willingly. They will dig in for a long stay, even if they are uneasy. We will need to make sure that Jesus has a firm place with us. This we do by faithfulness at worship, by prayer, by the nurture of his Word and Supper, and by service with our Lord to all who are in need. All this is so repulsive to the low rabble in our hearts that they well may give up on us.

"Jesus rebuked him [the unclean spirit], saying, 'Be silent, and come out of him!' And the unclean spirit . . . came out of him" (Mark 1:25-26).

His Will and Ours

DAY

14

I will what thou will'st—only keep me sure
That thou art willing; call to me now and then.
So, ceasing to enjoy, I shall endure
With perfect patience—willing beyond my ken,
Beyond my love, beyond my thinking scope;
Willing to be because thy will is pure;
Willing thy will beyond all bounds of hope.

When Jesus in the Garden of Gethsemane cried "not as I will, but as thou will," his own will did not die. He was embracing his Father's will. There is a difference between surrendering and embracing. To give up your own will to someone is one thing; to join your will with another is something different. You still have your will.

When God created us with free will, he made us different from a dog that has no will but his master's, different from the bird that yields only to instinct. Even when we sin we have wills, wills that disobey their Maker. Never are we reduced to being mere mammals, cousins of the rat. We may be in rebellion, but we are princes in rebellion.

It has been said that God does not love a weary collapse. He does love our wills to merge with his will. Then we become partners and friends. He is not a tyrant; we are not cowering slaves. We are his daughters and sons.

To know his will at all times is not possible. We need to pray, "Keep me sure that thou art willing." Without being sure of his will, we still have to choose a course, often with a prayer that he will "call now and then" and that he will forgive if we have misunderstood. And he will.

"But his delight is in the law of the Lord, and on his law he meditates day and night" (Ps. 1:2).

Mary Hull Mohr

JOHN DONNE

 OHN DONNE (1572–1631) is perhaps best known as a 17th-century love poet. But he also wrote religious poetry. He probably would most like to have been remembered as a preacher.

Donne did not start out to be a clergyman. Rather, he would have preferred a position in the court of James I; but he finally accepted an appointment as a clergyman of the Church of England when it was apparent that no high-ranking secular positions were going to be offered to him.

It would be a mistake to assume, however, that Donne entered the clergy without religious interests. In his love poetry, he consistently used religious metaphors, while in his religious poetry he used metaphors of earthly love. For him life was all of a piece.

Much of his religious poetry was written before he became a clergyman. It is deeply personal and characterized by his conviction of his own sin. But the poetry is not morbid, because alongside this conviction of sin is an assurance of God's mercy and an understanding of human redemption through the death and resurrection of Jesus Christ.

Donne created his sermons, *The Devotions Upon Emergent Occasions,* and his "Hymn to God the Father" after his ordination. He was made a deacon and priest of St. Paul's Cathedral in 1615 and became dean of St. Paul's in 1621. Eventually he became one of the most acclaimed preachers of his time. Donne's contemporary biographer, Izaak Walton, called him "a Preacher in earnest; weeping sometimes for his auditory, sometime with them: always preaching to himself, like an Angel from a cloud."

Donne's sermons strike the 20th-century reader as complicated. He uses vivid imagery and long, involved sentences. He was sometimes criticized even in his own time by Puritans who felt that his style was too "high." But as a clergyman, Donne did not speak down to his parishioners. His were the concerns of the day and he rooted his discussion of those concerns in a careful reading of the Bible. As in his religious poetry, his central themes were sin and the redemption of that sin through the death and resurrection of Jesus.

Betrayal

I am Thy son, made with Thyself to shine,
Thy servant, whose pains thou hast still repaid,
Thy sheep, Thine Image, and, till I betrayed
Myself, a temple of Thy spirit divine.

(Donne 1978)

In this section of his second "Holy Sonnet," Donne reflects upon the glory of his creation and the shame of his own sinfulness. In the images of son, servant, sheep, image, and temple, he captures what it is that human beings were created to be.

We are children of God, blessed with a rich inheritance of love and gifted with the promise of full lives, lives that can shine as the stars shine in the heavens.

We are servants—servants of God to be sure, but servants also to each other. That servanthood can also be a rich blessing as we experience the joys of giving of ourselves to others.

We are sheep, tenderly cared for by a Shepherd who counts each one of us as special. Although we may stray, we know that our Shepherd will seek us out and bring us back to the safety of the fold.

We are images of God, created not to be gods but to carry God's love to others in this world. As such we are a special creation.

We are temples, sanctified by God's love for us. We are places where God's Holy Spirit comes to dwell, where that spirit finds its fulfillment in human life.

Still, with all of that promise, we have betrayed ourselves. We have rebelled against our Creator. We have chosen a different path from the one God created us to take. We have become children of our own desires. We serve our own needs and follow shepherds who do not care about our welfare. We are not temples, but rather banks where we store our talents so that they will be there when we need them. And we begin to lose the lustrous image of God.

Is it any wonder that Donne despairs of himself and us and wonders if God will grant him mercy?

Dear God, we are aware of the power of sin in our lives, a power that often prevents us from seeing your purpose in our lives. Help us to understand what it means to be children of God so that we may live out your promise for us. In Jesus' name, amen.

Forgiveness

Wilt Thou forgive that sin where I begun,
Which is my sin, though it were done before?
Wilt Thou forgive those sins through which I run,
And do them still, though still I do deplore?
When Thou hast done, Thou has not done,
For I have more.

(Donne 1978)

To meditate on sin and guilt is no longer considered healthy. And yet Donne's conviction of sin in the first stanza of "A Hymn to God the Father" strikes a responsive chord. His frank acceptance of original sin, the sin which is his though "it were done before," is a conviction about the human condition. We know in our hearts that because we are human beings we participate in much of the suffering that is part of our world. We have fancier words than "sin" to describe the dreadful things that we can do to each other, words such as "racism," "sexism," and "economic exploitation."

Donne, living in another time and place, would have used different language than this. But his conviction that he bears responsibility for the sins of humanity is still meaningful for us. We need to hear his words.

We more often reflect about the "sins through which I run," sins we can remember and perhaps control. These are our individual sins, the ones we always hope to do something about. We resolve not to pass on harmful stories we hear about friends. We decide to become peacemakers in our congregations rather than take sides in bitter controversies. We make many efforts to change ourselves into better people.

And yet, in this first stanza of this poem, Donne puts together our individual sins and those sins we share as the people of God, past and present. In doing so he raises questions about our sense that we can indeed make ourselves sinless. Could it be that only God's forgiveness can be the answer? Yes, Donne says. And his absolute conviction of his own sinfulness makes even more amazing his faith in the power of that forgiveness.

Dear God, help us to acknowledge our sinfulness. But also make us aware of the power of your forgiveness in our lives. In Jesus' name, amen.

Assurance

<table>
<tr><td>

D A Y

3

</td><td>

Wilt Thou forgive that sin by which I have won
Others to sin? and made my sin their door?
Wilt Thou forgive that sin which I did shun
A year or two, but wallowed in a score?
When Thou hast done, Thou hast not done.
For I have more.

(Donne 1978)

</td></tr>
</table>

In this second stanza of "A Hymn to God the Father," Donne is still meditating on his sin. He first speaks of the sin of tempting others. We are reminded of the obvious and rather silly things that we do, such as convincing ourselves that a luxurious, peaceful morning at home on Sunday will do us and our family more "good" than church. Perhaps we feel more guilty when we think about the time we wormed some damaging bit of information out of an acquaintance who had promised to hold a confidence. Or, because a friend has been diagnosed as an alcoholic, we regret our expression of contempt for those who refused alcohol at our last party.

But more insidious is the kind of model our life has become, particularly to those who look up to us in our homes, our workplaces, our communities. We make clear in our actions that we believe that wielding power is more important than caring for people. We convey subtly to our children the power of money and suggest that it is the only measure of success. We are impressed by labels on clothes rather than by the person inside of those clothes.

Yes, we have "made my sin their door." And we also understand what Donne is referring to when he talks about falling back into sin. How easy it is to recover the bad habits that we felt we had overcome: to abuse our bodies by overeating, to close our eyes to the needs we see around us, to forget to honor those we love.

And yet, finally Donne's verse is not about those sins at all. It is again about God's forgiveness of those sins and our assurance of that forgiveness.

Dear God, forgive us for those times when we have been responsible for the sins of others. Have mercy on us when our best resolutions fail. Hear us when we call out to you. In Jesus' name, amen.

Illumination

*I have a sin of fear, that when I have spun
My last thread, I shall perish on the shore;
Swear by Thyself that at my death Thy Sun
Shall shine as it shines now, and heretofore;
And having done that, Thou hast done.
I have no more.*

(Donne 1978)

Despair is finally our greatest sin. In this final stanza of his poem, Donne reminds us that despair is the sin that paralyzes, that incapacitates, that ties us down to a living death. That is the sin that destroys us. Donne's biographer Izaak Walton says that Donne was ill when he wrote this poem. If so, he was describing his own conviction of sin as he faced death and his own fear of perishing because of sin. But we don't have to have a physical illness to fear the despair that grips us when we confront sin.

For some of us, this despair is very real when we contemplate the problems of the world; perhaps the despair is even greater for those of us who have been active in movements we had hoped would alleviate such problems. Sometimes the despair grips us when we look at the problems in our own families: broken relationships, verbal and physical abuse, lost opportunities. Or perhaps we despair when we contemplate problems even within the church: unfulfilled promises, worldly ambitions, waste of material and spiritual resources. Whatever the cause, we all experience the sin of despair and face the fear of perishing that Donne describes.

Finally, how beautiful Donne's words of promise are for us here. Where before he had talked of forgiveness, now we have the image of a blinding light filling our lives, a light that penetrates into all parts of the world.

His Son has become our Sun, the source of all goodness. God's promise has been fulfilled and the light that penetrates all of our dark places (places Donne has exposed in the poem) finally becomes not the heat of punishment, but the shining of a new day. And it is that reassurance that illuminates Donne and gives us and him forgiveness for all sins.

Dear God, may we also have the conviction that you have us in your arms. And although we fall short of your glory, may that glory become part of our lives through the death and resurrection of Jesus Christ. In Jesus' name we pray, amen.

Sunset and Sunrise

DAY 5

Hence is't that I am carried towards the West
This day, when my soul's form bends toward the East.
There I should see a Sun, by rising, set,
And by that setting endless day beget.

(Donne 1978)

Donne places and dates this poem very exactly: "Good Friday, 1613. Riding Westward." In the poem the narrator is engaged in a very specific activity on a very specific day. He is riding toward the West on Good Friday. And yet we also are in the poem. For the rider is each one of us on the day on which Christ died; riding away from the horror of that death of God.

And just as the narrator cannot tear himself away from that event, so too we, as Christians, are drawn to that death, even as we ride away from it. Donne describes what we would see if we would turn our faces: "That blood . . . made dirt of dust, . . . that flesh . . . ragg'd and torn, and his miserable mother."

The spectacle of the death of God is more than we can bear, so we do not confront it directly. Donne says he is being propelled toward the West by "pleasure or business." The vagueness of this description also suits our preoccupations. We busy ourselves with our routine obligations. We feel good about the time we spend on good causes, healthful exercise, community activity. We do not contemplate the death of God. To do so would call our very existence into question. It would be to see our blood no longer coursing through our veins, giving us health and vitality, but spilling out onto the ground, sapping our bodies of all strength. It would be to look into the mirror and see not a fresh, lively face or even a wrinkled skin, but ragged and torn flesh. We are frightened by such reality.

And yet Donne says, "Because you are human, your soul's eyes bend toward the East." Look with the eyes of your soul and see that the Son of God is truly dead. But also observe that God's Sun defies all that we know about nature and rises never to set again. We can only know this new and endless day by experiencing the sunset.

Dear God, turn our eyes toward the East that we may know the pain of death, but also the rebirth into your endless day. In Jesus' name, amen.

Mercy

"But God hath made no decree to distinguish the season of his mercies. . . . He can bring the Summer out of Winter, though thou have no Spring; though in the ways of fortune, or understanding, or conscience, though you have been benighted till now, wintered and frozen . . . now God comes to thee, not as in the dawning of the day, not as in the bud of the spring, but as the Sun at noon. . . . All occasions invite his mercies and all times are his seasons" (Potter and Simpson 1953).

In this sermon, preached on Christmas in 1624, Donne talks about the radical mercy of God. Although God has created nature, here Donne describes a God who works outside of nature, who enters our lives in ways that defy human understanding. The kind of mercy that Donne describes for us is not the kind that follows the laws we understand; it is not in the natural cycle of things.

Rather this mercy is sudden and unpredictable. It is intense, coming upon us without warning, warming us in ways we are not prepared for.

For those of us who live in northern areas, the seasons are the most predictable parts of our lives. Oh, we may have warm winters and cool summers and deplore the fact that we had too short a spring, but we know that spring follows winter and that summer comes before the autumn. There is a kind of rightness about the passage of time. We know that it is circular and repetitive, that we can depend upon its regularity and predictability.

Donne shakes us out of a sense of predictability about God's mercy. He reminds us that it has no colds or warms or in betweens. It has no mornings or evenings or nights. It is outside of our natural experience. It is not tied to our time or to our place.

Rather God's mercy is unconditional and intense. We do not watch mercy's bud blossom into the full flower. We can not get ready for the brilliant sun of mercy's presence by waking in the early dawn and preparing ourselves for the heat of the day. We must accept that which we cannot understand, prepare ourselves for the transforming power of God's mercy in our lives, confident of its rightness for us.

Dear God, help us to live lives that are receptive to your mercies. Keep us open to their unexpectedness and their intensity. In Jesus' name, amen.

Conversion

Yet dearly I love You, and would be loved fain,
But am betrothed unto Your enemy:
Divorce me, untie or break that knot again,
Take me to You, imprison me, for I,
Except You enthrall me, never shall be free,
Nor ever chaste, except You ravish me.
(Donne 1978)

We like to think of grace as falling upon us as Shakespeare says, like "gentle rain from heaven," a warm, cleansing experience that leaves us happily contemplating a new life with God. For Donne, and probably for many of us, the true experience of God's grace is much more painful. In powerful metaphors, Donne in this "Holy Sonnet" forces us to think not only of God's power but also and perhaps primarily of our resistance to that grace.

In our image of the gentle rain, we stand in a field with our faces upturned waiting to receive the grace of God. In Donne's imagery we are controlled by the forces of evil. It is not that we don't want to lift our faces to God. We do, but we are bound to God's enemy. It won't do, says Donne in the beginning of this poem, for God to simply "knock, breathe, shine, and seek to mend." More radical measures are needed.

Divorce, imprisonment, and rape: these are the painful, even repulsive, images Donne uses to describe the mercy of God. These actions are necessary because of our bondage. "But we are not such bad people," we say. "We do the right things most of the time." Perhaps Donne is speaking most especially to us in this poem. He wasn't a bad person either. Oh, perhaps he was a bit too ambitious. He had written some love poetry that was a bit too forthright. But he was a responsible man, faithful to his wife and friends. The conversion this poem describes sounds much too radical for such a man.

But the power of God's grace can transform lives. We people in the mainline churches perhaps have something to learn from our sisters and brothers in churches that emphasize "conversion experiences." We need not deny that we are already baptized into God's grace, but at the same time we need to be ready to receive afresh that transforming power that God's grace can be in our lives.

Dear God, imprison me so that I may be free to work your will in the world. In Jesus' name, amen.

Our Church

Dwells she with us, or like adventuring knights
First travel we to seek, and then make love?
Betray, kind husband, Thy spouse to our sights,
And let mine amorous soul court Thy mild Dove,
Who is most true and pleasing to Thee then
When she is embraced and open to most men.

(Donne 1978)

Where is God's true church? This question is no easier for us to answer today than it was for Donne 375 years ago. Perhaps it is even harder, since we have more kinds of churches and more religious expressions than he could have dreamed of.

The contradictory impulses Donne describes in the first two lines above describe our dilemma as we seek that true church. Should we undertake the search "like adventuring knights" and ride out to visit all available churches? We know many people who do. Commentators on the religious scene have suggested that we live in a church supermarket in which people go up and down the aisles, picking and choosing what fits their "life-style."

The alternative is to simply settle into the church in which we were reared, thus accepting our parents' choice. With this alternative, we accommodate ourselves to what is familiar.

Donne suggests that the Holy Spirit dwells in the church that embraces the greatest number and is the most "open." There is something in me that wants a little more precise theological definition of what it means to belong to a church, a more discriminating sense of what it means to be a church member.

Although mildly shocking, Donne's imagery is also lovely. Our desire for union with other believers, our need for a home where we can be lovingly received, is captured by the sexual metaphor Donne uses. He reminds us that the Bible speaks of the church as the bride of God. But rather than thinking of this bride as exclusively married to God, God "betrays" her to us so that we too can share in her embrace. Donne reminds us that the church should offer herself with this openness. And as members of the church, we also need to embrace others openly, unstintingly.

Dear God, help us to understand your spouse the church, to accept those who come to her, and to recognize the different forms she takes in our lives and in the lives of others. In Jesus' name, amen.

Doubt

Doubt wisely; in strange way
To stand inquiring right is not to stray;
To sleep, or run wrong is. On a huge hill,
Cragged and steep, Truth stands, and he that will
Reach her, about must, and about must go;
And what the hill's suddenness resist, win so.

(Donne 1978)

Most of us fear to doubt, and yet doubting is part of the search for truth. We especially fear doubt in the young, as if the questions they raise will inevitably lead them to a permanent loss of faith. Few of us live every day and confront every problem confident that our accumulated wisdom has led us to positive truth.

No, doubt is a part of life. In his "Satire III," Donne has captured this reality by his image of truth standing on a high hill, cragged and steep. The road to that truth is a difficult and circular one. It is not straight up the hill, but around and around it. Life is pictured as a journey around, as well as up, that hill.

Where does life around that hill lead us? In today's world, it inevitably leads us to some who do not believe. Often we become close to such people, admire them, respect them, and as those ideas become ours, we find ourselves doubting. Or we encounter times of great sadness and pain, when the old answers will not do, when our ready responses to life are no longer adequate. So we doubt. Or we simply become involved in this world. We become busy acquiring things and running after pleasures of many kinds. One day we wake up and discover that we doubt. We are traveling around the hill.

But as we travel slowly around the hill, we are steadily moving up it as well. The only mistakes that we can make, says the poet, are to go to sleep or to run too quickly. No, we "about must, and about must go." Doubt is a part of such a journey. We must learn to accept it in ourselves and—just as important—accept it in others, as part of the journey to truth.

Dear God, accompany us on our journey to truth. Take us through the times of doubt, so that we may climb that hill to the Truth. In Jesus' name, amen.

The Dying of Death

Thou art slave to fate, change, kings and desperate men,
And dost with poison, war, and sickness dwell;
And poppy or charms can make us sleep as well,
And better than thy stroke; why swell'st thou then?
One short sleep past, we wake eternally,
And death shall be no more; death, thou shalt die.

(Donne 1978)

Death often seems all-powerful. We spend millions of dollars in health care and in research to fight it. Many of us pay close attention daily to food and exercise in order to prolong our lives.

What is this power? Can we control it? We know, intellectually at least, that death is inevitable. Yet most of us believe the inevitable can be postponed. Some of us even believe that science will one day conquer death, so that we will live indefinitely.

For Donne, death was more immediate. By the time he had written this poem, he had experienced at least one devastating plague in London. But such periods of sickness only intensified the sense of loss that must have been present in a daily life attended by infection, death from childbirth, and disease.

Donne's reflection on the power of death comes not from any belief in the ability of science to postpone it or overcome it, but from his faith in God. In this address to death, he reminds death that it is caused by a multitude of other things, and therefore does not call the shots. And it also has a rival that teaches us something about death: sleep. Ironically, death is also finally subject to death. Eternal life conquers it. Death is really only a "short sleep past," a sleep from which we will wake to discover that indeed death has no power but has been overcome by life, life in Jesus Christ.

"Now if we be dead with Christ, we believe that we shall also live with him: knowing that Christ being raised from the dead dieth no more; death hath no more dominion over him" (Rom. 6:8-9 KJV).

The Resurrection

"To have knowne Good, to have believed it, to have intended it, nay to have preached it to others, will not serve, They must have done good" (Potter and Simpson 1953).

These lines come from the conclusion of an Easter sermon Donne preached in 1625. His text is about the last judgment, a judgment at which those who have done good deeds will be rewarded in the final resurrection.

The last judgment was very real for Donne. Throughout his religious poetry and his sermons, a sense of the importance of that day for all people is clear. In this Easter sermon, therefore, he talks not so much about Jesus' resurrection as about the resurrection of all of us, made possible by his.

Donne talks about the many spiritual resurrections we undergo in our earthly lives. We are resurrected from ignorance when we come to know God's Word. We are resurrected from a love for sin as we come to know God's plan in our life. We are resurrected from despair as we come to know God's love in our lives.

These resurrections result in fruits of the spirit, the "doing Good" of the Scripture text below. It is "they who have done good" who will experience the resurrection at the last judgment, says Donne.

The mystery of the last judgment is not much discussed these days, although we affirm it every time we say the Apostles' Creed. It remains for most of us just that: a mystery. We need sometimes to be reminded of its healthy stress on the importance of the body in our religious faith. This emphasis on the material is also evident in the focus on those good deeds that are consequences of our spiritual resurrections on this earth. Donne's healthy earthiness helps us to understand that God came into this world in human flesh and that it is as humans that we express God's love in this world.

"All who are in the tombs will hear his voice and come forth, those who have done good, to the resurrection of life" (John 5:28-29).

Connections

Tis all in pieces, all coherence gone;
All just supply, and all relation
Prince, subject, father, son, are things forgot,
For every man alone thinks he hath got
To be a phoenix, and there can be
None of that kind, of which he is, but he.
(Donne 1978)

Some have compared our own times to those of Donne. In the early 17th century, new discoveries in science, particularly in astronomy, were shaking old beliefs. In a poem Donne calls "The Anatomy of the World," he explores the implications of some of the new discoveries.

Donne was perhaps a bit ahead of his time in recognizing that such discoveries would eventually affect relationships in society. In the lines above, he deplores the beginning of a new sense of individuality. He realized people would no longer think of themselves first in relationship to others; rather, they would think of themselves as autonomous individuals.

But this change affected mostly the lives of men. Women continued to think of themselves in relationship to others: as mothers, wives, sisters, daughters. In our time, we have become aware of the danger of only thinking of ourselves as related to others. We need to treasure the gifts God has given to us as individuals, the talents that enrich us and that we can share with others.

But we also need to appreciate the gift of relationships. Perhaps even more than Donne, we see the dangers of an individuality that isolates, that cuts one off from a sense of being a part of the whole people of God.

We would not want to return to a world in which we had to define ourselves as subject to another person. But we do want to see our connections as human beings. It is in our relationships to others that our individuality can be most clearly expressed. God's command to love others can only be real in lives that are lived as part of a larger world.

Dear God, help us to respect the individuality of all persons, women as well as men; but also help us to see how our many relationships can enrich and develop our lives together as the people of God. In Jesus' name, amen.

Part of the Continent

"No man is an island, entire of itself; every man is a piece of the continent, a part of the main" (Donne 1978).

The temptation to make islands of our lives is a powerful one. Islands are places of escape. They represent for us idyllic retreats where we can indulge our fantasies and take refuge from the hectic pace that drives our lives. On islands we seem to be capable of going it alone, protected by water from unwelcome invasions.

But Donne says, "We are not islands, but pieces of the continent, parts of a whole." There is no retreat from other parts of God's creation. We are connected to each other. We are part of each other.

We cannot think of our actions as private, affecting only us or our family. We contribute to the whole of God's creation. Just as no country in today's world can afford to consider its own future apart from the world situation, so no individual can go it alone. About this we have no choice.

Why do we have this illusion of privacy? Why this belief that we can create our own lives in any way we wish if we do not consciously harm others? Our desire to control our own futures on our own private island is strong. But this desire to control is, in fact, a sign that we are out of control, that we are not willing to be a part of God's plan, a part of his creation, a part of the continent.

Dear God, help us to control our desire to create our own little worlds, to make islands out of our own families, our own communities, our own churches. Teach us to feel at home in the continent of your creation. In Jesus' name, amen.

Listening

 "Any man's death diminishes me, because I am involved in mankind, and therefore never send to know for whom the bell tolls; it tolls for thee" (Donne 1978).

When I was a child, the death of anyone in our community was announced to all by the tolling of the church bell. The number of times that the bell tolled was the same as the age of the dead person. Consequently, in our small town, the bells told who had died.

Donne is talking about the same custom in these lines from his *Devotions.* But he reminds us that those bells do not just announce the death of another. Because I am a part of God's creation, those bells are also ringing for me.

We listen to the bells not only because they tell us about the life and death of someone we have known. They also tell us something about our life and death because we are related to the one who has died. Donne connects us here to our mortality, to the fragility of our lives. He reminds us that the death of another is also our death, the affliction of another's pain is also our pain.

But if that is true about death, it is also true about life. We are also connected to an immortality, to that which gives strength to our lives. He reminds us that the birth of another is also our birth, the rejoicing of another in happiness is also our joy.

Bells call us to many things. When we are children they call us to classes. In our communities they call us to church. On the streets, they often call us to give money to worthy causes. Sometimes they signal the distress of a fire. We have them placed in our homes to herald the arrival of friends and relatives. At Christmas time we especially think of them as announcing the arrival of the Christ Child.

Dear God, open our ears so that we may hear your bells. Open our eyes so that we may see your creation. Open our hearts so that we may reach out to others in both our joys and our sorrows. In Jesus' name, amen.

Allan Sager

MEISTER ECKHART

MEET Meister Eckhart (1260–1329). He was not only a highly trained philosopher and theologian, but also a mystic, a preacher, and a poet. He cultivated rhetorical effects, bold paradoxes, unusual metaphors, and neologisms to stir his readers and hearers from intellectual and moral slumber.

A member of the Dominican Order, Eckhart earned the title of honor, "Meister," while teaching at the University of Paris, where he attracted notice by the contentious role he played in current theological controversies. He was posthumously condemned by a papal decree issued on March 27, 1329, after a papal trial. Scholars today agree he was unjustly condemned. In 1980, the Dominican Order formally requested that Rome lift its censure of him. It seems to have been his fate to arouse both deep affection and uncompromising hostility.

With Eckhart's condemnation, his thought went underground. There it influenced Martin Luther and many others. However, his effort to develop a holistic spirituality that combined deep cosmic mysticism with prophetic consciousness was lost for many years in mainstream Christianity.

For Eckhart, God is both ultimate depth and inaccessible height. God is ineffable for Eckhart—incomprehensible, the "superessential intellect." To know God, he affirms, one must enter into "the darkness of unknowing."

Eckhart's thinking is dialectical and so his language is paradoxical, even shocking at times. Persons who prefer clear either/or distinctions, a coherent rationalistic system, or sentimental nudgings will be disappointed. The man who has written, "I pray God to rid me of God," cannot be read with ease or detachment.

An original and creative thinker, Eckhart's chief themes were creation-centered: blessing, cosmos, compassion, beauty, healing, darkness, emptiness, creativity, celebration, justice, and humor. His wit and insight capture not only our minds, but our hearts as well.

Equality and Unity

"Love will never be anywhere except where quality and unity are. Between a master and his servant there is no peace for there is no real equality. And there can be no love where love does not find equality or is not busy creating equality. Nor is there any pleasure without equality. Practice equality in human society. Learn to love, esteem, consider all people like yourself. What happens to another, be it bad or good, pain or joy, ought to be as if it happened to you" (Fox 1983).

For such words, Meister Eckhart was declared a heretic. You don't speak of equality and unity in the 13th or any century without reprisal.

Among other things, Eckhart has been called a feminist. As early as seven centuries ago, he declared that one gender did not have superiority over the other. But if Eckhart had been asked in an interview if he was far ahead of his time, he would probably have thrown back his head and guffawed, "What, me? Ahead of my time? I'm already 13 centuries behind the New Testament."

He likely would have pointed to Jesus' respectful interaction with women. He surely would have reminded us of St. Paul's declaration that we are all one in Christ Jesus. That notion of being "one in Christ" covers both issues—equality and unity.

Think of how many of the world's conflicts and ills have to do with humanity's refusal to acknowledge equality and unity as givens in Christ. All of us who have been baptized into Christ are members of his one body, members one of another. Both in Romans 12 and 1 Corinthians 12, the body imagery is instructional. "But God has so composed the body . . . that there may be no discord in the body, but that the members may have the same care for one another" (1 Cor. 12:24-25).

St. Paul knows that we will never come to equality and unity without that higher gift, that more excellent way. And so 1 Corinthians 12 leads directly into the great love chapter, 1 Corinthians 13.

If I this day am to love, I will remember that love will never be anywhere except where equality and unity are.

God of Love, in your very being as Triune we find equality and unity. You call us in Christ to love as he loved. Make us restless wherever injustice reigns. Make us loving so that equality and unity, gifts divine, may be manifest also among us. Amen.

Body Consciousness

DAY 2 *"The soul loves the body"* (Fox 1983).

The body is far more important than Western theology or spirituality has conceded. The negative attitude of Western Christianity toward the body is not biblical.

The authors of Scripture saw the human person as embodied. It was the Greeks and the church fathers influenced by Greek philosophy who distinguished between body and spirit in a way that contributed to our modern separation of the two.

The neglect of body consciousness is an enormous obstacle both to human maturity as well as to spiritual growth.

"But what has all that theology and philosophy and history to do with my life today?" you rightfully ask. "I normally let those topics alone for others to fuss over."

If you and I look objectively at our treatment of our bodies, we may begin to squirm. How many of our actions are truly loving? When I subject my body to substances known or believed to be harmful, surely I am not doing that in the name of love. When I ignore signals from my body that I need more rest, what does my refusal to listen betray? When I keep telling my body that I am too busy to get proper exercise, what is my body to believe about how I am disposed towards it?

When we begin to poke around with questions such as these, we may begin to have some second thoughts. Perhaps some of our thinking about our bodies has, after all, been tainted with unbiblical ideas.

God gave us bodies, fashioning us from the dust of the earth. To care responsibly for what God has provided is to love God and to honor one of God's good designs. To neglect my body today makes me less fit to love my neighbor tomorrow.

Wise and faithful God, in your wisdom you gave me life, which is embodied. You never elevated the spirit at the expense of the body. I confess that too often my actions reflect less than a high and holy love for my body. By the incarnation of your Son, you hallowed the sacred bodily design. Making new resolves to better care for my body isn't good enough, Lord. Rather, come into my life with your transforming power so that you live in and through me. Then at once I shall love the body and the God whose idea it was. In Jesus' name and for his sake I pray. Amen.

Thankfulness to God

"If the only prayer you say in your entire life is 'thank you,' that would suffice" (Fox 1983).

Credit Meister Eckhart with a bellybutton theology. Only God has no bellybutton. The rest of us have a bellybutton right there in our centers to remind us that life is gift—entirely gift. And the proper response to gift is gratitude—hence, the "thank you" prayer.

Gratitude does not come easily for us. Our culture is bent on economic growth, and economic growth is dependent upon the constant stimulation of our appetites to want more. We're conditioned to be "graspy," to believe we can only show our worth by showing off our acquisitions. Millions of dollars are spent on advertising that propagandizes us to believe we must add the latest gadgets and exotic experiences to our hoard of gadgets and experiences. Little wonder that petitions to "give me" or "help me get" come much more naturally to our lips than songs of thanks and praise.

Have you ever wondered why it is that we have to teach our children to say "thank you"? Ought it not just be a natural, reasonable thing to do, given the gifted character of life? Shouldn't even children be able to figure out how much that is undeserved flows to them?

But it is precisely that giftedness to which we are blinded by sin. So curved in on ourselves are we, children included, that our prideful egos convince us that we're only getting what we deserve; we are the center around which our own little universe revolves.

But our bellybutton reminds us, at our center, that we are not that center of the universe.

So "thank you" is primal and primary! Does "thank you" come even before "forgive me"? Yes! Our courage to be penitent rests upon the assurance of God's grace freely shown us in the face of Jesus Christ. That's the gift above all gifts for which our whole lives become the only appropriate "thank you."

Today, treat each person you meet with the gloves of "thank you." Today, commune with nature with a "thank you." Today, say "thank you" to the living God from whom all blessings flow.

Good and gracious God, your showers of blessings never seem to end. Sadly, in contrast, I appear to tire of saying "thank you." I confess my ingratitude. I ask you to grant me that which I so obviously need: a grateful heart. I pray in the strong name of the Christ whose Spirit I desire. Amen.

Captured by Love

DAY 4 *"God is like a person who clears his throat while hiding and so gives himself away. God lies in wait for us with nothing so much as love. Now love is like a fishhook. A fisher cannot catch a fish unless the fish first picks up the hook. If the fish swallows the hook, no matter how it may squirm and turn, the fisher is certain of the fish. Love is the same way. Whoever is captured by love takes up this hook in such a fashion that foot and hand, mouth and eyes, heart and all that is in that person must always belong to God. Therefore, look only for this fishhook, and you will be happily caught. The more you are caught, the more you will be liberated"* (Fox 1983).

God as the Divine Fisher? I'm not sure I like that image, Meister Eckhart. Using bait and cunning? Wanting us to impale ourselves on the hook of love?

But then, Eckhart does speak of being "happily caught." That puts a different construction on the entire business. Do you think Eckhart rather assumes that all of us get caught by one thing or the other? To live is to commit ourselves to values and goals of some sort. Once we take up a value or goal, it is as though we have been caught by it, with our attentions, interests, and energies all devoted to it. And Eckhart well knows that most such commitments are binding, not liberating. Not so with that Divine Fisher. Strange the hook that frees those already in bondage.

Consider again the lines of that hymn so fraught with paradox:

Make me a captive, Lord, and then I shall be free;
Force me to render up my sword, and I shall conqueror be.
My will is not my own till thou hast made it thine;
If it would reach a monarch's throne it must its crown resign.

My heart is weak and poor until it master find;
It has no spring of action sure, it varies with the wind.
It cannot freely move till thou hast wrought its chain;
Enslave it with thy matchless love, and deathless it shall reign.
(Service Book and Hymnal, 508)

Lord Jesus, you are the truth that sets us free. Thank you for a love that is both capturing and captivating. At times we squirm under your lordship, but mostly we rejoice in that paradoxical realization of being most free when we are most caught by you. Amen.

Letting Go My Isaacs

DAY 5 *"God is not found in the soul by adding anything but by a process of subtraction"* (Fox 1983).

For commentary on Eckhart's provocative line, I can do no better than to adapt some lines from Edward J. Farrell's *Disciples and Other Strangers* (Dimension Books) titled "And Everyone Has His Own Isaac."

I want Abram for my friend, said God. I would make him a people great, more than the sea-sands, a people and a new land and a blessing. I will give him Isaac, said God.

And Abraham, looking up, loved back. I will build altars in the land you gave me, friend. And Abram moved his tent by Mamre, at Hebron built an altar to the Lord.

Then God took Abram out of doors, My childless friend, said God, Look up at the countless stars. And God said, Abram, I am going to pluck a son from you, a son to give you sons. You'll have more sons than stars, said God, before we're through.

So Abram put his faith in God and it was reckoned virtue.

But God left Abram waiting, gave him time Time almost to count the stars.

Later God thought: I cannot leave him counting stars forever. Already Sara laughs at me. It is time. It is time I gave him Isaac, said God.

And Abraham became the father of a son, Isaac. A hundred years of unspent fatherhood he poured all out on Isaac. And laughing Sara's breasts grew warm and full. Themselves they gave to Isaac.

There was no more counting stars for God's poor friend. He had the seed for all the flowers of earth. God had given Abraham his Isaac.

And God watched Abraham with love. Watched him as he played with sheep and land. And later on, He spoke: I am the Pack-Rat God, said God, and now, Abraham, I want Isaac.

But we are friends and you gave Isaac, Abr'am said.

I know we are, said God. But I want Isaac.

Till Abr'am cried, The stars so countless and the many sands and would you take my one son Isaac?

And God would only answer back: I want Isaac.

And Abraham, because he was a friend of God's said, God, Take Isaac.

God, help me let go whatever Isaacs compete with loving you. Amen.

Caution: Verbal Idol Making

DAY 6 *"I pray God to rid me of God"* (Fox 1983).

Who is this Eckhart anyway? The original "Death of God" theologian?

He also said, "The most beautiful thing which a person can say about God would be for that person to remain silent from the wisdom of an inner wealth. So, be silent and quit flapping your gums about God."

And more: "Truly God is a hidden God. All the names which the soul gives to God, it receives from the knowledge of itself. But the ground of the soul is dark. The ineffable One has no name."

Whatever else Eckhart may be saying (and often his meaning is multilayered), he is surely reminding us that words about God, including the names of God, are not God! "The map is not the territory," I learned in general semantics. And in the case of God, the "map" may, at best, only describe the territory remotely. We are wise to pray, at least on occasion, the Eckhart petition to remind us of that.

We must let go of culture's images of God to find the unknown, unnameable God. Words should lead beyond themselves, as icons that open vistas to what is beyond them. When we regard words as handles on the divine, then we know we have engaged in verbal idol making. Anything that functions as though it could contain and control God is more a hindrance than a help to our spirituality.

Eckhart would have us "sink deeply into the ineffable depths of the unfathomable ocean that is God." Perhaps we don't use words such as "ineffable" and "unfathomable" often enough in our religious life.

We say that God is both revealed and hidden. Most often we Protestants overplay what is revealed and underplay what is mystery. We certainly ought to make good efforts to understand God. But we must never presume that those efforts, no matter how diligent and inspired, can break open the mystery that is part of God's godness. God refuses to be mastered or controlled.

Almighty God, you surpass all that we can know. You've blessed us with a mind and want us to love you with it, but you refuse to allow us to control you through our mental images. In deep, reverent silence I worship you now and pray that you use the silence to rid me of all that is not of you. Amen.

God Is Eternally Young

D A Y
7

"When we say 'God is eternal,' we mean: God eternally young. God is ever green, ever verdant, ever flowering. Every action of God is new, for he makes all things new. God is the newest thing there is; the youngest thing there is. God is the beginning and if we are united to him we become new again" (Fox 1983).

Why, it's almost a challenge to think of God as young. Don't the images of age come more easily to mind as characterizations of God? In my earliest mental pictures, God looked more like my bearded grandfather than one of my youthful peers. After all, hasn't God been around a long, long time? That implies age.

"Eternally young." "Ever green." God made deciduous trees. They're especially beautiful in the fall as their leaves become splashed with colors from nature's palette. But then they scatter, leaving the tree unclothed to face the wintry blasts. In sharp contrast stand the evergreens. They do shed needles along the way, but they always keep their garb of green. Are you saying, Meister Eckhart, that God is somehow like that? Always full of life? Forever new?

I'm beginning to like the image, Meister Eckhart. But you said something more, something that speaks to my life. You said, "If we are united to him we become new again." That sounds a lot like something we find in the 15th chapter of the Gospel according to John. "I am the vine, you are the branches. He who abides in me, and I in him, he it is that bears much fruit" (John 15:5).

Each fall when we harvest grapes, I harvest also the reminder that those grapes would never form such delightful, luscious clusters if life were not coursing through that vine. The new harvest is on the old vine's new growth.

The God who remains forever new makes new all those who abide in God. What a precious promise! That promise itself remains ever green.

Lord, I thank you for this new day, which is still young no matter what the clock may say. It is a gift from you, as green and living as the evergreens. They help me to think of you, God, as eternally young, and to know that your great promises are both everlasting and ever green. All praise to you! Amen.

Trusting God

"Why is it that some people do not bear fruit? It is because they are so busy clinging to their egotistical attachments and so afraid of letting go and letting be that they have no trust either in God or in themselves. Love cannot distrust. It can only await the good trustfully. No person could ever trust God too much. Nothing people ever do is as appropriate as great trust in God. With such trust, God never fails to accomplish great things" (Fox 1983).

Letting go and letting be? Now, now, that's a mighty big order. For example, a parent mindful that some day the children will be launched knows what a challenge it will be to let them go and let them be without "egotistical attachments."

Psychologists tell us there is much we can do to let go of stress and disease. When Jesus asked, "Do you want to be made well?" he implied that health has to do with being willing to let go of disease. Can it be that at times we hang onto the familiar, though it causes us pain, rather than risk the unfamiliar, though it may promise gain?

Risking. Ah, there's the rub. To trust is to risk. Along comes Meister Eckhart with the reminder that love cannot distrust, and that none of us can ever "trust God too much."

Trusting God this day may mean letting go of my plans and my dreams, to live trustingly under the serendipity of God's good providings. Trusting God this day may mean being aware that much needless pain in marriage and family is caused by refusing either to let go or let be. Trusting God this day means that I await the good trustfully. Trusting God this day means that there is nothing else I can do that is more appropriate than to trust God greatly.

Lord Jesus, you call me to follow you. But I don't know in advance exactly where you are going. I want to trust you. Yet so often my egotistical attachments keep me holding on when I should be letting go. Only when I'm trusting you am I capable of bearing fruit. I don't exactly understand, Lord, how this all works, but I'm trusting you that it does. Thank you for never failing to accomplish great things. Amen.

Openness to God's Gifts

DAY 9 | *"Be prepared at all times for the gifts of God and be ready always for new ones. For God is a thousand times more ready to give than we are to receive"* (Fox 1983).

Some of us are evidently not as ready as Meister Eckhart was to receive new gifts from God. One of our hymns, "Spirit of God, Descend upon My Heart," is very specific about what gets on our OK-to-ask-from-God list. "I ask no dream, no prophet ecstasies, no sudden rending of the veil of clay," it claims. But we do ask God, "Take the dimness of my soul away, . . . wean my heart from earth, . . . [and] teach me to love you as your angels love." Interesting, isn't it, what we are ready to receive from God and what we feign being too modest to request.

"Be prepared at all times for the gifts of God and be ready always for new ones." That sounds quite a bit like: "Eye hath not seen nor ear heard what the Lord has prepared for them that love the Lord."

In and through Christ, God has given the church all that is needed. We have "gifts that differ according to the grace given to us" (Rom. 12:6). We must each stand ready to receive what is to be ours. "All these are inspired by one and the same Spirit, who apportions to each one individually as he wills" (1 Cor. 12:11). If we are not open to the gifts God intends to apportion to us, the whole people of God will be the poorer.

Eckhart and those passages from the New Testament call me to be prepared—not to act—but simply prepared to be a recipient. That means relinquishing my self-reliance and willingly receiving what One infinitely wiser and greater than me has prepared.

Lord, I want to be open to receive whatever gifts you may have in mind for me today, whether they are packaged as pleasure or as dismay or hurt. Whatever the nature of the gift, I know that it comes from a source gracious to the core and a thousand times more ready to give than I am to receive. Thank you especially for the greatest gift of all times, Jesus. By the power of your Spirit, stir in me a hunger to relinquish more of my life to the reign and rule of Jesus as Lord of all. I ask it in his strong name. Amen.

Feminine Images of God

 DAY 10

"From all eternity God lies on a maternity bed giving birth. The essence of God is birthing" (Fox 1983).

More pervasive than any other feminine image of God is the image of God as a mother. Not only is the Creator depicted as giving birth to creation: Christ and the Holy Spirit are also depicted in similar roles. In Isaiah we see a most powerful image of God's anguish at the human failure to embody justice: "For a long time I have held my peace, I have kept still and restrained myself; now I will cry out like a woman in travail, I will gasp and pant" (Isa. 42:14).

In Deuteronomy we find an image of God as both male and female: "You were unmindful of the Rock that begot you, and you forgot the God who gave you birth" (Deut. 32:18).

Job again balances parental images of God, speaking of his fathering of the rain and her giving birth to the ice from her womb (Job 38:28-29). Earlier in the same chapter, Job asks, "Who shut in the sea with doors, when it burst forth from the womb?" (Job 38:8). Out of that all-encompassing womb, God has given birth not only to all human beings, but to the whole magnificent natural creation as well.

Jesus uses a birth image (John 16:21) to comfort the disciples as they considered difficulties ahead. A woman, he said, has sorrow when her hour has come and her birth contractions begin, but later her sorrow is turned to joy by the arrival of the baby. According to John's account, it was only minutes later that Jesus began to pray with the words, "Father, the hour has come" (John 17:1). What hour? The hour of Christ's pain and sorrow, the hour of the birth pangs as Christ-the-Mother.

Romans carries the imagery further. "We know that the whole creation has been groaning in travail together until now; and not only the creation, but we ourselves, who have the first fruits of the Spirit, groan inwardly as we wait" (Rom. 8:22). Here we find salvation depicted as a birth occurring not only within each individual, but also within the natural order as a whole.

And that's only a small sample of some mother imagery as applied to the Divine Feminine. Seven centuries ago, Eckhart said: "The essence of God is birthing."

Lord of the Universe, you transcend and yet contain both female and male, both masculine and feminine. In you the battle of the sexes can at last be stilled. All praise to you as the birthing One. As you this day lie on a maternity bed giving birth, prepare me to receive the new life you entrust to me this day. Amen.

Suffering

"How ever great one's suffering is, if it comes through God, God suffers from it first. And remember this: All suffering comes to an end" (Fox 1983)

Surely not all pain is of God. A lot of pain is unjust and springs from the injustices we inflict upon ourselves and one another. It hardly seems fair to credit God with the violence born in the human heart.

And then there is the pain that necessarily goes with all birth. As birthing is a cosmic experience, so suffering is a cosmic experience. You and I came into this world through a painful birthing. Sometimes we may be experiencing psychic suffering and not be immediately aware that the pain is a symptom that we are in labor and are about to give birth to some new stage in our existence.

Because all humans suffer and die, pain can open us to a cosmic consciousness. Pain can help link us with others, especially fellow sufferers. Pain can help us understand others; it schools us in compassion.

Pain can make us stronger, strengthening us for our journeys. Think about instances when you were made strong at broken places; those breaks were at first occasions for pain.

Pain can also help sensitize us anew to pleasure. Ask someone who has been hobbling along on crutches with a broken leg how pleasurable it is simply to walk unimpeded again down a garden path.

It is hard to remember that pain blesses us. That doesn't mean, however, that we should not seek to alleviate pain, especially needless, unjust pain.

People who experience chronic pain report that they are helped when they learn to embrace their pain rather than to deny it or to seek to anesthetize it. They learn to walk with it for a while, and then to let go of it. An analogy might be picking up an armful of wood, carrying it to the fire, and then letting go of it into the fire.

But, says Eckhart, amidst all the various counsels regarding pain, two stand out: First, if your suffering comes through God, God suffers from it before you. That's divine companionship of the first magnitude! Second, pain does not have the last word. It will end. God and you can outlast it.

Lord Jesus, you not only suffered for me, you suffer with me. Thank you for not allowing pain to separate us. And thank you for the assurance that pain is not eternal, but that you are. Amen.

Compassion

DAY 12

"You may call God love. You may call God goodness. But the best name for God is compassion" (Fox 1983).

The highest work God ever works is compassion. In the triune God we have a God of peace, a God of justice, a God of creativity, and a God of hope, but preeminently we have a God of compassion.

In compassion, justice and peace kiss. Unrelieved justice may be harsh, cold, unfeeling. Peace unrelated to justice is apt to be shallow sentimentality. Compassion contributes to peace to the extent that it honors each person as a person, as a child of the compassionate parent called God.

Compassion clothes the soul with the robe of God. We are called to the vocation of compassion by the great exemplar of compassion, Jesus Christ. We are empowered to be compassionate when we become vitally linked with Jesus, as branches in the vine (John 15).

God also wants us to be compassionate toward our own bodies, minds, and spirits. Take a moment to determine one way to be compassionate to your body today. That might have to do with the foods you eat or don't eat, with the amount of exercise you get, or with the amount of rest you enjoy.

Then think of one way to be compassionate to your mind. St. Paul gives a worthy prescription: "Finally, . . . whatever is true, whatever is honorable, whatever is just, whatever is pure, whatever is lovely, whatever is gracious, if there is any excellence, if there is anything worthy of praise, think about these things" (Phil. 4:8). Refusing to harbor negative thoughts can be one way to be compassionate to your mind.

Finally, determine one way to be compassionate to your spirit. Does that have to do with honoring your feelings? Demonstrating self-respect? Allowing the validation that is yours in Baptism to set you on your feet and send you to your tasks?

Those who follow compassion find peace for themselves, justice for their neighbors, and glory for God.

Lord, I don't understand how you can be both just and compassionate. My justice tends to be unbending and sometimes harsh. You are pure compassion. Yet your death for my sake is somehow linked with justice. I'm content to let justice and compassion dance together in glorious mystery. Meanwhile, I'll continue to praise you, my compassionate Savior and Lord. Amen.

Loving God Selfishly

"Some people, I swear, want to love God in the same way as they love a cow. They love it for its milk and cheese and the profit they will derive from it. Those who love God for the sake of outward riches or for the sake of inward consolation operate on the same principle. They are not loving God correctly; they are merely loving their own advantage" (Fox 1983).

We Americans have been conditioned to respect "the bottom line." That's where we find out what profit we've netted. This conditioning has contaminated our religion as well; people gravitate to religious leaders who promise great rewards for small signs of support and allegiance. We love the religious cow for the equivalents of milk and cheese.

Similarly, people in Jesus' day would have been more receptive to his way of being God had he followed a more glorious road. Come on, Jesus, give us a few more miracles to wow and enrich us. And then, Lord, we'll give you praise and whatever else you want in trade!

A life full of profit and free of pain—that would pack the churches. Jesus, your way of the cross isn't all that popular. You obviously did an inadequate job of market research before you decided on your religious strategy.

But Jesus *did* consider the options. The tempter provided that opportunity, as we read in Matthew 4. But Jesus was not willing to prostitute his divinity by dazzling the masses or by building a following based on free food. Loving Jesus for stones turned into bread is like loving our cow for grass turned into milk.

To love God as God and not as the dispenser of heavenly goodies; to follow Jesus on the way of the cross and not just in the Palm Sunday parade; and to allow the Spirit to fashion us without the side benefits of milk and cheese is a tall order—too much to expect of me alone.

Lord Jesus, in calling you Lord, I honor not only you but also your way of being and doing. You renounced the path of glory, the way of riches and fame so seductive to me. Set your cross before me, and help me to see that my quest for glory has also been crucified on that cross. Amen.

Stewardship and Accountability

"All gifts of nature and of grace have been given us on loan. Their ownership is not ours, but God's. God never gave personal property to anyone—not even to his Mother or to any other person or to any creature in any way. Treat all things as if they were loaned to you without any ownership—whether body or soul, sense or strength, external goods or honors, friends or relations, house or hall, everything. For if I want to possess the property I have instead of receive it on loan, then I want to be a master" (Fox 1983).

Meister Eckhart, I don't know if your ideas will sell very well in our 20th century. One of our cardinal principles is the right of private ownership. I have deeds to show that this home, that property, and the car I drive belong to me.

And more. My friends are my friends. The word processor on which I work belongs to me. Those framed certificates on the wall represent honors I have won. I'm quite proud of them. And my body? Well, I take pretty good care of me. After all, my body is a kingdom and in it I rule supreme.

See, I told you, Meister Eckhart, that your ideas are simply out of harmony with the way things are—the basic tenets by which we live. What belongs to me, I can do with as I choose. Right?

There's only one problem. Meister Eckhart's thoughts are more in harmony with biblical revelation than are the unquestioned maxims by which so many of us live. The psalmist says, "The earth is the Lord's and the fulness thereof, the world and those who dwell therein" (Ps. 24:1).

Fulness is simply another term for what Eckhart called *everything*. I own nothing. I am master of nothing. All is given as loan. All belongs to God. To receive something as loan is to obligate me to care for it, to manage it, in behalf of the owner.

That makes me a manager for God—a caretaker, a steward. Some day I will be called to give an account of my stewardship. What kind of a manager was I? The true owner will want to know.

Creator God, you alone are master. By your gracious empowerment, I intend this day to care responsibly for that which you have loaned to me. Thank you for your patience as I struggle with learning to be a steward. In the name of Christ I pray. Amen.

Mary Schramm

THOMAS MERTON

T HE one person whose life and writings have probably changed attitudes toward spirituality, monasticism, and contemplation more than any other is Father Louis of Gethsemani Abbey, Kentucky. He is better known to the world as Thomas Merton (1915–1968). In his autobiography, *Seven Storey Mountain,* and other early writings he wrote with a tone of triumphalism. Merton's major contributions, however, came from the mature Catholic monk who bridges East and West, and who is open to the truth of Protestantism and to secular writers.

As a young man, he attended Columbia University in New York City. Merton describes himself as a "worldly man" in these years, drinking beer and writing for the campus humor magazine.

Merton's reading included the works of St. Thomas, and he became more and more interested in religion. In 1938, at 23 years of age, he was baptized into the Catholic faith. As he began the search for his vocation he taught English, worked on a newspaper, and volunteered at the *Catholic Worker.* A visit to Gethsemani Abbey planted a seed, and when he was 26 he entered the Trappist abbey as a novice.

As the years went by, Merton felt more and more called to a solitary life and began to live in a small hermitage away from the abbey. He became a prolific writer. More than 60 of his books have been published. Hundreds of articles, a lifetime of extensive correspondence, and unpublished journals are also part of the Merton heritage.

This monk was a poet and a social critic. He had an artist's eye as evidenced by his sketches and excellent photography. In his writings one finds a combination of humor, deep faith, joy at simple things, and a righteous anger at the injustice in the world. He could laugh at theologians who were not happy unless "God was a problem," and convinced many of his readers that to be a contemplative is not to see a different world, but to see *this* world differently.

The selections from his writings that follow sample the breadth of Merton's interests and concerns. Had Merton been alive today, I feel certain he would have been more inclusive in his language because his insights, like his faith, reflected contemporary issues.

Solitude

"The world of men has forgotten the joys of silence, the peace of solitude which is necessary, to some extent, for the fullness of human living.

"If a man is locked out of his spiritual solitude he ceases to be a true person. . . . Man becomes a kind of automaton, living without joy, because he has lost all spontaneity. He is no longer moved from within, but only from outside himself. He no longer makes decisions for himself, but lets them be made for him.

"Such a man no longer acts upon the outside world, but lets it act upon him. He is propelled through life by a series of collisions with outside forces . . . a being without a purpose and without any deeply valid response to reality" (Merton 1975).

We run along the river in the early morning with ear phones drumming sounds other than nature's music in our ears. We enter our empty apartments and flick on the T.V. switch. Our children seem born with boom boxes attached to the sides of their heads—an added appendage that makes their bodies twitch and jerk as they become part of the music. An evening alone? We quickly call a friend to go to a movie or the shopping mall.

In the Old Testament the Sabbath was grace, but we have not yet claimed that daily grace. Our agenda is laid out. No time for solitude, no time to listen to the Spirit within. Because there is no time for centering there is no center, no direction. When there is no direction we are tossed and turned by any whim, any project, any idolatrous worship that catches our attention. Our lives become scattered and full of stress.

Without a center, without direction, we allow the world to squeeze us into its mold. Like Jello, we fit nicely into predetermined forms and shapes, or as Merton writes, we become like robots, always responding to outside stimuli, outside pressure, outside expectations. The world affects us much more than we affect the world.

When we are locked out of our spiritual solitude, we are like people who have lost the keys to their houses. We have no home, no roots, no space that is ours where we can grow in awareness of who and whose we are. Solitude allows God's Spirit within to call us to become the persons we were created to be so that we respond to the world's needs in ways that are our own. "Do not be conformed to this world, but be transformed by the renewal of your mind, that you may prove what is the will of God, what is good and acceptable and perfect" (Rom. 12:2-3).

Giver of all good gifts, fill me with peace that I may see the world through your eyes and respond with your love. Amen.

Validating Prayer

DAY 2 *"Perhaps we ought to be a little more critical of this whole concept: 'the spiritual life.' As long as thought and prayer are not fully incarnated in an activity which supports and expresses them validly, the heart will be filled with a smoldering rage, frustration and a sense of dishonesty"* (Merton 1968).

I notice more and more when I am asked to give a lecture I begin with a disclaimer. If I have been asked to speak about life-styles of sufficiency or nonviolence, I find myself beginning with "don't do what I do, but what I say." The discrepancies in my own life cause a gnawing in my gut. My highest aspirations do not line up with my actions and I find my life out of sync.

The same is true of our prayer life. Most of us, if we err in regard to solitude and activity, find that we are more do-ers than pray-ers. Because our busy-ness and saving-the-world activities take priority over quiet times and contemplation, we are not fed and nourished to overcome the stress of disappointments and small results. We burn out quickly.

Recently a friend from the U.S. on a trip to Central America asked a man in Nicaragua, "With all the work to be done, why is your village having a fiesta?" The peasant replied, "Obviously you are not in this for the long haul as we are."

God gives us resources for the long haul. We are to tap the depths of God within us who longs to grace us with the fruits of the Spirit's presence. A healthy spirituality keeps the balance of prayer, listening, and an active response. Our highest aspirations in prayer and contemplation are validated when we see the needs of a hurting world around us and respond.

Growth for an individual is to move to a neglected area of spirituality. If we are do-ers, we need to learn to become more contemplative. If we are only pray-ers, we need to enflesh those prayers in action on behalf of the world.

Our world is filled with unfulfilled adults who, from a living room couch, rage at the injustice much of humanity suffers. It is also filled with compassionate women and men who forget they are not in charge of bringing the kingdom of God because they have not yet learned how to pray. "Such is the confidence that we have through Christ toward God. Not that we are competent of ourselves to claim anything as coming from us; our competence is from God" (2 Cor. 3:4-5).

God of compassion, use my prayers *and* my life to do your will. Amen.

Sanity

DAY 3 *"I am beginning to realize that 'sanity' is no longer a value or an end in itself. The 'sanity' of modern man is about as useful to him as the huge bulk and muscles of the dinosaur. If modern man were a little less sane, a little more doubtful, a little more aware of the contradictions perhaps there might be the possibility of survival. But if he is sane, too sane, perhaps we must say that in a society like ours the worst insanity is to be totally without anxiety, totally 'sane'"* (Merton 1966).

Today on the news was a report of an Arkansas man who shot and killed 16 people—family and acquaintances. One watched with horror as bodies were removed from shallow graves and trunks of abandoned cars. The man had to be insane, we said to each other.

The dictionary defines sanity as being able to make sound, rational judgments, showing good sense. Adolf Eichmann, it was pronounced at his trial, was perfectly sane. Merton writes that he was obedient, loyal, had a profound respect for the law, and served his government well. In his sanity, Eichmann was able to thoughtfully send 6 million Jews to their deaths.

In 1945 the U.S. deliberately and thoughtfully used a Roman Catholic cathedral as ground zero and dropped a bomb that obliterated thousands of Japanese people. We make certain the men and women who control our missile systems are perfectly sane folks who pass their psychological tests and make good sense out of the Rorschach inkblot designs.

Who is sane?

Cultural assumptions of sanity often seem to be on a collision course with the sanity of God. The wisdom of God contradicts the sanity of an arms race. The folly of the way Jesus asks us to live is often times in direct opposition to a sensible adherence to many of the values of our society. Is it sane to return love for hatred, nonviolence for violent acts against us, or to live out a vision of *shalom* where all God's children have enough but none have too much?

The monk from his hillside at Gethsemani Abbey in Kentucky was an astute observer of humanity. Perhaps only contemplatives can recognize that to be sane is not necessarily to be wise in the ways of God. Paul spoke to this when he wrote to the Corinthians: "Where is the wise [person]? . . . Has not God made foolish the wisdom of the world? . . . For Jews demand signs and Greeks seek wisdom, but we preach Christ crucified, a stumbling block to Jews and folly to Gentiles, but to those who are called, both Jews and Greeks, Christ the power of God and the wisdom of God. For the foolishness of God is wiser than men, and the weakness of God is stronger than men" (1 Cor. 1:20-25).

Faithfulness

 "We know that in everything God works for good with those who love [God], who are called according to [God's] purposes" (Rom. 8:28).

James Forest, coordinator of the Fellowship of Reconciliation, corresponded frequently with Thomas Merton. In a letter dated February 21, 1966, and reprinted in *Sojourner's* magazine, Merton is affirming Forest's commitment to nonviolence and the ministry of reconciliation but gently confronts him (and us) with these words: *"You are probably striving to build yourself an identity in your work and your witness. You are using it to protect yourself against nothingness, annihilation. This is not the right use of work. All the good that you will do will come not from you, but from the fact that you have allowed yourself, in obedience to the faith, to be used by God's love. Think of this more and gradually you will be free from the need to prove yourself, and you can be more open to the power that will work through you without your knowing it"* (Merton 1978).

If we depend on the hope of results we no longer live out of faithfulness but will act only when we can assume effectiveness and success. Our call is to faithfulness. The God of history and the God of the future takes our discipleship and uses whatever God will for kingdom building. This freeing concept is the good news that we can risk our gifts and our actions, knowing that whether they bear fruit or not is God's business. Merton said it this way in the letter to his friend: *"If you can get free from the domination of causes and just serve Christ's truth, you will be able to do more and will be less crushed by inevitable disappointments. . . . Do not depend on the hope of results. . . . The real hope is not in something we think we can do but in God who is making something good out of it in some way we cannot see. If we can do God's will we will be helping in the process* (Merton Dec. 1978).

This is probably why Latin American theologian Rubem Alves tells us to plant dates instead of pumpkins. The results of living out God's truth are not always easily discernable. Dates are for future generations but it is we who must plant them. To live out God's truth of nonviolence may or may not have immediate results, but we continue to live out of a faith stance because it is in this kind of loving and living that God works.

Loving Christ, give me the patience and courage to embrace your foolish, self-giving way of loving. Amen.

Despair

<table>
<tr><td>D A Y
5</td><td>There are many reasons, I suppose, why we neglect solitude. We claim outside distractions, a family needing our attention, a job that makes many demands on our short 24-hour day. Or is our neglect of solitude a symptom of a deeper malaise—the</td></tr>
</table>

fear of facing ourselves and looking hard at the despair in our lives? Sometimes our solitude makes demands on us, demanding that we move into the darkness of our life instead of denying or avoiding it.

Both Jesus and John the Baptizer had their desert experiences. They embraced despair and temptation in these times of solitude and the call upon their lives was renewed. All of us experience times of emptiness and that flat feeling when we wonder if God is indeed in charge of our world or cares for us at all.

Merton was acutely aware of this human crisis. He wrote: *"The desert is the home of despair. And despair now is everywhere. Let us not think that our interior solitude consists in the acceptance of defeat. We cannot escape anything by consenting tacitly to be defeated. Despair is an abyss without bottom. Do not think to close it by consenting to it and trying to forget you have consented.*

"This, then, is our desert: to live facing despair, but not to consent. To trample it down under hope in the cross. To wage war against despair unceasingly. That war is our wilderness. If we wage it courageously, we will find Christ at our side. If we cannot face it we will never find Him" (Merton 1956).

The opposite of faith is not unbelief. The opposite of faith is despair. To despair is to disbelieve the resurrection or to forget that in his suffering and his resurrection Christ defeated the powers of evil and the principalities that rule the world. God will rule. Jesus knows what it is like for us to despair. In the garden and on the cross he cried out to a God who seemed to have forgotten him. That is why Christ is always with us in our struggle.

It is in our desert solitude that we embrace despair and hope comes alive.

"Who shall separate us from the love of Christ? Shall tribulation, or distress, or persecution, or famine, or nakedness, or peril, or sword? . . . No, in all these things we are more than conquerors through him who loved us. For I am sure that neither death, nor life, nor angels, nor principalities, nor things present, nor things to come, nor powers, nor height, nor depth, nor anything else in all creation, will be able to separate us from the love of God in Christ Jesus our Lord" (Rom. 8:35-39).

Rain

<table>
<tr><td>D A Y
6</td></tr>
</table>

One evening Merton left the monastery and sloshed his way through the cornfields to his special hermitage in the woods. He cooked some oatmeal on his Coleman stove and toasted a piece of bread over the log fire. It was raining and during the concert of rain on the metal roof he reflected on its sound and meaning: *"Let me say this before rain becomes a utility that they can plan and distribute for money. By 'they' I mean the people who cannot understand that rain is a festival, who do not appreciate its gratuity, who think that what has no price has no value, that what cannot be sold is not real, so that the only way to make something actual is to place it on the market. The time will come when they will sell you even your rain. At the moment it is still free, and I am in it. I celebrate its gratuity and its meaninglessness"* (Merton 1966).

Rain as a festival! Not an inconvenience or even a necessity to make my garden grow, but pure celebration. It has value simply because it is. It is gift. It has no price tag and its worth cannot be calculated. It is accepted purely as a grace from a gracious God.

How rare to see something as valuable that cannot be bought or sold. There are few enough things in our world that we celebrate simply because they are. Even our worth as individuals usually depends upon what we possess or how well we are liked. Our usefulness is calculated by our productivity to society.

Writer James Carroll says that to be called useless in society is the thing that stirs within us our deepest fear, and so we attack the uselessness in others. But it is in our uselessness that we are human. We are as useless as art and music and fairy tales and everything lovely. Our humanity, like the rain on the roof, is a celebration simply because God created us.

Merton, the poet, ends his essay, "Rain and the Rhinoceros," with these words: *"The rain has stopped. The afternoon sun slants through the pine trees; and how useless needles smell in the clean air!*

"A dandelion, long out of season, has pushed itself into bloom between the smashed leaves of last summer's day lilies. The valley resounds with the totally uninformative talk of creeks and the wild water.

"Then the quails begin their sweet whistling in the wet bushes. Their noise is absolutely useless, and so is the delight I take in it. There is nothing I would rather hear, not because it is a better noise than other noises, but because it is the voice of the present moment, the present festival" (Merton 1966).

The earth is the Lord's and the fullness thereof. Let us rejoice and be glad in it. Amen.

Contentment

<table>
<tr><td>D A Y
7</td><td>"I have learned, in whatever state I am, to be content. I know how to be abased, and I know how to abound; in any and all circumstances I have learned the secret of facing plenty and hunger, abundance and want. I can do all things in him who</td></tr>
</table>

strengthens me" (Phil. 4:11-13).

Contentment is that quality which allows us to live fully in the present, seeing the possibilities and the joys at hand. How much of our energy and time is channeled into planning for future events, future security, future prospects. A psychologist commenting on the millions of aerobic exercise tapes being sold (mostly to women) observed that women are not and never will be completely content with their bodies. Our car is never quite right, our apartment is not quite large enough, our salary is never adequate and our work is never as fulfilling as we want. Our children aren't as gifted as we had hoped, our spouse not as romantic as we dreamed, and our health not perfect. There are so many places to see, foods to try, books to read, classes to take and concerts to attend.

In *Conjectures of a Guilty Bystander*, Merton writes: *"Why can we not be content with the secret happiness that God offers us without consulting the rest of the world? If we are fools enough to remain at the mercy of the people who want to sell us happiness, it will be impossible for us ever to be content with anything. How would they profit if we became content? . . . The last thing a salesman wants is for the buyer to become content. You are no use in our affluent society unless you are always just about to grasp what you never have.*

"The Greeks were not as smart as we are. In their primitive way they put Tantalus in hell. Madison Avenue, on the contrary, would convince us that Tantalus is in heaven" (Merton 1968).

Tantalus, son of Zeus, was doomed to hell. As he stood in water wanting a drink, the water would recede beyond his reach. Wanting to eat, he could never quite reach the fruit that hung above his head from a tree.

Our own hell surrounds us when the tantalizing glitter of a materialistic world robs us of the contentment God has to offer. God's world is a beautiful world. If we have eyes to see and ears to hear we are doubly blessed. And if we have food to sustain our bodies, a place to rest, someone to love and meaningful work to do we are richer than the richest person on earth.

God's secret of contentment is for us to become aware of how much we are loved and that God gives us gifts and people who need us.

Gracious God, let me learn the meaning of the word "enough." Amen.

Reconciliation

"I have learned that an age in which politicians talk about peace is an age in which everybody expects war; the great men of the earth would not talk of peace so much if they did not secretly believe it possible, with one more war, to annihilate their enemies forever. Always, "after just one more war" it will dawn, the new era of love; but first everybody who is hated must be eliminated. For hate, you see, is the mother of their kind of love" (Merton 1961a).

Planning and executing just one more war is not new to 20th-century people. The sin of thinking that peace will come if we can only destroy the enemy or threaten their existence has been with humanity since creation.

After the Civil War Abraham Lincoln was talking about being reconciled to the South and one member of his cabinet, Thaddeus Stevens, banged his fist on the table and said, "Mr. President, I think enemies are to be destroyed!" Mr. Lincoln quietly responded, "Do I not destroy my enemy when I make him my friend?"

This is the gospel. God chose to reconcile us while we were enemies of God by the self-giving love of Christ on a cross. The way God relates to enemies is our model for reconciliation. Forgiveness, understanding, and compassion are the marks of what it means to follow Jesus.

"To the extent that you are free to choose evil, you are not free. An evil choice destroys freedom," Merton wrote. Our freedom is to align ourselves with the will of God. God's will for us is to be reconciled to our neighbor, our enemy, and our family member. This is, and will continue to be, a stumbling block for many who see their freedom threatened and think the only way to bring peace is to flex military muscles or manipulate the lives of those in less powerful countries.

It is difficult to describe the peacefulness that is ours when we take the first step in being reconciled to one from whom we are estranged. This peace that passes understanding is God's gift, who always calls us to love instead of hate, support instead of condemn, and be united with individuals and nations instead of divided. Enemy love is not something we can achieve by ourselves but is a gift of the Spirit. God never commands us to live a certain way without furnishing the spiritual resources to do so.

"But now in Christ Jesus you who once were far off have been brought near in the blood of Christ. For he is our peace, who has made us both one, and has broken down the dividing wall of hostility" (Eph. 2:13-14).

Give me the spiritual resources, Holy Spirit, to be reconciled to my enemies. Amen.

Humility

DAY 9 *"Many poets are not poets for the same reason that many religious men are not saints; they never succeed in being themselves. . . . In great saints you will find that perfect humility and perfect integrity coincide. . . . The saint is unlike everybody else precisely because he is humble. . . . Humility consists in being precisely the person you are before God, and since no two people are alike, if you have the humility to be yourself you will not be like anyone else in the whole universe. . . . It will not be a matter of mere appearances or opinions, or tastes, or ways of doing things. It is something deep in the soul"* (Merton 1961b).

Somehow in our religious training, we have been led to believe humility and groveling are synonymous. Our breast beating and "worm" theology that mistakenly pass for humbleness often prevent us from experiencing the grace of an integrated life.

Each of us was created with a unique combination of gifts and abilities. When we deny these gifts we deny our very essence. So often we spend time wishing we were someone else or able to do the creative things others seem to do so effortlessly. We give God glory when we accept ourselves as the person God intended for us to be—a unique created individual.

When we accept ourselves, with our specific gifts (and limitations) we are able to forget self and reach out to others. This is what humility is. We do not flaunt who we are, but accept God's gifts to us and begin to use those gifts for others. This is a freeing way to live. We can stop searching for ways to respond to God's love and begin to be who we are.

Merton had another comment that is helpful to remember. "Hurry," he said, "ruins saints as well as artists." How like us to be discontented with small steps, small results and to want immediate gratification and success. We live our lives so hurriedly that we rarely take the time to discover who we are. Solitude is one necessity for this discovery. It is when we shut up for awhile that God's Spirit within us can be heard.

"I bid every one among you not to think of himself more highly than he ought to think, but to think with sober judgment, each according to the measure of faith which God has assigned him. For as in one body we have many members, and all the members do not have the same function, so we, though many, are one body in Christ, and individually members one of another. Having gifts that differ according to the grace given to us, let us use them" (Rom. 12:3-6).

Thank you, parent God, for the gift of who I am. Keep me from selfish use of my gifts. Amen.

Prayer

A friend called today. "This has been a hard week," he said. "I need your support and your prayers."

At my work I supervise a dozen people. Many days I do not feel I do a very good job. "Have you prayed about it?" someone asks when I confess my ineptness at managing skills.

What is prayer? How am I supposed to pray? Does it make any difference? What am I doing when I pray? What if I can't seem to pray?

The most helpful advice I have read comes from spiritual director John Chapman: "Pray as you can. Don't pray as you can't." Then he adds, "The less you pray the worse it goes."

When Merton was asked to speak at a conference on "how to pray," he was very blunt. "If you want to pray, begin to pray. Start praying. Pray." In our busy lives we are often tempted to say that all of life is a prayer. Everything we do is for the glory of God. No one led a fuller life than Jesus and yet we read in Mark 1:35 that "in the morning, a great while before day, he rose and went out to a lonely place, and there he prayed." In between healing and preaching, Jesus knew the importance of a time for intimacy with God.

For Merton, prayer is the time "we abandon our inertia, our egoism and submit entirely to the demands of the Spirit, praying earnestly for help, and giving ourselves generously to every effort asked of us by God" (Merton 1971). Later Merton writes, "The theology of prayer begins when we understand that we are in trouble." Prayer begins with those moments of honesty when we stand naked before God, confessing our impotence or our self-importance, confessing our inability to make sense out of life and abandoning our wills to the one who created and redeemed us.

"Prayer does not blind us to the world, but it transforms our vision of the world and makes us see it, all people, and all the history of mankind in the light of God." Prayer is not an escape but a way of "keeping oneself in the presence of God and of reality, rooted in one's own inner truth."

For those of us who feel immature in our prayer life, Merton has a comforting word. "We do not want to be beginners. But let us be convinced of the fact that we will never be anything else but beginners all our life!" There are no easy answers, no short cuts to a life of prayer. One begins to pray, again, and by the grace of God we come in touch with the source of our life.

"Likewise the Spirit helps us in our weakness; for we do not know how to pray as we ought, but the Spirit himself intercedes for us with sighs too deep for words" (Rom. 8:26).

Contemplation

DAY 11 One of several books by Thomas Merton destined to become a classic of spiritual readings is *New Seeds of Contemplation*. *Contemplation* is a word often misunderstood even in religious circles. One would hardly consider encouraging your child to grow up to be a contemplative. We think of a contemplative as an oddity, one withdrawn from the world or in some state of constant religious ecstasy—someone you wouldn't invite for dinner.

Merton was aware of these prejudices and not only tried to define contemplation and the vocation of a contemplative, but devoted a chapter to what contemplation *is not*. I found his distinctions helpful.

■ Contemplation is *the highest expression of man's intellectual and spiritual life. It is that life itself, fully awake, fully active, fully aware that it is alive. It is spiritual wonder. It is spontaneous awe at the sacredness of life, of being.*

■ Contemplation is not *something that can be taught, explained, hinted at, suggested, pointed to, symbolized. It can only be experienced.*

■ Contemplation is *above all, awareness of the reality of the source of life and of our very being. It knows the Source obscurely, inexplicably, but with a certitude that goes both beyond reason and beyond simple faith. For contemplation is a kind of spiritual vision to which both reason and faith aspire.*

■ Contemplation is not *mere inertia, a tendency to inactivity, to psychic peace or sitting around with a vacant stare.*

■ Contemplation is *the awareness and realization, even in some sense experience, of what each Christian obscurely believes: "it is now no longer I that live but Christ lives in me."*

■ Contemplation is not *a trance, an opium or alienation from our true self. Contemplation is no pain-killer.*

■ Contemplation is *more than a consideration of abstract truths about God, more even than affective meditation on the things we believe. It is awakening enlightenment and the amazing intuitive grasp by which love gains certitude of God's creative and dynamic intervention in daily life* (Merton 1961b).

Merton is trying to help us become acutely aware of all of life. Perhaps a comment made by an Anglican Benedictine to my husband best sums it up. The monk and my husband were walking around the grounds of the monastery in Michigan and he said, "People come here and expect they will find that contemplation comes after years of disciplined training. They think it is some highly developed technique. I tell them they can be a contemplative beginning today. They must begin to look at everything through the lens of their faith in Christ."

God of love, open my eyes and my ears to the beauty and the anguish of the world you care for. Amen.

Tainted with Poison

"We must be wary of ourselves when the worst that is in man becomes objectified in society, approved, acclaimed and deified, when hatred becomes patriotism and murder a holy duty, when spying and delation are called love of truth and the stool pigeon is a public benefactor, when the gnawing and prurient resentments of frustrated bureaucrats become the conscience of the people and the gangster is enthroned in power, then we must fear the voice in our own heart, even when it denounces them. For are not all tainted with the same poison?" (Merton 1961a).

Similar words to these have appeared recently on the editorial pages of our local newspaper. Merton, the keen observer of humanity, the contemplative, the social critic, wrote these words over 25 years ago but they have a contemporary ring. The conditions he described seem to me to be the result of society living with many illusions. Perhaps more than anything we, as Christians, need to be *dis*-illusioned.

Illusion comes from the Latin word *ludare,* meaning to play games. We have convinced ourselves that ends justify means. Patriotic duty blinds us to truth, and morality is easily sacrificed to protect our way of life. Perhaps it is important to examine the illusion that we are a Christian nation, following the life and teaching of Jesus. When we become disillusioned about this, perhaps the repentance that is the precondition for a conversion experience will begin in us.

But it is the last sentence of Merton's comments that bothers me. How quickly we pass judgment on officials and bureaucrats, military advisers and local politicians. It is appropriate to be filled with rage about injustice and lies but do we not first need to carefully and prayerfully examine our own motives and our own sin? It may be true that those who rule us are simply a projection of ourselves. They reflect our morality and our values. We confess before God that we worship other gods: the idolatry of greed, of control, of militarism. Each of these areas of trust demands sacrifice and each will leave us seduced but with no security and no salvation.

Part of a healthy spirituality is to be disillusioned, to have our eyes wide open to the cultural values that collide with the way of the cross. It is not truth but pretense that poisons us as individuals and as a nation.

"And God spoke all these words, saying,

'I am the LORD your God, who brought you out of the land of Egypt, out of the house of bondage.

'You shall have no other gods before me (Ex. 20:1-3).

Almighty God, may your kingdom come, your will be done on earth as in heaven. Forgive us our sin as we forgive those who sin against us. Amen.

Happiness

"It is not that someone else is preventing you from living happily; you yourself do not know what you want. Rather than admit this, you pretend that someone is keeping you from exercising your liberty. Who is this? It is you yourself" (Merton 1961b).

Merton, the monk, from his vantage point in Kentucky, resonates with our universal human condition. It is so much more convenient to blame others for our inability to be happy. Many of us still blame our parents for imperfect childhoods, find spouses an easy target for our discontent, or imagine our present job and coworkers the reason for our miserable life. This will always be the case when we allow any one person or situation to fully control our level of contentment, or when we forget who and whose we are.

In *No Man Is An Island* Merton writes, "We cannot be happy if we expect to live all the time at the highest peak of intensity. Happiness is not a matter of intensity, but of balance and order and rhythm and harmony."

I suspect that it is easier to find this balance in a monastery than in our modern world of frantic haste with appointments to keep and deadlines to meet. For Merton, the balance included work and worship, study and leisure. He found "supreme value in the ordinary everyday routine of work, poverty, hardship and monotony." These, he said, help one to be contemplative and to experience inner joy because they allow us to center our whole being on God's love.

As we look closely at Merton's values, we become aware that it truly is in those times of want and pain that we draw closer to God. It is when we recognize the seduction of material well-being that we can spend more time in committing our lives to the deep needs of those around us. As for the monotony, Merton described the monastery as being "deliberately boring" because when we are no longer distracted, we are able to turn more fully to God in prayer.

On occasions in my life I have known this to be reality. Not long ago I realized I had a "boring evening at home." No one was there, nothing good on T.V., no book that interested me. I was struggling with stress and distress. I was blaming others for my unhappiness.

For three hours, with classical music playing, I did nothing but pray, cry, listen, and look deeply into my heart. With gratitude I recommitted my life to the God who created and redeemed me. The peace that passes understanding comes alive in moments like these.

For a time of prayer, sit quietly, eyes closed, conscious of your breathing. Spend 15 minutes aware of God's Spirit within you.

God's Love

DAY 14

"It is God's love that warms me in the sun and God's love that sends the cold rain. It is God's love that feeds me in the bread I eat and God that feeds me also by hunger and fasting.

"It is the love of God that sends the winter days when I am cold and sick, and the hot summer when I labor and my clothes are full of sweat; but it is God who breathes on me with light winds off the river and in breezes out of the wood.

"His love spreads the shade of the sycamore over my head and sends the water-boy along the edge of the wheatfield with a bucket from the spring . . .

"It is God's love that speaks to me in the birds and streams, and all these things are seeds sent to me from his will. If these seeds would take root in my liberty, and if his will would grow from my freedom, I would become the love that he is, and my harvest would be his glory and my own joy" (Merton 1961b).

It is the contemplative who can acknowledge the presence of God's care and love in all facets of life—from the sweat that soaks our clothes in the hot summertime to the cold rain of autumn. All creation gives God glory and does so without thought, without labor, and without awareness. Nature praises God simply because it *is*.

But what about us, Merton asks? We are called to be holy. To be human and to be holy are not necessarily the same thing. "Our vocation is not simply to be, but to work together with God in the creation of our own life, our own identity, our own destiny."

Paul speaks of this paradox when he writes, "Work out your own salvation with fear and trembling; for God is at work in you, both to will and to work for his good pleasure" (Phil. 2:12).

We are given the liberty to make choices. By God's spirit we come to know God's will and are free to respond to that will. We can become cocreators with God, helping to create our identity and become the person we were created to be, or we can submit to the illusion that we will find joy outside of God's will for our lives. "We are not very good at recognizing illusions," Merton writes, "least of all the ones we cherish about ourselves. . . . A life devoted to the cult of this shadow is what is called a life of sin."

We were created in the image of God. To "become the love that God is" is where we will continue to find our deepest joy and satisfaction.

Come, Holy Spirit, and let God's love flow through me. Awaken me to that love in all of life. Amen.

Richard Koenig

GERARD MANLEY
HOPKINS

I N the history of English literature, Gerard Manley Hopkins (1844–
1889) is regarded as a powerful and profound Christian poet. Of
the poets who celebrated the beauties of nature he is one of the
most admired. He is also known for inventing a new style of
poetry. Because of this, his writings are not always easy to grasp when first
read. But when read with a little patience and care, they pay rich dividends.

Hopkins was born in Stratford, England, the eldest of eight children of
a prosperous Anglican (Episcopalian) family. In 1863 Gerard entered Oxford
University to study classical literature. There he encountered the Oxford
movement which was shaking the Anglican church. The movement's adherents believed the Anglican Church had fallen into apostasy. Hopkins's
involvement in the Oxford movement resulted in his "going over," as it was
then called, to the Roman Catholic Church.

Hopkins's spiritual life while at the university was influenced by John
Cardinal Newman. For a few months after leaving Oxford, Hopkins taught
at a school established by Cardinal Newman but soon gave that up to enter
the Society of Jesus. He became a Jesuit priest in 1868.

In spite of wearying assignments, Father Hopkins managed to produce
poetry of a kind that continues to dazzle the mind and the ear. Ordained in
1877, he served as select preacher, missioner, or parish priest at various places
in England, including the slums of Liverpool.

Father Hopkins's final assignment, beginning in 1884, was to the University College in Dublin, Ireland. There, the isolation he felt, together with
feelings of melancholy he had wrestled with all his life, combined to evoke
from him some of his most moving but desolate poetry.

As a deeply committed Roman Catholic priest, Father Hopkins's poems
(here reprinted from *Poems & Prose of Hopkins,* Penguin Books, 1953) are
stamped by the dogma of the Roman church. At the same time, his poetry
expresses the faith common to Christians of all communions, along with
insights that enrich not only the Catholic church, but the Church catholic.

God's Grandeur

The world is charged with the grandeur of God.
It will flame out, like shining from shook foil;

....

There lives the dearest freshness deep down things;
And though the last lights off the black West went
Oh, morning, at the brown brink eastward, springs—
Because the Holy Ghost over the bent
World broods with warm breast and with ah!
bright wings.

When have you felt close to God? Many people will reply, "I have felt close to God when attending some festival worship service or when taking Holy Communion." In almost the same breath, those same people will add, "I also have felt God's presence when I stood on some mountaintop, or viewed the trees turning gold in the fall, or walked along the shore of a still lake or the ocean at night."

Few of us would disagree. Even though we live in a high-tech age, drive powerful cars, and are able to fly to the farthest reaches of the world, nature still speaks to us. The believer who has watched a sunset at the seaside or from some vantage point on the prairie feels that he or she is in the presence of God.

Sadly, that is not true for all. Modern life, with its fast-paced lifestyle, reliance on machines, and mad pursuit of wealth, has changed the way many people respond to the world about them. Indeed, modern life, with its fantastic ability to pollute, threatens the very existence of much of God's grandeur.

Father Hopkins's poem tells of the danger but also of the hope. There is, he says, deep down in nature "the dearest freshness"—the power of the ravaged earth and imperiled living things for revival. As at the creation, this power comes as "the Holy Ghost over the bent / World broods with warm breast and with ah! / bright wings." Another reason for wonder—and thanksgiving!

"Bless the LORD, O my soul! O LORD my God, thou art very great! Thou art clothed with honor and majesty, who coverest thyself with light as with a garment, who hast stretched out the heavens like a tent. . . . May the glory of the LORD endure for ever!" (Ps. 104:1-2, 31).

Your world is truly amazing, Lord—fresh, green, new in spite of all we do to it. Each spring sets my heart to dancing. Death is answered by new and beautiful bursts of life. What a joy it is to behold it again! It leaves us breathless but grateful. Praise be to you, our Creator and Preserver! Amen.

Pied Beauty

DAY 2

GLORY be to God for dappled things—
For skies of couple-colour as a brinded cow;
For rose-moles in all stipple upon trout that swim;

....

All things counter, original, spare, strange;
Whatever is fickle, freckled (who knows how?)
With swift, slow, sweet, sour; adazzle, dim;
He fathers-forth whose beauty is past change:

Praise him.

Father Hopkins, the same poet who sensitized us to God's grandeur in nature, now shifts our eyes to something else. Nature, he says, possesses a "pied beauty," a beauty coming from its variety of colors. There is order in nature, but within that order—what variety! Thousands of different kinds of insects, flowers, trees, birds, people. No two snowflakes ever alike! Everything with its own distinct stamp, mark, identity—you and me included.

Down through the ages philosophers, wise men, and thinkers have gravely surveyed the earth and the heavens, attempting to draw from them some clue as to God's existence, missing the fun of it all. The exuberant variety of nature we find should make clear to us that whatever else God may be, God is not boring.

God delights in variety and uniqueness.

As God enjoys "all things counter, original, spare, strange" so may we. We might reason that if God places such a premium on variety and uniqueness, then God values us in our uniqueness as well.

All of us are different, but together each of us contributes to that wild and enchanting variety that makes up God's wonderful creation. As Father Hopkins enjoins in the last line of his poem: "Praise him."

"O LORD, how manifold are thy works! In wisdom hast thou made them all; the earth is full of thy creatures. Yonder is the sea, great and wide, which teems with things innumerable, living things both small and great. . . . May the glory of the LORD endure for ever, may the LORD rejoice in his works" (Ps. 104:24-25, 31).

Your giraffe, O Lord, is amazing; your cat stalking about my house is no less so. What fun it is to watch them go! They are signs of your love. Among all the billions who live on this earth (you love them all), teach me to value myself as one loved equally. It is through the one Christ that I ask this. Amen.

The Divine Mystery

I kiss my hand
To the stars, lovely-asunder
Starlight, wafting him out of it; and
Glow, glory in thunder;
Kiss my hand to the dappled-with-damson west;
Since, tho' he is under the world's splendour and wonder,
His mystery must be instressed, stressed;
For I greet him the days I meet him, and bless when
I understand.

Men and women always have bowed in reverence before nature. The sun has claimed many worshipers, as have the moon and the stars. Even today this human problem remains—to penetrate nature's dazzling, bewitching appearances without making any part of nature into a god. In the words of Father Hopkins, nature points to the God who is "under the world's splendour and wonder."

We speak of God sometimes quite matter-of-factly, as if God were something quite obvious and as easy to come by as the daily paper. Even Christians, maybe Christians especially, are prone to that mistake.

If we pay attention to the Bible, the mistake will not be made. "No one has ever seen God," says St. John (John 1:18). Since God reveals himself, God can be known, but there are always aspects of God that remain hidden.

Yet God is not playing blind man's bluff with his creatures. The key to understanding, says the poet, is to allow the mystery of God to strike upon the heart, which God does through the Lord Jesus Christ, who came as "the very image of the invisible God" among us. When we meet God in Christ, we can meet God in his creation everywhere.

"The heavens are telling the glory of God; and the firmament proclaims his handiwork. Day to day pours forth speech, and night to night declares knowledge. There is no speech, nor are there words; their voice is not heard; yet their voice goes out through all the earth, and their words to the end of the world" (Ps. 19:1-4).

Too often, I confess, Lord, I have been too embarrassed to let loose the feelings inside me when struck by the mystery of your being. I have stood beneath the stars and said, "Isn't that beautiful?" when I really wanted to say, "O Lord, my God, yes, yes!"

You are my God. I do understand and I give you praise. Amen.

Not Out of His Bliss

NOT of his bliss
Springs the stress felt
Nor first from heaven (and few know this)
Swings the stroke dealt—
Stroke and a stress that stars and storms deliver,
That guilt is hushed by, hearts are flushed by and melt—
But it rides time like riding a river
(And here the faithful waver, the faithless fable and miss).

Who can make a flower? the little children ask in their charming carol. None but God, they say. Nature is thought of as testifying truly to its Creator.

But others disagree. As fantastically wonderful as nature is, its cause is still a mystery. We may feel after God in hope of finding him, but there is a veil that cannot be penetrated.

The key, the poet declares, is Jesus Christ, not the Christ of glory, but the one who suffers death upon the cross. We need to remember that revelation does not come from God's bliss. The poet warns, "Here the faithful waver, the faithless fable and miss."

But how should we have dared to think otherwise? The mystery hidden in the delight and grandeur of nature is not something artificial, antiseptic, sealed off from the world's pain. God was in Christ, reconciling the world to himself, says the apostle Paul. Redemption issues from suffering. The dark times we experience tempt us to turn away from the crucified God. But out of the "dense and the driven Passion, and the frightful sweat" (stanza 7 of Father Hopkins's poem), comes the victory.

Puzzling as it seems, God's greatest power is hidden in weakness and the cross is his moment of glory. Moments of pain, distress, or shock at an accident or disaster can turn out to be for us moments of intense closeness to God, if we do not take offense at the way God works. For it is through "stroke and a stress that stars and storms deliver, / That guilt is hushed by, hearts are flushed by and melt." Christ is there.

My thoughts about you, my God, usually take the same course. You are God, I am a human being, your creature. This I acknowledge. I think I know you, but do I? Help me to see you truly that I may truly know you as the God for me in all circumstances. In Christ of the cross, I pray. Amen.

The Source

I caught this morning morning's minion, king-
dom of daylight's dauphin, dapple-dawn-drawn
Falcon, in his riding
Of the rolling level underneath him steady air, and
striding
High there, how he rung upon the rein of the wimpling
wing
In his ecstasy!

. . . . .

Brute beauty and valour and act, oh, air, pride, plume
here
Buckle! And the fire that breaks from thee then
a billion
Times told lovelier, more dangerous.

Father Hopkins subtitles this poem about a falcon in flight "To Christ Our Lord." The falcon makes Father Hopkins think of Christ.

Christ was to the poet like the falcon in beauty, bravery, power. The combination is not the usual image we hold of Christ. Father Hopkins sees in the words and works of Jesus something else than moments in the life of a divine person. He sees human perfection. He sees Christ, the Man for others, holding before us a picture of what human life should be.

But the force of this particular poem comes in the lines following Father Hopkins's celebration of the falcon. It is in that word "buckle." That masterful, beautiful human person, God's own Son, did not keep what he was and had to himself. As God fought for his people in the Old Testament, delivering them from the bondage of enemies, so Christ fights for his people. And in that fight, the enemies being sin, death, and the powers of darkness, Christ "buckles," goes down in apparent defeat.

But only for a moment. The cross, as someone has said, did not put a period at the end of Christ's life, only a comma. Christ rises, and out of the battle he comes forth as a fire "a billion / Times told lovelier"—lovelier than even he was in his sublime earthly life. For now he is not a candle lit to illumine just one place in the universe but a shining star to be seen by all, a force to transform a fallen world, yes, a fallen universe.

Lord, I thank you for the words of the poet. Your work for me is both lovely and dangerous. I want it to be a danger to the ways in which I am not conformed to your image and will, in order to let the loveliness of your Spirit shine through me. From you comes all good. Make me good. Amen.

The Final End

With an anvil-ding
And with fire in him forge thy will
Or rather, rather then, stealing as Spring
Through him, melt him but master him still:
Whether at once, as once at a crash Paul,
Or as Austin, a linger-out sweet skill,
Make mercy in all of us, out of us all
Mastery, but be adored, but be adored King.

"Hallowed be thy Name," prayed Father Hopkins in the stanza at the head of today's meditation. But what is so striking is the way that Father Hopkins prays that God's name should be kept holy by us.

The poet does not pray some vague prayer for grace to be obedient. He prays for something more radical. He sees in himself a blindness to God's will and an opposition to doing God's will.

Desiring God to be lord and master over him, Father Hopkins prays God to do what is necessary to accomplish that goal. It might take the anvil of trials or the gentle brush of the Spirit. Whatever it takes, the poet asks God to use it: "Make mercy in all of us, out of us all / Mastery, but be adored, but be adored King," he cries.

Is this our prayer? So often we have approached God with our requests—for protection, for deliverance, for escape from trouble, for safety, for success. Our list of petitions is never exhausted. Do we ever pray for grace to adore God as fervently as we pray for those other things?

These heavy thoughts raise the stakes of the spiritual life. It is not fashionable to speak of God as master or king these days. But God masters not to dominate but to free—free us from ourselves in order to be able to adore, to wonder, and to love.

Let God be God! "Ascribe to the Lord, O heavenly beings . . . ascribe to the Lord the glory of his name (Ps. 29:1-2).

I am frightened, Lord—frightened by what I am asked to ask for. Can I dare to pray for the grace to hallow your name, to fear, love, and trust you above all things? Suppose in order to reach that height you had to take away some of the things I dearly love and trust. Would I still praise you? I say yes, O God. Be with me as my prayer is answered, that I may be blessed in the way it is answered. In Jesus who prayed that not his will but yours be done. Amen.

New Nazareths

Of [Mary's] flesh he took flesh;
He does take fresh and fresh,
Though much the mystery how,
Not flesh but spirit now
And makes, O marvelous!
New Nazareths in us

. . . .

New Bethlehems, and be born
There, evening, noon, and morn—

. . . .

Who, born so, comes to be
New self and nobler me
In each one. . . .

"O holy Child of Bethlehem, descend to us, we pray, cast out our sin, and enter in, be born in us today." So we have sung at Christmas many times in celebration of the time when the Word took flesh and dwelt among us. The Jesuit priest and poet, Father Hopkins of England, developed the same thoughts in a different but equally beautiful way.

Born of the Virgin Mary, Jesus took on flesh. But that does not end the mystery, says the poet. Christ continues to take on flesh again and again when people are born again by the Spirit through water and the Word. New Nazareths are made, new Bethlehems happen, as people come to faith in the Christ who was born for them at that time and place long ago.

The Protestant hymn writer prayed that Christ would cast out sin and enter in. The Jesuit poet extends the thought and sees Christ's entry resulting in new selves, nobler persons, whenever it happens. Christians become "little Christs," taking on the form of him who lived not for himself but for God.

Wonder of wonders, that is what has happened to us. You and I are the sites of new Nazareths and Bethlehems. Now, in St. Paul's words, it is not we who live but Christ who lives within us, empowering, and enabling us to newness and love. Be glad.

I confess, Lord, that I forget who I am. The thought that in Christ I am a new creation is often too much for me. Help me see who I am because of whose I am. I do not ask in order that I be somebody, but in order to be *for* somebody who needs the touch of Christ. Amen.

Each of Us Different

As kingfishers catch fire, dragonflies draw flame;

....

Each mortal thing does one thing and the same;
Deals out that being indoors each one dwells.

....

I say more: the just man justices;
Keeps grace: that keeps all his going graces;
Acts in God's eyes what in God's eye he is—
Christ—for Christ plays in ten thousand places,
Lovely in limbs, and lovely in eyes not his
To the Father through the features of men's faces.

Being in a crowd at a baseball game, sitting in a subway car or a bus, or waiting in the doctor's office, we have all studied the faces opposite us. We see all kinds of faces—some glowing with youth, others grey with age. Some are marked with worry, others made-up in high fashion. The variety we human beings display never ceases to fascinate us. There are so many of us, all different.

One time Father Hopkins spotted a beautiful bird in flight, wings flashing back the sun's rays. It was a kingfisher. About the same time, the poet also observed the spectacular performance of a dragonfly. Such sights never failed to impress Father Hopkins, but this time, as sensational as they were, the appearances evoked a different response. Bird and insect caused Father Hopkins to ponder the special role that each creature plays in the great scheme of things. The activity of both the kingfisher and dragonfly he saw as something welling up from inside of them: "Each mortal thing does one thing and the same: Deals out that being indoors each one dwells."

Looking at our brothers and sisters and seeing people do their special thing, we are face-to-face with expressions of God's love. Looking around us, we are constantly greeted with the sight of Christ in a new guise.

How wonderful!

I like people, O Lord, and I try to appreciate each individual and treat him or her with kindness. But, Lord, it has seldom occurred to me to look for the face of Christ in them, just as it is something strange for me to think of myself that way. What a wonderful difference that makes. The more we see each other as individuals, the more your divine, saving goodness opens to us, and the more we know our Lord.

Thank you, dear God. Amen.

The Great Sorrow

Sometimes a lantern moves along the night,
That interests our eyes. And who goes there?
I think; where from and bound, I wonder, where,
With, all down darkness wide, his wading light?

Father Hopkins never ceased to be fascinated by people. So many different kinds of people, so vital and creative. The people he happened upon were to him like people you might see carrying lanterns or flashlights in the darkness: you know they are there; their lights drive shafts of light through the gloom, but soon the darkness will shut them off from your sight again.

The poet is facing up to a grim, sad truth: "Death or distance soon consumes" the people we encounter. No matter what "rich beams" they "rain against our much-thick and marsh air," "death or distance buys" these fellow human beings completely. They are gone. And like the worker at the office or the factory who left the company last month, we have a hard time remembering their names even when we try.

Is there no one who keeps them in mind? Later in the poem that began this meditation, Father Hopkins answers:

Christ minds: Christ's interest, what to avow or amend
There, eyes them, heart wants, care haunts, foot follows kind,
Their ransom, their rescue, and first, fast, last friend.

We are not forgotten. We have one who is our "first, fast, last friend," one whose eye stays upon us.

Hold this thought. Hold it not only for situations when you must face death, like the times when you stand at the graveside of a loved one or a friend. Hold it as you live and go through your everyday activities. Christ your friend is there with the most powerful light of all to push back the darkness that borders human life. That light is God's eternal and undying love. It will never be extinguished.

"Today the world lost a great (artist, leader, teacher, businessperson, scholar, entertainer)." Lord, we have heard those words many times about many people, and each time it happens, we feel something of ourselves has been lost. It's the feeling that everything is going, never to be seen again. But then comes the promise of your friendship, O Christ. And the light of hope is lit again. We praise you. Amen.

The Great Hope

Enough! the Resurrection,
A heart's clarion! Away grief's gasping, joyless days, dejection.
           Across my foundering deck shone
A beacon, an eternal beam. Flesh fade, and mortal trash
Fall to the residuary worm; world's wildfire, leave but ash:
           In a flash, at a trumpet crash,
I am all at once what Christ is, since he was what I am, and
This Jack, joke, poor potsherd, patch, matchwood, immortal
   diamond,
           Is immortal diamond.

We human beings are mortal. Both our presence and even the memory of our presence appear doomed to oblivion, swallowed up by the "enormous dark" of death. We sense that. No one likes to dwell on it, but it is there. Some psychologists say that our attempts to deny death cause much mischief. People do strange things, often without knowing it, when they feel threatened by annihilation.

Enough, says the poet. Through the miracle of the resurrection our Risen Lord comes upon the scene, introducing into our death-haunted world the promise of everlasting life.

The immensity of the miracle the poet describes in the words "flesh fade, and mortal trash / Fall to the residuary worm; world's wildfire, leave but ash." No matter how complete the destruction of our "lowly bodies," as St. Paul calls them, may be, those bodies will be restored, remade, glorified, given immortality as we are raised new.

When St. Paul preached the resurrection at Athens, his audience laughed. The reaction in many quarters today is the same. Sometimes the laughter rises from within ourselves, though silently for fear of disturbing fellow members of the congregation or our own family.

Our Lord understands. But that is why he told Thomas, the first one to struggle with the Mount Everest of Christian promises, "Blessed are those who have not seen and yet believe."

Higher and higher you bid me reach, dear Father. I think of my loved ones who are gone. They are silent in their graves, as I will be too. But now through the raising of Jesus you tell me we will all be raised to join in praising you together. Such is the power of your love. What hope! Amen.

The Inner Reason

In a flash, at a trumpet crash,
I am all at once what Christ is, since he was what I
am.

"Christ is my Savior. He is the Savior of all."

So Christians have confessed from earliest times. What did he do to be our Savior? "He died for us, on our behalf," the Church replies, "and thereby paid for our sins, and 'not for ours only but also for the sins of the whole world'" (1 John 2:2).

Later on, as Christians pondered what the Lord had accomplished for them, they drew from the event of Christ new insights, new ways of explaining his saving work. They said that in becoming a human being, the divine Christ permeated human life with God's life, the way a powerful dye colors an entire container of liquid. It is because of who Christ was as the divine Son of God that the work of Christ has such a powerful effect.

This union of the divine and human is what Father Hopkins hails as the inner secret of the resurrection: "I am all at once what Christ is, since he was what I am."

It is not resurrection or the work of Christ as some distant happening that saves us. We are saved because Christ entered into that realm where sorrow and suffering reigned, namely, our world. Freedom could not have been won had he not come to us. The rescue would not have happened had he not been who he was. But because he was and is the Son of God and our risen Lord, the poet can say (picking up on words of St. Paul and St. John), "In a flash, at a trumpet crash, / I am all at once what Christ is." We are given new life. The Savior defeats death to restore, to quicken, to make alive, to make new.

"For the Lord himself will descend from heaven with a cry of command, with the archangel's call, and with the sound of the trumpet of God. And the dead in Christ will rise first; then we who are alive, who are left, shall be caught up together with them in the clouds to meet the Lord in the air; and so we shall always be with the Lord" (1 Thess. 4:16-18).

Jesus reigns, adored by angels;
Man with God is on the throne.
Mighty Lord, in Thine ascension
We by faith behold our own.
(*The Lutheran Hymnal*, 218)

In Place of Peace

DAY 12

When will you ever, Peace, wild wooddove, shy wings shut,
Your round me roaming end, and under be my boughs?
When, when Peace, will you Peace? I'll not play hypocrite
To my own heart: I yield you do come sometimes; but
That piecemeal peace is poor peace. What pure peace allows
Alarms of wars, the daunting wars, the death of it?

Many Jewish people say *shalom* when they meet and when they say good-bye. *Shalom* is not a word unfamiliar to Christians. When we want to emphasize the full meaning of peace, which is what *shalom* means, we often resort to using the Hebrew word because its meaning includes not only "peace" but "wholeness," or "complete well-being."

The liturgy used in many Sunday worship services begins and ends with the word peace. But as much as we desire it, peace, like a bird, seems to fly away. We wonder when we will ever enjoy the peace that surpasses all human understanding, as our Christian faith promises.

Father Hopkins found himself wondering the same thing. He confessed that peace does come sometimes, but impatiently declared "that piecemeal peace is poor peace." He said peace should be a stronger force in him than it was, saving him from the anxiety born out of the struggle with life. Peace should be permanent, lasting.

The poem is a veiled protest to God for not granting the peace the writer knows he needs. In the second part of the poem, Father Hopkins answers his own complaint in lines that make us aware of how God helps in such situations. He sends something in place of peace that proves to be an additional blessing.

If peace for some reason is taken away the Lord does not leave us without a special spiritual gift to see us through! Patience grows into ("plumes" is the way the poet puts it) peace in time. And when peace does arrive, it will not be for just a short while; it will last. That is God's way with God's people in the Lord Jesus, whose final will for us is *shalom*, peace.

Lord, I will admit it. I, too, having asked for peace that did not come, have felt disappointed. I keep forgetting that whenever you withhold one thing you give another. Let me display and cherish patience, if not peace, and then let me in your good time experience your peace once again. Amen.

Spring

DAY

13

Nothing is so beautiful as Spring—
When weeds, in wheels, shoot long and lovely and lush;
....
The glassy peartree leaves and blooms, they brush
The descending blue; that blue is all in a rush
With richness. . .

As one of our foremost poets of nature, Father Hopkins raises a hymn to spring, and a glorious one it is.

"Nothing is so beautiful as Spring," he states and then goes on to produce images for us to make us share his belief—plants turning green and growing, birds nesting and singing, spring lambs racing in the fields, trees putting forth their leaves, the blue sky providing a canopy and backdrop to it all. We have seen enough things like that to make it easy for us to agree. We are ready to join in a hymn to God the Creator.

But Father Hopkins's poem about spring does not take that direction. For this poet-priest, spring brings to mind something else, something that might not have occurred to us.

> *What is all this juice and all this joy?*
> *A strain of the earth's sweet being in the beginning*
> *In Eden garden—*

For Father Hopkins, these lines show that the glories of spring bring to mind the earth and humankind before sin entered the world. We catch a glimpse of that world as it came from the hand of the Creator, when it was fresh and new and unspoiled, when God looked about and saw everything and called it good. Spring is the time when the world is close to being what God meant it to be.

It does us good to share the mind and feelings of the poet. We see what a catastrophe befell us when sin entered. We see what is in store for us as we wait with eager longing for the restoration of all that is promised in God's redemption.

Nothing is so beautiful as spring—at present. But the beauty of spring is only a preview of coming attractions when we shall behold beauty itself in the love of God.

I am moved, Father, by the glories of your world. People say, "It can't get any better than this." Looking about me and knowing what you have done in Christ, I say, "It can and will get even better than this." And I bow my head in joyful adoration. Amen.

Beautiful Savior

DAY
14

Summer ends now; now, barbarous in beauty, the stooks rise
Around; up above, what wind-walks! what lovely behaviour
Of silk-sack clouds! has wilder, wilful-wavier
Meal-drift moulded ever and melted across skies?

I walk, I lift up, I lift up heart, eyes,
Down all that glory in the heavens to glean our Saviour.

"Beautiful Savior" is a favorite hymn of many. In the second and third stanzas of that hymn, we sing that the creation is fair but that Jesus, our Savior, is fairer still. The beauty of the world is second to the beauty of the Lord who, in love, gave himself for us to redeem us.

Father Hopkins, too, is reminded of the beauty of Christ in nature. But for him nature as it is observed in the fall of the year is one with Christ. Christ's presence in nature is what gives it beauty. So great, so powerful, so all-encompassing is the glorified Redeemer in his love for our fallen world, that he penetrates it and makes it glow and shine. As Father Hopkins looked up and saw the shocks of wheat—"stooks"—standing in the fields, the clouds scattered in fanciful patterns across the sky, the hills of Wales (where he was at the time), in the priest sees the Savior.

Some seeing the Savior depicted in paintings, have thought him beautiful in his humanness. Others have thought him beautiful in his sacrifices for us. Father Hopkins's vision denies neither of those two images of the Lord Jesus. However, following the cross was the resurrection, where Christ joined the natural and the supernatural in glory. The imagination takes off when it thinks of him this way:

> *The heart rears wings bold and bolder*
> *And hurls for him, O half curls earth for him off under his feet.*

Lord, I have often taken your name upon my lips, but too few have been the times I placed your presence, your self, before my eyes. I have seen pictures of you in your ministry and on the cross. But then you disappear from my sight. Help me to see with new eyes that I am surrounded with your presence because you fill all things. Then I shall be drawn into you to know the joy of God. Amen.

William Smith

AUGUSTINE

UGUSTINE (354–430) was born some 40 years after Christianity had become the acknowledged religion of the Roman Empire under Constantine. His birthplace was Numidia, a Roman province in North Africa.

His father, Patricus, reasonably well off, remained a pagan until shortly before death, when he was baptized. Augustine's mother, Monica, on the other hand, was a Christian of tremendous piety. As his mother prayed, Augustine dedicated his life to the service of Christ and the church. She made him a saint and his sanctity eventually resulted in her being canonized.

By the end of the fourth century the decadence which had afflicted Rome had spread to the northern African provinces, especially to the great port of Carthage, at whose university Augustine studied. He excelled there and soon became a highly regarded teacher of rhetoric. Then he transferred to Rome because he found Carthage students too turbulent. In Rome he could find an academic position that would lead to great status and power. There was yet another darker motive: he wanted to escape from the watchful eye of his mother, and indulge himself more freely.

In Rome he was appointed to the Chair of Rhetoric in Milan. This brought him in contact with the imperial court and, even more importantly, with the saintly Bishop Ambrose. Under Ambrose's influence Augustine began to study the Scriptures, noting particularly the spiritual meaning of Old Testament stories. This played an important part in his final deliverance from the heresy of Manicheism and his ultimate conversion, described in the *Confessions*. Augustine returned with Monica to North Africa, resolving to dedicate the remaining years of his life wholly to the service of Christ. But his gifts were too celebrated and precious for him to be left in peace.

He was 43 years old when he became Bishop of Hippo. Thenceforth, he was endlessly involved in the responsibilities of his office and the often bitter controversies of his time. In the year 410 Rome had been sacked. Augustine was forced to turn to the question of the relation between earthly cities like Rome, which rise and fall, and the heavenly city, or city of God, which is everlasting. This question resulted in his great work, *The City of God,* in which he concluded that in Jesus Christ, the presence of God who has come to us in human form, we have a "window in the walls of time which looks out on to this Heavenly City."

We Are Drawn to Praise God

D A Y
1

One of Augustine's greatest contributions to Christian literature is his book *Confessions*. With such an ambiguous title, one may ask, Is Augustine intending a confession of sin? Of faith? Or is this simply his autobiography? While all of these elements are found in *Confessions,* it is not Augustine's primary concern to reveal himself and his faith in God. The focus of the *Confessions* is God! It is God who is before him and about whom he writes. The book starts with praise of God and ends with praise of creation—a creation that is good, created by a God who is wonderfully good. The heart of the book, then, is the confession of praise.

Why do we sing praises to God? Is it because we have a God before whom we tremble? "No!" says Augustine. It is something else. We must praise God out of our experiencing God's goodness, God's greatness, God's beauty. It is the expression of one's heart filled with the love of God (Rom. 5:5). The heart feels who this God is and is drawn to praise God. Praise is an inevitable expression of that awareness. So the book begins, *"Thou art great, O Lord, and greatly to be praised."**

Augustine asserts that our God-given, inner beauty and our desire to praise God are no longer present in their original form. However, he sees "traces of the trinity" in the inner soul of each individual, just as he does when he views the beauty and grandeur of God's creation as a whole. Though darkened by original sin, wonderful attributes can be found in all people.

The book is centered in the praise of God who was there all along in Augustine's life, mysteriously guiding and directing him, and who, he was convinced, would continue to direct him in his very active life as long as he lived.

Can you think of times when you have been especially conscious of this desire to praise God in your life?

*Quotations from Augustine throughout this chapter have been translated from Latin by the author. The sources are listed in the bibliography.

We Are Created to Be with God

DAY 2

"Since we are a part of your creation, we wish to praise you. The thought of you stirs us so deeply that we cannot be content unless we praise you, because you made us to be with you and our hearts are restless until they rest in you."

Here is one of the fundamental "traces of the trinity" for Augustine. We are created to be with God. We might say that no person is really human without God, according to Augustine. Without God, the humanity of that person is, if not lost, at least diminished. Our only proper place is to be with God.

Augustine would claim that a restlessness is "built into" every human being, that there is an awareness, at some level in every person, that one has no real being, no true existence without God. He prays: "O God, I should have no being at all unless you were in me, or rather I should not be unless I had being in you." Augustine's own restless yearning, his pining for this loving, unchangeable God, is expressed in this prayer: *"You are never new, never old, and yet all things have new life from you. . . . Who will grant me to rest content in you? To whom shall I turn for the gift of your coming into my heart and filling it to the brim so that I might forget all the wrong I have done and embrace you alone, my only source of good."*

How has this "inner restlessness" been expressed in your life? Can you reflect on those moments when you have been most aware of "yearning and pining" for God to come into your heart and fill it to the brim with his loving presence?

In Love God Creates and Sustains

 Augustine finds hints or evidence of the presence of God, "traces of the trinity," from the very beginning of his life. He sees them in his mother's sacrificial love, the love of one who pointed him to the first ray of divine light, the light which is Jesus Christ.

"The comfort of my mother's milk maintained my life. Yet neither did my mother nor my nurses fill their own breasts, but you, O Lord, did so, and afforded nourishment fit for my infancy, even according to your planning and riches which are arranged even to the lowest order of things."

From his mother Monica's little lamp of faith he saw the first light of God, the first light of Jesus Christ, the first light of the Holy Spirit. We, also, who at the beginning of our existence have all these infant needs can reflect later (as Augustine did) with deep warmth and gratitude for God's love coming to us through a mother's love. Some of us, however, may bear deep scars, spiritually as well as emotionally, because we were deprived of such love.

For Augustine, evidence of the presence of God could be seen, not only in the first work of divine love by which God created him and brought him into this world, but also in that next work of God's love in which he was sustained by the comfort of his mother's milk.

What experiences do you recall from your early life that have helped you see God's work of divine love in creating and sustaining you?

God's Severe Mercy

D A Y
4 Augustine looked back on his life and saw the whole of it under God's guidance, always with mercy, but this mercy was, in some cases, severe. Yet those experiences that looked like punishment turned out to be based on God's love, and the severity of the experience turned out to be precisely the best medicine, the best way to educate him inwardly. He saw this, for example, when he reflected on his life as a schoolboy. He had unusual intellectual gifts and the ability to think deeply. He was, however, lazy and irresponsible in making use of his gifts and received punishment because of it. He prayed that God would rescue him from the punishment, but his prayers were not answered as he hoped. The problem was that he knew and understood that he had insight given by God to avoid those punishments, but he refused to apply himself just the same.

At this time his Baptism was deferred. The initial reason for this was due to an illness he had. But a deeper reason for further delay was that his mother was very concerned about the seriousness of his rebellious behavior in general, not only in his school work. She held to the widespread notion in the North African church of that time that sins after Baptism could not be forgiven. Augustine, as a boy, thought about this and realized that it would be better if he were saved by Baptism immediately, because of his own concern about the way his life was going. He was, even at that time, aware of the pain and misery which sin creates. The more understanding he gained of the reality of sin in his life, the greater became his grasp of the incomparable value of salvation. Here is another sign of the presence of God in the formation of his life—his understanding of the great joy in salvation through Christ. Through the "severe mercy" of God in permitting him to go through this and many other much more painful experiences, he could grasp the greatness of Christian salvation.

Is it really difficult for you to describe some instances of the "severe mercy" of God as you look back on your life?

The Name of Jesus Christ

<table>
<tr><td>D A Y
5</td><td>Augustine, in his years of higher learning, became a very zealous student. During this time another "trace of the trinity," an indication of God's continued activity in his life, occurred in his study of a book by Cicero. It was called the *Hortensius*</td></tr>
</table>

Augustine, in his years of higher learning, became a very zealous student. During this time another "trace of the trinity," an indication of God's continued activity in his life, occurred in his study of a book by Cicero. It was called the *Hortensius* (*hortensius* means "gardener"). This book contained an invitation to a meaningful life. It was not propaganda for a special school of philosophy, but a call to a lifelong search for true wisdom. Augustine characterizes the influence of the book this way: *". . . that book changed my feelings and changed my prayers to you, O Lord. It altered my wishes and my desires. All former empty hopes lost significance for me, and I was yearning with incredible ardor of heart after the immortality of wisdom. I began to rise up so that I might turn to you, O God. . . . How did I burn then, my God, how did I burn to flee from earthly delights to you. Yet, I was unaware of what you were doing with me. For wisdom dwells with you."*

The most remarkable thing in all of Augustine's experience in reading *Hortensius* was how he found himself missing the name of Christ. Didn't he know that Cicero lived before the birth of Jesus? Clearly, this work was written before the Christian era. Yet he says: *"The only thing to dim my ardor was the fact that the name of Christ was not there, for this name, by your mercy, O Lord, this name of my Savior, your son, my youthful heart had drunk in piously with my mother's milk and, until that time, had retained it in its depth; whatever lacked this name could not completely win me, however well expressed and polished and true appearing."*

In Augustine's soul the presence of God was planted so deeply that it could not be uprooted or eliminated. Jesus Christ had written his name indelibly on Augustine's soul through the loving hands of his mother, Monica. So much so, that there was in him an inward necessity to have God as his heavenly Father, and Jesus Christ as his Savior.

How has that inward necessity to have God as your heavenly Father and Jesus Christ as your Savior been formed in you?

Scripture's Profound Meaning

D A Y
6

After the experience that emerged from reading *Hortensius* and not finding the name of Jesus there, Augustine turned back to the Scriptures with the idea of studying them in a new way. He later recognized that his mind was too rationalistic, too arrogant, too shallow at that time to penetrate the sense of the word of God and bow in humility before it.

So he turned his religious quest toward the cult of the Manicheans who, with their mysterious, esoteric language, held great attraction for him. The muddled teaching of the Manicheans could not give Augustine any peace, however. Yet, even while he was immersed in that cult, another trace of God's activity of grace working in his life was taking place through two inner events going on simultaneously. First, he was beginning to read more philosophy. The more he read, the less attracted he was to the materialistic, nightmarish teachings of the Manicheans who taught that God was a big luminous body filling the universe with his bulk, and that Augustine, himself, was a fragment of this luminous body.

At the same time, he was looking at his own Christian heritage and was deeply bothered by what he thought was a basic teaching of the North African church. He assumed that the church held to the literal sense of the Old Testament without looking to any spiritual understanding of it. But then God graciously placed the great bishop of Milan, Ambrose, in his path when Augustine came to Milan to teach rhetoric. While listening to the preaching of Ambrose, Augustine saw that his criticism of the church on this point was based on misunderstanding. Ambrose's continual emphasis that the "letter kills, but the spirit makes alive" opened up new spiritual horizons for Augustine.

Augustine heard Ambrose preach that there were things of God that could not be proved and yet were to be believed, and that faith is necessary to heal the soul. Ambrose pointed Augustine to the fundamental value of believing, because without faith, one cannot understand anything of God. The Bible now became much more attractive to Augustine when he realized there are mysteries above human reason in Scripture. "When having lifted the mystic veil he (Ambrose) laid bare the spiritual meaning of those things which, taken literally, seemed to teach error."

Augustine began to see how, in Scripture, the "majesty of the secret and the profoundness of meaning were offered in words most open and in a style most humble."

When did this "profoundness of meaning" of Scripture "offered in words most open and in style most humble" first grasp you?

God Speaks to Us

It is obvious that a "trace of the trinity" in Augustine's pilgrimage of faith would be his conversion experience in the garden described in Book 8. This episode is often overly dramatized. This was not as cataclysmic an event for Augustine as is often portrayed. It was, rather, the culmination of God's working in him over a long period of time. It was a time when he was inwardly running in circles, coming closer to recognizing that he had to do something drastic about his life. Relief finally came when God had his way with Augustine. He knew that he could not live without Christ any longer. All his rational arguments against faith in Christ had evaporated.

Compare this scene with Augustine's last conversation with his mother, Monica, found in Book 9. The two of them contemplate the divine glory of eternal life after death, that which "eye has not seen, nor ear heard, nor entered into one's heart." This transcendent moment for Augustine sheds light on all past experiences of God's presence in his life from infancy to the present. In this moment both he and Monica were in a state of profound yearning to reach "with the mouth of the heart those mountains and streams flowing above," so that they might reflect on those great things according to their capacity. He and his mother came to the conclusion that the highest point of human pleasure is not worth comparing to the awareness of that eternal life of God's divine presence, which they had experienced in the silence of the soul.

This experience offered Augustine an awesome awareness that, by God's grace, the heavenly world and our earthly world are joined. This perception filled Augustine with an inward blessedness and strength, knowing that we humans are not left alone on earth in this life.

Because of this experience Augustine was able to say: "We are assured of our possession of these three things: eternal life, eternal truth, and eternal love, not on the testimony of others, but by our own consciousness of their presence and because we see it with our most truthful interior vision."

Resident Aliens

DAY
8

The basic trait in the "resident alien," as Augustine writes in his great work *The City of God,* is seeing one's true citizenship in the invisible city of God. This means a growing awareness for the believer that one lives out the whole of one's life here on earth as a temporary resident. For Augustine, however, this implies that we, as Christians, must accept an intimate dependence on the community around us; we must realize that our common life was created by people like ourselves, to achieve some "good" that we are glad to share with them, to improve some situation, to avoid some greater evil; we must be genuinely grateful for the favorable conditions that it provides. However, Augustine expected that as "resident aliens" Christians would always be aware of the tenacity of those links that bind us to the world.

But we need to remember in these reflections, based mainly on *The City of God,* that, far from being a book about flight from the world, it is a book whose recurrent theme is "our business within this common mortal life." It is a book about being other-worldly while living in this world.

If you were asked, as a Christian, what it meant to you to be "in the world but not of the world," what would you say? Have there been times when an awareness of "being other-worldly in this world" has been most real for you as a Christian? How did that awareness come about? What effect did this have on you inwardly?

Living as Resident Aliens

DAY 9 Should the Christian be like everyone else, totally involved in the affairs of the world and totally immersed in its passions and pursuits? Should the aims of the Christian include the search for enjoyment of life, for possessions, for high position and status in society? Or should the Christian aspire to something even higher, having some distance and detachment from these other aims and desires, without denying their relative value? These are the questions that Augustine poses in *The City of God.*

Augustine turned to the Scriptures for help in answering these questions: "I beseech you as aliens and exiles to abstain from the passions of the flesh that wage war against your soul. Maintain good conduct among the Gentiles, so that in case they speak against you as wrongdoers, they may see your deeds and glorify God on the day of visitation" (1 Pet. 2:11-12). Here the Christian is characterized as not really being a citizen of this world, but in some way an alien. The Christian is a citizen of another country, a citizen with full rights of citizenship there. The writer to the Ephesians says, "So then you are no longer strangers and sojourners, but you are fellow citizens with the saints and members of the household of God, built upon the foundation of the apostles and prophets, Christ Jesus himself being the cornerstone" (Eph. 2:19-20).

This attitude, which is developed and emphasized by Augustine, was a basic orientation of the early Christian. Now, a question for you in these reflections on the Christian as "resident alien": How might such an attitude in our lives, as modern Christians, not only offer us help in recovering from inward conflicts, psychic distortions and sickness, but lead us toward a greater sense of the presence of Christ in our lives?

Order in Me My Love

DAY 10 The soul of the "resident alien" is in permanent tension between two powers pulling the Christian inwardly in opposite directions. Augustine speaks of these powers as "two loves." The two cities, the heavenly and earthly, are founded by these two loves. The one is the love of oneself (characteristic of the earthly city). This love of oneself goes so far as to disregard God. The heavenly love, on the contrary, goes so far in loving God as to forget oneself. The one glories in oneself. The other glories in God. The one seeks glory from other persons. But the great glory of the other is God who is giving witness of his forgiving love in one's conscience. The one loves ruling, dominating, and subduing. The other, in contrast, seeks to serve another in love. The one has delight in its own strength. The other has God as its strength.

Augustine believed that there is a deep love for God hidden within the heart of every believer. This highest, most sublime love for God does not imply for Augustine, however, that such a love swallows up all other lesser loves. Rather, he saw all these other loves—love of one's betrothed, love of spouse, family, friends, love of beauty, art, music, nature—as flowing out of this love for God. Augustine would ask us, as modern "resident alien" Christians, to maintain our identity, not by withdrawal from this "earthly city," but by something far more difficult, by maintaining a firm and balanced perspective on the whole range of loves of which we are capable in our present state. He would ask us, as members of Christ's body of believers, his church, inhabitants of the City of God—now by faith, and in the life to come, by sight—to join him in a simple prayer he repeatedly prayed: "Order in me my love."

When would you find (or perhaps have already found) words like these most helpful and vital for you to pray in your own Christian life?

Intelligent Self-Love

<table>
<tr><td>D A Y
11</td><td>Augustine believed that the more the "resident alien" consciousness develops in the Christian, the less the person is tied to himself or herself in self-idolatry. He is aware that the more one makes oneself a false god, the more one makes God an</td></tr>
</table>

enemy. But if one really loves God, one loves those who are loved by God. This means truly seeing God as a God of love—being aware of how much one is loved by God.

But Augustine also sees a peculiar, very positive type of self-love in this "resident alien" consciousness flowing directly out of love for God. This self-love includes the desire for one's salvation, the desire to possess goodness of character and to be loving to one's neighbor, and the yearning to be near God and to be a citizen of the city of God. "The one who knows that he loves himself loves God. The one who does not love God, even if he loves himself, it can be truly said that he hates himself." "We love ourselves the more we love God." This, according to Augustine, is "intelligent self-love."

We, as modern Christians, know we are immersed in a culture that is particularly susceptible to an obsession with the self. We also know how such an obsession easily leads to what Luther spoke of as *the sin:* "the person turned in on himself or herself." On the other hand, what would be the benefits for you to remind yourself regularly of this kind of "intelligent self-love" that Augustine holds up?

Unceasing Prayer

DAY 12

How do we become aware of the "resident alien" consciousness in our lives as Christians? Augustine replies, *"Give me one who longs, who hungers, who is a thirsty pilgrim in this wilderness, sighing for the springs of the eternal City: give me such a person; that one will know what I mean."* He reminds us that God, who sees in secret and knows our hearts, is aware of these hidden groanings within us and will reward us (cf. Matt. 6:6). How will God reward us? For one thing, we can become aware that this very longing, this inner yearning, this sighing within, is our praying; and if this longing continues, our praying is continual too.

"It was not for nothing," says Augustine, *"that the apostle Paul said, 'Pray without ceasing' (1 Thess. 5:17). Can we unceasingly bend our knees, bow down our bodies, or uplift our hands that the apostle should tell us to 'pray without ceasing'? No, if it is thus he bids us pray, I do not think we can do so without ceasing. There is another way of praying, interior and unbroken, and that is the way of longing, of desire. Whatever else you are doing, if you long for that City, that eternal homeland, you are not ceasing to pray. If you do not want to cease praying, do not cease longing. Your unceasing desire is your unceasing prayer."*

Augustine was concerned that this longing not be allowed to grow cold through the preoccupation of our everyday life. He would encourage us "resident alien" believers to find ways of stirring up this longing at "certain fixed times so that it may be brought to a glow." Would it not be of comfort for you to believe that your very yearning for God's peace, your sighing within to know more fully of God's forgiving love, and your desire to fix your eyes more firmly on the eternal city of God—that this longing and desire within you is an expression of your unceasing prayer?

Our Love for God

DAY 13 We can see that the heart of Augustine's understanding of the "resident alien" consciousness of the Christian is expressed in "longing for the vision of God." *"Nothing that God can promise is of any worth apart from God Himself. What is all the earth, the sea, the sky, the stars . . . the hosts of angels? For the creator of them all I thirst, for Him I hunger. . . ."* Augustine refers to this "longing for the vision of God" at times as "pure love" by which he means loving God for God's own sake. *"The heart is not pure,"* he says, *"if it worships God for a reward. What then? Shall we have no reward for the worship of God? Assuredly we shall, but it will be God Himself whom we worship: His own self will be our reward, in that we shall see Him as He is. . . . If you worship God who freely wrought your undeserved redemption, if when you consider God's goodness toward you, your heart sighs and is restless with longing for God; then seek not from God anything outside God, God Himself suffices you."*

Augustine would try to illustrate this by pointing out that in serious illness we long for health, but when restoration of health comes, that longing is dispatched. In a similar way when we, as believers, attain the perfect health, which is life eternal in the City of God, "we shall feel need no longer, and therein will be our happiness. For we shall be filled with our God, who Himself will be to us all that our longings make us count most desirable here."

But now Augustine would ask about my daily pilgrimage as a "resident alien" Christian when the fulfillment is not yet; what is my good here and now? His answer: *"So long as you are not yet fast joined to God, set there your hope . . . cleave to God in hope. And here (in this life) setting your hope in God, what will you have to do? What will be your work, but to praise Him you love and to get others to share your love of Him?"*

Could you reflect on any persons or events in your life that have edified and strengthened you in faith? Can you think of times when you've shared your love for God with other people?

The Business of Praising God

D A Y

14

We began these reflections on Augustine with the note of praise from his *Confessions*. His final word in *The City of God* ends on the same note: "The blessedness of the inhabitants of the Holy City is to be always praising God." The praise of God is to be our basic vocation as "resident alien" believers in this world, the vocation through which we are to win others to God's love. The praise of God is our highest calling. The degree to which all our life's work does not express itself in the praise of God will be the degree to which we are drawn down to the love of self. The voice of praise is never silent in us unless we fall away from God. We know how often that voice of praise has been silent in us, as Augustine knew, too. That is why he continually reminded himself and his people in his sermons, letters, and other writings that the grace of God is not only the power of God's spirit of love working in us, but the mercy of God toward us, through our Lord's self-giving love on the cross for our sake. Augustine knew how this evoked in him, as a forgiven sinner, an ever stronger and renewed voice of praise.

He would remind us that this vocation of praise as "resident alien" believers is our "schooling" for the perfect praise of the Heavenly City. "And when that which is perfect is come our whole business will be the praise of God."

When you hear language like this last phrase of Augustine's, and in your imagination you transfer yourself as you are, to the choir of heaven, you can't help but wonder how such an activity can seem anything but empty and unreal. Augustine responds to that natural apprehension this way: *"Let us rest assured, we shall not be wearied by the praise of God nor by His love. If your love should fail, so would your praise; but if love will be everlasting, fear not that you will lack power ever to praise God whom you will have power ever to love."*

Robert Stackel

THOMAS À KEMPIS

I T IS CLAIMED that the devotional book *The Imitation of Christ* by Thomas à Kempis (ca. 1380–1471), has been, next to the Bible, the most popular spiritual reading in the whole world for over five hundred years. It has been translated into more than 50 languages and has been beloved by Christians of all different types.

It was written originally in Latin and hand copied for decades before the invention of the printing press. Although there are still more than seven hundred manuscript copies of his book in existence, most publications today are translations of a 1441 manuscript written by Thomas's own hand, which is the definitive text. The humility of Thomas kept him from signing his name to his writings.

Thomas was born in the little Rhineland town of Kempen near Düsseldorf (hence, Thomas from Kempen) in the year 1379 or 1380, the son of an artisan. When Thomas was 20, he felt the call to the religious life and applied for entrance into a new religious community called Mount St. Agnes near Zwolle. Eventually he took his vows and was ordained a priest in 1413. He fulfilled the usual round of monastic duties: reading and study, copying and writing books, and training of novices. As a priest dealing with people in the confessional and in counseling, he learned the depths of human sorrow and the heights of spiritual joy. He steeped himself in the knowledge of the Scriptures and in time became a master of novices, training them in the religious life. He also wrote about how the spiritual insights he had discovered related to the experiences of life. The *Imitation* grew out of his instructions to novices. We don't know much about the rest of Thomas's life. For more than 70 years he lived at Mount St. Agnes, dying there on May 1, 1471, after Compline, when he was 91.

The vast popularity of the *Imitation* is due to its simplicity, its deep spirituality, and its keen interpretation of Scripture. Its style resembles that of Scripture itself, and often Scripture is quoted in it. Its timeless truth speaks to all humanity. The book was written at a time when a new Europe was emerging and the laity were acquiring a more prominent role in the life of the church. The established institutions of the church could not handle the new situation very well, so Thomas wrote to penetrate the new order with a profound spiritual piety. His piety has a rich contribution to make to Christians of all ages, all cultures, and all places.

The Test of Truth

"If you would understand Christ's words fully and taste them truly, you must strive to form your whole life after his pattern."

If anyone wants to understand more perfectly the teachings of another person, one must live those teachings and so test them. To understand better the convictions of an environmentalist, one must practice living in a way so as to do the least harm to the environment and discover what kind of a feeling this brings. To understand better the principles of a vegetarian, one must practice eating no meat for a time to discover what impression that makes.

Jesus welcomes our putting his teachings to the test by practicing them in daily life. If they work out in actual life, then they must be true. Take forgiveness, for example, which Jesus taught and lived. When we forgive someone an intentional wrong, do we feel good about it in our hearts? Is the other person blessed by it? Is the world a better place because of it? Or think of self-denial for the sake of others. When we deny ourselves some pleasure in order to help someone in trouble, do we have a good feeling about it inwardly? Is the other person happier? Does this please God?

Jesus once said, "If any man's will is to do [God's] will, he shall know whether the teaching is from God or whether I am speaking on my own authority" (John 7:17). Notice that the verb is *do*, not just talk about it. To do it is to put it into practice in daily life. God wants us to test his teachings in the crucible of actual life. He, the creator of all life, knows that his teachings, when practiced, enrich life as nothing else can.

Lord Jesus Christ, you came that we might have life. Give us the will to live the truths you taught, and in living them to discover new depths of joy and peace and a new closeness to you, our way to God the Father. In your name we pray. Amen.

Sturdier than Granite

"Men pass away, but the truth of the Lord abides for ever."

It has been said that God has no eraser on the end of his pencil. What he writes never needs to be changed. What he says will outlast Mount Everest. Such a basic document as the Constitution of the United States had to be amended almost before the ink was dry; the Bill of Rights, the first 10 amendments, was added. On the other hand, the Ten Commandments have never been amended. If the Pacific Ocean were to dry up, the Ten Commandments would still be in force. Jesus said, "Heaven and earth will pass away, but my words will not pass away."

"Men pass away," Thomas wrote, "but the truth of the Lord abides for ever." He also counseled, "We should search the Scriptures for what is profitable to our souls and not for beauties of language." Cadence of language can be majestic, but accuracy of truth is more important. When Thomas says, "We should *search* the Scriptures," he means we should keep digging deeper into the Bible all our lives, even as he did.

During the exile of God's people in Babylon six centuries before Christ, an unnamed prophet struck the same chord in Isaiah 40:6, 8: "All flesh is grass, and all its beauty is like the flower of the field," he cried. "The grass withers, the flower fades; but the word of our God will stand for ever." King Solomon seconds that motion in his stately prayer at the dedication of the first Temple which he built in Jerusalem. "Not one word has failed," he prayed, "of all [God's] good promise" (1 Kings 8:56). The average person speaks thousands of words a day and many of them fail to be significant, but "not one word" of all God's promises has ever failed to be true and enduring.

Eternal God, whose words are more enduring than granite and whose truth abides from everlasting to everlasting, guide us in searching the Scriptures until we find ever more clearly your saving truth in Jesus Christ, your Son our Lord. Amen.

Uses of Adversity

"It is good for us at times to have troubles and adversities; for often they make a man enter into himself, so that he may know that he is in exile, and may not place his hopes in anything of this world."

Thomas had a positive approach to setbacks. Instead of whining over them, he advised discovering their use. Every trouble has some use for the person who is willing to seek diligently enough with the Holy Spirit's help to find it.

A father took his 12-year-old son out into the country for his first rifle practice. The son raised the gun and fired as his father had instructed him. The blast of the gun nearly scared the boy out of his wits, and the powerful recoil of the rifle threw him backward into his father's arms; his father, anticipating this very thing, had taken a position behind his son to catch him. It was with a new appreciation of his father that the boy pulled himself together again. Life is like that. The shock of some experience unnerves us, and the recoil throws us backwards. That is, it seems as though it is backwards, but when we find ourself in our Father's arms, who was waiting to catch us and support us, we discover that, spiritually, it is a forward experience.

Thomas described a person in this world as being "in exile." He meant that this world is not our home. We are only pilgrims traveling through this life. Our true home is in heaven. Therefore, we should not look primarily to anything in this world to restore us when we fall into trouble, but to God, our loving heavenly Father. Thomas counseled: "Therefore ought a man to establish himself so firmly in God that he has no need to seek many human consolations."

St. Paul knew the meaning of trouble. He spoke of his "thorn in the flesh" and prayed to God agonizingly and repeatedly for its removal. But God didn't take away his thorn. Instead, God gave Paul something far better, namely, this assurance: "My grace is sufficient for you, for my power is made perfect in weakness" (2 Cor. 12:9).

O Holy Spirit, turn for us life's disappointing setbacks into experiences that move us forward spiritually, through Christ, whose cross was turned into a crown. Amen.

On Looking Ahead

"A very little while and all will be over with you here. Ask yourself are you ready for the next life? . . . O the dullness and the hardness of the human heart, that dwells only upon things present, instead of providing rather for those which are to come! You should so order yourself in every deed and thought as though you were to die this day. . . . If you are not prepared today, how will you be tomorrow? Tomorrow is an uncertain day; and how do you know if you shall have tomorrow?"

The uncertainty of the length of a human life weighed heavily on Thomas, as it should upon us all. "When it is morning, think that you will not live till evening," he wrote. "And when evening comes, venture not to promise yourself the next morning. Therefore be always ready; and so live that death may never find you unprepared." He also wrote, "Of what use is it to live long, when we amend ourselves so little?" And then, "How happy and how prudent is he who strives to be in life what he would fain be found in death!" But also, "The time will come when you will desire one day or even one hour for amendment; and I know not if you will obtain it."

His words in *The Imitation of Christ* are like an echo of Christ's words in Mark about the end. "Take heed, watch," Jesus taught, "for you do not know when the time will come." Then Jesus told his disciples the parable about the master of a household going away on a long trip, putting the servants in charge, not knowing when he would return. "Lest he come suddenly and find you asleep," the parable ended, "I say to all: 'Watch' " (Mark 13:36-37).

Thomas continued: "Therefore, study so to live now that in the hour of death you may be able to rejoice rather than be afraid. Learn now to die to the world, that then you may begin to live with Christ." He concluded, "Think of nothing but your salvation; care only for the things of God."

Lord Jesus Christ, we long for your return to earth in glory. Keep us watchful, spiritually prepared, and always amending our life. Take us in your mercy to our home with the Father. We pray in your dear name. Amen.

Solitude and Silence

DAY

5

"Seek a convenient time to retire into yourself; and think often on the benefits of God."

A modern problem is that there is no "convenient time" to draw apart for a silent time with God in our overscheduled days. There isn't even time to get everything done that has to be done. Besides, we are afraid of silence. The television or radio must always be on. The portable boom box must shriek at ear-puncturing decibels. We are more afraid of silence than we are of noise.

As if speaking to our day, Thomas wrote, "He, therefore, who aims at inward and spiritual things, must with Jesus turn aside from the crowd." This is almost a mirror image of what Jesus told the disciples in Mark: "Come away by yourselves to a lonely place, and rest awhile" (Mark 6:31). Jesus' next sentence sounds like the twentieth century: "For many were coming and going, and they had no leisure even to eat."

Thomas insisted, "In silence and in quiet the devout soul makes progress, and learns the hidden things of Scripture." Then he added, "For whoso withdraws himself from his acquaintances and friends, to him will God draw near with his holy angels." And also, "If you would feel compunction to your very heart, retire to your room and shut out the noise of the world." This sounds like Jesus speaking in Matthew: "When you pray, go into your room and shut the door and pray to your Father who sees in secret" (Matt. 6:6).

When the prophet Elijah stood on the mountain, God wanted to speak to him (1 Kings 19:11-13). A mighty wind came up that split the hills, but God was not in the wind. Then came an earthquake, but God was not in the earthquake. Then followed a raging fire, but God was not in the fire. Finally there was "a still small voice." That was God speaking. Another Bible translation calls it "the soft whisper of a voice." How can we hear God's "soft whisper of a voice" unless we withdraw from the noise of the world and listen to him in the silence of his presence with an open Bible?

Heavenly Father, as your Son calmed the storm on Galilee, calm the storm of noise around us. In the silence of your presence speak so that we may hear even your soft whisper of a voice. In Jesus' name we pray. Amen.

Cultivate the Inner Life

<table>
<tr><td>D A Y

6</td><td>*"Many are [Christ's] visits to the man of inward life. With such a one He holds delightful converse, granting him sweet comfort, much peace, and an intimacy astonishing beyond measure."*</td></tr>
</table>

In his training of candidates for holy orders in the church, Thomas stressed the importance of the inner life. It is just as important for every Christian today. Cultivating the inner life with Christ is not so much a duty as it is a privilege which brings us divine comfort, peace, and union with Christ.

We often fall into the trap of judging someone by outward appearances. Even the venerable prophet, Samuel, once fell into that trap. When God wanted to pick a new king for Israel, he had the sons of Jesse pass before Samuel one by one (1 Sam. 16:6-13). When Eliab stepped forward Samuel thought he was the one. Eliab must have been handsome, strong, and of regal bearing—a Mr. America type. But God said to Samuel, "Do not look on his appearance or on the height of his stature, because I have rejected him; for the Lord sees not as man sees; man looks on the outward appearance, but the Lord looks on the heart." On that basis David was chosen king.

Jesus told us how to cultivate the inner life. "If a man loves me, he will keep my word," he taught, "and my Father will love him, and we will come to him and make our home with him" (John 14:23). God comes to us in Christ through the Holy Scriptures by the power of the Holy Spirit. The more we hear, read, study, and meditate upon God's Word with believing hearts, the deeper and richer our inner life will become and the closer we will be to our Savior God.

Thomas saw the heart and center of God's Word as the suffering death of God's Son for the sin of the world, followed by his victorious resurrection. So he wrote, "If you fly devoutly to the wounds of Jesus and the precious marks of His passion, you shall feel greatly strengthened in tribulation." And again, "Rest in the passion of Christ, and love to dwell within His sacred wounds."

O God, by the power of your Holy Spirit come ever more deeply into our hearts through your holy Word and cause our slain but risen Redeemer to sit on the throne of our lives, for his sake. Amen.

The Way of the Cross

D A Y
7

"He is gone before you carrying His cross, and He died for you upon the cross, that you also may bear your cross, and love to die on the cross. Because if you die with Him, you shall also live with Him; and if you are His companion in suffering, you shall be His companion also in glory. Lo, in the cross does all consist."

After the "Black Monday" stock market crash of October 19, 1987, historian Arthur M. Schlesinger Jr. identified one factor contributing to the crash as America's "unbridled pursuit of self-interest." In the '80s, he said, Americans tipped the balance they are continually adjusting between altruism and selfishness, and selfishness clearly won. Stock market whiz Ivan F. Boesky told a group of business students, "I think greed is healthy. You can be greedy and still feel good about yourself."

Thomas had a position diametrically opposite. "Why do you seek another way than this royal way, which is the way of the holy cross?" He added, "The more a man dies to himself, the more does he begin to live to God." He went further, "Nothing is more acceptable to God, nothing more salutary for you in this world, than to suffer willingly for Christ." That word *willingly* means that bearing the cross is a sacrifice we accept voluntarily, not some suffering that happens to us over which we have no control. Jesus chose to go to the cross for a dying world.

In fact, Jesus' whole life on earth was a cross. Listen to Thomas, "For even our Lord Jesus Christ Himself was not for one hour of His life without the anguish of His passion. . . . The whole life of Christ was a cross and a martyrdom." In deepest gratitude to him, we choose to bear our crosses, for Jesus taught, "If any man would come after me, let him deny himself and take up his cross daily and follow me." Thomas described the reward: "There is no other way to life and to true interior peace, but the way of the holy cross." We are to bear the cross willingly with patience if we wish to attain inner peace.

Lord Jesus, may your acceptance of Calvary's cross for us always be the model of our daily acceptance of self-denial for others. Amen.

The Blessings of God's Love

"Ah, Lord God, my holy Lover! when Thou comest into my heart, all that is within me shall exult with joy. Thou art my glory and the exultation of my heart. Thou art my hope and my refuge in the day of my tribulation."

Thomas treasured with all his heart God's love for him. He called God "my holy Lover." God's love was the pride and joy of his life. He wrote: "The noble love of Jesus impels a man to do great things, and ever excites him to desire that which is more perfect." How similar this sounds to St. Paul's "the love of Christ controls us" (2 Cor. 5:14)!

There is nothing in all creation like the love of God in Christ. He created us in his image and gave us immense resources to resist temptation. When we sin, in spite of it all, he grieves with a broken heart and keeps tugging at our souls through his Holy Spirit to return to him. When we return in repentant trust, he always welcomes us back with open arms for Jesus' sake.

What could impel a gifted person like Thomas à Kempis to a monastery to train beginners in the monastic order except the love of God in Christ? What could transform you into a humble, faithful, grateful disciple of the Savior except the love of God through his slain but risen Son? There is more encouragement, comfort, motivation, and empowerment in God's grace than we have ever begun to harness.

"Nothing is sweeter than love," Thomas wrote. "Nothing stronger, nothing higher, nothing wider, nothing more pleasant, nothing fuller or better in heaven or in earth; for love is born of God, and cannot rest but in God, above all created things." He also wrote, "A lover must willingly embrace all that is hard and bitter for the sake of his Beloved, and never suffer himself to be turned away from Him by any obstacle whatsoever." Can you imitate Christ in that way today?

Let your saving love, O God, so bathe our souls today that we may love others around us with an authentic imitation of Jesus' self-denying love. Amen.

Cast All Care on God

DAY 9

"My son, let Me do with you what I will; I know what is expedient for you. . . . Lord, what Thou sayest is true. Greater is Thy care for me than all the care I can take of myself. . . . For it cannot but be good, whatever Thou shalt do with me."

During World War II an English scrubwoman was asked how she slept so soundly through those terrible nights when German planes were bombing the city. Her explanation was: "The good Lord promised that he would watch over us, and I trust him. There's no sense in two of us staying awake all night."

Thomas similarly trusted in God's gracious providence. He wrote: "You must be as ready to suffer as to rejoice; you must be as glad to be poor and needy as to be full and rich." He also said, "Provided that Thou dost not cast me off for ever, nor blot me out of the book of life, no matter what tribulation befalls me, it shall not hurt me."

Peter put it in plain words in his first New Testament letter: "Cast all your anxieties on him, for he cares about you" (1 Peter 5:7). Paul wrote the same thing to the Philippians in different words: "Have no anxiety about anything, but . . . by prayer and thanksgiving let your requests be made known to God" (Phil. 4:6). Both of them remembered Jesus' teachings: "Do not be anxious about tomorrow, for tomorrow will be anxious for itself" (Matt. 6:34).

Anxiety and worry are pollution to the Christian. The London plane tree is beautifully adapted to living in pollution-laden city air. Its smooth leaves make it easy for the rain to wash off the city's grime. It sheds its bark periodically in large, flaky pieces, thus getting rid of impurities embedded in its bark. So too, Christians can let God's reign wash off the grime of anxiety and help shed worry and care like a plane tree sheds its bark. Anxiety cannot stick, for God has said, "I will never fail you nor forsake you."

O thou who sees the sparrows fall and clothes the lily, teach us to trust in your loving providence at all times. Our anxieties do not honor you; we confess with shame our lack of faith. Keep us ever in the hollow of your hand, through Jesus Christ our Lord. Amen.

God Is Sweet

DAY 10

"Thou art my God and my all! What would I have more, and what greater happiness can I desire? . . . For when Thou art present, all things yield delight; but when Thou art absent, all things grow loathsome. Thou makest a tranquil heart, and great peace, and festal joy."

Jaroslav Pelikan described Martin Luther as a "Christ-intoxicated" person. Luther was filled to overflowing with the grace of God in Jesus Christ. Dwight L. Moody once said that he wanted to be so full of the love of God that all the world would see what God could do with a totally dedicated person.

Thomas had trouble putting down the human passions within him to make more room for God in his heart. "As yet," he confessed, "alas, the old man is living in me; he is not wholly crucified; he is not perfectly dead. He still lusts strongly against the spirit and wages war within me." St. Paul knew well that war within. "For I do not do the good I want," he confessed to the church in Rome, "but the evil I do not want is what I do" (Rom. 7:19). Both men wanted most of all to let God fill their lives totally. Thomas wrote, "O when will that blessed and desirable hour come that Thou mayest fill me with Thy presence, and become to me all in all?" Paul worked for the day when God would "be everything to everyone" (1 Cor. 15:28). He witnessed to the gospel "until we all attain . . . to the measure of the stature of the fulness of Christ" (Eph. 4:13).

Thomas declared that God is "sweet." We ourselves may not often call God sweet, but the gifts he brings with his presence in our hearts through the Holy Spirit surely are sweet. Thomas says they include "a tranquil heart, and great peace, and festal joy." The psalmist boasted that the Word of God is "sweeter also than honey" (Ps. 19:10). Jackie Gleason, the comedian, had a frequently repeated saying, "How sweet it is!" The Christian believer, rejoicing over Christ within, filled with the presence of God, and possessing the gifts of the Spirit, can exclaim with bubbling enthusiasm, "How sweet it is!"

O God, whose sweetest gift is always yourself, flood our hearts with your gracious presence, filling every hidden crevice until deep within we may wear an unfading smile freshened by tranquility, peace, and joy, through Jesus Christ we pray. Amen.

When under Attack

<table>
<tr><td>D A Y
11</td><td>*"My son, stand firm, and trust in Me; for what are words but words? They fly through the air, but cannot do any real hurt. If you are guilty, resolve willingly to amend; if you are conscious of no fault, be ready to suffer this for God's sake."*</td></tr>
</table>

Astronomer Nicolaus Copernicus was a much reviled man in the sixteenth century because of his theory that the earth revolved around the sun. Everybody else was sure that the sun revolved around the earth. For the rest of his life he was ridiculed and attacked unjustifiably, even by the church. Most Christians at some time have been similarly criticized and rejected without good cause.

Thomas wrote of this problem saying, "But give ear to My word, and you shall not mind ten thousand words of men." Jesus taught, "Blessed are you when men revile you and persecute you and utter all kinds of evil against you falsely on my account. Rejoice and be glad, for your reward is great in heaven, for so men persecuted the prophets who were before you" (Matt. 5:11-12). Even Jesus, in healing an afflicted man, was accused of being in league with the prince of devils.

During the War between the States there was a fort along the coast in the South that could not be destroyed by cannon from ships at sea because its sponge-like wood simply absorbed the cannonballs. Christians can absorb the cannonballs of unfair criticism and thus render them harmless. Thomas wrote: "For I am the Judge and Discerner of all secrets; I know well how the matter passed; I know who inflicted the injury and who suffered it." He added, "To Me, therefore, should you run in every judgment." That word *run* means to lose no time in referring the matter immediately to God. Peter gave this counsel, "Therefore let those who suffer according to God's will do right and entrust their souls to a faithful Creator (1 Peter 4:19). God knows who is in the right and who is in the wrong. He reads the heart's secrets like an X-ray machine.

Thomas concluded, "Although I am not conscious to myself of anything, yet I cannot hereby justify myself; for, except through Thy mercy, no living man shall be justified in Thy sight."

Merciful Father, help us to forgive others as we have been forgiven by you, and teach us to leave it up to your perfect justice when we are falsely accused by others for Jesus' sake. Amen.

Let Grace Abound

 DAY 12 *"Son, My grace is precious; it does not suffer itself to be mingled with outward things or with earthly consolations. Therefore, you must cast away every obstacle to grace, if you desire to receive its infusion."*

Speaking to 2000 graduates of the University of South Carolina, United States Senator Mark Hatfield of Oregon said that materialism is "the greatest enemy of humankind." He called success in terms of acquiring material things "the golden calf of this modern age." Former Massachusetts Senator Paul Tsongas, speaking to graduates in another school, warned, "If you think happiness can be found chasing money, this country hasn't the capacity to survive." Jesus put it this way, "You cannot serve God and mammon."

Thomas wrote in the *Imitation:* "For you cannot attend to Me and at the same time take delight in transitory things." Linking materialism with self-love, he continued, "If you perfectly conquer yourself, you shall more easily subdue all other things. The perfect victory is to triumph over oneself." It must have been inspired by Jesus' words, "Do not be anxious about your life, what you shall eat or what you shall drink [or] . . . what you shall put on. . . . Seek first [God's] kingdom and his righteousness, and all these things shall be yours as well" (Matt. 6:25, 33).

The grace of God in Jesus Christ can be blocked from streaming into our heart by a love of the things of this world. For such persons Christ died in vain. Paul wrote to the Corinthians, "By the grace of God I am what I am, and his grace toward me was not in vain" (1 Cor. 15:10). Thomas concludes, "This vice of inordinate self-love is the source of almost everything that has to be radically destroyed. If this evil be vanquished and subdued, there will at once follow great peace and tranquility."

Giver of amazing grace, let nothing in this world impede the flow of your saving and transforming grace into our hearts, bringing eternal life. Through your Son our Lord. Amen.

Life at the Cross-Road

"My son, in proportion as you can go out of yourself, so will you be able to enter into Me. Just as the desiring no outward thing brings inward peace, so does the forsaking of yourself inwardly bring union with God."

Thomas reminded his readers that Jesus told his followers that whoever keeps his commands is the one who loves him. Those who hold to Jesus' teaching are really his disciples. They will know the truth and the truth will make them free. To those who overcome, Jesus will give the right to sit with him on his throne.

In his *Imitation of Christ,* Thomas amplified those words with "I will have you learn the perfect renunciation of yourself to My will, without contradiction or complaint." Much depends on *how* a person bears the cross. Resentfully? Complainingly? With self-pity? Or cheerfully, patiently and without complaint? Scripture says, "Jesus . . . for the joy that was set before him endured the cross, despising the shame" (Heb. 12:2). He rejoiced in heart, though tortured in body, that he was emancipating all believers from sin and that he was fulfilling his Father's will. A cross isn't as heavy when those twin joys—ministering to others and doing God's will—are in the heart.

Jesus taught, "If any man would come after me, let him deny himself and take up his cross and follow me" (Matt. 16:24). Thomas replied, "Let us follow Him like [mature adults]; let no one fear any terrors; . . . and let us not stain our glory by flying from the cross." Thomas has a beautiful passage: " 'Follow Me,' Jesus says: 'I am the way, the truth, and the life.' Without the way there is no going; without the truth there is no knowing; without the life there is no living. I am the way which you should follow, the truth which you should believe, the life which you should hope for. I am the way inviolable, the truth infallible, the life everlasting."

Lord Jesus, grant that we may follow you in bearing the world's contempt. Help us to be instructed by your life, for it is the source of salvation and true holiness. Amen.

Faith Has Clenched Fingers

DAY
14

"I had rather be poor for Thy sake than rich without Thee. I had rather be a pilgrim upon earth with Thee than possess heaven without Thee. Where Thou art, there is heaven; and where Thou art not, there are death and hell."

In addition to the above words, Thomas wrote, "Thou art my hope, my confidence, my comforter, and in all things most faithful." It is obvious that Thomas clung to God for dear life.

In Portland, Maine, a commuter airline pilot named Henry Dempsey was aloft in flight when he heard a rattle in the back of the plane and went to investigate, leaving the copilot at the controls. As Dempsey leaned against the rear door, the plane struck some air turbulence. The door suddenly flew open, sucking him out at 4,000 feet. He had the presence of mind in a split second to grab the railings of the stairway door, and there he hung upside down as the plane cruised along at 190 miles per hour. When it made an emergency landing, Dempsey's face was one foot above the concrete runway. An airline spokesman said that the pilot's hands were clenched so tightly around the railings of the stairway door that they literally had to be pried off. Said the pilot the next day, "I was thrilled to see the sunrise."

Suppose that we clenched the promises of God so tightly that our fingers of faith would literally have to be pried off if ever we were to be separated. Here's a promise of God in Hebrews: "I will never fail you nor forsake you" (Heb. 13:5). If life turned you upside down in some sudden disturbance, faith could hold onto that promise with clenched fingers and bring you down safely. Nothing can pry loose the curl of our fingers around Christ. Holding onto him, we shall always see another sunrise.

Thomas prayed: Protect and preserve the soul of Thy poor servant amidst the many perils of this corruptible life, and by Thy accompanying grace direct him along the path of peace to his native country of everlasting light. Amen.

Walter Wietzke

BLAISE PASCAL

 LAISE PASCAL (1623–1662) was the third of four children. His father, Etienne, a local government official in Clermont, was influenced by the new light of the Renaissance. He was devoted to ancient languages and mathematics, interests critical in his son's development.

Professor Emile Cailliet wrote in *Pascal: The Emergence of Genius:* "The inner drama in the life of Blaise Pascal consisted, on the one hand, in his repudiation of scholastic theology and the incursion of human reason into the domain of faith, and of his ambition, on the other hand, to fashion a rational theology for himself" (Cailliet 1945).

So while this brilliant, young, scientific genius and religious giant resisted the idolatry that enthrones secular reason, he was himself anything but anti-intellectual. His was to be a theology hammered out in the tension between faith and reason. He avoided the pernicious contemporary heresy that allows people to forget learning and substance, basing faith only upon sincerity or feeling.

At age 13 he astonished a room full of distinguished scholars by "demonstrating the thirty-second proposition of the First Book of Euclid, having rediscovered for himself every one of the principles that preceded it." This is the young man who at age 19 invented the calculating machine and who later invented the barometer and omnibus.

But it is his contributions in the field of religion that emerge with great significance for all within the church today. His theology deals with two basic things, the condition of humanity and God's grace in Jesus Christ. "At the heart of Christianity he saw Christ Himself. 'In Him lies all our virtue and felicity.' Apart from Him is naught but vice, misery, error, darkness, despair! And his heart's desire was to lead men to Him," wrote C. S. Duthie.

We are left with no systematized record of Pascal's work. He died young, at 39, and his *Pensees*—a collection of notes and essays on religious and philosophical matters—was published in 1670. It has been described as "a formless mass of papers" and was put together by a bookbinder who could not even read!

On August 19, 1662, the day of his death, his diseased throat received for the final time the Holy Sacrament. His last words were, "May God never abandon me."

The Essence of Christianity

<table>
<tr><td>DAY
1</td><td>*"The Christian religion, then, teaches men these two truths; that there is a God whom men can know, and that there is a corruption within their nature which renders them unworthy of Him. It is equally important . . . to know both these points; and it is equally*</td></tr>
</table>

dangerous for man to know God without knowing his own wretchedness, and to know his own wretchedness without knowing the Redeemer who can free him from it. The knowledge of only one of these points gives rise either to the pride of the philosophers, who have known God, and not their own wretchedness, or to the despair of atheists, who know their own wretchedness, but not the Redeemer" (Pascal 1958).

With rapier-like efficiency Pascal penetrates to the heart of the matter—"there is a God whom men can know, and . . . there is a corruption within their nature which renders them unworthy of Him."

Why should either proposition become a matter of public dispute? Probably because humans do not attribute enough to God and they attribute too much to themselves. A high comfort level almost always accompanies general talk of God. It is when conversation gets specific that objections arise: "Do you really think God would confine Himself to a single incarnation?" "What about non-Christian understandings of God?" Pascal never wavers—God makes Himself known in one Redeemer—like it or not. So, while people seem generous and broadminded by introducing other possibilities, they are not taking God seriously. Biblically speaking, they will not claim as much as God claims for Himself.

But when they take measure of the human being, it seems many people are wearing rose-colored glasses. Hard evidence to the contrary, many are caught up in the "all people are good" way of thinking. If you try to deal with the ambiguities and contradictions of that opinion, you will surely be chided for your narrowness and negativism.

Gustav Vigeland's work is a case in point. He had been commissioned to do sculpted works of art depicting life in Norway. Located in Frogner Park in Oslo, the statues are a classic display of the human condition— love, care, anger, hate, violence. They are very realistic. However, the response of the populace to these sculptures was disarmingly sullen.

Back to Pascal—he says you have to know the human condition and you have to know the Redeemer of the human condition. Wretchedness or despair without the Redeemer will only incite a negative reaction and leave you with no hope.

O Lord, give me the eyes of faith so that I see myself as you see me. Amen.

Jesus Christ—the Revealed God

<table>
<tr><td>D A Y
2</td><td>*"I admire the boldness with which these persons undertake to speak of God. In addressing their argument to infidels, their first chapter is to prove Divinity from the works of nature. . . . But for those in whom this light is extinguished, . . . who . . . find only obscurity*</td></tr>
</table>

and darkness; to tell them that they have only to look at the smallest things which surround them and they will see God openly. . . . is to give them ground for believing that the proofs of our religion are very weak . . . Nothing is more calculated to arouse their contempt.

. . . Scripture . . . says, on the contrary, that God is a hidden God, and that, since the corruption of nature, He has left men in a darkness from which they can escape only through Jesus Christ, without whom all communion with God is cut off" (Pascal 1958).

Attempting to "prove God" by pointing unbelievers to the realm of nature is, in Pascal's mind, an exercise in futility. In this regard he is an echo of Luther who, in the *Table Talks* says, "Men seek God everywhere, but not seeking Him in Christ they find Him nowhere." This is a thesis Christians have to keep in the forefront of their thinking—necessarily so since a lot of inane talk is carried on in the marketplace, in university dormitories, and in neighborhoods, dealing with the subject of God in general! But, as theologian Joseph Sittler once reminded us, "that kind of conversation doesn't do a damn thing for their damned souls."

The hidden God must also be talked about in terms of revelation. Has he revealed himself? If so, when, and how? The issue is whether the uniqueness of God's self-disclosure is found only in Jesus Christ. Karl Barth, in dealing with this issue, focuses upon the confession of faith found in the second article of the Apostles' Creed. He says three things that are useful for us: (1) God cannot be known save as He reveals Himself. (2) The God revealed in Jesus Christ must be apprehended by faith. [So Jesus says to Simon Peter, "flesh and blood has not revealed this to you, but my Father who is in heaven" (Matt. 16:17).] (3) The God revealed in Jesus Christ and apprehended by faith, is still unfathomable!

Before Ceding Everything to the Positive Thinkers

DAY 3

"The nature of self-love and of this human Ego is to love self only and consider self only. But what will man do? He cannot prevent this object that he loves from being full of faults and wants. He wants to be great, and he sees himself small. He wants to be happy, and he sees himself miserable. He wants to be perfect, and he sees himself full of imperfections. He wants to be the object of love and esteem among men, and he sees that his faults merit only their hatred and contempt" (Pascal 1958).

If one wishes the undisturbed and veneered view of life advocated by positive thinking, if one's ego needs are such that the self must feed on a diet of highly complimentary words, then one dare not read Blaise Pascal. Not that Pascal is overly negative; he has a biblical balance in his appraisal of human beings and in his understanding of God's grace. His biographer, Cailliet, writes, "Pascal places himself between . . . two extremes: First, 'that impiety of Luther. . . . We co-operate in no way whatever in the matter of our salvation, any more than inanimate things'; secondly, 'the impiety of Molina's school which will not admit that it is by the strength of divine grace that we are enabled to co-operate in the work of our salvation; and which thereby destroys the principle of faith established by Saint Paul.' "

In *Pensees,* Pascal reduces the matter to this: "the Christian faith goes mainly to establish these two facts, the corruption of nature, and redemption by Jesus Christ." It is the human condition we are concerned with here, and the Frenchman holds up the mirror in which truth is reflected with disarming candor. "In a word, the Self has two qualities: it is unjust in itself since it makes itself the centre of everything; it is inconvenient to others since it would enslave them; for each Self is the enemy, and would like to be the tyrant of all others" (Pascal 1958).

The moralists are always stomping around trying to find the essence of sin in certain commodities—alcohol, tobacco, cosmetics, cinema—Pascal finds it in the human ego.

Perspective on Life—Human Disproportion

D A Y
4

"The whole visible world is only an imperceptible atom in the ample bosom of nature. No idea approaches it. We may enlarge our conceptions beyond all imaginable space; we only produce atoms in comparison with the reality of things. It is an infinite sphere, the center of which is everywhere, the circumference nowhere. In short it is the greatest sensible mark of the almighty power of God, that imagination loses itself in that thought" (Pascal 1958).

Here's a seventeenth-century man anticipating twentieth-century conversations on an expanding universe. Within the whole of the cosmos he ponders the existence of this fragile human atom. In relation to all else what is this being's worth? Very little!

All prideful efforts to measure human significance in terms of time and space—in a universe where time is a fraction on a spectrum of ageless aeons, and where space has virtually become a meaningless term—are steam-rolled into nothingness.

Once I stood on a shale ledge in eastern Wyoming. At my feet were hundreds of thousands of fossilized crustaceans—remnants of an ocean floor. Before me stretched endless wilderness, no other human being in sight, no ear to hear my voice, no evidence of civilization. The psalmist's question became my question: "When I look at . . . the work of thy fingers . . . what is man that thou art mindful of him?" (Ps. 8:3-4). Exaggerated self-importance was reduced to point zero.

Today our children are being reared in a learning atmosphere that dwarfs this experience a thousand times over. Elementary school youngsters are taught to think in dimensions we hardly dreamed of—galaxies beyond galaxies—infinity! Earth, once considered a large and important place, is seen as Pascal saw it, "an imperceptible atom in the ample bosom of nature." His concluding remarks are these: *". . . let man consider what he is in comparison with all existence; let him regard himself as lost in this remote corner of nature; and for the little cell in which he finds himself lodged, I mean the universe, let him estimate at their true value the earth, kingdoms, cities, and himself. What is a man in the Infinite?"* (Pascal 1958).

Perspective on Life—Human Proportion

DAY
5

"Man is but a reed, the most feeble thing in nature; but he is a thinking reed. . . . All our dignity consists, then, in thought. By it we must elevate ourselves, and not by space and time which we cannot fill. Let us endeavor, then, to think well.

"It is not from space that I must seek dignity, but from the government of my thought. . . . By space the universe encompasses and swallows me up like an atom; by thought I comprehend the world" (Pascal 1958).

In a brief notation Pascal wrote that there are "two contrary reasons": "Without that we understand nothing, and all is heretical; and we must even add at the end of each truth that the opposite truth is to be remembered." What he is dealing with, and what we must deal with, is the idea of paradox: the utilization of two seemingly contradictory statements, both needed to express the truth.

In the foregoing meditation we explored half a paradox—from one point of view humans are cosmic nothings, pathetic victims of nature. Now we have to turn that upside down and say, "No, this two-legged animal, so feeble and frail, is not only nature's victim, but also nature's master." Master? Wherein lies the mastery? Surely it isn't in terms of duration, which is most often only three-score years and ten. Surely it isn't in proportional strength; the lowly grasshopper outdoes us many times over. The physical power of other creatures puts us to shame. No, mastery lies in the human capacity to think. Thought makes the difference.

Everything originates from the mind of God, the ultimate mind. That is the significance of the biblical accounts of creation. Everything began as a thought, a divine thought. However, every child born of woman endowed with normal capacities of reflection and judgment shares the Creator's glory and becomes part of the Creator's plan for the world. Thought makes us active participants in the creative activity of God.

The Indefensibility of Casual Atheism

"Let them at least learn what is the religion they attack before attacking it. . . . In order to attack it, they should have protested that they had made every effort to seek Him everywhere, and even in that which the Church proposes for their instruction, but without satisfaction. . . . We know well enough how those who are of this mind behave. They believe they have made great efforts for their instruction, when they have spent a few hours in reading some book of Scripture, and have questioned some priest on the truths of the faith. After that they boast of having made vain search in books and among men. But, verily, this negligence is insufferable.

"Therefore . . . I make a vast difference between those who strive with all their power to inform themselves, and those who live without troubling or thinking about it" (Pascal 1958).

Unbelief has to be a major concern of the Christian church. Whether it is functional unbelief inside the church or militant atheism and agnosticism outside of the church, the actuality of unbelief is something we simply have to deal with. Like Pascal, we too can respect honest dissenters who, having searched and read and argued cannot yet say, "I believe." But these tend to be in a decided minority.

Far greater in number are those who wear the unbelieving mantle, not because people of faith have failed to answer their questions, not because Christian doctrine is inadequate, but because they simply do not want to be involved. It is not an intellectual problem; it is a problem of moral choice. These people are the target of Pascal's criticisms. He cannot abide lazy agnostics. He says, "This carelessness in a matter which concerns themselves, their eternity, their all, moves me more to anger than pity; it astonishes and shocks me; it is to me monstrous." We could say that "one can be and remain an agnostic if indeed one is searching for the truth and cannot find it. But when the search is a sham, nonexistent, then claims of being an agnostic fall."

There have been some, exhausted by past experiences, who wail, "The reason I am not a Christian, not in the church, is because of what happened to me when I was young. Parents made me worship, made me recite the creed, etc." They allege that great intellectual difficulty keeps them from believing, but it is a put-on. Pascal blows them away: "Let them at least learn what is the religion they attack, before attacking it."

He also has a postscript for Christians—do not be too glib in your talk about God! God, the hidden God, is "so disguised . . . that He will only be perceived by those who seek Him with all their heart . . ." In short, let's have no cheap talk from unbelievers or from believers.

A Word to Those Who Cannot Cope

D A Y
7

"*Nothing is so insufferable to man as to be completely at rest, without passions, without business, without diversion, without study. He then feels his nothingness, his forlornness, his insufficiency, his dependence, his weakness, his emptiness. There will immediately arise from the depth of his heart weariness, gloom, sadness, fretfulness, vexation, despair*" (Pascal 1958).

Pascal seems to be describing what, in these days, we call "burn-out." Burn-out suggests an inability to cope rather than exhaustion from labors. What we find is that many people are psychologically debilitated and overwhelmed even before they even begin a task. Either the enormity of the challenge, or the perceived enormity, appears so staggering that they cannot face up to it. So, emotionally, they retreat, and as they do, guilt overcomes them. The word of excuse—*burn-out.*

In June of 1530 Martin Luther wrote to his young friend, Hieronymous Weller, who was overtaken by a spirit of melancholy. "Depression destroys many and is good for nothing. . . . The Lord does not confuse you . . . therefore, do not succumb to evil but courageously oppose it. In this struggle the best pattern is not to give attention to these thoughts and dwell on them, but to oppose them and like a hissing goose despise and go by them. . . . Wherefore you will do the right thing if you choose diversions with others, or find some other enjoyment, and . . . have no scruples regarding games or play."

There are good and not so good reasons why some people feel as they do. We would all be well advised to deal with their situation by heeding the analyses and counsel of Pascal and Luther.

Lord, help me to throw myself into my work with passion, preparation, and abandon; into my home life with love and zeal, and into play with a freed conscience. Then, when the bedding hour comes, let me turn the world and its cares back to you while I sleep the sleep of a carefree child. Amen.

Seeking the Wrong Thing

<table>
<tr><td>D A Y

8</td><td>*"We sail within a vast sphere, ever drifting in uncertainty, driven from end to end. When we think to attach ourselves to any point and to fasten to it, it wavers and leaves us; and if we follow it, it eludes our grasp, slips past us, and vanishes forever. Nothing stays*</td></tr>
</table>

for us. This is our natural condition, and yet most contrary to our inclination; we burn with desire to find solid ground and an ultimate sure foundation whereon to build a tower reaching to the Infinite. But our whole groundwork cracks, and the earth opens to abysses. . . . Let us therefore not look for certainty and stability" (Pascal 1958).

There is an intrinsic human lust for certainty and stability! Deep in the heart is a desire for an undisturbed, tranquil existence. Therefore incursions of sickness, the presence of acerbic personalities, events which threaten serenity and comfort, are all seen as intrusive and destructive.

Early on I was taught an old German adage—*"Der alte Adam ist ein Systematiker"*—the old Adam always covets a secure system. But this is not where life is to be found and it is certainly the antithesis of life in Christ. Rather than security, Christians are called to risk. Rather than tranquil life on shore, days are to be spent, as it were, on the wild, restless sea—amid waves, storms, and sharks with only the astral point of a star to guide us.

In a wonderful monograph, *The Lee Shore*, comment is made on Bulkington, helmsman on the Pequod. "I looked with sympathetic awe . . . upon the man, who . . . just landed from four years' dangerous voyage. . . . In the port is safety, comfort, hearthstone, supper, warm blankets, friends, all that's kind to our mortalities. . . . But in landlessness alone resides the highest truth, shoreless, indefinite as God—so, better is it to perish in that howling infinite, than be ingloriously dashed upon the lee, even if that were safety! For worm-like, then, oh! who would craven crawl to land! . . ."

O Lord, give us the capacity to experience fierce joy of living in a citizenry preoccupied with pensions and with finding security through wealth. Amen.

Candor and Charity

DAY 9 *"Human society is founded on mutual deceit; few friendships would endure if each knew what his friend said of him in his absence, although he then spoke in sincerity and without passion. . . . Man is then only disguise, falsehood, and hypocrisy, both in himself and in regard to others. He does not wish anyone to tell him the truth; he avoids telling it to others . . .*

"I set it down as a fact that if all men knew what each said of the other, there would not be four friends in the world" (Pascal 1958).

In one sense Pascal is right—"if all men knew what each said of the other, there would not be four friends in the world." People of candor make others uncomfortable. Candid expressions of the truth are not what others want to hear, so truth tellers become a threat and people fear their company.

But lest we think that only the strict, unrestrained truth should be spoken in our families, churches and society, we need to listen to St. Paul's critical qualifier. In his letter to the Ephesians he uses the phrase "speaking the truth in love" (Eph. 4:15). Paul recognizes that while love can become saccharine and innocuous if truth is absent, truth by itself can be harsh and destructive, unless tempered by a goodly portion of charity.

Generally we do not encounter another and say, "you have an offensive odor," or, "boy, are you fat," or, "you look terrible," or, "have I ever told you how ignorant I think you are?" All these comments may indeed express the truth. But human society is founded on a sense of charity that makes allowances for others, and makes love of the neighbor second only to the love of God. Such love doesn't assume that the other is essentially loveable; sometimes the other is downright unloveable. It simply assumes others need love as much as they need truth.

Truth and love are never, ever, to be made mutually exclusive. "By this all men will know that you are my disciples, if you have love for one another" (John 13:35).

Complacent Doubters

DAY 10 *"We do not require great education of the mind to understand that here is no real and lasting satisfaction; that our pleasures are only vanity; that our evils are infinite; and lastly, that death, which threatens us every moment, must infallibly place us within a few years under the dreadful necessity of being forever either annihilated or unhappy. . . .*

"Let us reflect on this, and then say whether it is not beyond doubt that there is no good in this life but in the hope of another; that we are happy only in proportion as we draw near it; and that, as there are no more woes for those who have complete assurance of eternity, so there is no more happiness for those who have no insight into it.

"Surely it is a great evil thus to be in doubt, but it is at least an indispensable duty to seek when we are in such doubt; and thus the doubter who does not seek is altogether completely unhappy and completely wrong" (Pascal 1958).

Pascal says: "it is a great evil thus to be in doubt." What then do we do with the man who said to Jesus, "I believe, help my unbelief"? (Mark 9:24). The Gospel writer seems to accept the fact that belief and unbelief are commonplace and in tension at the very heart of life. That is my conviction. Doubt is for the life of the spirit what bile is for the life of the body. If a person becomes bilious, he or she will grow ill from excessive bile flow—but the production of no bile renders us incapable of digestion and we also grow ill from its lack.

Pascal, however, takes on the complacent doubters, and at this juncture we should stand shoulder to shoulder with him. He is right when he says, "it is at least an indispensable duty to seek when we are in . . . doubt." You see, there are two kinds of doubt. There is an unresolved, unchallenged kind of doubt that paralyzes us and renders us incapable of action. It is illustrated by the philosopher's donkey standing at point X. Beyond the beast are two bales of hay, one at position A, the other at position B. Both are equidistant, the same size, under the same light intensity. The donkey cannot decide which way to go and ultimately starves to death. The donkey does not pursue the "indispensable duty to seek."

The other kind of doubt is illustrated by the hunter atop a fence. On one side is a grizzly, on the other side a pack of wolves. It is painful to sit astride the wire. But he must decide. A calculated risk must be taken on one side or the other. Indecision is no real option.

Our society has more than its share of people trying to be complacent doubters. Their neutral, uncommitted state is basically a fiction. Their kind of doubt is indeed an evil.

Another French Error

"The most important affair in life is the choice of a calling; chance decides it. Custom makes men masons, soldiers, slaters. . . . We choose our callings according as we hear this or that praised or despised in our childhood. . ." (Pascal 1958).

In 1929 Cole Porter wrote a musical comedy, "Fifty Million Frenchmen." When show lady Texas Guinan and her troupe were denied entrance into France to present the production in 1931, she is reputed to have said: "It goes to show that fifty million Frenchmen can be wrong."

Add one more error to the French list—Pascal's estimate of "calling." He who was so right on so many things bids fair to be corrected here. "Chance decides calling. . . ." Not so! rather choice. From our perspective everything starts with a good understanding of calling. Martin Luther thought of calling not as "occupation" (masons, soldiers, slaters)—but as the beliefs that inform your existence. Recently George H. O. Madsen wrote a piece titled "Being and Doing": "What am I going to be? What am I going to do?" No generation escapes these questions. To those who wonder about such things the church has a word that bears on yesterday and today: Who am I?

"[This] is really a question of Whose am I? To whom do I belong? . . . We belong to God. . . . That word was spoken aloud in the midst of family and friends around a baptismal font. . . .

"What am I going to do? Our 'doing' flows from our 'being'. . . . To think that there is only one possibility for Christian 'doing' is to betray the liberating gift of 'being' in Christ. . . ."

Calling is not the vagary of chance; it is informed, reflective, choice.

It may not have been an error to keep Ms. Guinan's troupe out of Paris in 1931, but it is an error to include and uncritically baptize Pascal's ideas of "calling" in the late twentieth century.

Apes and Angels

"It is dangerous to make man see too clearly his equality with the brutes without showing him his greatness. It is also dangerous to make him see his greatness too clearly, apart from his vileness. . . . Man must not think that he is on a level either with the brutes or with the angels, nor must he be ignorant of both sides of his nature; but he must know both" (Pascal 1958).

We are caught in a tension where we are drawn to one of two extremes—either identifying with the beasts of the earth or living as if we don't belong to this world—apes or angels.

In a fifteenth-century document, "Asceticism in the Desert" we have this humorous and telling account: "John the Little . . . spake once unto his brethren: 'I would fain undertake a life as safe as that of the angelic hosts; they labour not, but serve and praise God without ceasing.' So he drew off the clothes that he wore, and went into the wilderness. And when he had spent a week there, then he came back to his brethren. And when he knocked at the door, the brother said before opening: 'Who is there?' Then said the other: 'I am thy brother, John.' . . . His brother answered, saying: 'John is become an angel, and cometh henceforth no more among men.' . . . John, hearing this, knocked again and said: 'I am John': yet he opened not, but let him suffer until morning without the cell. Then he . . . opened unto him and said: 'John, if thou art a man, then thou must work and earn thine own meat. . .' [and] he begged forgiveness . . . saying: '. . . I have sinned.'"

There is a much greater propensity today to model life after apes than angels. The Olympics, to illustrate, are wonderful—to a point. "Farther, faster, higher" are shibboleths for the youthful mind. So preoccupied are we with race tracks, gymnasia, health spas, and weight rooms, that selfhood is now reckoned in terms of animal form and strength—which are at best transitory.

Life with the Son of Man is our model. He affirmed earthly existence, but he did not make it ultimate. Life with Him and the heavenly Father, here and hereafter, was his dominant concern. Even with all its faults, I love the world of athletics and will until the day I die. But once in a while it doesn't hurt to cease playing Tarzan and give some thought to the angels.

The Argument of the Wager

 Long before any of us saw the light of day, Christians were betting their lives on a reality they couldn't prove. One of the most eminent gamblers was Pascal. Cailliet summarizes what is often called Pascal's wager: *"God exists or He does not. . . . You must take sides on the issue. You must bet. You have no choice. . . .*

"By wagering for God, if God does not exist, the player loses after all only a finite value of dubious quality; at the most he takes the risk of merely leading a life that is on the whole noble and advantageous; but in making the wager against God, if God exists, he will lose 'an infinity of life infinitely happy' and vice versa. It is the decision for God, the supreme step, that Pascal wants to obtain from the indifferent whom he has just buttonholed; he wants a full and unconditional surrender" (Cailliet 1945).

Each of us confronts the ultimate question of *who*. Who will inform your existence? Who will own you? To whom will you give your life, your eternity? From Pascal's perspective there is only one worth considering, our Lord Jesus Christ.

For the past three centuries pagan naturalists and devotees of science and technology have fired their broadsides at the body of Christ. They assume that the day of the Nazarene is past. Their calculation is that this lay French Christian represents a last ditch effort to give continuity to a passing tradition. But Christ is not dead and neither is his church. Bishop Dibelius put it well: "The idea that the age of Jesus . . . has come to an end and that now new truths will prevail is a delusion. Truth is not tied to time. Jesus Christ is the truth for all time."

Resurrection

"What reason have they for saying that we cannot rise from the dead? What is more difficult, to be born or to rise again; that what has never been should be, or that what has been should be again? Is it more difficult to come into existence than to return to it?" (Pascal 1958).

His reflections on sin and grace, his insistence on the uniqueness of God's appearance in Jesus Christ, and his discourses on truth and love all underscore that Pascal is the consummate Christian. It is not surprising, therefore, that he crowns all else with his opinions on death, resurrection, and life eternal.

Pascal argues in opposition to real life opponents, especially atheists. His challenge to them is a blunt one. Which is the more difficult, to produce a man or an animal, or to reproduce it? He cannot prove resurrection; it is a matter of faith, a miracle. But he sees the initial formation of life as the greater thing, its renewal as the lesser.

Joseph Sittler wrote: ". . . If we live, we are the Lord's; if we die, we are the Lord's. This is a faith, not an empirically established truth. . . . Intellectually, I cannot put any content into the word *live* after I die. Because the only life I know is the finite one that I live before dying. . . . What life beyond death might be, I have no notion. . . . Something continues, but what that will be I'm perfectly willing to leave in the hands of the Originator."

He speaks with incredible dispassion. This old carcass has to go. The new form? Purely a matter of conjecture. But that is not important; the promise is important, and it is real, very real! "Because I live, you will live also" (John 14:19) is all we need. We can leave it at that.

Gracia Grindal

FLANNERY O'CONNOR

F LANNERY O'CONNOR (1925–1964) was born in Milledgeville, Georgia. In 1945, after graduating from Georgia College in Milledgeville, she attended the writing school at the University of Iowa in Iowa City where she earned an M.F.A. By the time she had completed her degree there she had already published her first short story, "The Geranium." After she left to work at the writing colony, Yaddo, near Saratoga Springs, New York, it became apparent to those who knew her and read her work that she had a major talent. Until 1950, she lived with Robert and Sally Fitzgerald, prominent teachers and writers in Connecticut. There she developed her gift and wrote stories and novels. In 1950, when she was diagnosed as having lupus, an autoimmune disease, she moved home with her mother to live on the family farm until her death. Though she suffered greatly from the disease, she was able to complete a significant contribution to literature.

A devout Catholic all her life, she was conversant with most of the theology of the day. But she did not write theology. Fiction was her gift and she used it to show what happens to people in the secular culture when grace smashes into their lives. This shocked many people who did not approve of her violent picture of the faith. She regarded their criticism with good humor and a wry distance. When she died at the age of 39, she left behind a small, but highly distinguished body of fiction which sets her in good company with the best of American writers, from Nathaniel Hawthorne to William Faulkner.

God's Presence Among Us

D A Y
1

"One of the awful things about writing when you are a Christian is that for you the ultimate reality is the Incarnation, the present reality is the Incarnation, and nobody believes in the Incarnation; that is, nobody in your audience. My audience are the people who think God is dead" (O'Connor 1979).

Flannery O'Connor was keenly aware that she wrote as a Christian. She knew that for moderns, God was dead. As a Christian she could not write as though God were dead; to do so would have been a great denial for her. So she wrote novels, short stories, essays, letters, all of which are radical, violent visions of how God works in this world. Moderns, she knew, prefer a spiritual god, if any, one whose powers are limited, and who does not have to do with the real life people live every day.

The fact that Jesus did become flesh and dwell among us—pitched his tent among us, as John says in his Gospel—has always upset the conventional worldly wise. God would be less bothersome, these people say, far away, vacantly looking down at us from remote distances. To imagine that God is present with us in our daily lives, humiliated and crucified by us, seems utterly beneath God, the God who created the earth and heavens.

Those who try to save the reputation of God from this scandal need once again to consider how this scandal is the only thing that saves us. It is the only way that God can finally get at us. As we are hammering the nails into our Savior's hands and feet, we hear God's saving word to us in Christ, "Father, forgive them, for they know not what they do."

God became human to win us over, to make us new creatures. This comes as good news when we have exhausted all our anger and defenses against this gracious act in Christ Jesus. When, weary with our own ideas about God, we lay down our hammers and plead for God to save us, it is then we come to know how powerful the weakness of God is, how saving it is for us who once were dead. God is not dead; without God's word, we are.

How grand that all of life is made new in Christ Jesus. Praise God for the incarnation of Jesus, into whose death and resurrection we are now made one.

"And the Word became flesh and dwelt among us, full of grace and truth; we have beheld his glory, glory as of the only Son from the Father" (John 1:14).

Suffering for the Faith

D A Y
2

"You don't serve God by saying: the Church is ineffective, I'll have none of it. Your pain at its lack of effectiveness is a sign of your nearness to God" (O'Connor 1979).

Luther said that one of the marks of the church is suffering. Marked with the cross of Christ, Christians live out their Christian vocations, doing what they have been called to do, if not always with joy, at least, always in humble obedience to God's call to serve the neighbor. Changed by our new life in Christ, we see things differently, understanding the difference between ultimate and penultimate concerns.

For some, the ineffectiveness of the church, its unresponsive bureaucracy and failure to be everything we expect and hope it will be, pains more sharply than we might have thought possible. How it hurts to see the great difference between our dreams and the actuality of the church.

O'Connor speaks to that situation. To leave the church because it is not perfect is like leaving a beloved because he or she is not perfect. A disappointed love is a bitter thing, but never to have loved at all is worse, most of us would agree. To love is to risk disappointment. Not to love is to fear life. Risking love, we discover a richness we had not known before.

O'Connor's letter speaks of the way love changes us. But this love is more fierce in us because, as she says, it is a sign of the nearness of God. Jesus has promised to dwell in us, with the Father. No wonder we are filled with a restless longing for the unblemished, the pure. No wonder the mark of a Christian is suffering. Christ who now dwells in us has put to death the old Adam and Eve so that we have died to self and our own sinful purposes. This death is daily and it pains us, but in that pain is life.

Christ's life in us fills us with a holy impatience to serve the neighbor, to bring the good news. Oddly enough, it is this holy impatience which drives us back again and again to the Word and to church on Sunday morning to be fed so we can be sent out on our way, back to serve the world.

"And if children, then heirs, heirs of God and fellow heirs with Christ, provided we suffer with him in order that we may also be glorified with him. I consider that the sufferings of this present time are not worth comparing with the glory that is to be revealed to us. We know that the whole creation has been groaning in travail together until now; and not only the creation, but we ourselves, who have the first fruits of the Spirit, groan inwardly as we wait for adoption as sons, the redemption of our bodies (Rom. 8:17-23).

150

Sin's Mystery

<table>
<tr><td>D A Y
3</td><td>*"Part of the mystery of existence is sin. When we think about the Crucifixtion [sic], we miss the point of it if we don't think about sin"* (O'Connor 1979).</td></tr>
</table>

What ever happened to sin? Karl Menninger asked in a book. What is sin? Luther says that sin is the failure to take God at his word. Unbelief. Sin comes when we try to build our own systems of survival. The failure to believe takes many forms—from the proud, disdainful rejection of God by the superman to the fearful failure of the victim of abuse to believe God's grace is for her.

O'Connor says that "part of the mystery of existence is sin." She is not touting sin as a kind of mystery one longs for and wishes to explore. She is speaking, rather, of that most profound rebellion in the human heart that does what it would not, and does not do what it would. The lie easily told, the filching of money from the till, blasphemous conversations at the golf course which seem quite unworthy of a Christian—we remember those with regret and wonderment. Why, we ask, did I do something I know to be wrong? Why? Was it a slip, or am I just naturally bent toward evil even though I know otherwise? Why?

The human heart is a factory of idols, Luther said. It was his way of saying that we will do almost anything to avoid the one true God, sinning by failing to fear and love God above all things.

In this day and age, people are demonstrating a great interest in being religious on their own terms. They are trying to get in tune with the earth, with what is natural, with the good spirits that hover around us all. They suffer from self-imposed laws they must observe to please these gods. But actually they are their own god, for these gods can be manipulated into doing what we want if we just do the right thing enough times.

One sees the root of sin in the idol factory: the failure to believe in the living God, who will not be manipulated into doing what we desire, but who will, at the great cost of Jesus, have us to be his own and live in his kingdom.

What amazing grace, this event, when, while we were yet sinners, Christ gave himself for us so that we might live.

"While we were still weak, at the right time Christ died for the ungodly. Why, one will hardly die for a righteous man—though perhaps for a good man one will dare even to die. But God shows his love for us in that while we were yet sinners Christ died for us" (Rom. 5:6-8).

Baptism's Death and Resurrection

"All voluntary baptisms are a miracle to me and stop my mouth as much as if I had just seen Lazarus walk out of the tomb. I suppose it's because I know that it had to be given me before the age of reason, or I wouldn't have used any reason to find it" (O'Connor 1979).

O'Connor demonstrates a profound sense for the radical nature of baptism, clearly understanding the life and death nature of it. Thus, adults look like Lazarus when they volunteer for baptism. Christians know that baptism is a dying and rising into the death and resurrection of Christ. To choose death—baptism—seems an incredible thing, especially since this death is the death of the old self, the ego, that part of us bent on its own survival and flourishing.

To want to do that defies all reason, O'Connor says. In fact, she knows that if she had not been baptized as a baby, before the age of reason in her own life, she would have resisted baptism. Reason is never the way to faith, in O'Connor's thought. Reason sees faith as folly and a stumbling block. Nothing does make sense about the faith, if one is to make a reasonable argument for it. One cannot argue another into the faith, or into accepting this undeserved grace. Reason would demand that at least we deserve this grace, in some way. So we try to get the old Adam and Eve whipped up to work for God's love.

Luther wrote, in his great explanation of the Third Article of the Apostles' Creed in the *Small Catechism:* "I believe that by my own reason or strength I cannot believe in Jesus Christ, my Lord, or come to him. But the Holy Spirit has called me through the Gospel, enlightened me with his gifts, and sanctified and preserved me in true faith."

Neither O'Connor nor Luther believed that one could come to faith on one's own, or by one's own reason. Faith is a gift, a violent rebirth, or resurrection, like Lazarus raised from the stinking tomb. It is not something any one of us has the power to effect. It is a gift; sheer, undeserved, wonderful gift. A gift that saves us and gives us life. For that we can only praise the Lord.

"Do you not know that all of us who have been baptized into Christ Jesus were baptized into his death? We were buried therefore with him by baptism into death, so that as Christ was raised from the dead by the glory of the Father, we too might walk in newness of life" (Rom. 6:3-4).

Fools for Christ

"But let me tell you this: faith comes and goes. It rises and falls like the tides of an invisible ocean. If it is presumptuous to think that faith will stay with you forever, it is just as presumptuous to think that unbelief will. Leaving the Church is not the solution, but since you think it is, all I can suggest to you . . . is that if you find in yourself the least return of a desire for faith, to go back to the Church with a light heart and without the conscience-raking to which you are probably subject. Subtlety is the curse of man. It is not found in the deity" (O'Connor 1979).

This remarkable passage from O'Connor's letter to a friend who had written her that she was leaving the church is filled with a wise sense for the faith. O'Connor's young friend was probably prepared for much of what she heard. But she must have puzzled over the idea that subtlety is not found in the deity. This seems to go against everything we might have ever learned about God. If God is human beings raised to the nth power, we might imagine that God's subtlety would surpass anything we could imagine. Not true, O'Connor says.

She is, of course, right. It was the serpent who was the most subtle of all creatures. It was his very cunning arguments that appealed most directly to Eve who wanted to know about God, to be like God. God had made a simple law; Satan tempted Eve to disobey the law by pointing out that God would be threatened by her knowledge.

This is a terrible blasphemy against God, the one who had created her. But it seems reasonable, so she eats of the fruit, for she saw it "was good for food, and that it was a delight to the eyes, and that the tree was to be desired to make one wise" (Gen. 3:6). This complicated reasoning brings her death. As O'Connor points out, this subtlety is our curse. God is not so subtle. God demands obedience from us, as creatures. This seems to be too simple a demand and we, ever since Eve, have resisted such obedience, appearing to be bound to our need for freedom from this simplicity. O'Connor's friend is going to leave the church because it seems too simple. She will use her reason to make the charge that faith is foolish. Exactly!

God's wisdom does appear to be foolishness to the wise. But it is a foolishness which saves. Jesus died on the cross so we might live. Foolish? To the subtle, perhaps. But to Christians, it is the only truth to live by.

"We preach Christ crucified, a stumbling block to Jews and folly to Gentiles, but to those who are called, both Jews and Greeks, Christ the power of God and the wisdom of God. For the foolishness of God is wiser than men, and the weakness of God is stronger than men" (1 Cor. 1:23-25).

Two-Edged Sword

 "This notion that grace is healing omits the fact before it heals, it cuts with the sword Christ said he came to bring" (O'Connor 1979).

O'Connor was not in the least sentimental. Her stories deal directly with the power of grace to shatter people and change them violently. This causes some good people to become squeamish about reading her work. They want a gentler vision of the church and God's grace. But she will not give them one.

She is right not to. Her vision of the powers of God's grace is purifying and radical. The idea that Christ simply takes us as we are and does nothing to us is not very Christian. From the very first God is out to re-create us. In baptism, we are put to death in Christ's death so that we may rise again with him each day. To think this is an entirely painless undertaking is foolish.

God is out to change us. One image of this is God as the potter who shapes the clay. This shaping and remaking of the lump of clay into a useful pot is hard work. The potter's hands slap and caress the wet clay until it takes the shape the potter has felt within the clay.

Or we may speak of God as being like a fire in us, burning out the dross, cleansing us with the intense heat of the refiner's fire. The purging that goes on in the refining fire is violent and yet beautiful. God's work in us is like that. The idea that God's grace is simply a sunny addition to our already nice lives misses that most terrible of facts about human beings: we have all sinned and come short of the glory of God. There is no standing before the fire of God's love for us on our own. Only Christ can spare our being consumed by the flames. His life in us saves us, even while it changes us utterly. For this we thank God.

"For the word of God is living and active, sharper than any two-edged sword, piercing to the division of soul and spirit, of joints and marrow, and discerning the thoughts and intentions of the heart" (Heb. 4:12).

Reason and Faith

<table>
<tr><td>D A Y
7</td><td>*"I certainly don't think that the death required that 'ye be born again,' is the death of reason. . . . One of the effects of modern liberal Protestantism has been gradually to turn religion into poetry and therapy, to make truth vaguer and vaguer and more and more*</td></tr>
</table>

relative, to banish intellectual distinctions, to depend on feeling instead of thought, and gradually to come to believe that God has no power, that he cannot communicate with us, cannot reveal himself to us, indeed has not done so, and that religion is our own sweet invention" (O'Connor 1979).

Here O'Connor deals with the question of the modern age: how can I believe something that is irrational, that seems at its very root, foolish. Her strong sense of the radical powers of grace would not allow her to change her theological understanding of the faith into feeling rather than a thoughtful appreciation for the paradoxes of the faith.

To think, as she did, that God is revealed in history, and continues to be present in this world through the word and sacraments, is to be completely out of step with modernity. For this reason her fiction was so violent. She had to convince the typical American through her stories that God's grace took real forms in this life, that God's grace has real consequence in this life.

Christians today, 25 years after O'Connor wrote these words, know exactly what she meant. The claim we make that Jesus is Lord and present in human existence today seems to be ludicrous to the powers of this world. What evidence is there, our secular friends will ask us, that Jesus is present in this terribly sinful and meaningless world?

It is useless to explain that God's power is in weakness. This does not compute for the modern. But even as the modern consciousness has given way to the post-modern consciousness, which seems ready for "out of body experiences," or other communications with the spiritual realms, religion has become even more what O'Connor predicted it would be: "our own sweet invention." Many people around us who would never walk inside a church or read the Bible, much less say a creed that has been handed down over generations, feel perfectly free to invent their own religion, one which gives them no offense because it has no power.

"It is a fearful thing to fall into the hands of the living God" (Heb. 10:31).

The Best Medicine

DAY
8

"About the Lourdes business. I am going as a pilgrim, not a patient. I will not be taking any bath. I am one of those people who could die for his religion easier than take a bath for it" (O'Connor 1979).

Few people have been as funny about their faith—and as fierce—as O'Connor. At first glance, we might expect that she would be quite serious. In her early 30s she was diagnosed as having lupus, a disease of the immune system that causes the body to degenerate. But even in her final illness she saw things around her that genuinely amused her.

She was not amused when an elderly cousin insisted she travel to Lourdes to take the cure. "Only about 40 ahead of me so the water looked pretty clean. They pass around the water for 'les malades' to drink & everybody drinks out of the same cup. As somebody said, 'the miracle is that the place don't bring on epidemics.'"

She wrote her good friend Sally Fitzgerald about the trip with some dread. "It is Cousin Katie's end-all and be-all that I get to Lourdes and if I am dead upon arrival that's too bad but I still have to get there."

The Fitzgeralds, who were in Europe at the time, agreed to meet them in Milan. O'Connor wrote them to confirm the plan. "Could you meet us in Milan? Left for two minutes alone in foreign parts, Regina (her mother) and I would probably end up behind the Iron Curtain asking the way to Lourdes in sign language. I cannot bear to contemplate it."

When she told a friend that the bishop had asked her to write up her trip for a Catholic paper, she concluded: "I don't think he has thought this through."

We can be sure the report would have been very funny and thought to be inappropriate for devotional literature. But it would have been Christian for it would have reveled in the great plenitude of God's creation and the Christian comedy which we see all around us when we understand that God is the author of all things and our significance comes from God, not ourselves. That is the best news of all.

"A cheerful heart is a good medicine, but a downcast spirit dries up the bones" (Prov. 17:22).

The Scandal of Faith

"If I set myself to write about a socially desirable Christianity, all the life would go out of what I do. And if I set myself to write about the essence of Christianity, I would have to quit writing fiction, or become another person" (O'Connor 1979).

In this letter to a Catholic sister who taught English in "some outpost in the Dakotas," O'Connor discusses the problems of her being thought of as a Christian writer. To make the faith desirable, according to her, would be to misrepresent it completely. On the one hand, it would give believers respectability or make them seem not so foolish. On the other hand, it would deform the faith.

As she writes later in this same letter, "it was the devils who first recognized Christ and the evangelists didn't censor this information. They apparently thought it was pretty good witness." This is scandalous to us because we would like to be the first to make such a recognition. At the same time, we know that we do not.

We do see evangelists who have tried to make the Gospel acceptable, even desirable. It is easy for us to see that they are wrong. What is difficult to understand is that the Gospel also is sure to offend us as well. Even when we understand its essential offense, we forget that it will offend us.

To describe the essence of theology, O'Connor understood, would be to do a different thing than write fiction. Fiction indirectly reveals the heart of the matter; fiction writers do not write discourses on good and evil, or theological treatises. Their work can become the occasion for such treatises, but they are themselves never the treatises.

As O'Connor points out in this same letter: "The tendency of people who ask questions like this is always toward the abstract and therefore toward allegory, thinness, and ultimately what they are looking for is an apologetic fiction." This was not her calling; O'Connor wanted to write fiction that showed how grace worked in the world, in people. To do that she had to "make the corruption believable before [she could] make the grace meaningful."

For this reason we read O'Connor: to see clearly the way grace works on sinners to shock them into life. Grace reveals our sin to us even as it saves us and works its power in us. This is a religion for sinners, no one else. No wonder our questions end in praise and doxology.

"For Christ did not send me to baptize but to preach the gospel, and not with eloquent wisdom, lest the cross of Christ be emptied of its power. For the word of the cross is folly to those who are perishing, but to us who are being saved it is the power of God" (1 Cor. 1:17-18).

Knowing the Truth

"I don't much agree with you . . . about suffering teaching you much about the redemption. You learn about the redemption simply from listening to what the Church teaches about it and then following this to its logical conclusion" (O'Connor 1979).

In this letter O'Connor speaks to the skewed theology of the cross which many people carry around with them. Looking for suffering, they almost seem to covet it since it brings them closer to Christ, they say, and teaches them what he has done for us. Once again, we see O'Connor's utter lack of sentimentality and her rather tough approach to the faith.

Following the teaching of the church on the redemption brings one directly into contact with suffering, through no effort on the part of the Christian. She explains this in the context of her character Tarwater in her novella *The Violent Bear It Away*. "People are depressed by the ending of *The Violent Bear It Away* because they think: poor Tarwater, his mind has been warped by that old man and he's off to make a fool or a martyr of himself. They forget that the old man has taught him the truth and that now he's doing what is right, however crazy" (O'Connor 1963).

It is bracing to think of the consequences of knowing the truth and acting on it. This is not the same as going to look for the truth, as O'Connor inferred from her correspondent's idea. Truth has found the prophet and now he is bound to speak it. This brings him no end of suffering, suffering he cannot really understand.

In this same letter O'Connor says, "I haven't suffered to speak of in my life and I don't know any more about the redemption than anybody else. All I do is follow it through literally in the lives of my characters."

In less than a year after writing those remarkable sentences, she will be dead from lupus after years of suffering from the illness, years of hospitalization, harsh medications that wearied her body, but never her spirit. For her, faith was a gift, the teaching of the church a way into life.

"For we are God's fellow workers; you are God's field, God's building. Let each man take care how he builds upon it. For no other foundation can any one lay than that which is laid, which is Jesus Christ. Now if any one builds on the foundation with gold, silver, precious stones, wood, hay, straw . . . the Day will disclose it, because the fire will test what sort of work each one has done. If the work which any man has built on the foundation survives, he will receive a reward. If any man's work is burned up, he will suffer loss, though he himself will be saved, but only as through fire. Do you not know that you are God's temple and that God's Spirit dwells in you?" (1 Cor. 3:9-16).

Being Known

"Love and understanding are one and the same only in God. Who do you think you understand? If anybody, you delude yourself. I love a lot of people, understand none of them" (O'Connor 1979).

In answer to a frequent correspondent who struggled with the faith, O'Connor gets at the heart of the modern problem. Apparently the woman has complained that she is stuck with people she neither loves nor understands. This comment is filled with the vain hope that one can find people you both love and understand. It is of such notions that Americans are lost in high divorce rates and the breakup of families and communities. How much richer O'Connor's flat-out statement that she does not understand anyone.

On reflection we know that it is precisely the people we think we understand that we find most deadly dull and uninteresting. It is the closest of friends and lovers who remain unplumbed depths for our exploration. Formal business letters do for those with whom we are barely acquainted. Good friends can speak to each other every hour on the hour and not exhaust each other.

As a teacher of writing I am always amused by students who come to me with stories in which they reveal shocking things about their parents or friends. "You see," they say, alive with their discovery, "he was really . . ." and they fill in with some psychological term that is supposed to introduce me to the essence of the person. They are always puzzled when I tell them that I could care less about that, what I want to know is why the character in the story is wearing an L. L. Bean jacket.

That always tells me more about the character than any psychological analysis could, though it does not help me understand him fully. The detail just gives me a quick glimpse into the person's soul. But then it closes and is enveloped in mystery.

This is the excitement of the Christian life: longing for complete knowledge while admitting the mystery of the other. When at last we are raised up and made new, we will be changed, but still ourselves. Then we are promised, in 1 Corinthians 13, that we will know, even as we are known. Does this mean we will understand each other completely? Perhaps, but until the last judgment we will not know. Until then we can only live in faith and hope.

"For now we see in a mirror dimly, but then face to face. Now I know in part; then I shall understand fully, even as I have been fully understood" (1 Cor. 13:12).

Diversities of Gifts

DAY 12 *"I do pray for you but in my fashion which is not a very good one. I am not a good pray-er. I don't have a gift for it. My type of spirituality is almost completely shut-mouth. I really dislike books of piety most of all. They do nothing for me and they corrupt most people's ear if nothing else. . . . This book of C. S. Lewis on prayer is a good one but I don't like to pray any better for reading it"* (O'Connor 1979).

At this time in her life, O'Connor was recovering from surgery, extremely dangerous for anyone with lupus. The resultant infections and damage to her system were to cause her death in two months. Still she was filled with good humor and, though weak, was pleased to note that her finest story "Revelation" had just been published.

Her remarks on her own prayers are instructive to us. Even as one who had been steeped in Catholic traditions of spirituality and heroic men and women of prayer, she is smart enough to know that this is not her gift, nor is it something she should even aspire to. Her gifts were elsewhere.

Few, if any, American writers have so confronted readers of American literature with the paradoxes of grace and faith. One can say without fear of too much contradiction that she shocked most of her readers, secular and religious, with her uncompromising vision of the human dilemma. She knew that shock came from readers who may have thought of themselves as understanding the faith, or even being pious, and yet could not brook the stark world she gave them. Books of saccharine piety give readers false impressions of the faith, or "corrupt" their expectations. Devotional books which gloss over human pain with answers that are not wrung from deeply felt experience and understanding give people false hope and reduce almighty God to a powerless grandfather in the sky. This was not O'Connor's God and we can be thankful for that.

"And God has appointed in the church first apostles, second prophets, third teachers, then workers of miracles, then healers, helpers, administrators, speakers in various kinds of tongues. Are all apostles? Are all prophets? Are all teachers? Do all work miracles? Do all possess gifts of healing? Do all speak with tongues? Do all interpret? But earnestly desire the higher gifts. And I will show you a still more excellent way" (1 Cor. 12:28-31).

The First Shall Be Last

D A Y	" 'Revelation' was my reward for setting [sic] in the doctor's office. Mrs. Turpin I found in there last fall. Mary Grace I found in my head, doubtless as a result of reading too much theology" (O'Connor 1979).
13	

By all accounts O'Connor's greatest short story, one of the best of all short stories, is "Revelation." It is the story of a middle-aged woman named Mrs. Turpin whom we first meet in the doctor's office with her husband who has a bad leg. As she is waiting in the office, she notices a young student, Mary Grace, reading a book called *Human Development*. Mrs. Turpin notices the glum expression on Mary Grace's face and wishes she would smile. Mary Grace glowers back. Mrs. Turpin then occupies herself in innocent chatter about who is better: white trash, blacks, or her. She is fairly clear about where she stands in relation to everyone else, but she is not sure about some others.

Her pious prattle finally exasperates Mary Grace so much that she throws her book at her and calls her "an old wart hog out of hell." The epithet is so wounding to Mrs. Turpin that she faints. But she spends the next few days fussing about it. Finally, standing in the pig yard, feeding the hogs, she has a vision of heaven which further shakes her confidence that she is better or worse than white trash or the blacks.

She sees the saints marching into heaven, and leading the group, she sees blacks, followed by white trash and then, finally, her group. As they are marching in, their distinguishing marks are being washed away.

The story is funny and quite to the point. What it does is enflesh further the story of the banquet where the first are made last, and the last, first. There is a bracing rightness to the story. But most shocking, and then most comforting, is the picture of the saints losing their individual features.

Sometimes we do weary of each other and humorously regret having to spend eternity with each other as well. But God promises to change us and make us new. Heaven is the promise of redemption and salvation to all. With that promise comes radical newness and change—bad news and good news all at once. Finally, a revelation most gracious and moving.

"There you will weep and gnash your teeth, when you see Abraham and Isaac and Jacob and all the prophets in the kingdom of God and you yourselves thrust out. And men will come from east and west, and from north and south, and sit at table in the kingdom of God. And behold, some are last who will be first, and some are first who will be last" (Luke 13:28-30).

Delighting in the Lord

D A Y
14

Few American writers have been as taken with the grotesqueries of American life as O'Connor. She pored over the newspapers to find stories of odd human behavior. Some of these stories became the occasion for her own stories. She loved the absurdities of the small southern town, appropriating phrases and scenes in the daily life around her for some of her greatest stories.

As a Christian she knew that it was in the hard physical fact of personal encounter that Christ was to be found and where grace would abound. She spoke repeatedly of her lack of interest in the abstract or spiritual. What she loved about life was its incongruities.

American letters are richer for her wonderful observations of life as it was lived around her. She enjoyed the farm where she and her mother lived: the various animals, the peacocks, the hired help, the local society. One can tell in her letters and speeches how thoroughly she enjoyed her mother—whom she refers to as "my parent"—and her decided opinions about things. She mocks pious religiosity when it is phony and yet was an obedient Catholic of the '50s.

Knowing she was the occasion for devotion would have amused her. Yet, her radical presentation of the gospel in narrative and letters jolts us with its absolute dead aim for the gospel. Her short stories and novels are a major contribution to American life and literature. God used her gift to teach many of us to understand and acknowledge grace in new and surprising ways. For this we must thank God and read her fiction over and over again. Like God, her fiction never ceases to delight its readers. Blessed be her memory.

"Blessed is the man who walks not in the counsel of the wicked, nor stands in the way of sinners, nor sits in the seat of scoffers; but his delight is in the law of the Lord, and on his law he meditates day and night. He is like a tree planted by streams of water, that yields its fruit in its season, and its leaf does not wither. In all that he does, he prospers. The wicked are not so, but are like chaff which the wind drives away. Therefore the wicked will not stand in the judgment, nor sinners in the congregation of the righteous; for the Lord knows the way of the righteous, but the way of the wicked will perish" (Ps. 1).

James Limburg

HASIDIC STORIES

GROUP of Jewish people were discussing their rabbis. "Our rabbi is so spiritual," said one of them, "that for him, the streets of heaven are as bright and as clear as the streets of his own home town." "Oh, but your rabbi has it all wrong," said another. "Our rabbi says that if you really understand the things of God, it is just the opposite. The streets of your home town will look as bright and as clear as the streets of heaven."

That second person was a *hasid*. The word means "pious one" and designates a member of a revival movement that took place within Judaism, centered in Poland, beginning just before 1750.

The situation of Jews in Poland at that time was not good. Most of them had fled from persecution in Germany. They did not own land and were very poor. Many had been disappointed by the appearance of a false "messiah" who had promised much, but who then denied the Jewish faith and converted to Islam. Morale sank lower and lower.

Since external conditions were so bad, Jews withdrew more and more into the world of the Bible and the Talmud, a collection of post-biblical writings. Worship took the form of meaningless memorization and empty routine. Religion was reduced to mindless habit, to matters of the head and not of the heart.

Into this scene came a most remarkable leader. Born in 1700, he worked in the Carpathian mountains digging clay. For a time, he and his wife managed an inn. He had no formal education. His name was Israel ben Eliezer. At the age of 36 he set off a revival within Judaism and became known as the *Baal Shem Tov* which means the "Master of the Good Name," that is, the name of God. His followers were known as "pious ones" or, in Hebrew, *hasidim*.

The Baal Shem Tov traveled from town to town, helping the poor, healing the sick and, always with his pipe at hand, telling stories. The Judaism of his day emphasized the study of holy books; he said that God was much more interested in holy people. The religion of his time had become dry and stodgy; his followers sang, danced, and even turned somersaults in the streets! Synagogue preaching had become too harsh, he said; his was a smiling Judaism.

The hasidic movement spread among Jews throughout Eastern Europe. Soon other leaders emerged, carrying on the tradition of the Baal Shem Tov.

God Loves Stories, Too

D A Y
1

"I love to tell the story," goes the refrain of the old hymn. Christian people love to tell stories, and to hear them, too. Most of us first learned about God and Jesus Christ by hearing stories. Someone may have read Bible stories to you in your home or you may have learned them in Sunday school.

It is not surprising that Christians should love stories. Jesus was a master storyteller. He was a Jew, and Jews share with Christians all those favorite stories from the Old Testament.

We begin with a Jewish story that mentions four of the leaders of a Jewish revival movement that took place in Eastern Europe in the 1700s. The story is about the power of stories:

When the great Rabbi Israel Baal Shem-Tov saw misfortune threatening the Jews it was his custom to go into a certain part of the forest to meditate. There he would light a fire, say a special prayer, and the miracle would be accomplished and the misfortune averted.

Later, when his disciple, the celebrated Magid of Mezritch, had occasion for the same reason to intercede with heaven, he would go to the same place in the forest and say: "Master of the Universe, listen! I do not know how to light the fire, but I am still able to say the prayer," and again the miracle would be accomplished.

Still later, Rabbi Moshe-Leib of Sasov, in order to save his people once more, would go into the forest and say: "I do not know how to light the fire, I do not know the prayer, but I know the place and this must be sufficient." It was sufficient and the miracle was accomplished.

Then it fell to Rabbi Israel of Rizhyn to overcome misfortune. Sitting in his armchair, his head in his hands, he spoke to God: "I am unable to light the fire and I do not know the prayer; I cannot even find the place in the forest. All I can do is to tell the story, and this must be sufficient." And it was sufficient. God made people because God loves stories (adapted from Wiesel 1967).

We should not be surprised if we love to tell and to hear stories. We are created in the image of God. And, according to this tale, God loves stories, too!

Read the story of the prodigal son in Luke 15:11-32.

Our Heavenly Father, we thank you for those parents and teachers who told us the stories of the Bible and our Christian faith. Help us to hear them rightly, and then to tell them faithfully to others. Amen.

The Prayer That Was Whistled

D A Y 2 | One of the aims of the hasidic movement was to put some life and enthusiasm back into the worship of God. Religion had become a mechanical ritual. What was missing was a genuine and spontaneous praising of the Lord.

Once on Yom Kippur, the holiest day of the year, Rabbi Israel was leading the congregation in prayer. But everything seemed to go uphill. The Rabbi couldn't pray, nor could anyone in the congregation. The prayers, it seemed, didn't reach any higher than the ceiling of the little synagogue.

It happened that on this day a shepherd boy had been tending his sheep on a hill near the synagogue. He heard the sound of the chanting of the prayers and came down to see what was going on. Looking in the door, he saw a gathering of men and women, some of them holding prayer books, absorbed in their devotions.

The boy walked in and sat in the back of the synagogue. The chants were beautiful, he thought. The sun was bright, the sky blue, and he felt like praising God himself. Since he couldn't read Hebrew, and since he didn't know any prayers by heart, he did the only thing he knew how to do when he was happy and enthusiastic: He put two fingers in his mouth and let go a long, shrill whistle!

Of course the entire congregation turned around to see what this disturbance was all about. They looked to discover the shepherd boy, sitting alone, smiling, on the back bench of the synagogue. Two of the leaders of the synagogue got up, intending to scold the boy and take him out.

But Rabbi Israel asked them to sit down, and turned to the congregation with a smile on his face. "At last," he said. "Our worship service is now finished. At last there was someone in our midst who could offer an unselfish and genuine prayer to God!"

Read Psalm 150 and consider whether there is even a place for praising God with a long, shrill whistle.

Gracious God, you have given to us food and clothing, house and home, money and possessions, believing parents, children, good government, seasonable weather, peace and health, good friends and neighbors. For all of these we give you thanks and we praise you! Amen.

Knee Deep in Wonder

 DAY 3

It was Rabbi Nachman of Bratzlav who one day noticed one of his followers rushing about in the marketplace, busy with the ordinary affairs of the day.

Nachman came up to him. "Haikel," he said, "you are so busy. Tell me: what have you seen here today?"

"Oh, Rabbi," Haikel answered, "I have seen merchants selling, peasants buying, just the usual business of the market on a very busy day."

"But Haikel," said Nachman, "have you taken time to notice the sky? The sky is beautiful today. What is the use of all this rushing and bustling about, if you don't take time to look at the sky?"

A psalmist once looked at the sky and wrote, "O Lord, our Lord, how majestic is thy name. . . . When I look at thy heavens, the work of thy fingers, the moon and the stars which thou hast established . . . O Lord, our Lord, how majestic is thy name in all the earth!" (Ps. 8:1, 3, 9).

In another story, it was told of the *Magid* (preacher) of Mezritch that he began each day by walking down to the pond at dawn and staying there for a while. "Why does your master do this?" one of his followers was asked. "He goes down to the pond each morning to listen to the songs with which the frogs praise God," the hasid replied. "He wants to learn them, and it takes a long time to learn those songs."

"Look at the birds of the air," Jesus said. "When you look at a bird, you are looking at a good theologian," said Luther. "Birds keep busy building their nests and gathering their food and they never let worry about tomorrow rob them of their song."

Read Matthew 6:25-34.

God, our Creator:
> Field and fountain, vale and mountain,
> Flowery meadow, flashing sea,
> Chanting bird and flowing fountain
> Call us to rejoice in thee. Amen.
> (*LBW* 551)

The ABC's of Prayer

D A Y
4

Jesus told a story about two men who went up to the Temple to pray. One of them was quite proud of his piety and his blameless life-style. He properly gave God credit for all of this, praying, "I thank you, God, that I am not greedy, dishonest, or an adulterer, like everybody else. I fast two days a week, and I give you one tenth of all my income." The other person praying in the Temple was a tax collector, a representative of the Roman occupation, especially despised by the citizens of the land. When he prayed, he stood off at a distance. He did not even lift his eyes to heaven. He said simply, "God, have pity on me, a sinner." It was this humble man, said Jesus, who was in the right with God (Luke 18:9-14).

A hasidic story tells about the prayer of a poor, simple woodcutter. He was in the forest, and it was evening and time to pray. But he had forgotten his prayerbook. What could he do? He didn't know any prayers by heart. He decided to pray anyhow, and his prayer went like this:

"Lord, I am a simple, stupid man. I am so stupid that I have forgotten my prayerbook. Worse yet, I don't know any prayers by heart. But you, O Lord, know all the prayers, even before we say them. So I will do this. I will recite the letters of the alphabet, and you put the prayer together." So he began his prayer, going through the Hebrew alphabet: "Aleph, bet, gimel, dalet, hey . . ." And, concludes the story, of all the prayers that God heard on that day, the prayer of the woodcutter in the forest was most precious.

Each time I teach the Hebrew alphabet to a new class of students, I tell them this story. And when I hear that story Jesus told, about the tax collector, I also think of that woodcutter in the forest, furnishing God with the letters, and trusting a loving heavenly Father to put the prayer together.

Read Luke 18:9-14.

Father in heaven, we come before you as children who are often lost and who need your help. Teach us to pray. Forgive the things we have done that were wrong. Help us to find the way again, through Jesus Christ. Amen.

When Meyer Stamped His Foot at God

This is a story about a rabbi named Meyer, and how he once stamped his foot at God.

It was Meyer's custom to pray for especially bad sinners, asking God to forgive them. And, the story goes, when Meyer prayed for a sinner, God always did forgive! Except for one time. Once there was an especially shameful sinner, and Meyer prayed, and God refused to grant forgiveness.

What did Meyer do? This one time (and the story emphasizes that this happened once, and only once), this one time only, Meyer actually stamped his foot at God! And the sinner was immediately forgiven.

The story continues: "If you are a father or a mother, you will understand this. Remember how delighted you were when your little child first stamped a foot at you. Only the first time, of course, and it had to be the last time. Well, it was just the same sort of joy that this little Meyer gave our Father which is in heaven . . ." (adapted from Langer 1961).

When I first discovered this story, I thought of what Jesus said about prayer. When his closest followers asked him, "Teach us to pray," Jesus answered, "When you pray, begin this way: 'Our Father . . .'" We are to come before God as children come before a father or mother. And maybe once (it could only be once, of course), maybe once a child could stamp a foot to get a mother or father's attention! The parent just might admire such boldness.

Luther explains the "Our Father . . ." of the Lord's Prayer in his catechism: "God thereby tenderly encourages us to believe that he is truly our Father, and that we are truly his children, so that we may boldly and confidently come to him in prayer, even as beloved children come to their own dear father."

Jesus told some stories about how to pray. Read Luke 18:1-8.

Lord, teach us how to pray: Our Father in heaven, hallowed by your name, your kingdom come, your will be done, on earth as in heaven. Give us today our daily bread. Forgive us our sins as we forgive those who sin against us. Save us from the time of trial and deliver us from evil. For the kingdom, the power, and the glory are yours, now and forever. Amen.

But You, Where Are You?

DAY

6

Elie Wiesel tells this story about the beadle (caretaker) of a synagogue in Eastern Europe, during World War II. This was a time when synagogues were being burned and when Jews were being driven from their homes.

This is the story of a ghetto that stopped living, and of a beadle who lost his mind. It was the beadle's custom to rush to the synagogue each morning, to ascend the bimah (a platform in the front) and shout first with pride, and then with anger: "I have come to inform you, Master of the Universe, that we are here." Then came the first massacre, followed by many others. The beadle always emerged unscathed. As soon as he could he would run to the synagogue, and pounding his fist on the lectern, would shout at the top of his voice: "You see, Lord, we are still here." After the last massacre, he found himself all alone in the deserted synagogue. The last living Jew, he climbed the bimah one last time, stared at the Ark, and whispered with infinite gentleness: "You see, I am still here." He stopped briefly before continuing in his sad, almost toneless voice: "But You, where are You?" (Wiesel 1972).

All who have read the psalms will recognize this caretaker's prayer. It is the desperate cry of one who doesn't know which way to turn, and who can only turn to God. This is not a theoretical question *about* God, asking "Why doesn't God . . ." This is a personal question, *to* God, asking, "But You, where are You?" It is the same sort of question that begins Psalm 22: "My God, my God, why have you forsaken me?"

All who have heard the story of Good Friday will recognize this cry. It is the cry of one who had wrestled long in the garden with the task God had laid upon him. It is the cry of Jesus on the cross, so intense that the Gospels remember it in Jesus' native language: "Eloi, Eloi, lama sabachthani?" (Mark 15:33).

Read Psalm 22.

Lord, hear our cries from the Gethsemanes of our own lives, and enable us to hear the Good News of Easter Sunday so that we can praise you once again. Through Christ our Lord, amen.

The Baby-sitter

DAY

7

This is a story about the time that Rabbi Levi Yitzhak became a baby-sitter.

It happened that the famous rabbi was to be the featured speaker at a synagogue in a little town somewhere in Poland. A woman in the town had heard much about the learned rabbi and was eager to hear what he had to say. She was rushing to get ready, but could not get her little baby to stop crying. So she carefully propped the child up in its crib, kissed the baby good-bye, and rushed off to get to the synagogue service on time.

The rabbi himself came walking along that street on his way to the services. As he neared that house, he heard a child crying. He walked up to the house, knocked, and no one answered. The door was not locked, so he went inside. He walked over to the crib, picked up the crying baby and held it in his arms, singing a lullaby until the child fell asleep.

Meanwhile, those at the synagogue were wondering what had happened to the rabbi. When he finally arrived and the services could begin, he told them about the crying baby and what he had been doing. He explained, "After all, it is much easier for God to wait than for that child."

Our own children are grown up now. But a picture that once hung in a bedroom where three boys slept still hangs in our home. The picture shows Jesus, who was also called "Rabbi," surrounded by children. People were bringing their children to Jesus so that he could hold them, put his arm around them and pray for them. The disciples, trying to protect Jesus' time, scolded the people and told them he was too busy to see the children. Every Sunday school child remembers what Jesus said: "Let the children come to me and do not stop them, because the Kingdom of heaven belongs to such as these" (Matt. 19:14).

Read Matthew 19:13-15.

Lord, in our busyness help us to remember children, so that our care for them might be modelled after your own love for us all. Amen.

What Do You Have for the Poor?

DAY
8

One of the marks of the hasidic movement was a special concern for the poor. In their stories, we meet orphans, beggars, and poor widows, and hear how people of the community helped them. This story was told about a rabbi whose name was Moshe.

It was Moshe's custom to go from place to place collecting money to give to the poor. One day he entered a tavern where a group of men were sitting at a table, drinking and playing cards. They were a rough and surly bunch, carnival workers, drifters, all sorts of hucksters. "But even such people should not pass by us," says one version of the story. "We should love them and not despise them. And if possible, we should give them the chance to help others by giving money for the poor, too."

So the rabbi walked up to the men politely asking for a contribution. At first, they paid no attention and simply went on with their game. When he asked again, they dismissed him with a curse and some rough language. Finally, when the rabbi asked a third time, one of them got up, walked over to the rabbi, knocked him to the floor, and began pounding on him with his fists.

When he was finished, Rabbi Moshe got up from the floor and spoke to the group one more time. "All right," he said, "that was for me. Now what do you have for the poor?" The ruffians were quite disarmed and gave the rabbi a generous contribution.

The theme of concern for the widow, the orphan, and the poor runs through the entire Bible. The laws of Deuteronomy specify that when a field is harvested, any scraps dropped should be left for the poor and the widowed (Deut. 24:19-22). The prophets insisted that the rulers and people of Jerusalem watch over the rights of the poor and care for them (Isa. 1:10-17; 1:23; 3:13-15). The psalms remind the political leadership of their obligations toward the powerless (Ps. 72:12-14). Jesus said that when we help the hungry and the hurting we are helping him (Matt. 25:31-46).

Read James 1:25—2:26, which calls for a faith that is active in doing something for the poor and hungry.

Lord, give us eyes to see those who are hungry and hurting around us and throughout the world, and ears to hear their cries for help. Then give us the imagination and the energy to help, not only with words, but with acts. Amen.

Apologize to the Next Beggar

D A Y
9

Rabbi Zishi was an authority on matters of the faith, famous because of his insight into spiritual matters but also because of his habit of going about dressed like a beggar.

Once Zishi was travelling to address some of his followers in a neighboring town. He got into a train car and sat down. Then two wealthy gentlemen dressed in expensive suits got on the train and started looking for a place where they could sit together. Seeing what they thought was a poor beggar sitting by himself, they walked up to him and rudely told him to move to the rear of the car. He did, and the two sat down together.

When they arrived at their destination, the wealthy pair noticed a huge crowd waiting at the station. "There must be some famous person on the train," they said. They were amazed when they saw the crowd rush forward to meet the man they took to be a poor beggar. They discovered that this man was the famous rabbi.

They felt terrible for the way they had treated the rabbi. So they pushed their way through the crowd until they came up to Zishi. "Rabbi," they said, "we want to apologize. We treated you so terribly! But how could we have known? We didn't mean to insult you. We thought you were just a poor beggar. Please forgive us."

"I can't forgive you," said Zishi, "because you didn't insult me. You insulted a poor beggar. So the next time you meet a beggar, apologize to him."

True religion, the Bible makes clear, has something to do with how we treat the poor. Defend the widow and the orphan, said Isaiah (1:17). Let there be justice for the poor in the courts, said Amos (5:10-15).

Jesus made an astounding statement about the sick, the poor, and the hungry. He said that the way we treat these people is the way we treat our Lord (see Matt. 25:31-46).

Read Matthew 25:31-46.

Lord, we know the story of how your Son Jesus became poor and lived among us, giving his life so that we might live. Now enable us to see the lonely and the hurting who live among us, that we might help them not only with words but with actions. Amen.

If Not Higher

DAY

10

There were some fantastic rumors going around concerning the rabbi in the town of Nemirov. During each morning of the High Holidays, the rabbi was nowhere to be found. His followers said: "Why, it is clear. He ascends to heaven each morning, to be with God!"

The story about the rabbi was told and retold and spread through the whole area. Then it happened that a certain skeptic came to the town. He decided to put an end to this silly story about ascending into heaven by making a scientific investigation.

The skeptic sneaked into the rabbi's house one evening and hid under his bed. Finally morning came. This was to be the time when the rabbi would ascend to heaven to be with God. The skeptic heard the rabbi get up and recite his morning prayers. Then he saw him do a strange thing. The rabbi went to a closet and took out an old jacket, worn trousers, and boots and put them on. Then he took an axe and an old sack from the closet. He looked like a woodcutter about to set out for the forest.

The rabbi left the house and the skeptic followed him at a distance. They passed by the houses in the sleeping village and came to the forest at the edge of town. The rabbi gathered some wood, chopped it into small pieces, and filled his sack. Then he walked deeper into the forest.

The rabbi came to a small house. He knocked and the skeptic heard the weak voice of an old woman, "Who is it?" "It's Vassil, the woodcutter," the rabbi answered gruffly. "O yes," said the voice, "but I can't get out of bed." "Never mind," said the rabbi, "I'll bring the wood in." "Could you light the fire, too?" the voice asked. "I suppose," answered the rabbi, and the skeptic saw him light a fire and heard him recite the morning prayers.

The rabbi left the forest, left his woodcutter's clothes at home, and went about the normal activities of the day.

Then an amazing thing happened. The skeptic showed up at the synagogue for worship. He joined the congregation. Whenever someone would tell the story of the rabbi ascending to heaven, the skeptic no longer laughed. He would add, quietly, "Yes, if not even higher."

Read Philippians 2:1-13 and listen for an echo of the theme of the story about the rabbi from Nemirov.

Lord, we know that your Son Jesus Christ became poor, so that we might have the riches of eternal life. Give us eyes to see the poor and hurting around us, and the energy and imagination to help. Amen.

The Sabbath Smoker

Rabbi Levi Yitzhak was noted for interpreting every act in the most charitable possible way. Once he was walking along the street and met a young man smoking a pipe. Lighting a fire was forbidden on the Sabbath. The Rabbi spoke gently to the young man, "Surely, my good friend, you have forgotten that this is the Sabbath." "No," said the fellow, "I know perfectly well what day it is." "Why then," the rabbi continued, "you must have forgotten the commandment that does not allow us to light a fire on the Sabbath." "No," the young man said, somewhat defiantly, "I know all the commandments very well." "I see," said the rabbi, "but you must feel bad about what you are doing." "No, it doesn't bother me at all," the young man said, and took a big puff on his pipe. Refusing to be provoked, the rabbi turned to God in prayer: "Lord, did you hear this fine man? True, he violates one of your commandments. But you must admit one thing: No one can get him to tell a lie!"

When Levi Yitzhak led services in the synagogue, he did not stand in one place but would run back and forth, praising God, even dancing. Once in a while he would go down into the congregation, grab someone by the coat collars and shout, "Whom do you serve?" The worshiper, shocked and a bit frightened, would answer, "Why, I serve the Lord, the maker of heaven and earth." Then the rabbi would turn to God in joy and say, "Do you see, Master of the Universe, how your children love you and serve you? Where in all the earth is there a people so wonderful as your people?"

What does it mean to interpret charitably all that a person does? A woman with a bad reputation once came up to Jesus and began washing his feet. There were some who thought Jesus ought to have nothing to do with her. But Jesus saw in her a person who wanted to get a fresh start and who was sorry for what had become of her life. "Your sins are forgiven," he said, and told her to go in peace.

Read Luke 7:36-50.

Lord, forgive our gossip, our slander, our carping, and our criticizing. Teach us to see each person we meet as a child of God, to speak well of that person, and to interpret charitably all that he or she does. Amen.

Why Try to Be Moses?

DAY 12 Zusia was a young rabbi. He was in his first congregation and was discouraged with how things were going. When he preached, people would look out the window or doze off. The young people thought he was too old-fashioned. The older people considered him too liberal. He didn't seem to be making an impact on the community. He knew that he wasn't much of a scholar.

Discouraged, Zusia went to visit an older rabbi. "Rabbi," he said, "I just don't know what to do. I am not a leader. I am not a scholar. I can't seem to get through to my congregation. What can I do?"

The older rabbi looked at him and said, "Zusia, when you get to heaven, God is not going to say to you, 'Why weren't you Moses?' But God is going to say, 'Why weren't you Zusia?' So why don't you stop trying to be Moses, and start being the Zusia God created you to be?"

I think of that story about Zusia when I read Psalm 139. While other creation psalms speak of God making the heavens and earth, indeed the whole universe, (Psalms 8, 104), the focus of Psalm 139 is limited to God and one individual. Or, more accurately, this psalm says, "God you created *me!*" Listen to what the psalm says: "Lord, you have examined me and you know me. You know everything I do. . . . You see me, whether I am working or resting; you know all my actions. . . . Where could I go to escape from you? Where could I get away from your presence?" (Ps. 139:1-2,3,7 TEV). Then at the heart of the psalm we hear, "You created every part of me; you put me together in my mother's womb" (v. 13 TEV).

God has not made you, or me, to be Moses. God has already had one Moses. But God did make you to be you, and me to be me. For this, we can join the psalmist in praising and thanking God.

Read Psalm 139:1-18.

Lord, I praise you because all you do is strange and wonderful. I thank you for giving me life, and for giving me new life through Jesus Christ. Amen.

The Text Written in My Heart

DAY 13 One afternoon there were a number of people gathered in the synagogue, studying a text from the Bible. The text was a difficult one and the questions were many. Was the text speaking of God's love for human beings? Or our human love for God? Should the text be understood literally or taken in a more symbolic manner? The discussion went on, and seemed to get nowhere.

Then the people gathered at the table heard a door open and heard footsteps. They looked up to see that they had a visitor, one of the great rabbis of their day.

How wonderful to see the rabbi! They welcomed him and he greeted them. Then they got to the point. The text. "Rabbi," they asked, "how should the text be understood? You must have been sent by God, just to help us with this text."

So the rabbi looked at the text. A glance was enough to bring it to mind. "Oh yes," he began, "a beautiful text, one of my favorites." And he began to speak about God the Creator. He went on to tell the story of how God had called Abraham and formed a people. He continued by telling of Joseph, then of Moses and the Exodus, pausing every so often to say, "May God be praised."

After a time, those gathered around the table began to look at one another. Something was bothering them. True, the rabbi was speaking beautifully about God and God's people.

But—the text!

Finally one had the courage to interrupt. "That is all very fine, Rabbi," he said, "but what about the text?"

"Oh," said the rabbi, putting his hand to his forehead. "The text. You mean the text written in this book. I was speaking about the text written in my heart."

Read Matthew 13:51-52.

Gracious God, we give you thanks for the story of your love for us, written in the Bible. Grant that as we hear and learn it, it may be written in our hearts, too. Through our Savior, Jesus Christ, amen.

Tear Up the Invitations!

The rabbis taught that every person ought to be waiting, watching, expecting the Messiah to come any day. When that day came, the Messiah would come to Jerusalem, and the people of Israel from all over the world would go there to meet the Messiah.

Levi Yitzhak, rabbi in the town of Berditchev, watched and waited each day for the Messiah to come. It happened that it was the time for the wedding of his daughter. She was busily writing out invitations. Her father walked up to the table where she was writing, and began to read one. Suddenly he became angry and tore the invitation into pieces. "Tear up the invitations," he said. "You can't send them out this way!"

"But why?" his daughter asked. "What is wrong?"

"Look what they say," said her father: "Rachel, the daughter of Levi and Sarah Yitzhak will be married on August the 3rd. The wedding will take place at the synagogue in Berditchev."

"Why yes," said the daughter, "that is all correct."

"Why no, of course it is all wrong," said her good and pious father. "Write it this way: 'Rachel, the daughter of Levi and Sarah Yitzhak will be married on August the 3rd. The wedding will take place in the holy city of Jerusalem.' Then," he continued, "at the bottom you should add: 'P.S. If it *should* happen that the Messiah has not come by that time, then the wedding will be in Berditchev.'"

As Christians, we believe that the Messiah has already come in the person of Jesus. We look back to Jesus' life, death, and resurrection. But we also look forward to the time when Christ will come again. When will that be? Jesus said: ". . . of that day or hour no one knows, not even the angels in heaven, nor the Son, but only the Father" (Mark 13:32).

We aren't told the day. But we are told to be ready. Jesus told a story about ten young women waiting for the bridegroom to arrive at a wedding. Five were prepared with extra fuel for their lamps, but five were not. All ten dozed off and, in the night, the bridegroom came. Those who were not prepared were out of luck. Jesus concluded, "Watch out, then, because you do not know the day or the hour" (Matt. 25:13).

Read Matthew 25:1-13.

Lord, teach us to accept each new day of life as a gift, and to live each day as if it might be the day when we meet you. Amen.

Jane Strohl

MARTIN LUTHER

ARTIN LUTHER (1483–1546) was born in Saxony, and his parents saw to it that he received a good education. He was embarking on studies for a career in law when an extraordinary experience elicited from him a vow that changed the course of his life forever. Caught in a violent thunderstorm, Luther prayed to St. Anne for assistance, promising that if he were delivered from danger, he would become a monk. He was and he did, astonishing and dismaying his friends and family.

Luther entered the Augustinian cloister in Erfurt. His superior, Johann von Staupitz, then determined that the gifted young man should return to school to take his doctor's degree and teach. Luther became a professor of Scripture at the University of Wittenburg. Luther wrote near the end of his life that a new understanding of Romans 1:17 led him to a resolution of the conflict tormenting his conscience: "Then, finally, God had mercy on me, and I began to understand that the righteousness of God is that gift of God by which a righteous man lives, namely, faith, and that this sentence—the righteousness of God is revealed in the Gospel—is passive, indicating that the merciful God justifies us by faith. . . . Now I felt as though I had been reborn altogether and had entered Paradise" (Luther 1951).

One might describe Luther's career as a lifelong pastoral malpractice suit against the Roman Catholic hierarchy of his day, whose doctrine of grace, in his opinion, deprived believers of true consolation and robbed Christ of His rightful honor as Savior. Yet the years brought conflicts with other groups in which he felt called to champion the cause of the gospel as he understood it. Luther's theology was polemical, his style often inflammatory. The heirs to his legacy often feel compelled to apologize for him. Indeed, a fair and critical evaluation of his work requires that one acknowledge inconsistencies, errors of judgment, and attitudes that are disturbing. But the same fair and critical eye cannot help but recognize the force of his confession and the keen insight of his spiritual guidance. Luther challenges each generation to measure its understanding of the gospel against the message he found to be the heart of Scripture: "For the person is justified and saved, not by works or laws, but by the Word of God, that is, by the promise of his grace, and by faith, that the glory may remain God's, who saved us not by works of righteousness which we have done, but by virtue of his mercy by the word of his grace when we believed" (Luther 1957).

St. Christopher's Burden

 "When one receives the faith, one does not allow oneself to imagine that there will be difficulty in this. . . . It appears to one as a tiny child, pretty and well formed and easy to carry. For the Gospel shows itself at first as a fine, pleasing, friendly, and childlike doctrine, as we then saw at the start, when everyone seized upon it and wanted to be evangelical. There was such longing and thirst for the Gospel that no oven's heat could match that of the people then. But what happened? The same situation occurred as befell Christopher, who did not learn how heavy the little child was until he had entered the deepest water" (Luther 1906).

Luther preached these words in a sermon delivered to the Elector of Saxony and his party just before their departure for the Diet of Augsburg in 1530. This gathering was summoned by the Emperor Charles V, so that the evangelicals, those who had embraced Luther's teaching, would have to give account of the faith that was in them. The stakes were very high, for if the Emperor was unconvinced by their testimony, he could use military force against his Protestant subjects. There were certainly some among their opponents who would have been glad to see him do so.

In this sermon Luther sought to prepare his friends and their prince for the trial that lay ahead. He tells them of St. Christopher, who, according to legend, bore the little Christ with joy and ease at first. Yet his burden did not always weigh so lightly upon him. As he forded deep water, Christopher felt himself dragged down by the child. The gospel, says Luther, is lovely and irresistible to the believer at the start. But to hold fast to the Word is not easy. To confess Christ before those who challenge our conviction, to trust God in the midst of suffering, to press on with our burden of faithfulness when the waters of confusion flow deep and the currents threaten to carry us under—these too are part of what it means to be a Christian. Luther acknowledges to his hearers that they enter the waters at great risk, but he also reminds them of the promises of God, extending like strong, stout branches from the opposite shore to support them in the tide.

Lord Jesus Christ, never remove the weight of your presence from our lives. Let us lean upon you in our times of weakness and trial, and bring us safely through them. Amen.

The Augsburg Confessors

DAY 2

"There is nothing else we can give God, for he possesses everything and what we own, we have from him. We can give him nothing but praise and thanksgiving and honor. . . . Praise is really a work and fruit of faith, concerning which St. Paul teaches in Romans 10[:10]: 'For man believes with his heart and so is justified, but he confesses with his lips and so is saved. . . .' St. Paul here seems to want to say: To believe in Christ secretly in your heart and to praise him in a private corner is not true faith. You must confess openly with your lips before everyone what you believe in your heart. A confession may cost you your head, for the devil and men do not like to hear it and the cross is a necessary part of this confessing . . ." (Luther 1974).

Luther confirmed what he says here about confession in his response to the events at Augsburg some eight years later. Although he was unable to attend the 1530 Diet, he rejoiced greatly when he heard from his friends that the Augsburg Confession had been read aloud in the presence of the Emperor and the German princes. Attempts to silence the evangelicals were thwarted, for at that moment the gospel was boldly proclaimed for all to hear. Philipp Melanchthon, the author of the Augsburg Confession, worried that such a public declaration might make reconciliation even more difficult, if not impossible. He dreaded the possibility of plunging Germany into civil war over the religious issues dividing Catholics and Protestants.

Yet Luther praised Philipp and the other adherents of the evangelical cause. They had not failed in their duty, even though they could not insure a peaceful settlement with the Emperor. God was calling them to confess the gospel, and this they had done without reservation. In Luther's view, one could do one's neighbor no kinder service than to speak the truth, God's saving word, publicly and plainly, at whatever risk it might entail. To avoid conflict, or be reticent so as not to inflame tempers is often crucial for keeping life in community civil. Luther insisted, however, that our confession of Christ cannot be compromised for such a peace.

Gracious Lord, put on our lips the words that you would gladly hear, words of praise and proclamation to give honor to you and hope to our brothers and sisters. Amen.

Keeping Watch

"The Word moves quickly; prayer is fervid; hope endures; faith conquers so that we are compelled to boast, and if we were not flesh and blood, we would be able to sleep securely, remembering the saying of Moses: 'You have only to be still, and the Lord will fight for you.' For even if we, being most watchful, wanted to take counsel, and say and do everything differently, if the Lord did not fight, we would stay awake in vain. Truly with him fighting, we will not have slept in vain. And it is certain that he is giving battle. . ." (Luther 1941).

Throughout the Diet of Augsburg Luther cautioned his friend Philipp Melanchthon not to worry so much. He reminded Philipp that the cause for which they were contending was God's and that the outcome lay in God's care. Philipp was not the lord of the future. Rather than drive himself to distraction trying to control events, he could best serve God by resting and taking the leisure his overwrought spirit needed.

The Diet of Augsburg was not the last attempt to resolve the religious differences dividing Germany. In succeeding years Emperor Charles V summoned a number of colloquies at which representatives of the Catholic and Protestant parties sought to hammer out an agreement. Nor was the Diet of Augsburg the last time Melanchthon was on the spot as a defender of the evangelical faith . . . and ever an anxious one. Luther's words to Melanchthon offer comfort and caution. One needn't worry overmuch for the gospel—it is doing its work, driving prayer, kindling hope, sustaining faith. Given the power of God's Word, there is no need for Melanchthon to lie awake at night worrying about its future.

Human nature being what it is, it comes hard to us to surrender to such confidence, to rest securely in the promises of God. It is not that our careful planning and deliberate efforts are unnecessary; God's will is not effected without us. Yet as Luther reminded Melanchthon, we do not act alone. Because God is with us, we can both fight the good fight *and* take our rest. We can commend to our Lord our efforts and our failures, our energy and our weariness.

Gracious God, may your will be done and done through us. Teach us so to trust your vigilance that we may know peace when we work and when we rest. Amen.

Christmas

<table>
<tr><td>D A Y

4</td><td>"In my sin, my death, I must take leave of all created things. No, sun, moon, stars, all creatures, physicians, emperors, kings, wise men and potentates cannot help me. When I die I shall see nothing but black darkness, and yet that light, 'To you is born this day the</td></tr>
</table>

Savior' [Luke 2:11], remains in my eyes and fills all heaven and earth. The Savior will help me when all have forsaken me" (Luther 1959a).

This passage is from one of Luther's sermons for Christmas, the season when we celebrate the Incarnation . . . a wondrous birth . . . a new life. And yet Luther talks of death, not of coming into the world but of leaving it. He speaks of the utter loneliness of mortality, the bitter darkness of the grave.

The greatest joy of our existence, and often its greatest trial, is living in relationship with other people. Year by year we learn just how dependent we are on the wisdom, affection, loyalty, and service of others. We may pride ourselves on our independence, but rarely can we "do" for ourselves. Our ability to think and to love comes in response to persons who are not us, to lives that are not ours.

But when it comes to dying, says Luther, whether they wish to or not, all who live must abandon us. No human power, no knowledge, no skill can hold us back from death. We live with and for others, but we die alone. Or do we? "The Savior will help me when all have forsaken me," proclaims Luther. It is in Christ we live and move and have our being, and it is in the compass of His mercy that we die. As earthly life fades from us and we, in mounting weakness, lose our sense of belonging to it, a light kindled long ago becomes our world: "To you this day is born the Savior," who is Christ your Lord in death as in life.

Gracious Father, thank you for the gift of your Son, our Savior Jesus Christ. May the light of His grace and truth guide our ways in this world, comfort us in our fear and grief, sustain us in our dying, and glorify us in your kingdom. Amen.

Doubt

DAY 5 *"But when one's head begins to swim, when one is obliged to taste the experience and bring it into one's life, then understanding comes very dear. It is well nigh unbearable that we should lose the Christ in us, the one we believe to be God's Son who died and rose for us, and that he should die to us, as happened to the apostles throughout the three days. Then there takes place a miserable crucifixion and dying, when Christ dies in me and I also to him. As he says here: 'You will not see me, for I am going from you,' that is, I am dying; so you will also die because you see me not and thus will I be dead to you and you to me. Only then do we really know extraordinary, deep, grievous sorrow"* (Luther 1913).

Luther talked about God as being both hidden and revealed. As the Christmas communion liturgy proclaims, the God whom we see revealed in Jesus Christ comes to us so that we may come to worship, love, and trust the God whom we do not see.

In the witness of Scripture, the history of humankind, and the sorrows of our own private stories we see reasons not only to be mystified by God's ways but distrustful, even terrified of God. The Gospel is compelling evidence to the contrary, says Luther, but even after Christ's entrance into our lives, we do not feel unfailingly secure. The snares of doubt can still encompass us. We shall know the kind of emptiness and despair which afflicted the disciples after the Lord's crucifixion. Yet foretelling his absence, Christ also promised his return: "A little while, and you will see me no more; again a little while, and you will see me." So we must hold onto the promise in our time of loss and lean upon the faith of our friends to sustain us.

Lord Jesus, it is not easy for us to bear the times when we feel you absent from our lives. Yet to know uncertainty and grief, to fear abandonment by the One we have trusted and loved is to follow in the way of the disciples and indeed of you yourself. Grant that we too may be restored to joy and raised to new life. Amen.

The Word

```
D A Y
  6
```

"Therefore our life is simply contained in the bare Word; for we have Christ, we have eternal life, eternal righteousness, help and comfort, but where is it? We don't see it. We neither possess it in coffers nor hold it in our hands, but only in the bare Word. Thus has God clothed his object in nothingness" (Luther 1906).

Our desire to retain control over things great and small is the root of what Luther identified as our besetting sin, works-righteousness. It is so easy, he said, to slip from receiving a gift to earning a reward. We want to build salvation out of our own works and initiate, determine, and control. We want to give ourselves identity and to create meaning for our lives by our efforts and achievement. Yet God will not have it so. It is not that God denies us our own active role in the world. We must never underestimate the importance of our works, but we must avoid false understandings of them as well. It is blessed to give to our neighbors through an active, creative life, but when it comes to God, it is more blessed to receive—that "bare Word" of promise, which we can neither see nor seize and hold in our own safekeeping.

Our salvation is, as Luther puts it, clothed in nothingness. It is God's gift, borne by the seemingly insubstantial sound of a voice. We never know when we shall hear God's word in, with, and under the many human words addressed to us. We never know when that word will echo so resoundingly in our hearts, stilling pain, unmasking sin, and sowing hope, that our lives take an unexpected direction. The hardest fight is to accept that we cannot control this word. We must let God be God.

Gracious Lord, keep us steadfast in your Word. Give us ears to hear, wisdom to understand and courage to respond. Teach us confidently to receive what you would give and to surrender to you the control we covet for ourselves. Amen.

Righteousness

D A Y
7

"You see that the First Commandment, which says, 'You shall worship one God,' is fulfilled by faith alone. Though you were nothing but good works from the soles of your feet to the crown of your head, you would still not be righteous or worship God or fulfil the First Commandment, since God cannot be worshiped unless you ascribe to him the glory of truthfulness and all goodness which is due him. This cannot be done by works but only by the faith of the heart" (Luther 1957).

Once again Luther is telling us that nothing should come between us and God, not even our good works. For though it seems that we might rightfully be proud of these, Luther insists that they cannot make us righteous. Indeed, if we depend upon them to give us claims before God, then our very "right doing" leads us into the worst of sins, the breaking of the first and chief commandment. To look to our own actions for our salvation is to have another god in place of the One who should command our hearts and receive our worship.

In our efforts to please God by keeping the commandments, we can all too easily defy God's will. We withhold something of ourselves. Surreptitiously we keep some element of control, hoping to respond to God's challenge with a righteousness of our own. We are loath to appear empty-handed, to acknowledge and offer to God our vulnerability. But this is what God asks of us. It is a fearsome demand for intimacy and honesty and trust. When we fall back on our works, we beg God's question. To lay aside all righteousness of our own and to rest solely on the promise that God wills to be our Lord in life and death, this is the worship God desires from us. This is the true source of all righteousness.

Gracious God, we give you thanks for being our God. Create faith in us to respond to your faithfulness. Let our good works abound but not come between us and your grace. In Christ's name we pray, amen.

Psalm 23

"The Lord certainly makes of me a strange warrior and arms me against my enemies in an unusual manner. I thought he should clothe me with a suit of armor, set a helmet on my head, put a sword in my hand and warn me to be cautious and on the lookout constantly, lest my enemies overtake me. So he sits me at a table and prepares for me a feast, anoints my head with precious balsam or (as is the custom in our country) crowns me with a garland, as if I should go rejoicing and dancing and not do battle with my enemies. And that nothing might be lacking, he pours me a bumper so that immediately I drink and become drunk, joyful, and high spirited. So the prepared table is my armor, the precious balsam my helmet, the proffered overflowing cup my sword with which I overcome all my enemies. Is this not a singular armor and an even more singular victory?" (Luther 1914).

Luther writes of the trials and hardships that attend faith. He lived in difficult times, when the threat of persecution was often real. But the dangers were not only external. As we have seen, Luther knew the doubt and fear that could beset the conscience from within and cause the believer great anguish. The confession of the gospel of Jesus Christ often weighed heavily upon him, like the burden of the Christ child dragging St. Christopher down. Yet the gospel, like the lovely child, was always a source of wonder and delight.

This commentary on Psalm 23 shows that along with temptation and opposition, Luther also knew ecstasy in his service of the Lord. He never ceased to marvel at the power of God, at the unexpectedness of God's ways, at the unparalleled joy God pours into human lives. Called to be watchful and constant, this soldier in defense of the gospel might well expect grim duty. Yet the Lord prepares him for his place on the front lines not with harsh discipline but with feasting and celebration.

Luther reflects on the momentous events of which he has been part and sees God carrying out great things through commonplace persons and actions. Looking at our own lives, we too can find cause for wonder and rejoicing at God's guiding hand. Yea, though we pass through the valley of the shadow of death, we do so as those dancing for joy.

Gracious God, refresh us at your table so that even in hardship we may go our way rejoicing in you. In Christ's name we pray, amen.

Life in Christ

D A Y 9 *"Thus, as long as the danger and uncertainty of death are present, so long am I to believe that Christ is my life, that is, the whole time that I am here on earth. Let no one evaluate this proclamation according to the hour, season or year—it never becomes null and void so that you dare say, 'Christ will be my life when the time comes for me to die, meanwhile I shall live as I please.' But you should know that the time has already come for you to make that crossing. You have already stepped into the sea with the children of Israel, and you must press on until you come to the shore, lest the enemy seize you under way"* (Luther 1911).

Some people come to know Christ in one dramatic encounter. Their hearts are pierced, their eyes opened, and never again can they return to their old ways and beliefs. One thinks here of St. Paul and his experience on the road to Damascus. For others of us, the process of conversion is far more gradual, at times imperceptible. God nudges, fascinates, and frustrates us in numerous incidents, making us mindful of our lives in new ways. The critical point may well come with some misfortune—the estrangement of a loved one, the failure of a career, the onset of illness. We are made keenly aware of our vulnerability and our powerlessness to set things right in our world. We learn that sometimes we must endure conditions and situations that are painful and unjust. We learn what it is to suffer and thus taste our mortality. Then we are drawn to a savior like Christ, one who loves in the midst of cruelty and brings life from death.

Yet Luther reminds us that Christ is our Lord not just at such times but every day. Life for Luther is a pilgrimage with God. It is not only at its unmistakably sharp edges, in times of sorrow and disappointment and on the verge of death, that one must dare to live in Christ. Every hour, every season, every year is crucial: "You have already stepped into the sea with the children of Israel and you must press on . . ."

Lord Jesus, be our life now and at the hour of our death. Every day is a crossing; in your mercy, guide and keep us safe. Amen.

The Resurrection

"But Christ, on the other hand, is a lord and prince of life beyond all the power of the devil. Therefore he leads his own and brings them with him to heaven, because they are in him, and they live and die and lie in his bosom and arms, not in the grave or in the power of the devil, except in the old being. Just as Christ also, though he lay in the grave, yet in a moment he was both dead and alive and rose again like a lightening flash from heaven. So he will raise us too in an instant, in the twinkling of an eye, out of the grave, the dust, the water, and we shall stand in full view, utterly pure and clean as the bright sun. This is what St. Paul certainly wants us to conclude and believe (though it is incredible and ridiculous to reason) as a sure consequence of the fact that Christ died and rose again" (Luther 1959).

Some people feel that Christian teaching about the hereafter has led to the neglect of this world and the endurance of wrong in the name of a better life to come. They insist that the new life in Christ is imparted to us here and now. We need not turn away from this world and fix our hopes on a new heaven and earth, they say. Rather, we can draw on the grace and guidance that are ours in Christ Jesus to transform the creation and realize human life in this world according to the new Adam. These are important understandings of the power and meaning of Christ's resurrection. Yet they often relegate the afterlife to an afterthought in Christian theology or dismiss it from consideration altogether.

We are drawn to contemplate the lordship of Christ in the light of eternity, to ponder what it means to confess Him as the prince of life. When we bury our dead, there is more at stake than the meaning of the resurrection for life in this world. Luther reminds those who gather to mourn that while they have good cause for sorrow, they have even greater cause for hope. Christ came into the world to claim us as the children of the living God; the claim holds good whether we walk the earth or lie in the grave. Where do we go when we die? We go to the One who is already with us.

Jesus our Savior, grant that by the power of your resurrection we may live and die boldly under your lordship. Amen.

Baptism

D A Y
11

"A child is baptized, not in order that it may become a prince; it is baptized in order that it may be saved, as the words say, that is, in order that it may be redeemed from sin, death, and the devil, that it may become a member of Christ, and that it may come into Christ's kingdom and Christ become its Lord. Accordingly, baptism is useful to the end that through it we may be saved. There you have the transcendent excellence of baptism. The first honor is that it is a divine water, and when you see a baptism remember that the heavens are opened. The fruit is that it saves, redeems you from sin, liberates you from the devil, and leads you to Christ. . . . Note well, therefore, that baptism is water with the Word of God, not water and my faith. My faith does not make the baptism but rather receives the baptism, no matter whether the person being baptized believes or not; for baptism is not dependent upon my faith but upon God's Word" (Luther 1959b).

Luther contended with those who insisted that the recipient of baptism had to be old enough consciously to believe and submit him or herself to a life of Christian discipline within the fellowship of other such persons. He preserved the church's long tradition of baptizing infants, recipients who certainly could not give the informed consent required by these opponents. He was unwilling to make faith a precondition, for how would one know when there was enough faith present to warrant baptizing? If I go through dark times which erode my trust in God, must I be baptized again when faith reasserts itself? No adult, says Luther, can dare to receive the sacrament on the basis of his or her own faith, for one is not baptized upon one's faith or that of someone else, but solely upon God's Word and command. Luther writes, "In my faith I may lie, but he who instituted baptism cannot lie." Thus, an infant has as sure a place at the font as any of God's children. In this washing by water and the Word, God acts to create the very faith the gospel requires.

Gracious God, we give you thanks that you have made us your own through water and the Word. Keep us in the covenant of our baptism so that daily we may die to sin and rise to new life in our Lord Jesus. In his name we pray, amen.

The Lord's Supper

"The need (which drives us to [the Lord's Supper]) is that sin, devil, and death are always present. The benefit is that we receive forgiveness of sins and the Holy Spirit. Here, not poison, but a remedy and salvation is given, in so far as you acknowledge that you need it. Don't say: I am not fit today, I will wait a while. This is a trick of the devil. What will you do if you are not fit when death comes? Who will make you fit then? Say rather: Neither preacher, prince, pope, nor emperor compels me, but my great need and, beyond this, the benefit" (Luther 1959b).

Luther worried about the infrequency with which many Christians came to the Lord's table in his day. Some felt no need, and Luther sternly cautioned them that such an attitude was a clear indication of peril. When one's spirit is not troubled by the consciousness of sin and experiences no hunger for mercy and reconciliation, then one is desperately in need of grace. At such times we are the least competent judges of our condition and must be "sinners by faith," that is, we must take God's word as to the depth of our brokenness and alienation.

Others hesitated to receive the sacrament because of a painful sense of their unworthiness. According to Luther, they too suffered under a dangerous delusion. One does not determine when to be baptized according to the strength of one's faith, nor does one wait until one feels deserving to come to the Lord's table. The sacrament does not demand righteousness, it imparts it; it creates the faith it requires. Humility in this instance may not serve us well. Our conviction of unworthiness may foster the drive to make ourselves "fit" and thus to assume some responsibility for our own salvation, to merit in some small measure the benefits bestowed by the sacrament. Time and again Luther reminds us that God doesn't give grace on such terms. When you look at yourself and see your great need, let it turn you to Christ, not in on yourself. Let it carry you to the table, not drive you away. Forgiveness of sin and the gifts of the Spirit wait for you there, the very things you need to be fit for service and salvation.

Gracious Lord Jesus, teach us to know our great need, bring us to your table, and fill us with your grace. Amen.

Sin and Sanctification

 DAY 13 *"Contrariwise, we teach and comfort the afflicted sinner after this manner: Brother, it is not possible for thee to become so righteous in this life, that thou shouldest feel no sin at all, that thy body should be clear like the sun, without spot or blemish; but thou hast as yet wrinkles and spots, and yet art thou holy notwithstanding. But thou wilt say: How can I be holy, when I have and feel sin in me? I answer: In that thou dost feel and acknowledge thy sin, it is a good token; give thanks unto God and despair not. It is one step of health, when the sick man doth acknowledge and confess his infirmity. But how shall I be delivered from sin? Run to Christ the physician, which healeth them that are broken in heart, and saveth sinners"* (Luther 1953, 1956).

Luther expected believers to struggle with their discipleship, to labor daily to conform their lives to Christ, and to make real progress. When you are giving thanks, reflect over your own life and recognize the number of harmful attitudes and actions you have rejected, the set of new habits you have cultivated because of Christ's challenging presence in your life. Taking stock in this way can be so encouraging. Even as we see how much remains to be changed, we can look forward with hope because of the transformations that have already occurred under Christ's guidance and care.

Yet Luther knew better than to let people dwell on their sanctification, for it can also be disheartening. The life of discipleship is not one of steady advance. Too often our old faults reassert themselves. We find ourselves acting in selfish, cruel ways that we thought we had put behind us once and for all. We crave more excitement, more beauty, more wealth in our lives, and we sacrifice our integrity to get them. Time and time again God's Word sounds out in judgment upon us. It pierces the heart, and we feel shame. How can I be holy, the frustrated believer cries, when I cannot escape sin? I thought I was moving toward heaven, but here I am in hell again. Ah yes, says Luther, but this hell is the forecourt of paradise. "It is one step of health, when the sick man doth acknowledge and confess his infirmity." And the next step takes one to Christ and his healing righteousness.

Lord Jesus, be near us when sin rages so that we may turn to you to find hope, forgiveness, and the power to amend our lives. Amen.

Unbelievers

"For everything happens according to Christ's counsel, will, and ordaining. Without and beyond him nothing occurs. If something good transpires through pious princes and rulers, Christ sets it in motion and advances it. Should something evil take place through wicked rulers and tyrants, as, for example, some of the dear saints having spilled and still spilling their blood, he decrees it. How it comes about, however, that he holds everything in his hands, rules, creates, effects, propels, and preserves, and yet not all people are godly, this belongs to the invisible rule of the invisible God, which it is not fitting for us to investigate" (Luther 1911).

Because our relationship to Christ is so fundamental to our existence, we want other people to experience Christ's presence as we have. Indeed we are charged to bear witness to him so that others too might hear the Word and be transformed by its power. Yet the mystery remains—why, as Luther writes, are not all people godly?

Some of the blame may well lie with us. Perhaps our efforts at evangelizing have been clumsy, our message unclear, and our manner insensitive. Certainly we need to attend to such matters. Yet all our art and wisdom cannot guarantee the success of our mission. The source of the Word's power is God. We may sound it in the ears of our neighbors, but only God can seal it in their hearts. Even when we think we are coming to Christ and making a decision for him on our own, it is God bringing us and creating in us new powers of love and faithfulness. So what are we to say of those who seem to remain unmoved? Have they rejected God or has God rejected them?

It may not be a very satisfying answer that Luther gives, but it is an honest one. We accomplish nothing by trying to second guess God. Moreover, it is too simple, and hence false, to say that unbelievers are such by their own choice and thus solely responsible for their fates. When we recognize that "everything happens according to Christ's counsel," we must acknowledge that this counsel often mystifies, even terrifies us. Yet it assures us that Christ has the power to do what he has promised, that is, to save. When faced with the mystery of God's ways, we can only commend all of humankind to the certainty of God's grace.

Gracious Lord, claim for your own all whom you have created. This we ask in Christ's name, amen.

Vernon Schreiber

BROTHER LAWRENCE

E WAS a kitchen cook who became the spiritual director of his superiors. He objected to being published and left behind letters more cherished with each passing century. He scrupulously fulfilled his vows of obedience and became the freest of spirits. He described himself as a "clumsy lummox" who broke everything but sculpted his life into a thing of beauty. He spent his last 40 years inside monastery walls and became a pioneer carving out a new highway to God. He offered himself to the Lord in a spirit of subjection and self-denial and was surprised to find a life of joy. Expecting nothing, he found so much that he often said to God, "You have outwitted me." His name was Brother Lawrence (1608 or 1611–1691).

Born Nicholas Herman, in Lorraine, France, he was, according to his own report, converted at the age of 18. Gazing at a tree in early spring, knowing that soon it would burst forth into buds and then leaves, he became overwhelmed with the awareness of the providence and power of God and by God's grace, was filled with a love for God that never diminished.

As a young man he served as a soldier in what came to be known as the Thirty Years War. He was wounded and discharged. He then decided to give his life wholly to Christ, first choosing the life of a hermit. He soon saw that this was not for him and applied for admission to a Carmelite monastery. He was admitted and became a full member of his order in 1642.

He did not immediately burst forth into lofty thoughts about God. He learned what all must learn: "One does not become holy all at once." But then something happened and he began to experience "a profound interior peace." He had learned to practice the presence of God. When he died his painful death, it was with the full confidence that he would soon see Him whose presence was never absent.

His holiness and his humility were recognized both at the monastery and beyond it. His superior, Abbe Joseph de Beaufort, vicar general of Cardinal Louis Antoine de Noailles, came to him and learned from him. This worthy man later recalled these conversations and sought to put together with them the few scraps of writings and letters which Brother Lawrence had not destroyed. This effort resulted in the slim volume known as *The Practice of the Presence of God.*

The Presence of God

DAY 1 *"Were I a preacher, I should, above all other things, preach the practice of the presence of God; and were I a 'director,' I should advise all the world to do it, so necessary do I think it, and so easy, too"* (Symons 1941).

We are always in the presence of God because he is present everywhere. He is present when we hear his Word proclaimed, walk in the woods, or sit at table. But we can also enter *into* communion with God or, as Brother Lawrence would put it, into the presence of God.

Brother Lawrence would not deny that we are helped to enter into the presence of God through hearing the Word. His whole life was grounded in acts of devotion. In the innocence and purity of his heart, however, he went beyond prescribed prayers. He entered into the presence of God by means of "a habitual, silent, and secret conversation with God."

Such communion can take place because we have within us a space for spiritual growth. It is at the very core of our being. Through Holy Baptism the Holy Spirit has come to dwell there. The reality of the Spirit's presence takes hold of us when through prayer we center on God within us and enter into communion with him.

But how shall this be done? Brother Lawrence wrote that two childlike qualities prompted Jesus to pray, "I thank thee, Father, Lord of heaven and earth, that thou hast hidden these things from the wise and understanding and revealed them to babes" (Matt. 11:25). The first quality was humility—he surrendered his body, soul, and mind to God. The second was the boldness which made it possible to step into the presence of God and converse with Him. The child's instinct is correct. The Father is ready to embrace us.

"To thee, O Lord, do I lift up my soul. O my God, in thee I trust . . . Cast me not away from thy presence, and take not thy Holy Spirit from me" (Pss. 25:1-2; 51:11).

Prayer and Life Are One

D A Y	"*The time of business does not with me differ from the time of*

D A Y 2

"*The time of business does not with me differ from the time of prayer, and in the noise and clatter of my kitchen, while several persons are calling for different things, I possess God in as great tranquility as if I were upon my knees at the Blessed Sacrament*" (Symons 1941).

Brother Lawrence believed that we can pray with our hands unfolded, that prayer and life are one. He looked upon his kitchen and business assignments as part of his religious life and discharged them accordingly. He saw it that way because for him prayer was being in the presence of God, not merely having one's mind filled with pious phrases. That was his fundamental message for all of us.

We might consider some assignments "unspiritual" or "beneath" the dignity of those who are described as spiritual giants. Brother Lawrence thought otherwise. On one occasion he speaks of a trip to buy wine in Burgundy. He did not consider himself to be a person who had "a turn for business," but this did not cause him uneasiness. He simply turned it over to God, saying that "it was His business he was about."

His candor and lack of false piety is also seen in his description of working in the monastery kitchen. He didn't really like such work. In fact, he had "a great aversion to it." But in spite of that he could say that "he had found everything easy in the fifteen years he had been employed there."

Brother Lawrence demonstrated how the Mary and Martha can live side by side in us. When we must endure the strain, drudgery, and even humiliation that can accompany our work, then the Martha in us will learn that it is important, even necessary to pray while cooking supper. Leaving behind mere talk about the dignity of labor, the Mary in us will learn what it takes to pray while standing at Martha's side (Luke 10:38-42).

O Lord, when we find ourselves in the frenzied and overheated kitchens of life, help us to carry on knowing that we are in your presence, called to do all things, great and small, to the glory of your name. Amen.

Confusing the Means with the End

 In conversation with the Vicar General, Brother Lawrence said: *"It was lamentable to see how many people mistook the means for the end, addicting themselves to certain works, which they performed very imperfectly, by reason of their human or selfish regards"* (Symons 1941).

Clergy and lay people who serve as leaders in a congregation are not immune to the experience of great spiritual dryness. While feeding others, they are kept from feeding themselves. Their thoughts are fixed on the means, on what they are doing and saying, and not on God, who is the true end. Knowing that this is not how it should be, they may turn hopefully, even desperately, to devotional guides and inspiring readings. But even as they read them, they find themselves thinking of how they could use these words to help others. So in the habit of giving, they no longer know how to receive.

So caught up forming committees, serving on boards, and dealing with questions about salaries, they come to look upon themselves as a principal actor instead of people to be acted upon.

Brother Lawrence did not place the blame on the duties assigned to us. He knew that the secret lay in never forgetting the end of what one is doing: to be in communion with the Lord. He knew that if we are to reach that end, there must be times when we lay aside all tasks, standing back and gazing upon that image which is the end, the heart of the faith: the cross of Christ. In it and through it we see the mystery of that wondrous love which led St. Paul to exclaim, "Far be it from me to glory except in the cross of our Lord Jesus Christ" (Gal. 6:14).

Perhaps it was his own sense of spiritual dryness that led the Vicar General to come to Brother Lawrence and then to write down so carefully what had been said, including the words, "We should await, without anxiety, the remission of our sins through the blood of Jesus." Perhaps he would most willingly pray with us, "Hold high before us, O Lord, your cross, to the end that, by its inspiration, our lives may confess our hope." Amen.

Peace through Pardon

Brother Lawrence had confessed to him, the Grand Vicar tells us, *"that when sometimes he had not thought of God for a good while, he did not disquiet himself for it; but after having acknowledged his wretchedness to God, he returned to Him with so much greater trust in Him as he had found himself wretched through forgetting Him"* (Symons 1941).

Brother Lawrence once said that the practice of the presence of God is an easy thing to do. If this was all he said, we might resent him as one of those Christians who make everything sound so easy. For most of us it is not and, it seems, never will be. Least of all our prayers.

It is Brother Lawrence's willingness to be honest about himself and his failures which makes him such an authentic Christian. Why then should we be surprised that we, too, must confess that we are not yet perfectly trusting children of God who are always eager to commune with him? This is no reason to give up on ourselves and charge ourselves with unbelief. Unbelief is the refusal to turn to God, while our discouragement is but a sign of a troubled heart that still wants to reach out to God.

We ought to be encouraged by our brother's report to the vicar that "when he failed in his duty, he simply confessed his fault, saying to God, 'I shall never do otherwise if Thou leavest me to myself; it is Thou who must hinder my failing, and mend what is amiss.' That after this he gave himself no further uneasiness about it. . . . That he was very sensible of his faults, but was not discouraged by them, that he confessed them to God, but did not plead against Him to excuse them. When he had so done, he peaceably resumed his usual practice of love and adoration" (Symons 1941).

As we consider these words we see that Brother Lawrence did not first of all see himself as an "achiever." Despite his years of cheerful service, despite his life of ceaseless prayer, he always saw himself as a recipient, receiving rest in the grace of God, free from worry, full of love.

O God, give us that understanding of ourselves which is both the counsel and the comfort of the Holy Spirit in your holy word: "If we say we have no sin, we deceive ourselves, and the truth is not in us. If we confess our sins, he is faithful and just, and will forgive our sins and cleanse us from all unrighteousness" (1 John 1:8-9).

Prayer Is Listening

DAY 5 Brother Lawrence told the Grand Vicar *"that his view of prayer was nothing but a sense of the Presence of God, his soul being at that time insensible to everything but Divine Love; and that when the appointed times of prayer were past, he found no difference, because he still continued with God, praising and blessing him with all his might, so that he passed his life in continual joy"* (Symons 1941).

It doesn't take much to tempt us to give up on our prayers. Sometimes, when we hear the ardent prayer of others or read prayers which are so beautiful and expressive compared to anything we might say, we are cast down. All we can perceive is our own inadequacy and inability to know how or what to ask. So, we think to ourselves, why bother at all? Such a sense of helplessness, however, may be the best thing that can happen to us, because now we are ready to turn to God in the one way that matters: giving over to Him everything.

In such a moment we may be most ready to understand the nature of Brother Lawrence's discovery about practicing the presence of God. He learned that prayer is more than words. Prayer involves waiting. Prayer often means closing our lips so that our dear Lord might have His turn to speak. We need to allow him the opportunity to break into our thought processes. It is a good thing to be silent at first, resting in the awareness that we are in the Lord's presence. It is the wise and mature Christian who knows how important it is to be an attentive child waiting for the Father to speak. "Be still and know that I am God!" (Ps. 46:10). If we are willing to wait and be silent, becoming, as Brother Lawrence advises, "like a dumb paralytic beggar at a rich man's door," we may find ourselves in conversations we never dreamed possible.

Such communion with God, Brother Lawrence says, cannot be shut off simply because one is done with formal prayer at a given hour. It is the joy of knowing that the Lord is going with you along the way. Who knows when he might not have another word to say?

> Eternal Spirit of the living Christ,
> I know not how to ask or what to say;
> I only know my need, as deep as life,
> And only you can teach me how to pray.
> (*LBW* 441)

Faith's Logic

"How can we pray to Him without being with Him? How can we be with Him but in thinking of Him often? And how can we often think of Him unless by a holy habit of thought which we should form? You will tell me that I am always saying the same thing. It is true, for this is the best and easiest method I know; and as I use no other, I advise all the world to do it. We must know before we can love. In order to know God, we must often think of Him; and when we come to love Him, we shall then also think of Him often, for our heart will be with our treasure" (Symons 1941).

Although he was hardly a trained theologian, Brother Lawrence speaks to us as a Sherlock Holmes of the seventeenth century as he answers, "Elementary, my dear Christian," and proceeds to tick off the steps in his logic: (1) To know God one must enter into a "holy habit of thought." (2) The more we then love, the more we will think of our Beloved. (3) Thus God will become more and more our treasure.

Brother Lawrence spoke much of experience, but he never separated experience from thought. He wrote in his very last letter, "And as knowledge is commonly the measure of love, the deeper and more extensive our knowledge shall be, the greater will be our *love*: and if our love of God be great, we shall love Him equally in grief and in joy" (Symons 1941).

Christian experience comes through knowledge which is incomplete without experience. Miriam Murphy writes, "Early Christians did not die in the Coloseum because they were expert theologians but because they knew him who dwelt within them and would overcome death."

May it be on our behalf that the Apostle prays, "that Christ may dwell in your hearts through faith; that you, being rooted and grounded in love, may have power to comprehend with all the saints what is the breadth and length and height and depth, and to know the love of Christ which surpasses knowledge, that you may be filled with all the fulness of God" (Eph. 3:17-19).

The Past Blotted Out

|DAY|
|7|

"*Overcome by remorse, I confess all my wickedness to Him, ask His pardon and abandon myself entirely to Him, to do with me as He will. But this King, filled with goodness and mercy, far from chastising me, lovingly embraces me, makes me eat at His table, serves me with His own hands, gives me the keys of His treasures and treats me as His favorite*" (Delaney 1977).

As we hear Brother Lawrence speak of his joy in the presence of God, we might be led to think that our good brother sailed through life on a perpetual spiritual high. This was not the case. It was rather that he did not find it necessary to linger in the land of regrets.

Perhaps Brother Lawrence would especially appreciate a little story about a duck in the barnyard. A brother and his younger sister had gone to their grandparent's farm. Outside, the boy threw a stone at their prize duck, never expecting to hit it. But he did. In fact, he killed it. In a panic, he hid it behind the woodpile out back. But his sister saw him, and let him know it.

That day and the next, whenever Grandma assigned a chore to sister, she would say, "Oh, Billy will be glad to do it for me, won't you, brother?" Then, as he stood at the sink, or swept the floor, she would walk by and whisper, "Remember the duck!"

Finally, he could stand it no longer and confessed to his grandmother what he had done. "Billy," she said, "I knew it all along. I saw it happen from the kitchen window, and I forgave you long ago. I've just been waiting for you to tell me about it."

For too long people will allow an inner voice control their lives as they hear it say, "Remember the duck!" We ought to rejoice instead in the steadfast love and mercy of God. Theologian Helmut Thielecke wrote an apt description of God as "The Waiting Father." Our God is the Father who stands on the hill waiting for us to come to our senses. Seeing us from afar as we turn back towards home, we are welcomed as his very own. God has prepared for us day by day the feast of love and pardon at the table of Holy Communion.

We come to you, O Father, trusting in your promise that "if any one does sin, we have an advocate with the Father, Jesus Christ the righteous; and he is the expiation for our sins, and not for ours only, but also for the sins of the whole world" (1 John 2:1-2). Amen.

All for the Love of God

Brother Lawrence said *"that he found the best way of reaching God was by doing ordinary tasks, which he was obliged to perform under obedience, entirely for the love of God and not for the human attitude toward them"* (Delaney 1977).

We all know how easy it is to do the right thing for the wrong reason. Jesus spoke about this problem when he described the people who pray, give to charity, or engage in fasting, all for the same reason: to be seen by others. They have their reward, he said. They are seen by others.

The fault of such people seems so obvious that we overlook the more subtle ways in which we are subject to the same failing. Early on we learn that devotion to God and being helpful to others is one road to approval. We may also become people controlled by the expectations of others, filled with anxiety as we wonder what they might be thinking. From this anxiety it is but a short step to resentment as we begin to complain that people "don't appreciate how hard I am trying." Little wonder that for some, what passes for "religion" has become a state of bondage instead of the freedom which Christ came to bestow upon those who follow Him.

At this point, we would do well to turn to the apostolic invitation: "Whatever your task, work heartily, as serving the Lord and not men, knowing that from the Lord you will receive the inheritance as your reward; you are serving the Lord Christ" (Col. 3:23-24).

Paul is stating the simple truth that happiness rests in serving God, not in pursuing the approval of those around us. Peace comes when we are given a task to do and we do it for him who is our companion, friend and savior.

O Lord, grant that my life of Christian service will not become burned-out because I have forgotten my first love of You. Refresh and renew me through your love so that I may again put my whole heart into whatever You have given me to do. Amen.

Good Medicine

"My good Mother: If we were accustomed to the regular exercise of the presence of God, all the ills of the body would be lessened; God often permits us to suffer a little to purify our souls and to bring us to him. . . . It grieves me to see you suffering so long; what lightens somewhat my sympathy for your suffering is that I am convinced it is proof of God's love for you" (Delaney 1977).

Brother Lawrence is full of surprises. He knew then what people today are hailing as a startling new discovery: the influence of a joyous spirit upon a physical malady. He joyfully proclaimed that the presence of God is good medicine, working wonders both spiritually and physically.

As the Proverbs remind us, "A merry heart doeth good like a medicine" (Prov. 17:22 KJV).

Brother Lawrence is not calling on us to deny the reality of pain or illness. He simply offers an antidote: "Love eases pain and when one loves God, one suffers for him with joy and courage." His only point is that it works wonders to adore God at all times, to trust in him without reservation, and to be assured of his unchanging love. I, too, have seen such holy laughter confound a pessimistic prognosis.

Trouble can become for us the anvil of God on which his Word strikes sparks as He says to us, "No, I won't let you go your own heedless way! Are you mine or not?" Through the Word we may then be led to say with renewed joy, "Yes, I do belong to God in the midst of this trouble. For in Jesus God has given us the promised Messiah who with us bears our griefs and carries our sorrows. It is he who has been bruised for our iniquities. By his stripes he brings healing to us all. Even in my troubles I am more than a conqueror through him who loves us" (compare Isa. 53:4-5; Rom. 8:37).

Heavenly Father, we need not deny our pain or our cause for sorrow, for we know you are with us and are filled with joy through the power of your presence. Amen.

Press On

D A Y 10

"That the end we ought to propose to ourselves is to become, in this life, the most perfect worshipers of God we can possibly be, as we hope to be throughout all eternity" (Symons 1941).

Brother Lawrence wrote very little about looking forward to the joys of heaven. Is not heaven being in the presence of the Lord? If that is so, what makes us think we must wait for it? We can begin to enjoy its pleasures right now. Knowing the presence of the Lord is a present reality, not merely a future hope.

One beautiful hymn prays for the Lord's presence at our waking, in our working, upon our homing, and then concludes:

Lord of all gentleness, Lord of all calm,
   Whose voice is contentment, whose presence is balm,
Be there at our sleeping, and give us we pray,
   Your peace in our hearts, Lord, at the end of the day.
                              (*LBW* 469)

Like the hymn, for Brother Lawrence being in the presence of the Lord around the clock was the goal of life itself. At the same time, with St. Paul, he might say: "but I press on, hoping to take hold of that for which Christ once took hold of me. My friends, I do not reckon to have got hold of it yet. All I can say is this: forgetting what lies behind me, and reaching out for that which lies ahead, I press towards the goal to win the prize which is God's call to the life above, in Christ Jesus" (Phil. 3:12b-14 New English Bible).

Always press on. This is the word of encouragement from these giants of the faith as we take our first stumbling steps. "In the end we will acquire a habit which will allow us to perform our acts effortlessly and with great pleasure" (Delaney 1977). Press on, until at last we shall see Him face to face.

O Lord, lead us to know by faith your presence in our lives today until at last we attain, with all the company of heaven, the full vision of your glory. Amen.

An Interior Joy

Brother Lawrence writes of himself, *"He is now so accustomed to this divine presence that he receives continual aid from it in all circumstances; for almost thirty years his soul has been filled with interior joys so continual and sometimes so great that to contain them and prevent their outward manifestation, he has resorted to behavior that seems more foolishness than piety"* (Delaney 1977).

Whence comes such joy as Brother Lawrence writes about? It comes out of union with Christ, a union we deepen through the practice of prayer. The aim of such prayer is not to make our Lord a push-button God who does what we say, but One in whom we live and who lives in us—a communion that is sacred, loving, joyful. We want the "love of God poured into our hearts through the Holy Spirit which has been given to us" (Rom. 5:5) not for selfish reasons, in the sense of personal glory, but for the sake of the self God sees as our potential.

One day a visitor stood on the coast of England and looked out over a vast stretch of mud in which ships tilted at crazy angles. He wondered what could be done. The heaving of an anchor or the hoisting of a sail would mean nothing. It was impossible to haul in enough water to fill the basin. Then, as he watched, the tide swept in. As the waters splashed against their side, the ships came to life again.

It is exactly in those moments when we feel we have been left totally "high and dry" that the flood tide of God's love can make us ready to sail again.

This is why Brother Lawrence would urge us to be open to and pray for the presence of God at all hours. Through communion with the Lord the heart is delighted as in no other way.

Holy Spirit, through the knowledge of God's inexhaustible love fill me to the brim with your gift of joy. Amen.

A Little Talk with God

"It would be pertinent for those who undertake this practice to make up interiorly short ejaculations such as, 'My God, I am all yours,' 'God of love,' 'I love you with all my heart,' and any such words that love may beget on the spur of the moment." (Delaney 1977).

Jesus once spoke of people who would take the kingdom of God by violence. Many of us would seize it and conquer it through our knowledge and ability to use words. We meditate on what we read and hear. We take notes. But there is another way. It is something more intuitive. A friend has put the formula this way: "Rest in God as He rests in you." She calls for a time of quiet and listening. We need a time of waiting for God's response as we give ourselves over to quietness.

Through a simple resting in God, growth comes as growth always must come: slowly. If a wound heals best when it heals slowly, and if only slowly does the seed grow and mature into a beautiful tree, then why think that the beauty of God's holiness can be attained through a religious cram course? As Brother Lawrence, with a trace of humor, says of Sister N—, "She appears to me to be full of good will, but she wants to go faster than grace. One does not become holy all at once."

O Lord, help us to encourage one another, to forgive one another, to be patient with one another, and to delight in one another, to the end that we might help each other into a deeper communion with You, the source of every good gift. Amen.

Who Shall See God?

DAY
13

"By the presence of God and by this interior gaze, the soul comes to know God in such a way that it is . . . always engaged in this divine presence." (Delaney 1977).

Can a mortal human being see God? Moses asked to see him, but was denied, except for a glimpse of the Lord's departing glory. Furthermore, the Gospel has declared, "No one has ever seen God" (John 1:18). If we are speaking of a visual record received by the retina, most certainly it is impossible to see God.

And yet, seeing not, we see God another way. We see Him by faith. We behold him through what Brother Lawrence describes as the soul's "interior gaze." It is a seeing just as real as anything caught by the mechanism of the eye and brain.

This is the vision which is promised in our Lord's beatitude spoken in the Sermon on the Mount. He speaks of the "pure in heart," the people who "shall see God." While the absolute and total fulfillment of Jesus' promise shall take place only at the end of time, it shall also happen as we turn to him with unquestioning obedience and heartfelt adoration. It is then that, seeing not, we see.

We only know that at the end, as Joseph Sittler suggests, this seeing certainly will *not* be the discovery that God looks like us, only on a much grander scale. Such a claim would be both blasphemy against God and idolatry of mankind.

What we shall see goes beyond the limits of human language. We simply know that we will see God as his glory becomes our light and his presence our life. In the meantime, through the Father's disclosure of himself in his only Son, through this act of sheer grace, we are able to pray,

> O my soul,
> Why these eyes shut so tight?
> Open them now and thus begin
> To see Him who will be your Light
> Through all your days in heaven.

Centering on God

DAY 14

"I cannot imagine how religious persons can live satisfied without the practice of the presence of God. For my part, I keep myself retired with Him in the very center of my soul as much as I can; and while I am so with Him, I fear nothing" (Symons 1941).

As we leave Brother Lawrence, let us remember that he was not out to foster one particular "method" of devotional life. Only one thing really mattered to him: seeking the presence of God. Concerning this goal, he would not tolerate indifference. He once told his superior he could visit him any time without fear of bothering him, if what he truly desired was union with God. But if that was not the case, this kitchen cook admonished the vicar general that he "ought no more to visit him" (Symons 1941).

Brother Lawrence reminds us that our goal will not take place by our talking about prayer, but only by the *doing* of it. To that end, the following exercises may help us to center on God and enter into communion with God:

1. Sit back in a relaxed manner, your back straight and both feet on the floor, your whole body as relaxed as possible, leaving your soul free. Thank and praise God for all he has done through the day.
2. Reflect for a moment on a passage of Scripture.
3. Concentrate your consciousness on the loving presence of Christ within your inner self. Think of how much you love and honor him. Exclude other thoughts as best you can. "Seek the things that are above, where Christ is, seated at the right hand of God" (Col. 3:1).
4. Breathe deeply and rhythmically, since this in itself brings calm and peace. Speak softly the names of the Lord. Say little things such as, "My God, I am all yours," "God of love, I love you with all my heart," "My Lord and my God, heal me and free me."
5. As you are relaxed and centering on the presence of God within you, you may wish to make use of a favorite and simple prayer. It may simply be the doxology or a prayer to the Lamb of God who takes away the sins of the world.

Then, whether it is in such a moment set apart, or in the newly found peace that attends our given tasks, our life becomes this prayer: Whether we sleep or wake, work or play, may we ever know, O Lord, "the mystery hidden for ages . . . but now made manifest to his saints . . . which is Christ in you, the hope of glory" (Col. 1:26-27).

Herbert Brokering

ST. FRANCIS OF ASSISI

H
E WAS born into the family of a rich cloth merchant in a small Italian town in the Umbrian Valley. Pietro Bernardoni and his French wife, the Lady of Pica, baptized their son Giovanni. Later his wealthy father changed the name to Francesco and we now know him as St. Francis of Assisi (1182–1226). He grew up a spoiled son, full of humor, generosity, wit, charm. He was a raucous, musical, sensual troubadour, a prodigal.

In the act of becoming a knight at age twenty-two, he forsook the glamour of sword, shield, and death. A new light came into him, the light and sight of a child. This new eye for all life would never leave him. He heard voices and saw visions that lead into a desert journey. Francis was listening to God.

From a crucifix he heard a voice commanding him to repair a nearby chapel on the verge of ruin. The priest would not accept the prodigal money which was his father's, so Francesco turned to begging. With stones received through begging, he rebuilt the church.

Francesco was mocked, returned what he had to his father, and stripped himself of all possessions. In rags he became a new person. The transformation was a ritual of baptism. Pietro Bernardoni is no longer his father; Francesco's Father is in heaven. He did not give a tithe: he gave everything. He was a fool but not foolhardy. He was streetwise and then memorized songs of red-winged blackbirds. His earthly father was a cloth merchant but his Father in heaven made him a man of the cloth—it was tattered and torn, and it was often a towel.

Sister Earth

Be praised, my Lord, for our sister Mother Earth,
Who sustains and guides us,
and brings forth fruits of many kinds,
with many colored flowers of grass.

(Cornelia 1985)

The earth is kind. Gardens, meadows, woodlands gladly give more than we need. Mother earth is Sister, partner in the family. Earth plays and lives with her human siblings. We cheer when the buds burst; we thank for the fruit we eat. The one who gives us what we need is part of our family. Mother earth is partner, Sister.

Earth is a pantry. She has access to what is good. We have a right to the bounty of all the earth. We need the lap and arms and warmth of Sister Mother Earth. Earth is kinder than a friend; earth is Sister.

Earth is a minister to the human spirit. She uses all her gifts and forms. Earth can be Mother and Sister in long night watches. In a storm she can make strangers one close family. All nations will gather in awe around her eclipse. Rain can make thankless people praise. We are all in the mercy of Sister Earth. She is God's full-time minister.

St. Francis spoke lovingly of earth. He was earth's brother. We are to greet earth with dignity and call her by her endearing name. We find in earth our daily life and food. We find in earth our work and play and all mysteries. We find in her an abundance.

> Dear mother earth, who day by day
> Unfolds rich blessings on our way,
> Oh, praise [God]! Alleluia!
> The fruits and flow'rs that verdant grow,
> Let them his praise abundant show.
> Oh, praise [God]!
>
> (LBW 527)

"The earth is the Lord's and the fullness thereof, the world and those who dwell therein" (Ps. 24:1).

Sister Water

DAY
2

Be praised, my Lord, for Sister Water,
most useful is she, and humble,
and precious and chaste.
(Cornelia 1985)

Praise the Lord for water says St. Francis. By nature water is precious and chaste. For St. Francis all water was inspired. Jesus was washed in water, so all water belongs to Christ. In the same way, all nature is God's nature. Francis had no more possessions than the lowest creation. So he loved all things, and the lowliest of all loved him in return. Francis knew the water loved him.

There is nothing water will not wash clean. There is no thirst it will not heal. Water is the drink for rich and poor. The rose garden in Washington, DC and your lawn need the same water. Queens, prisoners, and actors wash in one water. Water and towel are a sign of forgiveness. Jesus amazed his disciples in the Upper Room with Sister Water and the towel.

Water is a common character in spiritual dramas. God's people still have favorite water holes, cups, fountains, lakes. All know a struggling creek, rampaging river, collapsed cistern, and dry well. Picture water stories of salvation. Through water God saves the world and family of Noah, the nation of Israel, the prophet Jonah, the army of Gideon, the woman in Samaria. Sister Water is a main character in Scriptures and church history.

> Let water be the sacred sign
> That we must die each day
> To rise again by his design
> As foll'wers of his way
> (*LBW* 195)

"Have you entered into the springs of the sea, or walked in the recesses of the deep?" (Job 38:16).

Our Lord's Mother

We are all our Lord's mothers
when we carry him about
in our heart and person by means of love
and a clean and sincere conscience,
and we give birth to him
by means of our actions which should shine . . .

(Cornelia 1985)

Christ entered space: a geographic location, historical site, creature space, human space, racial space, covenant space. Each generation seeks some humble, simple, concrete, worship space in which to say: "Christ has entered here." God knows our need for an incarnate One to come to our space so we can hear: "a child is born for you." We say the same in creeds when we confess that Christ is truly God and truly human.

Mary gave space within herself to be the Lord's mother. We have admired, even adored her parent role. Francis bids us be Christ's mother, and keep alive and warm what is Christ. Mary rejoiced for the child in her. Christ in us transforms us and cheers us. We are not the same when we confess that Christ lives in us. In faith we can hold God so intimately.

A lawyer came to Jesus at night with a faith question. Jesus answered with a picture of rebirth. Of all images at hand, Jesus asked that the man be born anew. Jesus would only ask in this way to one whom he so loved. The lawyer needed a mother again.

Consider the space Mary readied for Christ. The room of this mother was not only in the house, in the synagogue, with neighbors, in study and play, in the shop of Joseph or at the table. First of all, Jesus was in the space of his own mother.

With the love of a mother we say, "Come Lord Jesus, be our guest," or sing, "Come into my heart, Lord Jesus." Who would not for love's sake want to hold and rock the Christ?

> What child is this, who laid to rest,
> On Mary's lap is sleeping?
> Whom angels greet with anthems sweet
> While shepherds watch are keeping?
> This, this is Christ the King.
>
> (*LBW* 40)

"Mary said, 'Behold, I am the handmaid of the Lord; let it be according to your word" (Luke 1:38).

Yours Is the Praise

DAY

4

Most High, mighty and good Lord,
Yours is the praise, the glory, the honor
and all benediction.
To you alone, Most High, do they belong,
and no one is fit even to mention your name.

(Cornelia 1985)

When we pray we may face a cross, a wall, a tree, a city, a friend, a painting, the Scriptures, a light. When Francis prayed the above words he saw the sun. The sun to him was entree to even more light. Through the sun he could see sights for praise and glory and honor.

When we pray we travel through insight. In secret, in silence, and while transfixed our thoughts go far and fast and close. The goal of prayer is God. The depth or height of prayer is to praise, to give glory, and to exalt. So prayer is aimed toward God.

Prayer is an astonishing mode of speaking. Though simple it is not commonplace. It is a surprise that we may know and speak the name of God. We should be astonished that God would be addressed. Francis was in wonder of God's name.

Francis knew what it meant to revel. He was in some ways the Lord's lifelong minstrel. What he did in prayer some saw as dance and clown. He never took the joy away from others, but saw delight and celebration as pointing to the Most High. Nothing stopped before reaching the High one.

Most High: what a name for God. And if Most High, then Most Low, Most Deep, Most Wide, Most Far, Most Near. Nothing is out of range. Nothing is too exaggerated. Nothing is too humble. Nothing is too aesthetic. Nothing is too little. Nothing is too much. We belong to the one Most High who slept in the straw. We belong to the one Most High.

Oh, that I had a thousand voices
To praise my God with thousand tongues!
My heart, which in the Lord rejoices,
Would then proclaim in grateful songs
To all, wherever I might be,
What great things God has done for me.

(*LBW* 560)

"And the city has no need for sun or moon to shine upon it, for the glory of God is its light, and its lamp is the Lamb" (Rev. 21:23).

Brother Wind

Be praised, my Lord, for Brother Wind,
and for the air, for cloudy, fair,
and every kind of weather,
through which you give your creatures sustenance.

(Cornelia 1985)

There are those who, like St. Francis, bless the wind: the tail wind that makes the flight on time, the wind that brings needed rain, and the wind to cool heat at dusk. There is also the wind to fly balloons or kites, the wind to dry a flood, and the wind to make leaves ripple at twilight.

Some watch clouds and praise God for Brother Wind. There is a country church high on a single hill where often blows a high wind. Some hang on to their hats and hurry through the door. Some face the wind and revel in it thankfully. Some read the wind as God's word for freedom, of the Spirit moving to and fro. Wind is their Brother.

Wind is a synonym for breath. When runners need a second wind they rejoice in the gift. When we need spirit, Brother Wind is there. We wait for the wind through the cry of newborn. Handel's "Messiah" always features a chorus of wind, harmonies learned from the wind in woods.

Brother Wind leads us by scent to roses, tree blossoms, and oceans. By the wind the dog can smell home. By the wind we know places, we smell that dinner is ready and candles are lit.

The wind and breath of God lives in us. There is spirit and breath as when God spoke to Ezekial saying that the dry bones would live when God put his breath in them. When we travel believing, we journey far and high with Brother Wind. We hear the Spirit speaking to us, calling us. We listen for constant songs of praise.

O rushing wind and breezes soft,
O clouds that ride the winds aloft:
Oh, praise him! Alleluia!

(*LBW* 527)

"Let everything that breathes praise the Lord! Praise the Lord!"

(Ps. 150:6)

Love

Be praised, my Lord,
for those who grant pardon
for love of you,
and endure infirmity and tribulation.

(Cornelia 1985)

These words were always in St. Francis's Friday prayer. Friday was the day to ask pardon, because on that one Friday they did not pardon him who pardoned them all. They did not love him, who said: "Forgive them; for they know not what they do" (Luke 23:34).

There is a shout of pardon to be heard; the pardon we seek we already have. In this pardon, we come to know the great love St. Francis knew. Because we are loved we seek more love, and will find it. We know the love out there by the love inside.

Francis had a way of loving Jesus: it was the way anyone wanted to be loved. There is a way to love Christ that makes others feel loved. When Christ is truly human then we learn how to be human to each other. In our devotion for Christ we learn to be devoted to each other.

Francis knew the key to love. He knew how lovable God is. He knew the joy love brings. He knew the simple acts of being loved. We know how direct love must be. Love surrounds and is within. Love begets love. Love begat creation. Love overwhelms. God knows all about love.

God takes the lead in love and pardon. God led Francis to the lepers. God leads us to the thirsty, the lonely, the imprisoned. God leads us down the frightening road to the lost. God leads us to the enemy. And when we arrive, God's work of reconciliation has already begun. God always leads us into love.

> O Love that will not let me go,
> I rest my weary soul in thee;
> I give thee back the life I owe,
> That in thine ocean depths its flow
> May richer, fuller be.
>
> (*LBW* 324)

"This is my commandment, that you love one another as I have loved you. Greater love has no man than this, that a man lay down his life for his friends" (John 15:12-13).

Brother Death

DAY
7

Be praised, my Lord,
for our brother the death of the body,
which no one among the living can escape.
Unhappy they who will die in mortal sin.
Blessed those who shall be found
in your most holy pleasure,
for the second death shall do no harm to them.
(Cornelia 1985)

It is said St. Francis prayed loudly. He faced the silence of death with a full voice. Christ is the first death. We die a second death and awaken to a long life. The second death will do us no harm.

Francis names the death of the body his Brother. Christ makes death our second Brother. No one can escape it, and it can do us no harm.

Some may recall from childhood the silence in a dark night just before sleeping. Noise and commotion of the day quiet into silence. Someone's final word or act of love fills the silence, and we go into the place of sleep. We fall asleep while trusting love.

We are not to die frightened by mortal sin. The notion of being "scared to death" is not to be nurtured. Fear, anger, and hate are not to put us to sleep. Christ brings death as brother.

Someone has been in the darkness and silence of death, to make death the brother. We are not the first to go there. Death did not keep Christ asleep. It is the same with us; we can believe the God of Brother Death.

Jesus lives! And now is death
But the gate of life immortal;
This shall calm my trembling breath
When I pass its gloomy portal
Faith shall cry, as fails each sense:
Jesus is my confidence.
(*LBW* 133)

"The life was made manifest, and we saw it, and testify to it, and proclaim to you the eternal life, which was with the Father and which was made manifest to us" (1 John 1:2).

The Wealth

You are all the wealth one can desire.
You are beauty. You are gentleness.
You are our protector.

(Cornelia 1985)

The sun had not yet risen. Morning was still behind the horizon. Francis would sing aloud of his wealth and protection in the night. Francis trusted God when there was little to see.

Francis found wealth with lepers. In the frayed edges of old garments he found the elegance of God. In what seemed to be crumbs he had a feast.

Where is the wealth of the Lord? We may need to close our eyes to see this bounty. We may need to fold our hands, be alone, and feel pangs of hunger to know God's wealth. The Lord is the wealth. Wealth is not something separate.

God is the richest of the wealthy. This is the wealth: beauty and gentleness. Francis was raised in the house of a clothier, a merchant of fine cloth. Yet there was a beauty he found to be greater than fine linen: it was in all that Christ had touched or seen. What Christ had set his eyes on turned to beauty, Francis learned.

Francis names the Lord "Wealth." There is no greater fortune. There is no greater asset, than the "Wealth." In Christ all things are drawn into the center. Everything from shadows to seasons to spirits to reasons has worth. We are totally immersed in wealth. What is most essential for life cannot be manufactured. It can be discovered. Great need can take us to great wealth quickly.

It is happening now. At this moment we can desire any wealth, any beauty, any protection. The wealth Francis is describing is the Lord. Prayer takes us into this wealth. Closing our eyes we can be there. Folding or reaching our arms we can be there. Saying one word we can be there in the middle of the wealth.

> For the joy of ear and eye,
> For the heart and mind's delight,
> For the mystic harmony
> Linking sense to sound and sight:
> Christ, our Lord, to you we raise
> This our sacrifice of praise
>
> (*LBW* 561)

"I will not leave you desolate; I will come to you" (John 14:18).

Blessed Sun

Be praised, my Lord, for all your creatures,
in the first place for Blessed Sun,
who gives us the day
and enlightens us through you,
beautiful and radiant,
giving witness to you, Most High.

(Cornelia 1985)

In first place of all things created for Francis was Blessed Sun. "Let there be light" is the first stanza of the hymn in Genesis. He could shout "Amen" to a beam of light.

Through Blessed Sun God gives us day. So we have long horizons, deep vistas, sharp shadows. We have high noon, twilight, dawn, and dusk. These stances of Blessed Sun are also ways we see; these are all kinds of enlightenment. There are high places and places deep. There are dim places and places clear. Blessed Sun is a sign of many ways to see.

Blessed Sun is our mentor. We too want to radiate, be enlightened, shine. We too want to grow, ripen, bloom, enliven. We want to see clearly in dim places. We want to face in the day what may haunt in the dark. We like the feeling of seeing some glory.

There is a higher light than the sun. It has more brightness, radiance, and beauty than a bright day. Through the Blessed Sun we see even more; we behold! There is a sight so bright that in its sudden moments we stammer with angels to exclaim: "Lo," and "Behold." We utter: we are silent.

Higher than Blessed Sun is the Most High. All day, all light, all enlightenment is a witness. To follow all forms of sun and light leads us to the Most High. All light is a spotlight on the Most High.

O Jesus, shine around us
With radiance of your grace;
O Jesus, turn upon us
The brightness of your face.
We need no star to guide us,
As on our way we press,
If you will light our pathway,
O Sun of righteousness.

(*LBW* 77)

"Lord, now lettest thou thy servant depart in peace, according to thy word; for mine eyes have seen thy salvation" (Luke 2:29-30).

217

Pardon Me

Be praised, my Lord,
for those who grant pardon
for love of you,
and endure infirmity and tribulation.

(Cornelia 1985)

Francis knew pardon. At Francis's worst times Christ was in best form, granting pardon. And during our worst times, Christ is with the downcast and the outcast, for Christ became the outcast.

Christ came to us to be human. Distance is erased. Differences are erased. The frown of God is gone. Curtains are torn in two. Partitions are abolished. God's rainbow shouts one will: Pardon. "Pardon me" is a Biblical word. All is changed now because Christ hung on the unpardonable shape, the cross.

Life can go on without our perishing. We can submit to tribulation. We can climb calvary. We can carry the cross. There is in us a life and love of Christ. It is in us and around us. Love goes before and after.

The greatest of all we possess is love. We are born into love; it is stronger than all else. Love converts water into wine, an acorn into a lumber yard, a convict into a disciple, a thief into a friend, a stumbling block into a cornerstone.

"Forgive our sins as we forgive,"
You taught us, Lord, to pray:
But you alone can grant us grace
To live the words we say.

Lord, cleanse the depths within our souls
And bid resentment cease;
Then, bound to all in bonds of love,
Our lives will spread your peace.

(*LBW* 307)

"For the commandments . . . are summed up in this sentence, 'You shall love your neighbor as yourself' " (Rom. 13:9).

The Journey

Bless this earth, dear Lord,
And every cave within it,
For here will come a host
Of lonely wanderers.
May this blessed mountain
Hold them tight until
The morning of their tomorrows
Breaks upon the crest
Of every Mount Subasio on the earth.
(Bodo 1972)

St. Francis lived near Mount Subasio. In flight of prayer his soul soared to its peak and glided through its tiny rock caves. In that mountain and its caves Francis saw clearly the journey of pilgrims on their way. The caves marked places of refuge along the way.

The rock caves were shelters for people who were made new in the journey. The caves were the empty graves of Christ, and Francis asked Christ to bless these tiny rooms of shelter and worship.

Those on the journey were drawn ahead by a dream. These dreams kept the wanderers seeking, going, climbing, singing. The dreams were many; the highest dream was to see God face to face. Francis and Christ walked this road together.

Sometimes we meet in caves of lonely wanderers. We are those who have nothing but the rock walls around. We are those stripped of everything important in all dreaming: we find ourselves safe in the empty tomb of Christ. It is Easter today. We meet those whose courage and singing draws us into their caves. There is no glamour there, but there is a fire, a light, a love, a dream being fulfilled.

The touch of Christ and the face of God are in the dream. We have a dream to follow; in our tiny blessed caves along the way, our dream is restored. The dream draws us on.

Come, my way, my truth, my life;
Such a way as gives us breath;
Such a truth as ends all strife;
Such a life as conquers death
(*LBW* 513)

"They said to each other, 'Did not our hearts burn within us while he talked to us on the road, while he opened to us the scriptures?'" (Luke 24:32).

The Dream

Lord, make me an instrument of your peace.
Where there is hatred, let me sow love,
Where there is injury, pardon,
Where there is darkness, light,
Where there is despair, hope
And where there is sadness, joy.

(Bodo 1972)

The sight of Francis, a poor beggar in the palace of the Turkish sultan, was a study of contrasts. He'd come to tell his majesty about Jesus. He'd come to tell of the peace he'd found along life's way. From his youth Francis was following a dream which he was now fulfilling. In the dream he'd stood as a beggar in the palace of a Turkish sultan to talk of peace. His words flowed from within like a rich wine.

Now beside the sultan whose prayers were to Allah, old Francis knew to pray: "Lord, make me an instrument of your peace." As his eyes lifted up he caught a sliver of bright light through the top of the tent; Francis could see the sultan was moved by the peace of Christ pouring from Francis' heart.

The sultan heard that the poor beggar from Assisi sought to balance the world's hatred. Francis told him not what the sultan wanted to hear, but the truth. This poem of peace lays paradoxes upon the great scale of justice. Francis does not ask to destroy despair, darkness, injury, or hatred. Where there is hatred, he would sow love.

We are going somewhere. This dream is more than images inside us. It is evident; the dream lives; people hear it in our words and see our eyes on fire. It is a road we will not leave. It is a long journey to tents of sultans and places of danger. We share a dream of peace, and then we go home.

Grant peace, we pray, in mercy, Lord;
Peace in our time, oh, send us!
For there is none on earth but you,
None other to defend us.
You only, Lord, can fight for us. Amen.

(*LBW* 417)

"And above all these put on love, which binds everything together in perfect harmony. And let the peace of Christ rule in your hearts, to which indeed you were called in the one body. And be thankful (Col. 3:14-15).

Jesus

O Lord, I beg of you two graces before I die—
to experience personally and in all possible fullness
the pains of your bitter Passion,
and to feel for you the same love
that moved you to sacrifice yourself for us.

(Bodo 1984)

For everything in Francis' life Jesus was in the center. It was in the cave that he first met Jesus. In the dark, the damp, the quiet—where it was easier to hear the voice of Jesus come from within. In the cave he found a hidden center of himself. Christ helped him into that inner place for strength and peace.

He embraced the Christ found in the center of the publicans and sinners, the center of the lepers and blind, in the center of the outcast. There was a stigma of Jesus which Francis wanted; he believed the markings of Jesus would be his surest sign of unity.

The Jesus whom Francis knew is the one who did not grab equality with God, and who took on the nature of a slave. It was mainly poor women and men who were Jesus' disciples. He had no house, no regular place to lie down, and died in a robe that was not his own.

In his last days, friends carried Francis down to the valley of the little church, St. Mary of the Angels. He lay there stripped of his habit on the cold floor with the thought and hope to die naked as Christ. He would not be hoisted on the cross as Christ had been. He would die lying on cold stone, with the wound in his side.

There is something in this dream that is ours. For Francis, as for us, Jesus is the center. Jesus is the beginning, and Jesus is the end. In death we come full circle. The one who shared the open grave in our baptism, is the one who says: "It is I!" at the end.

> Jesus, priceless treasure,
> Source of purest pleasure,
> Truest friend to me:
> Ah, how long I've panted,
> And my heart has fainted,
> Thirsting, Lord, for Thee.
> (*LBW* 458)

"He said to them, 'But who do you say that I am?' Simon Peter replied, 'You are the Christ, the Son of the living God' " (Matt. 16:15-16).

Communion

There should not be, anywhere in the world,
a fallen brother,
no matter how far he has fallen into sin,
who will ever fail to find your forgiveness for asking,
if he will but look into your eyes.
And if he doesn't ask for forgiveness,
you should ask him if he wants it.
And should he come back to you a thousand times,
you should love him more than you love me,
so that you may draw him to God.

(Bodo 1984)

Francis lived with ordinary people. He knew their ordinariness. For him poverty was par for life's course. For him community was a communion of ordinary beings, united not by their high estate, but their poverty. They were with high self-esteem and of low estate. There were none too low to be in the body, none whom Jesus will not gather to the table.

For Jesus hunts the hidden one. Jesus in communion is relentless. He is the shepherd who hunts the one lost, until it is found. Jesus is the one who has a party when the coin is finally discovered. Jesus is the parent waiting for the child to come home, and then hosts a celebration.

As you, Lord, have lived for others,
So may we for others live.
Freely have your gifts been granted;
Freely may your servants give.

(*LBW* 364)

"As the Father has loved me, so have I loved you; abide in my love. If you keep my commandments, you will abide in my love, just as I have kept my Father's commandments and abide in his love. These things I have spoken to you, that my joy may be in you, and that your joy may be full" (John 15:9-11).

Wilfred Bockelman

ELTON TRUEBLOOD

T HINK of Elton Trueblood (full name, David Elton Trueblood), and in addition to being the author of more than 30 books, other identifying words that come to mind are Quaker, Yokefellow, philosopher, and mystic, to name just a few.

Trueblood was born in 1900 near Indianola, Iowa. His ancestors, John and Agnes Trueblood, arrived in North Carolina from England in 1682. They were Quakers and most of their descendants are still of that faith today.

After being educated at Penn College, Oskaloosa, Iowa, Hartford Theological Seminary, and Harvard University where he received a Ph. D., Trueblood taught religion and philosophy at several colleges and universities. He also served for a number of years as chaplain and professor of religion and philosophy at the prestigious Stanford University before he moved to Earlham College in Richmond, Indiana in 1946, and served there until his retirement in 1966. He continued actively in lecturing, writing, and developing such concepts as Yokefellows.

All of his writings and activities have a common and readily identifiable thread running through them. In his autobiography, he describes how he came to found Yokefellows: "As I came to middle age, two separate dangers were simultaneously impressed upon my mind. I saw, at the same time, both the futility of empty freedom and the fruitlessness of single effort. Affirmatively stated, the latter led to the idea of the small fellowship, while the former led to the idea of voluntary discipline, in conjunction they led to the recognition that hope lies in the creation of an order."

That new order was the Order of the Yoke, commonly known as Yokefellows. It combines a high sense of individual and personal discipline with commitment to working in fellowship with others. Even the titles of some of his books illustrate this double emphasis; for example, *The Company of the Committed* and *The Incendiary Fellowship*.

There will be those readers who would prefer more about the doctrine of salvation, but for Trueblood that is always a beginning point that he doesn't emphasize over and over again. He is more interested in living that Christian life as a witness in today's society.

It is obvious that his books were written before the days of sensitivity to sexist language. But what makes them classics is that the fundamentals hold for all generations in spite of cultural differences.

The Greatest of These Is Caring

D A Y
1

"Modern man can be helped immeasurably by the realization that at the heart of all that is, stands not mere power, but a Person. We have all been aware of the temptation to think of God in impersonal terms, on the mistaken assumption that this has somehow liberated us from childish superstition. . . . The odd consequence is that in this understandable effort, we have moved down rather than up, since a person can know a force while a force cannot know a person or itself. A person is not a being with a body, though we, as finite persons, happen now to inhabit bodies. A person is any being, finite or infinite, capable of reflective thought, or self-consciousness, and of caring. The greatest of these is caring" (Trueblood 1970).

As a child we perhaps pictured God as a tall, strong man with a beard. Or perhaps we imagined God with feminine attributes, even as the Bible does—a mother in travail in childbirth, a woman sweeping the house looking for a lost coin, a mother hen watching over her chicks. Then as we grow older and more educated we feel the need for a more sophisticated image of God. God certainly isn't an old man with a beard, strong as he may be. We begin to think of God in more impersonal terms, as a great force in the world, as the "ground of our being."

Part of our problem comes from the fact that even though we cling to the belief that God is a person, our human language fails us. The only way we can think of a person is through the persons we see, beings with arms and legs and eyes. Yet, moving from a childlike image of God as a person to a more sophisticated, abstract image of force, is a move downward, not upward. The essence of personhood is the ability for self-identification and relationship with others.

Even in the Biblical images of a mother in travail, a woman diligently seeking that which is lost, or the shepherd caring for the sheep, the common thread that runs through them all is the caring relationship. God is one who cares. The Psalms say it over and over. God's steadfast love endures forever.

"The Lord is merciful and gracious, slow to anger and abounding in steadfast love" (Ps. 103:8).

O God, you are far too big for me to understand, but I thank you that you love me and care for me. Amen.

Eternal Mind and the Suffering Servant

D A Y
2

"We tend to proceed with a spiritual naivete, unaware of the sources of our convictions. When we extol service as the mark of greatness, we honor a humility which is more noble than pride, but seldom realize that we might not have understood that it is these very ideas that provide us with some understanding of the Maker of heaven and earth. What if the Eternal Mind, underlying all reality, were indeed the Suffering Servant, with the spirit of the little child. The astounding revelation is that this is true" (Trueblood 1968-69).

Our image of power usually includes thoughts of armies or bombs and the capability of making others do our will through sheer force. God is powerful because God can throw universes out into space and keep them going with minute exactness every second of the time. True, we know that power can easily lead to arrogance, and so even in the human sphere we recognize the strange paradox that extols service as a mark of greatness and honors humility as more noble than pride. Seldom, however, do we think of God's power in a similar way.

There's an old prayer assigned to one of the Sundays of the church year that goes, "O God, thou who showest thine almighty power chiefly in declaring mercy." Mercy? More powerful than creating a universe? But that's what God is like. The eternal mind, the Creator of the universe, is also the suffering servant.

The Master stoops and washes the feet of the disciples. The Lord of all takes children up in his arms when the disciples thought he should not be bothered. Love is the most powerful force in the world. While dying on the cross, Jesus prayed for those who crucified him. Love is the very essence of God, and it has the power to change lives.

The world will never understand this. Even lifelong Christians need to be reminded of this fact constantly. When God wanted to show people the real nature of the divine, God did not send a general leading an army. Well, in a sense it was an army, but not one with guns and tanks and planes carrying bombs, but rather an army of loving people, convinced that love is the most powerful force in the world.

"If I then, your Lord and Teacher, have washed your feet, you also ought to wash one another's feet" (John 13:14).

Lord, in washing your disciples' feet, you taught us not only to serve others, but showed us the very nature of God. Draw us ever closer to that God that we too may understand the true nature of power. Amen.

Still Our Best Hope

DAY 3 *"[Faith] must have certain features, and it must be held with both intellectual integrity and dedication by self-conscious groups of people. Herein lies the crucial relevance of what we mean generally when we refer to the Church, since endurance requires both a spirit and a fellowship. Little is gained without the spirit, and the spirit cannot be maintained by separated individuals. Therefore the Church or something like it must be cherished, criticized, nourished and reformed. The Church of Jesus Christ with all its blemishes, its divisions, and its failures, remains our best hope of spiritual vitality. However poor it is, life without it is worse"* (Trueblood 1961).

Perhaps the greatest strength that a person can have is the assurance that he or she is not alone. In a sense, that is both an active and a passive assurance. When things are going bad for you it's good to know that others are praying for you and are supporting you. You receive their support. That's passive.

On the other hand when you are committed to a cause that is too big for one person, it's again good to know that you have the active support of others committed to that same cause. The church is the best place for both kinds of support. That is not to say that the church is perfect. It is not. There may be times when there is little support of either kind. Part of this may be due to the fact that others in the church simply aren't aware of your hurts so they can comfort you, or of your dreams, so they can assist you. Simply knowing the reason for the lack of support may not be very helpful to you at the time, but at least it helps to explain that usually lack of attention is not deliberate.

The church is indeed "the company of the committed." That means that those of us in the church have a responsibility. We are dependent on each other, and together we are dependent on Christ, whose body the church is. In that church there is strength. The strength comes essentially from Christ, but it also comes from the strength we give each other. We do not all have the same strength. The apostle Paul says it so well, "For as in one body we have many members, and all the members do not have the same function, so we, though many, are one body in Christ, and individually members one of another" (Rom. 12:4-5).

Dear Lord, you are the Lord of the church. We are your representatives here on the earth. Help us to be drawn closer both to you and to brothers and sisters throughout the world who also belong to you, so that together we may worship you and be your faithful witnesses. Amen.

Saints and Sinners

"We need not pay much attention to critics of the existent church when they operate out of obvious hatred or when they have no alternatives to suggest. Mere diagnosis is too easy. But we can rightly pay attention to those who criticize the Church because they love her so deeply that they want her to achieve her true character. . . . The amazing truth is that God creates a community of saints out of sinful men and women. Those who are detached observers do not and cannot know this, but those who are really involved know it because they, themselves, are both saints and sinners. Close contact with a redeemed people makes us both weep and shout for joy, and do both at the same time" (Trueblood 1967a).

You have heard it said, "The reason I don't go to church is that there are too many hypocrites in the church." The accusation is correct, of course. There are hypocrites in the church. That's like saying, "The reason I don't like hospitals is that there are sick people in hospitals." The church is for hypocrites. Not only hypocrites, but liars, and cheaters, and just plain nasty people. But that's only half the story.

Most people in the church don't want to be that way. And they earnestly strive to improve. Paul said it this way to the Romans: "I can will what is right, but I cannot do it. For I do not do the good I want, but the evil I do not want is what I do" (Rom. 7:18-19).

In the church we find some of the best people in the world. Sometimes we also find great disappointments. That's why we have confession in the church and the assurance that God forgives sins. While at times we may grow tired of some of the criticism of the church even by those in the church, we can openly face up to our weaknesses, because we know we are saved by grace and not by being right or having the right answers.

Go anywhere in the world, and even though you may be in a strange community with languages and a culture you do not understand, whenever you find a Christian you have something in common. You may not like everything he or she does, but when you have a common relationship in Christ, misunderstanding is replaced by understanding and a new relationship.

We continue to be both saints and sinners, so as Trueblood says, "Close contact with redeemed people makes us both weep and shout for joy, and do both at the same time."

O Lord, we thank you for the church. It's not perfect. But there is forgiveness, and because we have the assurance of your forgiving love, let us not be too defensive when someone points out some of our weaknesses. Help us to be considerate of each other's weaknesses and pray for strength and healing for all. Amen.

The Temptation to Grandeur

DAY
5

"Few features of official religion, of any particular faith, are more open to ridicule than is ostentation. The Christian faith, which began with an emphasis upon simplicity and humility, as vividly illustrated by the acted parable of the washing of the disciples' feet, has succumbed, in various generations, to the temptation to grandeur. Christ saw it coming and gave advance warning, though the warning has been seldom heeded" (Trueblood 1975a).

One of the problems confronting Christians is to allow good things to get in the way of better things. Good music and art, beautiful church buildings, effective and efficient organizational structure to enable the work of the church to be done well, are all good things. God gave specific instructions for the building of the Tabernacle so that it was attractive. When Solomon built the Temple, there was nothing too good for God. Jesus swept away the criticism of those who thought that the woman who anointed him with costly oil was wasteful. God does not have a depression complex. He literally lavishes us with good things.

There can, however, be a temptation to grandeur, for at times, it can be emphasized so much that the basis of Christianity is lost. Simplicity, humility, and washing of disciples' feet are of the essence of the Christian faith. A full recognition of that temptation should lead us to seek a balance between those activities that are absolutely essential to the faith and those that may be helpful but not absolutely essential.

There will not always be agreement on the identification of the two. We are often in danger of looking down on those who may have different opinions. There is indeed room for grandeur in worship, for the God we worship is majestic. The Wise Men sensed that and brought their gifts of gold, frankincense, and myrrh.

But just as God chose a lowly manger in Bethlehem rather than a palace in Jerusalem as the birthplace for the Saviour, so we also need to pause from time to time and ask whether we are tempted by grandeur and ostentation. The washing of disciples' feet is more expressive of the power of love than a parade of army generals dressed in full uniform.

Psalm 150 and Amos 5:21-24

O God, you are marvelous and majestic beyond all words. Since words cannot give full expression to your glory we thank you for the gift of the arts to beautify our worship. May they always be a means to an end and not the end itself. Give us an appreciation of simplicity and humility, as shown us by Jesus himself when he washed the feet of his disciples. Amen.

Life in Scorn of Consequences

D A Y
6

"We understand much of the distinction between religion and other phases of our lives when we sense the profound difference between faith and belief. Faith is closer to courage than it is to intellectual assent. Faith is easily understood by the gambler . . . because the gambler stands to win or lose by his play. This was brought out in Kirsopp Lake's now classic definition, "Faith is not belief in spite of evidence, but life in scorn of consequences." Faith, as the plain man knows, is not belief without proof, but trust without reservations" (Trueblood 1967b).

A definition of faith that many of us have been brought up on is, "Faith is believing what we can't prove." I can't prove that the sun will come up tomorrow morning, but I have faith that it will. It may be overshadowed by clouds, but I still know that the sun is up there somewhere.

But there is more to faith than just knowing intellectually that something is so or will happen even though I don't have absolute proof. Faith also means *acting* on what I believe. Because I believe the sun will come up tomorrow and because I believe I will wake up in the morning I will act accordingly. I will work today and know that what I don't get finished, I can still work on tomorrow.

However, what if the sun hadn't come up for 100 days in a row? Would I still believe that there was a sun, and would I still continue to plant crops? What if the doctor told me I had only a few months left to live? Would I continue to go on living as though every day mattered?

Martin Luther once said, "If I were sure that the end of the world would come tomorrow, I would plant a tree today." There is a "nevertheless" about faith. There may be times when all the evidence points to there not being a loving God, but the "nevertheless" of faith says with Job of the Old Testament, "Though he slay me, yet will I trust in him." More than just believing that intellectually, faith provides the courage to live that conviction, to live "in scorn of the consequences." Faith, then, is stronger than belief. I may believe that a circus performer is able to push a wheelbarrow with a person in it across a high wire. That belief turns to faith when I am willing to be the person in the wheelbarrow and trust without reservation.

Romans 8:31-39

Oh Lord, I believe; help thou my unbelief. At times we are weak. We know also that you understand our weakness. Our simple prayer is, "Forgive our lack of trust and give us the courage of faith." Amen.

Learning to Pray by Praying

"It is not irrational to suppose that God's cosmic purpose includes such a self-limitation of His power that some events do not occur apart from the prayers of finite men. Then, with the major barriers lowered, or at least made less formidable, we are ready to learn to pray by praying. If we take seriously the wisdom about entering as a little child, our prayers need not be grand or polished. It is helpful to know that we shall not be heard for our much speaking. Indeed, a great part of prayer need not involve words at all, for words are not the music, but only the movements of the conductor's baton. As our contemporary world becomes ever more noisy, silence is hard to find, but it can be found if we really prize it" (Trueblood 1968-69).

Prayer is both the simplest and the most profound of spiritual activities. Jesus himself tells us to think of prayer as talking to a loving father. This presupposes that there is a good relationship between parents and children. Unfortunately, this is not always the case, but when the relationship is a good one, the image of praying to a loving parent is powerful.

We can do something about improving that relationship. Jesus came to show us what God was like: loving and compassionate. But no matter how loving a person may be, if we deliberately avoid that person, then a loving relationship cannot be established.

A child often has an easier grasp of prayer and a greater faith that prayers will be answered. Children will learn that prayer is not magic, but that evening prayers bring closeness to God, and memories of childhood prayers stay with them for a long time.

Prayer also raises profound questions. Is God really moved by our prayers? If so, then are we not bigger than God if we can move God to do things? Even scientific research that is being done today illustrates how God often uses prayers in behalf of other people. In the human body itself, for instance, it has been shown that a good attitude will cause the brain to produce endorphins that bring healing. And the prayers of many people concentrating on a specific person releases a power within that person.

No matter how profound or how simple prayer may be, it will remain something of a mystery. We learn to pray by praying. Sometimes the words may come hard, or they may not come at all, but an attitude of prayer brings a feeling of the presence of God. Out of quietness often comes great strength. (Luke 11:9-13)

Lord, sometimes it's difficult to pray. Our mind wanders. We can't find the right words. We even wonder if it does any good at all to pray. Give us that childlike faith that believes that you hear prayers. Amen.

Greater When It Comes as a Surprise

<table>
<tr><td>D A Y
8</td><td>*"Personal happiness must never become our chief end or goal. The purpose is not to be happy, but to perpetuate what is best for human life. Of course happiness usually comes in such a procedure, but it comes as a by-product. Emerson says wisely that the beauty of the*</td></tr>
</table>

sunrise or sunset is greater when it comes as a surprise by the way" (Trueblood 1953).

We hear much about happiness these days, and books are written telling us how to achieve it. There is a difference of opinion as to exactly what happiness is. The dictionary gives these definitions: good fortune, pleasure, contentment, gladness. Many people have the impression that if you have good fortune and pleasure, then you are glad and content.

Rabbi Harold Kushner, author of *When All You've Ever Wanted Isn't Enough*, says, "The reason you shouldn't put all of your trust in stocks is not that the stock market may crash and you lose everything, but that even if it kept going up and you gained a fortune, it would not guarantee happiness." Good fortune and pleasure alone do not always bring happiness.

There are some who question the translation of the Beatitudes in *The Living Bible*, using the word *happy* instead of *blessed*. Blessedness and happiness are not the same, at least not according to the popular definition of happiness. Blessedness brings a deeper dimension. One of the dictionary definitions of blessedness is indeed happiness, but others have a deeper meaning. To be blessed means to be divinely favored. True happiness exists when in the midst of trials and bad fortune and when life seems anything but pleasurable, you can still have a good feeling.

Paul wrote to the Philippians, "I know how to be abased, and I know how to abound; in any and all circumstances I have learned the secret of facing plenty and hunger, abundance and want" (Phil. 4:12). Perhaps that's also why he could say, "I can do all things in him who strengthens me" (Phil. 4:13).

It's not wrong to seek happiness. The trick is to know where to look for it. Trueblood gives us a clue. It's more likely to come as a surprise, as the by-product of having done a noble deed.

Philippians 4:8-13

Lord Jesus, you have given us the true recipe for happiness by serving others. Please give us your servant spirit. Amen.

Self-Expression—a Two-Edged Sword

DAY 9

"Just as our popular philosophy is ambiguous about happiness, it is likewise ambiguous about self-expression. Just what do we mean by it? Which side of ourselves do we propose to express? The idea of self-expression does not really help us, since the beastly side can be expressed just as the potential nobility can be expressed. Anyone who expressed all his thoughts and obeyed all his impulses would surely reveal himself as an utter fool" (Trueblood 1953).

One of the marvelous characteristics of us as human beings is that we are made in the image of God: we can think and are free to choose between right and wrong. Another one of the marvels is that we all have individual characteristics. No two of us are exactly alike. Our own personality, therefore, is precious both to us and to God. We can and ought to use it to glorify God. We also ought to enjoy our personality.

Recently a lot of emphasis has been placed on self-expression, so much so that it has almost become a cult. But just as there is misunderstanding about happiness, so there is misunderstanding about self-expression. We have two sides to express. Which side should we express?

Human beings did not stay in the state of perfection in which God created us. Unpleasant as it may sound, there is sin in the world. There is sin in us. We do not always act out of the highest of motives. Should we be given free reign to encourage the self-expression of our baser nature?

On the other hand, psychologists tell us that great damage can be done if we constantly suppress urges for self-expression. Many of us know people whose personalities have been damaged because they have never felt free to express themselves.

How to solve the problem? We begin with thanksgiving for the marvelous creation of human beings. We pray for guidance that we may use opportunities to "bring out the best in us," always realizing that the gifts we have come from God. We recognize that when we express ourselves we need to be sensitive to other people whose self-expression may be at odds with ours. In fact, one of the best ways of using our self-expression is to encourage expression in others. It would be a dull world if all were alike. We ourselves are enriched by the self-expression of others.

1 Corinthians 12:12-26

God of creation, may we never be ashamed of our individual gifts or put on a false modesty that would deny your very creation of those gifts. But may we be sensitive to the needs of others and encourage them to think highly of themselves also. Amen.

Discipline—A Source of Strength

DAY 10

"As we analyze the experiences of the faithful and courageous minorities we find that there is one factor which all have in common, the acceptance of discipline. The Orthodox Jews have the discipline of the refusal to eat pork, or the separate Sabbath, and of the specially donned clothing during prayer. All this makes them a people apart, sometimes persecuted and despised, but the discipline, however trivial it may seem, is a source of strength. The faithful Roman Catholic has the discipline of confession, of early mass, of the Friday fast. This last may be largely fictitious since fish is regularly substituted for meat, but the very reminder is helpful to many. In any case it is beneficent to have the ordinary Western rule of self-indulgence and doing what you please limited at even a few points" (Trueblood 1948).

Trueblood wrote his *Alternative to Futility* before the Second Vatican Council, at a time when Catholics generally refrained from eating meat on Friday. There are still Catholics who think that something was lost when they gave up that practice.

We tend to take New Year's resolutions lightly, or jokingly refer to what we give up for Lent. These disciplines may become trivialized but they don't have to become that way. Discipline can bring strength.

I was attending a worship service once in a church in the Bronx. The community had changed, the public schools had become badly run down, there was little discipline. The pastor told me before the service, "You may be surprised to see the 10- to 13-year-old kids singing our liturgy from memory. This is the only time of the week when they know what comes next." They appreciated the discipline of having memorized something.

Prisoners in concentration camps during World War II often expressed appreciation that they had been made to memorize Scripture and the Catechism in their youth. They didn't like it at the time, but the discipline of having been made to memorize gave them something to hang on to.

Athletes know about discipline. So do business executives and virtually everyone who is successful. Discipline requires willingly submitting to some rules and regulations that may inhibit us for some short-term activities, but strengthen us for long-range accomplishments.

1 Corinthians 9:19-27 and Philippians 3:12-16

Lord Jesus, you disciplined yourself, taking the form of a servant. Help us to submit to the kind of discipline that will strengthen our character so that we may be witnesses to your power. Amen.

Streams Rather Than Swamps

<table>
<tr><td>

D A Y
11

</td><td>

"Was the strict Quaker discipline of an earlier day a mistake or not? It is hard to know. It is easy to see why the strictness kept a man like Walt Whitman from joining the fellowship even though he was deeply drawn to it on other grounds. . . . But, having

</td></tr>
</table>

recognized these difficulties, we must also admit that the older Quaker discipline was a source of enormous moral strength. It was like high, straight banks, which make a stream run swiftly instead of spreading into swamps. In the lives of John Woolman, Elizabeth Fry, John Greenleaf Whittier, and many more the disciplined simplicity of speech, clothing, and manner of life released energy for social concern. We have now given it up, but what have we put in its place?" (Trueblood 1948).

Discipline has become so outmoded that it is useful to devote two days to the subject. When I was a child, a question often asked about teachers was, "Is she—or he—strict?" Children liked teachers who were not too strict, while parents appreciated those who were more strict.

Strictness and discipline mean insisting on exactness and precision. They call for greater effort, not being satisfied until the best is accomplished. It's true, strictness and discipline can be taken to the extreme, and then it's questionable whether it makes the Christian faith attractive or not.

The argument is often used, "Why make it so hard for people to get into the church? Why set up all kinds of rules and regulations? Are they really necessary?" For instance, if church functions interfere with school or sports events, won't it turn people—particularly young people—against the church if they are forced to go to catechism classes instead of sports events?

These are not easy questions. Parents and children need to consider them seriously. They present an excellent opportunity to discuss what is important in life. One problem is that it is easy to give in to pressures on either side and then years later regret the decisions that were made.

A river needs the discipline of banks or it becomes a swamp. When an engineer plans to build a bridge over a stream 50 feet wide, he can't say, "The bridge ought to be somewhere between 40 and 60 feet long." It needs to be quite precise. Life is as important as a bridge. It needs the disciplines of a bank to keep it from becoming a swamp.

Ephesians 6:10-20

O God, it is so easy to neglect the discipline of prayer or Bible reading or doing deeds of love. Renew our priorities so that these things may not be chores, but joyful means to an energized commitment. Amen.

The System That Sets Us Free

"That system of life is good which sets men free, which releases divinely given powers, which provides for the nourishment of the spiritual life in all its phases. That system is evil which denies brotherhood and ceases to look on separate men as absolute ends, sacred in and of themselves. . . . Our belief in the sacredness of human life must be transmuted into a powerful love which makes us break the chains which bind men because we really care. In this way we shall gain the power to know blasphemy when it appears and to go beyond" (Trueblood 1975b).

Usually when we think of our devotional life, we somehow separate it from our everyday work. Yet we spend a larger amount of our time at work than at any other activity—hobbies, family, church, even sleeping.

Spirituality is, in a sense, an awareness of the presence of God and our response to that presence. If we're not aware of God's presence in the workplace, how can we respond? How can we have any spirituality?

Most of us work within some kind of system. That system both limits us and gives us opportunities and challenges. Some things in that system may be beyond our control, but we also have the obligation to help shape that system. It is in our daily work as we help shape that system that we need to be reminded of Trueblood's insights about the sacredness of human life, the sacredness of those who work with us.

Jesus didn't talk much about supernatural events. He talked about things that people saw around themselves in everyday life: shepherds and widows and runaway sons, lost coins, and mustard seeds, sly servants and generous Samaritans, full barns and beaten travellers.

If our devotional time draws us away from our daily work, it should do so only momentarily, to strengthen us so that we may reenter the "system" with renewed vigor for serving God there. And one way to serve God, as Trueblood says, is to work for a system that sets people free, that releases divinely given powers, that provides for the nourishment of spiritual life.

Colossians 3:12-17

God, Creator of the world, you have called us to be managers of the world. We are each called to various occupations and vocations in which we exercise that stewardship. Grant that we may never think of our daily work as being second rate. It is there that we serve others, and by serving them, serve you. Give us insights into how we can best witness for you in that system so that it may become a holy place. Amen.

Sunday No Substitute for Wednesday

DAY 13

"Part of what we need in economic order is a revival of common honesty. It is conceivable that men of our time might come to take pride in meticulous care in the keeping of promises and strictness with themselves in matters of integrity. There have been periods like that before and they could come again, but they will not come of themselves. We are making a start in this direction when we give the widest possible dissemination to the idea that no amount of piety on Sunday will take the place of integrity on Wednesday" (Trueblood 1952).

Piety is no substitute for performance. There is need for both, and God is interested in both. Martin Luther once said that a Christian shoemaker does not exercise his Christian vocation by putting crosses on the shoes he makes. He makes good shoes, because God wants good workmanship. A Christian maid does not exercise her Christian vocation by singing a hymn while she sweeps the floor. She does it by doing a good job of sweeping because God likes clean floors.

We sometimes get so absorbed in our talk about piety that we apply it only to activities within the church or to behavior that may offend other pious people. Piety is a perfectly good word. The dictionary defines it as reverence for God. Integrity is another good word. It is defined as soundness of moral principle and character, uprightness and honesty.

We really do not live in two worlds, a secular world of our work and occupation and a spiritual world of our prayer life. The two belong together. God is as interested in our work as in our prayers. And it is in our work that we need to develop honesty and integrity and skills so that the work may be well-pleasing to God. Sloppiness in one can easily lead to sloppiness in the other. We cannot excuse our carelessness and goofing off at our work on Wednesday by going to church on Sunday.

America has been going through a period of carelessness, of being satisfied with slip-shod work, or not taking pride in meticulousness. That tendency has spiritual dimensions as well as practical, economic implications. It helps explain why other countries are getting ahead of us in many areas. Fortunately, there is a reawakening to the need for integrity and honesty. Wednesday and Sunday need to go together.

O God, you are no stranger to work. You have ordered the world in such a way that we help you take care of it. That sounds almost like blasphemy, but you yourself have told us that it is so. We thank you for the honor you have bestowed on us with this assignment. Give us now a willingness to fulfill our daily tasks with integrity and joy. Amen.

The Priority of Family

DAY 14 *"No matter how much a man may be concerned with his work in the world, he cannot normally care about it as much as he cares about his family. This is because we have, in the life of the family, a bigger stake than most of us can ever have in our employment. We can change business associates, if we need to, and we can leave a poor job for a better one, but we cannot change sons. If we lose the struggle in our occupational interests, we can try again, but if we lose with our children our loss is terribly and frighteningly final. A man who cares more for his work than he cares for his family is generally accounted abnormal or perverse and justifiably so. He is one who has not succeeded in getting his values straight; he fails to recognize what the true priorities are"* (Trueblood 1952).

Important as our work may be, our families are more important. The two are related, of course. Work is important to support family, and so at times adjustments must be made for short-range family sacrifice so that work can prosper to make possible a better long-term care for family.

But it is easy to get hooked on work and forget family. Then values need to be straightened out. *Values*—that's the key word. Harmon Killebrew, the famous home run hitter, says that his father never complained when the boys tore up the grass while playing baseball. "It's more important to grow boys than to grow grass," he said.

It takes deliberate effort and planning to keep a proper balance between work and family. In a college commencement address given by a domestic relations court judge nearly 50 years ago, he said, "A man may be very successful in business but if his family falls apart, he will be a failure. On the other hand, a person may not have reached all of his goals in the business world, but if he has managed to rear a good family, he has been successful."

Perhaps that is a slight oversimplification because one person is never totally responsible for what happens in a family, but the point is well made. Family is the place where lasting relationships are built. My own father was never very successful as a farmer, but during the depression years he reared a family of children—all of whom lived in great harmony with each other and their parents all during their lives. That did not happen by accident. My father and mother had their priorities straight, and I am thankful.

Lord, the family is indeed a profound mystery. You have placed us in families. In families we learn about relationships. You yourself have told us that in the family we even have a picture of what God is like. Many things would drive us away from giving proper attention to family life. Give us a sense of values so that we may prize this great gift of family and through it find joy and a way of serving you. Amen.

JOHN BUNYAN

J OHN BUNYAN (1628–1688), son of Thomas Bunyan Jr. and Margaret Bentley, was born in the heart of the English midlands. He was to spend all of his life in this small, rural village of Elstow, which was next door to Bedford. John grew up in a poor, humble home. He who was to become a world-renowned author attended elementary school for about two years. At the age of 16, he joined the army of the Parliament fighting for the cause of liberty against the troops of the Government. His military adventure was more family than politically motivated. John Bunyan joined the army to get away from home!

Returning from the army, and becoming a tinker, a brazier, a traveling fixer and seller of pots and pans, John married the daughter of a devout Protestant. John said this about his marriage, "Until I came to the state of marriage, I was the very ringleader in all manner of vice and ungodliness." John's wife gave him a good push toward maturity. During these years his life was like a "seesaw" between hope and despair. During this time the Bible and Luther's commentary on Galatians prepared him for baptism. At the age of 25 he was baptized and joined the Baptist Church in Bedford. He was to remain a member of that church all his life—serving as deacon, lay preacher and pastor.

In 1660 he was arrested and the next 12 years of his life were spent in prison. But jail did not dampen his spirit nor weaken his devotion to ministry. From prison he sent forth book after book, all of which demonstrated remarkable knowledge of the Bible.

In 1672 John Bunyan was set free. He became the preacher/pastor of the Bedford congregation. In this small, simple place John Bunyan became the focus of a renewal movement and the rallying place for growing crowds of worshipers. He attracted people with his zeal, wit, and insight. He had a great sense of humor. He preached and ministered to all people with great passion and compassion. On a forty-mile trip to London he was drenched and chilled by a driving rainstorm. He caught a fever and, at the age of sixty, died.

These Words upon Your Heart

DAY 1 *"Read, and read again, and do not despair of help to understand something of the will and mind of God, though you think they are fast locked up from you. Neither trouble your heads though you have not commentaries and expositions; pray and read, and read and pray. . . . There is nothing that so abides with us as what we receive from God. . . . Things that we receive at God's hand come to us as things from the minting-house, though old in themselves, yet new to us. Old truths are always new to us, if they come to us with the smell of heaven upon them"* (Kepler 1952).

It is through words that we are encountered by God. This is what we mean when we say, "the Word of God is a means of grace." It is the means, the way, the method through which God meets us. God is revealed to us through human language.

So, early in the Bible we read these words from Moses, "And these words which I command you this day shall be upon your heart; and you shall teach them diligently to your children, and shall talk of them when you sit in your house, and when you walk by the way, and when you lie down, and when you rise" (Deut. 6:6-7).

"These words upon your heart" are the most valuable heritage the chosen people of God had. Virtually every crisis that God's people faced, the word of God was there to provide a lamp for the feet and light for the path.

Luke, the author of the Book of Acts, tells us that missionary Paul "argued with the people from the scriptures . . . explaining and proving that it was necessary for the Christ to suffer and to rise from the dead." It was in this congregation that Paul and Silas were described in those never-to-be-forgotten words: "These men, who have turned the world upside down, have come here also" (Acts 17:6).

"Read and read again. . . ." This counsel by Bunyan remains timely and on target. We have good intentions, but it seems we make little progress. Don't despair. Don't quit. Your reading of this devotional book may mark a new beginning of Bible reading for you.

Read Deuteronomy 6:1-9 and Acts 17.

Caesar or God?

DAY 2

"That which makes a martyr is suffering for the word of God after a right manner. And that is when he suffers not only for righteousness, but for righteousness' sake; not only for truth, but for love of truth; not only for God's word, but according to it; to wit, in that holy, humble, meek manner that the word of God requires" (Kepler, 1952).

"You will go to prison for six months," said the judge. So Bunyan went to prison for nothing worse than preaching in the little Bedford Baptist Church. But it was against the law. He told Justice Keeling, "If I was out of prison today, I would preach the gospel again tomorrow, by the help of God." So it was back to prison. This time for 12 years. And again for six months. He who gave us the great classic *Pilgrim's Progress*, spent one-fifth of his life in jail.

Martin Luther told the government: "Here I stand! I can do no other." Bunyan refused to give any promise that would bind his conscience and so he remained a prisoner for the best part of his adult life.

A few years ago I had some lengthy conversations with one of our sons. He did not want to register for the draft. My counsel was that he should register and if need be could make his stand later on. In retrospect my advice sounded much like that of Mr. Worldly Wiseman of *Pilgrim's Progress* who lived in the town of Carnal Policy. Worldly Wiseman: "But why will you seek for ease this way, since so many dangers attend it?"

One wonders how different our world would be if Bunyan had given in to Caesar? One wonders how different our world would be if more people would have said no to Hitler. Isn't Stanley Hauerwas right in his statement, "Auschwitz began when Christians assumed that they could be the heirs and carriers of the symbols of the faith without sacrifice and suffering" (*Truthfulness and Tragedy*, University of Notre Dame Press, 1977).

Bunyan is a good example for our time. For today the temptation is to hand over more and more of our decisions to Caesar.

Read Matthew 22:15-21.

The Throne of Grace

"Grace can pardon our ungodliness and justify us with Christ's righteousness; it can put the Spirit of Jesus Christ within us; it can help us when we are down; it can heal us when we are wounded; it can multiply pardons as we through frailty multiply transgressions" (Kepler 1952).

Somewhere I read the great twentieth-century theologian Karl Barth said something like this: "God's judgment doesn't bother us, we can handle that. But God's grace, that scares the devil out of us." It is hard for us to believe that God loves sinners while they are still sinners! It just doesn't make sense.

The elder brother in Jesus' beautiful story of the prodigal son was right. He had every reason to be angry. The "good news" for his rascally brother was most unfair. How can you run a world that way?

Yet for me and for many others, the most beautiful picture of grace in all of Scriptures is the father welcoming home his young son. We hear that the father does not wait for the son, but runs to meet him. And he doesn't even permit this wasteful rascal to finish his confession. He chokes it off with a big bear hug and then calls for the ring, the shoes, and the robe, all powerful symbols of instant restoration to the family. In this memorable homecoming we see the sheer goodness of God.

Bunyan experienced God's grace. He entitled his spiritual biography, *Grace Abounding to the Chief of Sinners*. This is one of his definitions of grace: "But do thou remember that the grace of God is his good-will and great love to sinners, in his Son Jesus Christ." He also compares the grace of God to a river: "so those who live by grace are compared to fish; for that, as water is that element in which the fish lives, so grace is that which is the life of the saint."

Jesus' great parable of the prodigal son was directed to people who, like the elder brother, were offended at the gospel. We may have a similar problem. Thus the story of the loving father becomes the story for repentant young people who are wasting their lives in "riotous living." But the "far country" can be a bank as well as a tavern. The elder brother is a powerful witness to the fact that one doesn't even have to leave home to be far from the father. "The far country," writes Augustine, "is forgetfulness of God." But God loves us even in the far country. Ours is a mercy, not a merit religion. Thanks be to God for the throne of grace.

Read Luke 15.

Grace of Fear

DAY
4

"It seems to me as if this grace of fear was the darling grace, the grace that God set his heart upon at the highest rate.... This grace of fear is the softest and most tender of God's honor of all the graces.... We cannot watch as we should, if we are destitute of fear.... This grace of fear can make the man that in many other things is not capable of serving God, serve him better than those that have all else without it" (Kepler 1952).

One wonders if we who have developed such a cozy familiarity with the Almighty can have any appreciation for Bunyan's "grace of fear." I read somewhere that Isaiah's tormented cry, "I'm of unclean lips and I dwell in the midst of a people of unclean lips," has been replaced by the comfortable, popular response, "Lord, I do the best I can, you know ... you know. After all you don't expect us to be perfect, do you?" C. S. Lewis called this a "flabby kind" of religion and so it is.

But the other side of that observation is that many of us desire something more substantial in our relationship with God than someone whom we can manipulate. Is there any way we can restore the tension between the lowly Lord who is our pal and the High and Holy One who is our Lord?

Maybe a beginning could be made if we would look more kindly on the word *fear* (or reverence, which is its basic meaning). Luther reminds us in the Small Catechism that the true interpretation of the First and chief Commandment, "Thou shall have no other gods before me," means simply this: "Thou shalt fear, love, and trust in God above everything else." It is Luther's contention that the Bible gives emphasis to these two points— fear of and trust in God.

Bunyan speaks of the "grace of fear." He also describes the "fear of the Lord as the pulse of the soul." So he urges us to pray, "Lord, unite my heart to fear thy name, and do not harden mine heart from thy fear."

Read Genesis 28:10-17 and Luke 9:28-36.

Fear Need Not Own Us

D A Y 5

"There are but few when they come to the cross, say Welcome, cross! as some of the martyrs did to the stake they were burned at. Therefore, if you meet with the cross in thy journey, in what manner soever it be, be not daunted and say, Alas, what shall I do now? but rather take courage, knowing that by the cross is the way to the kingdom. Can one believe in Christ and not be hated by the devil? Can one make a profession of Christ, and that sweetly and convincingly, and the children of Satan hold their tongue? Can darkness agree with light?" (Kepler 1952).

There is fear afoot in our world, but it is not the fear of God. I can't prove it, but I have the suspicion that the more casual we have become toward God, the greater our fears in and of the world. Death has always been a great fear, but in our time that is in danger of being replaced by our fear of living. Fear is reshaping the center and focus of our lives. It intensifies the greed in us. Fear empowers the arms race. Our massive military preparations to avoid war are making us prisoners of our own fears. Bunyan's character "Mr. Fearing" is insightful at this point: *"Mr. Fearing was one that played upon the bass. For my part, I care not at all for that profession that begins not in heaviness of mind. The first string that the musician usually touches is the bass, when he intends to put all in tune; God also plays upon this string first, when he set the soul in tune for himself. Only, there was the imperfection of Mr. Fearing, he could play upon no other music but this till toward his latter end."*

James Forest tells the story of young Mel Hollander who received the very bad news that he was dying of cancer and at the most had six months to live. He heard of a course at Union Theological Seminary for those who would be working with the dying. Mel registered for it and also for a course on the book of Revelation being taught by Daniel Berrigan. At the opening of Berrigan's class Mel was quite nervous. He was aware of his physical condition and fearful of what other people might say. Teacher Berrigan focused on him and asked: "What's the matter?" Mel, thinking the question was rude, responded: "I'm dying of cancer." There was brief pause and then Berrigan's response: "That must be very exciting." It was the moment of transfiguration for Mel. It wasn't that he was no longer fearful, but fear no longer owned him. (*Sojourners*, February 1980).

Read Romans 8:31-39.

Life in the Wilderness

D A Y

6

"The school of the cross is the school of light: it discovers the world's vanity, baseness, and wickedness, and lets us see more of God's mind. Out of dark afflictions comes a spiritual light" (Kepler 1952).

For most of chapter 15 in the book of Exodus, the children of Israel have a good time celebrating. But then they are in the wilderness. And it is not like our protected wilderness areas. No, the wilderness was a lonely place full of fear, danger, and suffering. The people of God became thirsty, hungry, and lost. They wanted to go back to Egypt, but instead spent forty years in the wilderness—as long as most of our careers.

Jesus had just been baptized. He heard the promise: "You are my beloved son in whom I am well pleased." The first result of that promise was trouble. The same Spirit who called him "beloved" now ordered him into the wilderness to be tested by the Evil One. As Israel, the old "Son of God," was tested through forty years in the wilderness, so also there was struggle and testing for Jesus Christ. Jesus went from the mountain on Sunday to the wilderness on Monday.

Because he persisted in preaching the word of God, which was contrary to the laws of the state, Bunyan was arrested and put into the county jail of Bedford. This was no modern prison, but a place of stench and dirt. The best part of Bunyan's life was spent in this place. The prisoner saw his suffering as an opportunity that might stir up "the saints in the country" to renewed dedication and faithfulness.

We like to think that life in Christ is an escape from wilderness living. Sometimes that is how the faith is proclaimed—salvation is equated with the American Dream. But that is an illusion. Though our testing experiences may not be as severe as they were for Jesus or Bunyan (if we lived in South Africa it would be different!), there is no way back to Egypt or forward to the promised land except through the wilderness.

The testing in the wilderness reveals what we are made of. The journey continues. But it continues with our Lord who in all ways was tested as we are.

Hope Has a Thick Skin

DAY 7 *"Despair undervalues the promise, undervalues the invitation, undervalues the offer of grace. Despair undervalues the ability of God the Father, and the redeeming blood of Christ his Son. Oh, unreasonable despair"* (Kepler 1952).

Our century began in an "orgy of optimism." That optimism died with the Great War, World War One—one of the most horrendous wars in history. In its wake, we feel we are left only with despair; as Henri Nouwen writes: "[We live in] a world clouded with an all-pervading fear, a growing sense of despair, and the paralyzing awareness that humanity has come to the verge of suicide."

In order not to despair, we may turn to either of two extremes. One is called cynicism. It seeks to save people from their own expectations. Today cynicism is being replaced by narcissism. Our cynics want to be left alone to enjoy themselves. On the other side of the fence we have the "credulous ones," shutting their eyes to the real world. One believes in believing, no matter the evidence to the contrary. One's expectations are guided by unquestioned assumptions.

So it is hard not to despair. Bunyan indicates his personal struggle with despair in these words, "I would say to my soul, O my soul, this is not the place of despair; this is not the time to despair in. . . . As long as there is a moment left in me of breath or life in this world, so long will I wait or look for mercy, so long will I fight against unbelief and despair."

So cynicism wants to get rid of expectation, and credulity wants to ignore experience. It is our faith that holds together both expectation and experience. The focal point of that tension is the cross of Jesus Christ. Faith doesn't lie about the world and will accept the struggle. It is in continual dialogue with its constant shadow—doubt. But in the struggle, faith does not give up on the promise.

Herein is our hope. "Faith is the assurance of things hoped for, the conviction of things not seen" (Heb. 11:1). Hope is faith fulfilled in the future. Preacher Bunyan writes: "Faith says to hope, Look for what is promised. Hope says to faith, so I do, and will wait for it too. Hope has a thick skin and will endure many a blow."

Read Romans 5:1-5 and 8:18-30.

Loving God with Our Mind

D A Y 8 *"The greatest part of professors nowadays take up their time in contracting guilt and asking for pardon, and yet are not much the better. Whereas, if they had but the grace to add to their faith, virtue, etc., they might have more peace, live better lives and not have their heads so often in a bag, as they have"* (Kepler 1952).

An outspoken individual, Daniel Webster said, "Education can make us into clever devils." Bunyan would have agreed. Of keen mind and good judgment, he seemed to be unduly suspicious of formal education. He read few books and justified his ignorance because it permitted the Spirit to work unhindered.

There is an old story about an airline pilot that goes like this: after the plane had gone through a terrible storm the pilot said to the passengers, "I'm sorry about the rough ride, but there wasn't much I could do about it. I think we are through the worst of it, although there are still a few problems. We have lost our navigational equipment. It appears that we are lost, but I want you to know that we are making good time."

"It appears that we are lost, but we are making good time," could well be the epitaph of our century. Clever devils are more concerned with ends than with the means to an end. Their first question is not: "Is this the right thing to do?" but rather, "Is this going to be effective?" This provokes the need for education to produce *wise saints*, not clever devils.

Of course we are not saved by our education. But neither does salvation place a premium on ignorance. To the woman of Samaria Christ said, "You worship what you do not know" (John 4:22). Too many of us are in that predicament today, fumbling and groping in a kind of theological fog with inaccurate compasses making us vulnerable to clever devils.

The great commandment reminds us to not only love God with our whole heart and soul, but also with our mind.

Read Matthew 22:34-40 and Ephesians 4:11-15.

A Sense of Sin

"He that will keep water in a sieve, must use more than ordinary diligence. Our heart is a leaky vessel; and therefore we ought to give the more earnest heed to the things which we have heard; lest at any time we should let them slip" (Kepler 1952).

In a recent newspaper article, George Drake, president of Grinnell College, wrote of a growing willingness in our society "to cut corners and to misrepresent the truth." He concluded: "We are ethically flabby." He went on to say, "Ethical values don't just happen . . . they require a disciplined effort, and it is not at all clear that we are making the effort" (*Des Moines Register,* Aug. 24, 1986).

This is how Bunyan saw the situation in his day: ". . . it is manifest that sin has a friendly entertainment by the soul, and that therefore the soul is guilty of damnation; for what do all these things argue, but that God, his word, his ways and graces, are out of favor with the soul, and that sin and Satan are its only pleasant companions?" Sin as "friendly entertainment" becomes in our time "flabby ethics."

Perhaps we have been quite naive of human sinfulness. Maybe we're unwilling to come to terms with the awesome truth about who we are and why we do the things we do.

I would like to suggest that we might recapture a "sense of sin" if today we would attempt to see sin as "self-deception." One of the basic reasons we are so vulnerable to deceiving ourselves is the great power of self-interest. This power prompts us to shape, explain, and understand the circumstances of our life to serve our needs. We build convincing illusions that hide our deception. These illusions are so useful and used so much that we begin to accept them as reality. So we say, "Business is business and I am entitled to a fair profit"; "don't look a gift horse in the mouth"; "one has to survive"; "that's politics"; "I'm a company person." So go our explanations and understandings.

"Behold, thou desirest truth in the inward being" (Ps. 51:6). Recognition of our self-deception can lead to the reorientation of repentance, and calls us to accept the responsibility for deceitful actions. Repentance is "truth in the inward being." "If we confess our sins, Jesus is faithful and just and will forgive our sins and cleanse us from all unrighteousness" (1 John 1:9).

Read Psalm 51 and 1 John 1:8-10.

Who Speaks for the Poor?

DAY 10 *"There are two sorts of good works; and a man may be shrewdly guessed at with reference to his faith, even by the works that he chooses to be conversant in. There are works that cost nothing, and works that are chargeable; and observe it, the unsound faith will choose to itself the most easy works it can find: for example, there is reading, praying, hearing of sermons, baptism, breaking of bread, church-fellowship, preaching, and the like; and there is mortification of lusts, charity, simplicity, and open-heartedness with a liberal hand to the poor, and their like also"* (Kepler 1952).

It has been pointed out that the most pessimistic statement Jesus made is his conclusion of the uncomfortable Rich Man/Poor Man story: "If they do not hear Moses and the prophets, neither will they be convinced if some one should rise from the dead" (Luke 16:31).

The rich man and the poor man die. But here is the great reversal. The rich man ends up in hell and the poor man is safe in the arms of Abraham. In many of Jesus' parables, the real point is revealed in the last sentence. The point of this story is the massive indifference and apathy on the part of the rich in regard to the poor. The real issue is not inequality, but inequality coupled with indifference. If the rich do not learn sympathy with the Bible in their hands and Lazarus at their gates, not even a voice from the dead will convince them.

Bunyan was a noteworthy example in his day, speaking for the poor, even remaining poor despite the income from the sale of his books. Who speaks for the poor today? Aren't we Christians supposed to have some equipment that helps us understand the tragedy of poverty? I don't have the answer to poverty but would suggest that we who follow the Lord Christ could begin by speaking and standing for the poor.

Read Jeremiah 13-17 and Luke 16:19-31.

The Call to Holy Living

DAY
11

"Remember, if the grace of God hath taken hold of thy soul, thou art a person of another world, and indeed a subject of another and more noble kingdom, the kingdom of God—which is the kingdom of the gospel, of grace, of faith and righteousness, and the kingdom of heaven hereafter. In these things thou should exercise thyself, not making heavenly things which God hath bestowed upon thee, stoop to things that are of the world; but rather beat down the body, to mortify thy members, hoist up thy mind to the things that are above, and practically hold forth before all the world that blessed word of life" (Kepler 1952).

Early in my ministry, I received a strong letter disagreeing with a church remodeling program, and taking me to task for many things. One of the comments in the letter was "Any pastor who has more than two suits in his closet is a hustler." To the best of my memory (one tends to remember those instances!), that is the only time my life-style was scrutinized. I have been asked what I believed, especially questions pertaining to the authority of the Bible. Other than the above letter nobody has asked me why we need two cars, two bathrooms, two television sets or how much of our income we give away. Of course it takes no genius to know why those questions are hardly ever asked. We have a kind of secret agreement, you and me. You don't ask me those kind of questions and I don't ask you.

Some years ago, theologian Jaroslav Pelikan wrote these words, "If I begin to ask myself what kind of church the world will need tomorrow—indeed, what kind of church God will need today—I cannot avoid the conclusion that it will be a church in which this summons to holiness is taken with utmost seriousness."

Yes, I am somewhat apprehensive about calling attention to the word "holiness." I am fearful of adding to the fervor and fanaticism of those who see themselves as God's chief prosecuting attorneys. But our faith does have ethical implications. How we "behave" as a Christian matters. Yes, we are justified by God's grace. But justified for what? Whatever happened to sanctification?

Read Romans 12.

Going Home in the Arms of the Savior

DAY 12 *"It was not the overheavy Load of Sin, but the Discovery of Mercy; not the Roaring of the Devil, but the Drawing of the Father, that makes a Person come to Jesus Christ: I myself know all of these Things"* (Kepler 1952).

One of the first sermon texts I assign to my preaching students is Luke 15:1-7. This well-known parable by Jesus is usually called the story of the "lost sheep." We didn't raise sheep on the farm where I grew up. My Dad, who was good with animals, did not like sheep. He regarded them as stupid, stubborn, and prone to mysterious diseases. Taking care of sheep was too frustrating and wasn't worth the time and effort.

I would like to suggest that the emphasis of our text is not upon sheep, but upon the shepherd. Neither is badness or goodness the point of this story. This story is not about a repentant or sorry sheep searching for its master. It's the other way around. The shepherd searches for the lost sheep "till he finds it." But even finding the lost one does not end the shepherd's task. No, now the shepherd must carry the lost one home. This story is not about reformation but restoration. This is what the rejoicing is all about.

Bunyan had a sensitive conscience and an active imagination. This combination created for him terrifying images and visions of the oncoming day of judgment. It was during these stormy years that he read Luther's commentary on Paul's epistle to the Galatians. This was one of the experiences whereby he was found by God. Later he described Luther's book as having been "written out of my heart." Years later he was to write his most important book, *Pilgrim's Progress,* and its opening sentence is quite revealing: "As I walked through the wilderness of this world. . . ."

In the assigning of this sermon text to student preachers, it is my hope that it will set the tone for their future ministry. It is hard not to get lost in the wilderness of this world. Our congregations are made up of people who are both shepherds and sheep. You and I are a mixture of being lost and found. Ours is not an "I found it" faith. It is just the opposite. We have a God who doesn't calculate the cost in searching for and finding us. Thanks be to God! We are in the arms of the Savior, going home!

Read Luke 15:1-7.

Teach Us to Number Our Days

<table>
<tr><td>

D A Y

13

</td><td>

"Let dissolution come when it will, it can do the Christian no harm, for it will be but only a passage out of a prison into a palace; out of a sea of troubles into a haven of rest; out of a crowd of enemies to an innumerable company of true, loving, and faithful friends;

</td></tr>
</table>

out of shame, reproach, and contempt, into exceeding great and eternal glory" (Kepler 1952).

I like to think that I am still a person who is in the middle of middle age. But our kids wreck that illusion with the tough question: "Dad, how many people live to be 128 years old?" It has been said that "middle age is not only later than you think, but sooner than you expect." That has certainly been the case with me.

My growing old happened in a hurry! Karl Menninger described the blunt truth in these words, "We all know that we are growing older. . . . But suddenly, all at once, we realize that we are actually old. Older was not so bad but old! That's a shock. Old is more older than we thought." It was Auden who said in his Christmas oratorio, "But that was when we were children, just a moment ago" (*The Complete Works of W. H. Auden*, Princeton University Press, 1989). Just a moment ago I was still playing softball. Just a moment ago I was a young pastor. This business of getting old happens in a hurry.

Bunyan died somewhat unexpectedly during his 60th year. The last words of his last sermon were these, "Consider that the holy God is your Father, and let this oblige you to live like the children of God, that you may look your Father in the face with comfort another day."

Have you ever wondered what your last words might be? Have you thought much about the aging, dying process—how you might handle it? As a parish pastor for many years, I have been with a number of people who have traveled through the "valley of the shadow." Some handled it well. Some didn't. I have wondered what made the difference. Perhaps the "heart of wisdom"?

Teach us, Lord, to number our days, that we may get a heart of wisdom.

Read Psalm 90 and 1 Corinthians 15.

The Resurrection

DAY 14 (John Bunyan died in London, after traveling there to bring about a reconciliation between a father and his son. He was buried in Bunhill Fields, Finsbury.) *"The doctrine of the resurrection, however questioned by heretics and erroneous persons, yet is such a truth, that almost all the holy scriptures of God point at and center in it"* (Kepler 1952).

"Death," said Aristotle, "is a dreadful thing, for it is the end." Theologian Joseph Sittler was convinced that "the fear of death is at the bottom of all apprehensions." History has recorded many great events, but there can be little question that the greatest is the resurrection of Jesus Christ. It has been called "history's turning point."

The resurrection event has been the focus of much controversy and many explanations. The much debated question is, "Did the empty tomb create the Easter faith or did the Easter faith create the empty tomb?" If you spend much time reading the various biblical accounts of the resurrection you will discover there disagreements in the descriptions of what happened.

"He is not here. He is risen." According to Mark's account the empty tomb did not initially create faith and understanding, but rather fear and terror. The resurrection is something that happened between Jesus and God and not God and the disciples. What can be historically verified at the death of Jesus is the death of Jesus. Later, after some time of reflection and prayer, there was the great resurgence of power and hope in the words and deeds of the early followers of Christ. Jesus' empty tomb is the focus and source of that hope and power.

I believe in the promise of the resurrection because of the biblical witness of the empty tomb and its results. I also believe in the resurrection because a God who loves us so much as to die for us is not going to be frustrated by death. In the Bible, the power of death comes under the control of God. With the apostle Paul, I confess, "If we live, we live to the Lord, and if we die, we die to the Lord; so then, whether we live or die, we are the Lord's" (Rom. 14:7-8). The best is yet to be!

Read Luke 24; Matthew 28:1-10; and Mark 16.

Stephanie Frey

JULIAN OF NORWICH

I F ONE is in search of precise biographical data about the woman named Julian, whose legacy to us is her manuscript "Revelations of Divine Love," there is little to be found. According to the manuscript itself, Julian of Norwich was a woman who lived during the fourteenth century and made her home in Norwich, England. Most manuscripts give a date of May 13, 1373, her 30th year of life, as the occasion upon which she experienced the set of visions recorded in her book. Julian was quite ill when the visions occurred, so ill that her priest had been sent to bring her a crucifix on which to gaze. The visions she received are all centered around the image of Christ on the cross.

At some point, Julian became an anchoress, and entered a monastic cell that was part of the Church of St. Julian at Norwich. As was customary she took the name of the patron saint of the anchorhold. She remained in the anchorhold at Norwich until the time of her death, thought to be between 1416 and 1419 A.D.

The contextual setting of her life is of great importance, even though there are few biographical details known. Julian lived during the time of the Hundred Years War, under the reign of Edward III. This was a time of decline in both church and state. Along with that, the bubonic plague was sweeping the countryside—and death was all around her. Some scholars speculate that because of the high death rate, and the fact that many children were growing up without their mothers, Julian might have been prompted to develop her well-known image of Jesus as our Mother. She herself may have longed for mothering, and without a living mother of her own may have sought that particularly in her Lord.

Julian's writings are of import yet today for several reasons: they give us a sharp view of the medieval mind and theological perspective, they present to us a fine record of an individual's personal and profound experience of God, and they can draw us into an understanding of the lifegiving nature of such deep prayer as this. While it may be that some of Julian's observations would suffer today under a careful doctrinal examination, her writing can nevertheless prompt us to affirm our own creeds, to live in her world for a while, and to consider the awesome majesty of God's great love for all of humankind.

Passion for Christ

DAY 1

"... I thought I had already had some experience of the passion of Christ, but by his grace I wanted still more. I wanted to be actually there with Mary Magdalene and the Other who loved him, and with my own eyes to see and know more of the physical suffering of our Savior, and the compassion of our Lady and of those who were there and then were loving him truly and watching his pains. I would be one of them and suffer with them. . ." (Julian 1966).

There is hardly a believer who has not at some time wondered just what it would have been like to have been in a crowd that heard Jesus teach and saw him heal, or to have been one of the disciples at that Last Supper, or among the women who stood at the cross and then made their way in the early morning darkness to the empty tomb. The gospel story is so compelling, and draws us so close to itself, that we long for a way of knowing more nearly what the passion of Christ was like. As with Julian, there may be in us, especially during Lent and Holy Week, that desire actually to have been there.

Try as we might, we will not have the experience of being with Jesus in the flesh, nor will most of us have the visions of Julian as she lay sick and near death in the fourteenth century. But the lively Word of God, read and proclaimed, tells us that the Holy Spirit, working faith in us, will draw us near to God, near to the heart of the gospel. God has promised to create and nourish faith in us—and to give us the gifts of the Spirit, which include understanding. In that way we can begin to have understanding of what Christ's passion was, because we will know that it was for the love of us that it took place. To know that and have confidence in that is a great gift.

God of all mercy, work faith in us. Give us hearts of compassion and eyes to see with clarity, that through the accounts of your passion we may come to understand your unending love for us. Amen.

God Is Our Clothing

"God is our clothing that wraps, clasps and encloses us so as to never leave us" (Doyle 1983).

The baptismal gown hung in the closet, long before Sarah arrived. She was coming from Korea, and the precise date of her arrival was not known. Not only had her parents gone about the task of making a nursery ready for her, they had also begun to prepare for her Baptism. The gown was crafted from the wedding dress of the woman who would be Sarah's mother—to signify that even though this child for whom they waited was not of their own flesh and blood, she was still "born" of their marriage relationship. So the white gown and cap hung there waiting for her to arrive, and in anticipation of the day she would be adopted into God's family through the gift of Baptism.

Many children wear baptismal garments that have been carefully handed down from one generation to another, or newly made by a devoted aunt or grandmother. It is far more than a quaint tradition, for it symbolizes as well the new creation who is born in Baptism—a person clothed in God's love and grace. In the waters of Baptism come a multitude of promises: the promise of God for forgiveness of sin, the promise of the Holy Spirit's presence in the life of the baptized person, and the promise of God never to forsake or abandon any who are marked with the sign of the cross.

When the baptismal waters are splashed over a child's head, a new creation is brought to life by God's gracious Word. God clothes the baptized one in garments of promise, garments of new life, and of salvation. And God wraps and encloses that one in great arms of love. "I will greatly rejoice in the Lord, my soul shall exult in my God; for [God] has clothed me with the garments of salvation, has covered me with the robe of righteousness, as a bridegroom decks himself with a garland, and as a bride adorns herself with her jewels" (Isa. 61:10).

Gracious God, we rejoice in the garments of salvation with which you clothe us in Baptism. Help us to live our lives as your new creation with joy, giving thanks to you who have wrapped us in your love and grace. Amen.

Resting in God

"God is the True Rest who wants to be known. God finds pleasure in being our true resting place" (Doyle 1983).

How often people speak of the frantic pace of daily life in our time, the timeclocks of the workplace and the various clocks of family life. There are school schedules, work schedules, sports schedules, church schedules. The times given over to silence for meditation during Sunday worship are brief, as we feel the edginess of people for whom silence is foreign and perhaps even fearsome. How do we learn to rest? To rest from our daily schedules and even more important, to rest in God? Augustine knew the problem well: "My heart is restless until it rests in thee."

You and I belong to a God who rests: "And on the seventh day God finished his work which he had done, and he rested on the seventh day from all his work which he had done. So God blessed the seventh day and hallowed it, because on it God rested from all his work which he had done in creation" (Gen. 2:2-3).

And we have a Savior who invites us to rest: "Come to me, all who labor and are heavy laden, and I will give you rest. Take my yoke upon you, and learn from me; for I am gentle and lowly in heart, and you will find rest for your souls. For my yoke is easy, and my burden is light" (Matt. 11:28-30).

God is the one who promises to fill us and refresh us in those times of spiritual dryness. This God will be there in the silence of our rest. This God beckons us not to fear. This God "wants to be known," and is the one we can trust to cradle us in the everlasting arms, where there is true peace and rest.

O God, you rested when you were finished with this marvelous creation which gives us sustenance as well as delight in its mystery and beauty. You invite us now to rest from our work, and find a resting place in you. Help us quiet ourselves, and let the silence be filled with your promise and your peace, so we might be refreshed by you and your gospel of life. Amen.

You Will Not Be Overcome

D A Y
4

"God did not say: 'You will not be tempested. You will not labor hard. You will not be troubled.' But God did say: 'You will not be overcome'" (Doyle 1983).

It does not take long in life for a person to encounter a situation in which they ask the question, "Why me?" In the face of a doctor's report that issues a death sentence, or the tragic accident of a friend, or the heartbreak of having a child who wanders off into a difficult world of his own, that question comes quickly. The often unspoken part of that question is, "Why me?—I'm a Christian! What have I done to deserve this?"

In our day, there are those who preach the "victorious" Christian life—and who paint that life as a one lived perpetually on the mountaintop, on the crest of a wave, or on the "sunny side of the street." But the victory in the Christian life is a victory over death—not over the fact that we still live between the times of Christ's life on earth and his coming again.

Instead, our life as baptized people of God propels us directly into this "between-the-times" world in which we live. There is no need to seek out suffering, for it will come in one way, shape, or form to every person who has a heartbeat. We would be naive to think that the Christian life is free of such tyrannies.

Paul writes: "But we have this treasure in earthen vessels, to show that the transcendent power belongs to God and not to us. We are afflicted in every way, but not crushed; perplexed, but not driven to despair; persecuted, but not forsaken; struck down, but not destroyed; always carrying in the body the death of Jesus, so that the life of Jesus may also be manifested in our bodies" (2 Cor. 4:7-10).

In the face of suffering we still have hope, because God has loved us and gone even to the cross for us. We will not be overcome. We have the freedom to sing the song of others who have striven to throw off the chains of oppression: "We shall overcome. . . . Deep in my heart, I do believe, we shall overcome one day."

Almighty God, you have given us a treasure in earthen vessels: the undying hope we have in the gospel of Jesus. Carry us through the sufferings of this life, and give us a vision of a day when death and war and injustice will be no more. Amen.

The Pain of Sin

"But I did not see sin. I believe it has no substance or real existence. It can only be known by the pain it causes. This pain is something, as I see it, which lasts but a while. It purges us and makes us know ourselves, so that we ask for mercy" (Julian 1966).

It is striking how many times the effects of sin and wrongdoing are felt physically: guilt tightens the stomach, broken relationships bring a real ache to the heart, words too quickly spoken hang in the air and we feel desperate to be able to reel them in like line on a fishing rod. Julian writes, "Sin . . . can only be known by the pain it causes." A simple and true statement! How easily the effects of sin can be felt in our own discomfort and wrongdoing, and in the emotional pain or "dis-ease" wreaked upon those whose lives are touched by that sin. Perhaps the physical discomfort we experience in such times is itself part of God's judgment in that moment. Perhaps it does serve, as Julian contends, to help us know our need and ask for forgiveness.

Julian goes on to say: *"The passion of our Lord is our comfort against all this—for such is his blessed will. Because of his tender love for those who are to be saved our good Lord comforts us at once and sweetly as if to say. . . . 'All will be well, and all will be well and every manner of thing will be well'"* (Doyle 1983).

The psalmist provides us a marvelous portrait of the God whose memory becomes poor when it comes to keeping track of our sin, and who takes pleasure in offering forgiveness. Julian's confident words that all will be well find an echo in the psalm: "The Lord is merciful and gracious, slow to anger and abounding in steadfast love. He will not always chide, nor will he keep his anger for ever. He does not deal with us according to our sins, nor requite us according to our iniquities. For as the heavens are high above the earth, so great is his steadfast love toward those who fear him; as far as the east is from the west, so far does he remove our transgressions from us" (Ps. 103:8-12).

Gracious and loving God, we rejoice that you look with compassion and tenderness upon our sin. We ask your forgiveness for all that has been hurtful to the neighbor, and pray that you will continue to work your way within us, to bring us to faith and new life. Amen.

At Home with God

DAY 6	*"Flee to our Lord and we shall be strengthened. Touch him, and we shall be cleansed. Cling to him, and we shall be safe and sound from every danger. For it is the will of our courteous Lord that we should be as much at home with him as heart may think or soul*

desire" (Julian 1966).

The story of the woman with the flow of blood, told in Luke 8, is the story of a woman who did flee to Jesus for strength, who touched him, and was cleansed. She was a woman who lived her life on the outside edges of community. She had been made an outsider, deemed unclean due to her hemorrhage. But within her, even after 12 years of exclusion from community, there burned a strong hope. If she could only make her way to Jesus, touching even the fringe of his garments, she was confident she would be healed.

The woman's faith was such that as she furtively moved through the great crowd of people pressing around Jesus, and as she reached out and touched the hem of his garments, he felt his healing power go out from him. Jesus asked, "Who was it that touched me?" Full of the shame she had carried with her for years, the woman came out from the crowd and fell at his feet, confessing that it was she who had touched him. She also declared that she had been healed immediately. Jesus did not shame her for her boldness, but instead said simply, "Daughter, your faith has made you well; go in peace" (Luke 8:48).

We can only imagine and hope that after this encounter the woman became an "insider" again, and that she was able to put aside her shame and stand tall in the knowledge that she belonged to a healing Savior. Jesus' quiet words of compassion and welcome spoken to her became words of safety and refuge. Jesus himself became a "home" to her.

Jesus, our risen and living Lord, still works such healing among us through the work of the Holy Spirit. Jesus also gives that gift of healing to us whenever we eat the Lord's Supper and hear the words, "given for you" spoken to us. He is the one to whom we can flee and cling, and in whom we can find a place safe and sound from every danger.

Gracious and loving God, grant that we may have the bold and confident faith of the woman who sought you out for healing. Grant that we may flee to you and cling to you. And when our faith is not strong, we pray that you will continue to cling to us. Amen.

Our Faith Is a Light

<table>
<tr><td>D A Y
7</td><td>*"Our faith is a light. . . . Because of the light we live; because of the night we suffer and grieve. . . . When we are done with grief our eyes will be suddenly enlightened, and in the shining brightness of the light we shall see perfectly. For our light is none other than*</td></tr>
</table>

God our Maker, and the Holy Spirit, in our Savior, Christ Jesus" (Julian 1966).

Julian well understands that faith in God brings light to our lives. If faith is light, it is born of the light of Christ who overcame the darkness of our world by being born in a stinking stable in a backwater town like Bethlehem. If faith is light, it is born of the light of Christ who overcame the darkness of our world by being raised to life after three days in the grave. It is as if all of God's story through the ages rushes back and forth from dark to light.

God our Creator spoke a creative word over the chaos, and fashioned from that great darkness both day and night. That old scoundrel Jacob wrestled in the night with an unknown stranger—and by morning's light realized that it was God with whom he had wrestled. The people of Israel traveled both by day and night, and God lit their way at night with a great pillar of fire. The psalmist looked for day from the pit of night when his couch was filled with tears. And Good Friday was as dark as dark could be when Jesus hung on the cross. It wasn't until Easter morning that the glorious light of the resurrection filled that burial garden.

You and I move from darkness to light and back again countless times in our lives. Even in the darkest of times, the faith God is working to create in us brings light to the darkness. God has promised that even a "dimly burning wick he will not quench" (Isa. 42:3). God grants grace sufficient for our needs, and gives us the faith we need to walk the baptismal journey of our lives.

Enlighten our darkness, O God, and make the light of your gospel shine among us. Sustain our faith so it can give light to our days. Carry us through the various darknesses of our lives, so we may enter your light at life's end. Amen.

God Never Began to Love Us

DAY

8

"I saw that God never began to love us. For just as we will be in everlasting joy (all God's creation is destined for this) so also we have always been in God's foreknowledge, known and loved from without beginning" (Doyle 1983).

A friend reflected on the presence of children in her marriage by saying, "I can hardly remember what it was like not to have them. I feel as though they have always been here." That feeling is, perhaps, just a tiny glimpse of the way in which God stretches both backward and forward into eternity, entirely without a time of beginning and without a time of ending.

Even more mystifying is the notion that we ourselves have been known and chosen by God from before we were a "twinkling in the Father's eye." How can we, who have two parents who gave us life, and birth certificates that note the hour and minute of birth—how can we, with finite lives—have been known by God from the beginning? But Julian's words are borne out by the writer to the Ephesians: "Blessed be the God and Father of our Lord Jesus Christ, who has blessed us in Christ with every spiritual blessing in the heavenly places, even as he chose us in him before the foundation of the world, that we should be holy and blameless before him" (Eph. 1:3-4).

Even the psalmist sings of that marvel: "Thou knowest me right well; my frame was not hidden from thee, when I was being made in secret, intricately wrought in the depths of the earth. Thy eyes beheld my unformed substance; in thy book were written, every one of them, the days that were formed for me, when as yet there were none of them" (Ps. 139:14b-16).

God has known us, named us, called us from all time. God did not have to begin loving us, because God's love for us has always been. That is beyond our understanding, but so vital a knowing for us to have: God's love for us knows no beginning, no bounds, and no end.

God of love, you made us your own long before we had breath or form. We praise you for your marvelous work, for we are fearfully and wonderfully made. Grant that we may hear your call, and have confidence in it. Amen.

Knowing Our ABCs

D A Y
9

"In this life we are able to stand because of three things. . . . The first is the use of our natural reason; the second, the everyday teaching of the Holy Church; the third, the inner working of grace through the Holy Spirit. . . . God is the source of our natural reason; God the basis of the teaching of the Holy Church; and God is the Holy Spirit. . . . All of them are continually at work in us. . . . God's will is that we should know something about them here below: to know the ABCs as it were, and have the full understanding in heaven. All this will help us on our way" (Julian 1966).

Each one of us has been given the gift of a mind by which we can learn, receive information, and experience life. We have been given two other gifts that nurture us on the lifelong journey of faith. From Baptism on, we are surrounded by the Church—the gathering of God's faithful people. And from that Church we receive teaching and tradition.

While we remain children of God no matter what our age, we also are called to grow up into Christ, to mature in faith, to continue our learning whether we are 7 or 70. We need the basics, the ABCs, as Julian calls them—in order to move further on in the journey. The greatest treasure of all is that God's Holy Spirit promises to lavish us with grace, to shower us with gifts for learning and apprehending, and to lead us all the way home so we know we are not alone.

In his first letter to the Corinthians, Paul writes: "For now we see in a mirror dimly, but then face to face. Now I know in part; then I shall understand fully, even as I have been fully understood" (1 Cor. 13:12). Paul knows that we grow from childish thoughts and ways to those of adulthood. He also knows, however, that being human, we shall always only see dimly. It will be part of our final union with God after death that we fully understand all the mysteries of God. In the meantime, we are given the gifts of our minds, the teaching of the Church, and our hope in the promises of God to sustain us.

Holy and gracious God, we thank and praise you for your many gifts, especially today the gifts of the Church and its teaching. Help us to grow and mature in faith, even as we remain your children. Amen.

Let Your Prayer Be Large

DAY 10 *"It is the will of our Lord that our prayer and our trust be large. We must truly know that our Lord is the ground from which prayer sprouts and that it is a gift given out of love, otherwise we waste our time and pain ourselves"* (Doyle 1983).

The group gathered in the evening for worship, and the shadows hung dark and rich around the chapel as day's light began to fade. The worshipers began to sing the prayer from the vespers liturgy: "Let my prayer rise before you as incense, the lifting up of my hands as the evening sacrifice. . . ." As they sang, a dancer entered, and carried a bowl containing incense. She raised the bowl high and clouds of incense filled the room. Its pungent smell seemed to transport the worshipers into another time and space, and the ancient words of the psalm they sang became new. In that room, God was great and large—and the prayers God invited took on the largeness and greatness of the billowing smoke of incense.

We belong to a God who invites us to pray constantly (1 Thess. 5:17), and who invites us to ask for what we need, promising that it shall be given to us (Luke 11:9). And Paul urged his hearers to pray for one another. Clearly, it is God's will that the people of God should pray. Prayer opens us to hear God's Word. Prayer on behalf of other people not only strengthens them, but also enables us to love them and have compassion for them, and to work on their behalf. Prayer allows our own trust of God to grow. So often we make both God and our requests so small that we do not benefit from the greatness of God's mercy and God's ability to fill our hearts and provide for our need.

God is the very ground out of which our prayers grow. We pray because we know God is the source of all things. We may plant and water, but it is God alone who gives the growth. When we let our prayers and our trust be large, as Julian says, we can only be blessed by God's abundant grace.

Most gracious God, you invite us to trust you for all things and to pray without ceasing. Help us to let our prayers be as large and great as your promises. Let our prayers be sweet upon your ears. Amen.

Christ's Thirst for Us

DAY 11

"The spiritual thirst of Christ is a love-longing that lasts and always will until we are all together whole in him. For we are not now as fully whole in Christ as we will be one day" (Doyle 1983).

In Margaret Wise Brown's book for children called *The Runaway Bunny,* she tells the story of a bunny who wanted to run away from home, and told his mother of his plans. "If you run away, I will run after you. For you are my little bunny," said the mother rabbit. "If you run after me, I will become a fish, and swim away," said the bunny. "If you become a fish, I will be a fisherman, and I will fish for you," said the mother. "Then I will become a rock on a mountain, high above you," said the bunny. "If you become a rock on the mountain high above me," said his mother, "I will be a mountain climber, and I will climb to where you are." "If you become a mountain climber," said the little bunny, "I will be a crocus in a hidden garden." "If you become a crocus in a hidden garden," said his mother, "I will be a gardener. And I will find you." So the story goes, until at last the little bunny decides it might just be best to stay at home (Harper & Row, 1941).

The longing of the mother rabbit is a picture of the kind of love-longing God has for us. It is the love that seeks always to be with us, ahead of us and behind us. For God, through Christ Jesus, pursues us relentlessly to have us belong to him. God pursues us as a mother pursues her child, and as a lover seeks the beloved.

In the words "I thirst," spoken from the cross (John 19:28) Julian hears reference to a spiritual thirst. It is the thirst of the love-longing that God in Jesus has for us—that same quality of searching and seeking us out. It is that ongoing pursuit of us that will one day bring us to full union with God. Only then will we experience the true wholeness and healing of salvation won for us in Jesus' death on the cross—when Jesus showed the depth and breadth of his thirst to claim us as his own.

O loving God, thank you for always seeking us out when we try so desperately to run and hide from you. Bring us to yourself, and grant us the wholeness and healing only you can give. In Christ's name, amen.

Jesus Our Mother

<table>
<tr><td>D A Y

12</td><td>*"The human mother will suckle her child with her own milk, but our beloved Mother, Jesus, feeds us with himself, and with the most tender courtesy, does it by means of the Blessed Sacrament, the precious food of all true life"* (Julian 1966).</td></tr>
</table>

Perhaps the most celebrated and unusual image from Julian's writing is the portrait she gives of Jesus Christ as our mother. In this and several other passages she focuses on a mother "at work": a mother will feed a child, teach and discipline a child, comfort the child who is sad, and cleanse the one who needs to be washed.

Just as mothers work to feed their children, even producing food from their own bodies, so also Jesus feeds us. Julian speaks of Christ "nursing" us to maturity by feeding us from his own body through the means of the Lord's Supper.

It was at the meal table that Jesus took bread and wine, gave thanks for it, and gave it to each one seated there to eat. He told his disciple friends that this was his body and his blood. It was the great gift of himself to feed us and strengthen us.

In a strange way, Jesus does do the things we have long associated with the tasks of mothering. Julian uses that image to show the trust we might have in Christ, the same trust a child has in its mother.

Julian writes further of this: *"The human mother may put her child tenderly to her breast, but our tender Mother Jesus simply leads us into his blessed breast through his open side, and there gives us a glimpse of the Godhead and heavenly joy—the inner certainty of eternal bliss"* (Julian 1966).

Gracious God, in you we find one more motherly than our own mothers, and more fatherly than our own fathers. We give you praise and hearty thanks that you nourish and sustain us with your own body and blood, strengthening us for all we encounter in this life, and guiding us in ways that are in keeping with your will. Grant that we may receive your gifts with believing hearts. Amen.

The Old and the New

DAY 13

"In this life there is within us who are to be saved a surprising mixture of good and bad. We have our risen Lord; we have the wretchedness and mischief done by Adam's fall and death. Kept secure by Christ we are assured, by his touch of grace, of salvation; broken by Adam's fall, and in many ways by our own sins and sorrows, we are so darkened and blinded that we can hardly find any comfort" (Julian 1966).

Julian touches on a compelling truth in this statement: that even when we are confident that we are a "new creation" in Jesus Christ, we still struggle with the old self in us that persists in raising its head. Luther talked about being a saint and a sinner at the same time: a sinner because the struggle with the old self will not be over until we are joined to Christ, and a saint because God graciously views us through eyes that see us as blameless.

That struggle is age-old and difficult. How many times we make efforts to change and to be more faithful. Yet how easily our efforts meet their end. That is the "mischief of Adam's fall." It is persistent and gnawing.

But we have a word which stands over against all of that: "Therefore, if any one is in Christ, he is a new creation; the old has passed away, behold, the new has come" (2 Cor. 5:17). God is at work in us, from the moment of Baptism on, to fashion us into new people—people who trust God to open the future for us. There may not be much evidence of that new creation. But you and I see only from a human point of view. God's view is far different, and God has promised to persevere in making that new creation.

We have signs of the new creation whenever we are given the grace to think of the neighbor before we consider our own well-being, or whenever people are able to trust one another in relationship and open themselves to truth telling and dream sharing. The signs are there, quiet and subtle, but they are there. God is keeping the promise! The risen Christ does live in us!

God of all life, through your risen Son Jesus Christ you have made us each a new creation. Give us strength to refuse the schemes of the old self—and when we know we cannot, then assure us of your grace and comfort so we may see that Christ does live within us. Amen.

Thanks Be to God!

DAY 14 *"With prayer goes gratitude. Thanksgiving is a real, interior knowledge. . . . It brings joy and gratitude within. Sometimes its very abundance gives voice, 'Good Lord, thank you and bless you!' And sometimes when the heart is dry and unfeeling—or it may be because of the enemy's tempting—then reason and grace drive us to cry aloud to our Lord, recalling his blessed passion and great goodness. And the strength of our Lord's word comes to the soul, and fires the heart, and leads it by grace into its real business, enabling it to pray happily and to enjoy our Lord in truth"* (Julian 1966).

Anna was a woman whose entire life had been marked by her thanksgiving to God. At 101, she would speak of her gratitude that she and her sister, Clara, could live just two doors apart in the nursing home. She was grateful that they could be well cared for, and be in good health and of sound mind.

In the spring of her 102nd year the time finally did come for Anna, who had spoken confidently all along about "going home" to her Lord. At the meal following the funeral, friends—some who had had Anna as a Sunday School teacher over 50 years ago—gathered around her sister to speak words of thanksgiving about Anna. The words of praise were moving: "You and Anna always made me feel like royalty. . . . You were both women of grace. . . ."

Women of grace—that is precisely right. For the gratitude and graciousness of these two women came from living in God's grace, from living in the Word. It had become that "real, interior, knowledge" of which Julian speaks. It is the one thing that sustains through the spiritually dry seasons of our lives. "Time was," reflected Anna's sister, "I thought I could manage everything on my own. Finally, late in life, I learned that there was someone else who could manage it all better than I. Now I ask for help. And it is there."

Anna and Clara knew, as did Julian, that "the Word fires the heart," leading us deeper into the abundant promises of God's grace, and giving us hearts made for thanksgiving.

Gracious and loving God, thank you for the countless gifts of each new day. Make us good stewards of your gifts. Amen.

Arndt Halvorson

P. T. FORSYTH

PETER TAYLOR FORSYTH was a theologian, pastor, and educator whose fiery preaching and provocative writing stirred Great Britain from 1874 until his death in 1921. For a number of years after his death he was forgotten, but since 1940 he has been "rediscovered" and has been studied by many of today's church leaders and theologians.

His ability to address the center of the spiritual and theological question, his passionate defense of the gospel of the cross of Jesus, his remarkable command of language, and his evocative writing style combine to assure him a permanent place in the study of theology.

Born and educated in Scotland, he combines Scottish toughness and gentleness, practicality and mysticism, with an openness to the world outside—mainly German, Scandinavian and French thought.

He is most appreciated for his rescue of the great word *evangelical*. Evangelical theology was in danger of eclipse, so he wrote clearly that evangelical is not "old hat" but the constant pressure of a redeeming God upon the world. He wrote convincingly that the "good news" or "evangel" was that God has procured salvation for us all through the cross. Evangelical means gospel-centered, gospel-created, gospel-destined. This gospel rules and validates the Bible, and empowers the church and the Christian. The highest authority is the gospel.

Since he was a pastor for 25 years, he does not write to systematize his thought, but to apply it to our daily lives. Thus, his theology has a personal "bite" which gets us involved as participants, not spectators.

His love of language and the world of art, music and literature was deliberately sacrificed during his ministry as he experienced, with Paul, "I decided to know nothing among you except Jesus Christ and him crucified" (1 Cor. 2:2). But he could not deny his heart love for the poetic phrase, so his writing style is fascinating. It reminds us of the poetry of Gerard Manley Hopkins. While teaching a course in Forsyth's theology with Olaf Hanson, we would ask the class to collect from their reading some "quotable quotes." Their only complaint was there were so many.

His writings seem current, addressing the great questions of our time—such issues as authority, how to read the Bible, prayer, the cross and its significance, and the call to holiness by a Holy God.

Christk Owns the Future

D A Y
1

"Our first need is for a positive theology. A positive theology is an evangelical theology. Positive means moral in the great evangelical sense . . . not an influence but a new creation, not a career opened for the race but a finished thing. Positive Christianity first adjusts us to the holy and then creates the holy in us. It is evangelical because it does full justice to the one creative principle of grace" (Forsyth 1957c).

The late Hubert Humphrey said in an address to pastors: "Why don't you ever write me about what you're for? All you write me about is what you're against." It is so easy to find fault, to point out what is wrong in the name of religious opinions. But the nagging voice of criticism has never built anything that mattered.

By dying on the cross, Jesus demolished—shattered—the power of the negative. Death has no more power over us, nor does the devil, nor sin. This means that the future is as bright as the promises of God. Christ makes each day a new day—in every respect. When he died, he died once and for all. "It is finished," he said on the cross.

By rising from the dead, he created a new form of life. This new life is not stoicism, the grim ability to endure life. This new life is not ecstasy, that high-pitched emotionalism which enables us to float over life's problems. This new life is the confidence that the risen Christ owns the future, has hold of me, and is with me in everything. The new creation is a new dimension. It is fact, not mere fancy or mood. Thus we may groan under life's burden even as we live free from burdens.

Positive theology, then, is the calm confidence in the truth of the Christ story. This story supersedes all others. If the story seems to demand more of us than we can find in us, it performs a radical miracle within us. The story creates in us a desire to live for and under Christ as Lord. This desire is the key—soon we find that we are living under his lordship.

Lord Jesus, we thank you for bothering us through the years with your challenge to a higher life, and we thank you for giving us both the desire and strength to live this new life. Amen.

Through Death to Life

D A Y 2 *"With the abolition of death would vanish the uncertainty which educates faith, the mystery, the tragedy, which makes life so great, the sense of another world which gives such dignity and meaning to this. But, of course, it is not death that preserves this after all. It is the conviction that death is a crisis which opens a new phase of life. It is not the poverty and brevity of life that draws out its resources; it is its sense of fullness and power. We were created by God not out of His poverty and His need of company, but out of His overflowing wealth of love and His passion to multiply joy"* (Forsyth 1953).

In our unpredictable human existence, we need certainty. There is a resurrection that is certain, writes Paul, for life is cradled in uncertainty. The other basic need for our life journey is mystery. We need both.

Certainty alone results in the famous line of the poet, "A rose is a rose is a rose is a rose." Mystery alone results in vagueness, a habit of testing everything by how we feel or what we think we see in a mystic vision.

The resurrection combines these two needs.

It is a certainty that we shall die. The curtain will come down on our personal human dramas. Through the centuries human beings have tried to see beyond the curtain of death. This makes cemeteries and burial grounds fascinating subjects for study, but we have never found a single clue to the life beyond in these burial places.

The empty tomb of Jesus is the only burial place that shows anything about life beyond the curtain. "Death is swallowed up in victory" (1 Cor. 15:54b). We shall be like Jesus and we shall be with Jesus. Paul says we shall all be changed, in the twinkling of an eye, at the last trumpet. And this dramatic change will be more glorious, by far, than anything we have seen in this life.

It Isn't Fair

"Christ exhibited God, He did not expound Him. He was His witness, not His apologist. He did more to reveal than to interpret. And His revelation was in work more than in Word. He was the revelation. To see Him was to see the Father, not to see how He could be the Father" (Forsyth 1957b).

The Bible insists that we are saved by faith, not by sight. We believe that God is like Jesus, in Jesus, working through him—even though nobody in the 2000 years of Christian history claims to fully understand how it works.

We see God in worship more fully, more clearly than in detailed explanations. The language of the church is prayer, praise, and thanksgiving, rather than philosophical abstractions.

The artist captures the flight of an eagle more fully than the essayist. The musician captures the glory of life more precisely than the sociologist or psychologist—yes, very likely, more than the theologian. The poet sees beyond the "facts." Jesus, the artist, the musician, the poet, shows us God. We may not understand, but we cannot resist the glory.

In Jesus we see the triumph of love—and holiness.

The love of Jesus includes everyone—even me—without in any way compromising his holiness. Sometimes this angers us. We dare not—since we call ourselves Christians—challenge his right to love criminals, cheap-skates, homosexuals, communists, etc., but we do resent it, don't we?

Our image of God is dimmed by resentment or self-righteousness and the refrain, "It isn't fair." Then it is urgent that we spend some time just looking at and listening to Jesus. And though we still can't explain why—the world does seem to reflect his glory.

> He drew a circle that shut me out
> Heretic, rebel, a thing to flout
> But love and I had the wit to win,
> We drew a circle that took him in.
> Edwin Markham, "Outwitted"

"He who has seen me has seen the Father; how can you say, 'Show us the Father'? Do you not believe that I am in the Father, and the Father in me?" (John 14:9-10).

It's My Fault

DAY 4 *"The greater the favor that is done to us, the more fiercely we resent it if it does not break us down and make us grateful. . . . The effect of Christ's death upon human nature. . . is not always gratitude. Unless it is received in the Holy Ghost, the effect may just be . . . judgment . . . a death unto death"* (Forsyth 1957a).

Today we use the word *defensive* a great deal. We tend to be judgmental about persons who become defensive. It is a tacit admission of weakness and guilt. Our legal system seems to encourage people never to say, "It was my fault," or "I was guilty." We are encouraged to find extenuating circumstances. We seem to be in a human conspiracy to protect one another from the shame of saying, "I am to blame." Who wants to be a wimp?

This defensive system has levels, or degrees of crisis. At the top is the experience of being forgiven before we are accused. G. B. Shaw is reputed to have said, "I don't want anyone to die for me." "I can manage," we say. Ironically, if we do manage, continue to "stonewall," and yet are found guilty, we have only demonstrated that we can survive in prison.

Jesus came to set us free from the exhaustion of defending ourselves. He came to set us free to be what God had in mind when he created us.

Such a huge gift is very expensive. To receive such a pardon means accepting also his claim on us. He not only came to give us good things, he died to save us from having to save ourselves.

His love kills our self love and creates a love for him that in turn sets us free, and gives us self-respect. Conversion is dying with Christ to our pride and self-protection system, and living to and with him as ruler and redeemer.

O resurrected Lord, strengthen us so we dare to confess our wrongdoings and to trust only in your merciful, saving, life-restoring love. Amen.

The Phone Is Ringing

<table>
<tr><td>D A Y
5</td><td>*"All progress in prayer is an answer to prayer, our own or an-
other's. . . . In every act of prayer we have already begun to do
God's will, for which, above all things, we pray. The prayer within
all prayer is, 'Thy will be done' "* (Forsyth 1954).</td></tr>
</table>

Prayer is God's crowning gift. Yet—prayer is our main work. These two facts must always be held together.

Praying is our way of keeping contact with God. He made prayer possible when he came as one of us to live with us and to die and be raised for us. He is always available, always.

Sometimes, usually in untroubled times, we take this for granted. In these times our prayers often become a kind of chit-chat—expressing our views and feelings. Often we grow sentimental and tend to romanticize.

This kind of praying, though not what we would call vital prayer, is just fine with God. His main concern is that we keep the communication lines open. Sometimes we use the telephone just to hear a friend's or loved one's voice, after all.

When pleasant times cease, and we are besieged by bad news—a death, an accident, a moral lapse, a defeat, a frightening doctor's report, loss of a job—we must not panic and say, "Where is God now?" He is where he was in pleasant days, at the other end of the telephone line.

In such times, if we listen closely, our phone is ringing. God is calling. He is saying to us, "I am as near as breathing. Keep talking to me. My grace is still sufficient."

Keep talking—and listening. He has not changed or moved away. His will is that we let him love us, that we let his arms hold us, that we let his mercy wash away our sins and our fears.

His will is that we hear him calling us, by name.

"Rejoice always, pray constantly" (1 Thess. 5:16-17).

Jesus Loves Me, This I Know

<table>
<tr><td>D A Y

6</td><td>*"The first duty of every soul is to find not its freedom, but its master. . . . If within us we find nothing over us, we succumb to what is around us. . . . He is not an other; He is my other"* (Forsyth 1957c).</td></tr>
</table>

A boy once asked his teacher, "Is there any proof that Christianity is true?" The teacher answered: "Nothing can prove its truth by logic—but there is indisputable evidence of its truth. For Jesus can do the impossible. He can so change our hearts that we come to hate the evil and love the good."

This transformation is the foundation of our lives as Christian believers. As Christians we do more than hold strong opinions on moral issues; we are controlled by more than principles and ideas. We respond to him, a person, who loves us in a completely unique way.

He loves us sinners, as we are, sins and all. He never qualifies this love. He wants to burn into our awareness that nothing can prevent him from loving us.

He wants us to surrender our lives to him—voluntarily, that is. He knows that as we let his love into our heart of hearts, we will not ever want to do anything to pain him. So we do not seek to convince him that we deserve his love. To do that would be to provide an escape hatch from his mastery of our lives. If he loves us like that, we know a security that gives us peace and certainty in any situation—including approaching death.

So we turn to him with our fears and futility, our shame and sin, our anger and even our rebellion.

A young boy, who had a sister seven years older, and who took her position as elder sister seriously enough to be his sometime caretaker, was spending a holiday with his grandparents. When he went to bed they heard his prayers. He asked God to bless all his friends and relatives by name, but omitted his older sister's name. Grandma asked him why. He said, "It's such a relief not to have her telling me what to do and not do."

"But," asked grandma, "what do you think God thinks of that?"

"Oh," he replied, "I told God and he said he understood."

Who can resist such a loving God?

"But in your hearts reverence Christ as Lord" (1 Pet. 3:15).

Eternal Life Is Now

<table>
<tr><td>

DAY

7

</td><td>

"Immortality is really a destiny pressing on us by Christ in us. Our immortality lies on us with that kindling weight, that weight of glory, that weight of wings. Weight but not pressure. The wings that add to our weight, yet lift us from the ground. Ask—am I

</td></tr>
</table>

living as an immortal—not as one who will be immortal?" (Forsyth 1953).

As Christians we have the best of two worlds. As Mr. Forsyth writes elsewhere, "To live is Christ. To die is more Christ."

"What is heaven like?" the girl asked her mother.

"I'm not sure of the details," her mother answered, "but if it is better than this life, and it is, it must be glorious."

We have been side-swiped by eternity. In Baptism we were given God's promise to never leave us. He keeps his promise. We may, to be sure, forget this many times. Life may seem empty and purposeless. We often feel frighteningly alone. Yet, something intrudes, often at strange times, like the call of a bird for its mate, reminding us that there is another dimension to life than this seemingly endless round of going to work, cashing the pay check, and paying bills.

This call of God strengthens us to do more than "grin and bear it." We respond to something which causes us to help someone else, to pray for and reach out to someone else, to notice the flowers and the birds and the beauty of people. We dare to be concerned with issues and causes which cannot be really called "profitable"—but which are the essence of life.

This is poetry, to be sure, but the poet does see reality which is not visible to the earthbound. "A man's reach must exceed his grasp, or what's a heaven for?" asks the poet. The day is coming, yes is here even now, when we can see and know God face to face, and strangely, his face seems to be that of my neighbor!

"For to me to live is Christ, and to die is gain. . . . I am hard pressed between the two. My desire is to depart and be with Christ, for that is far better" (Phil. 1:21,23).

275

When the Gospel Happens

 "If the classic religion is Christianity, the classic type is the experience of the redeemer. It is not the sense of the experience that is the main matter, but the source of the experience. It is not our experience we are conscious of, but it is Christ. It is not our experience we proclaim, but the Christ who comes in our experience" (Forsyth 1957c).

"Must we have an experience of Christ to be called Christians?" people often ask.

To which the Bible answers, "The question is phrased wrong. To know Christ is to experience him, since he is a living person, for as we know, anytime we say we 'know' another person, we are saying we have experienced that person. It is not that we 'must'; we simply do."

Of course there are many ways of experiencing someone. It may be a mental stimulus, an emotional response, or a moral challenge, to name the most obvious. What matters is that the God of Jesus is never neutral. As Forsyth writes elsewhere, "Each time we hear the gospel, something happens to us, either for the better or for the worse." So we need not look for an "experience" for the sake of the sensation. Rather, we focus on him.

Most of us live our lives in the land between ecstasy and despair. We are given the gift of faith, which usually manifests itself as a kind of stubborn refusal to let the bleakness of unfaith prevail.

We live in his presence, that is. We study him. We "look to Jesus the pioneer and perfecter of our faith," as the letter to the Hebrews states it (12:2). He is the source of faith because he is its creator. He is the really real in this world of shadows. And who knows? This very day he may so erupt in our inner selves that we sing a song of hope which drowns the dirge of our misery.

Lord Jesus, you are the fairest, most reliable, most powerful of all the forces that seek to control us. Help us to relax in you, that we may live in and through you. Amen.

"Therefore, if any one is in Christ, he is a new creation; the old has passed away, behold the new has come" (2 Cor. 5:17).

We Must Eat

DAY 9 *"It is safer and better to pray over the Bible than to brood over self. And the prayer which is stirred by the cross is holier even than that which arises from the guilt which drives us to the cross"* (Forsyth 1957c).

There are always those in the church who grow impatient with written prayers, with the ritual of church worship, with the liturgy. They complain that such routine forms of worship are not personal enough, and apparently, not "spiritual" (whatever that is!) enough. We tend to expect every religious occasion to be what we call "soul-stirring," a memorable experience.

This attitude can cause great trouble. Sometimes we just don't feel like praying, or worshiping, or Bible study, or receiving the sacrament. If this feeling becomes the norm, we are in grave danger of spiritual shipwreck. We may lapse into "brooding over ourselves," dwelling on our problems and sins. Many a person who says, "I couldn't sleep last night," must in all honesty, add that it was because he/she was "brooding over self," and this is always fatal.

No—far better to have and keep a practice of a daily devotional time when the Bible is read, regardless of how we feel. Far better to keep inviolate the practice of regular, weekly (at least) worship with the congregation and using written prayers. As we say to sick people, "You must eat."

For God is always calling, always seeking us—and he uses the words, his word, to do this. This word says he went to the cross for us. He chose to do this. Sometimes we forget that.

"Attend to the public reading of scripture, to preaching, to teaching. Do not neglect the gift you have. . . . Practice these duties, devote yourself to them" (1 Tim. 4:13, 14, 15).

So, my savior God, remind me this day to listen to you through your book. Help me never to ignore your cross. Create in me this day a hunger for your word of love, so I may hear it again, and enjoy your company on my way. Amen.

The Greatness of the Small

"We reach heaven step by step, fighting all the way. What we need most of all for this life is the courage of the prosaic. As someone has put it, 'Above all, no heroics.' If we get into the habit of indulging in heroics, we too often end in a scream. Heroism is a great thing, but fortitude is greater still" (Forsyth 1971b).

Some days it seems like a mistake to get out of bed, we often say. It is tempting to pray with the psalmist for the "wings of a dove," or with the prophet for the "wings of an eagle." We look for a religion of escapism, and clothe our thoughts in the language of religious generalities. We turn off the news broadcast because it is "so depressing."

What should we do?

It is helpful to remember Martin Luther's definition of baptism as a daily renewal, a daily "being drowned" in the waters of God's mercy, so that we face this day as a fresh time to revel in God's glory and mercy. That is, we sever the ties with yesterday and its heavy burdens.

It is also helpful to take this day seriously—to face the mundane tasks facing us, with a prayer for the wisdom and strength the tasks are calling for.

We live with a Savior who reminded us of the beauty of the ordinary. "Consider the lilies of the field." He reminded us of the sanctity of the small and helpless. "Not a sparrow falls to the ground but your Heavenly Father sees." He demonstrated the availability of God by his use of the seemingly mundane. He healed with spit and mud, he validated the new birth by God with water, and became personally available through bread and wine.

Today he would have us use his strength to grub through the tedium of small things and to fight through those nagging doubts and resentments. His glory shines brightest in the little things.

"O that I had in the desert a wayfarer's lodging place, that I might leave my people and go away from them!" (Jer. 9:2).

"I can do all things through him who strengthens me" (Phil. 4:13).

Help Me!

DAY 11 *"First we cry from the depth of our need, then from the depth of our sin and despair, and finally deepest of all we cry from the depth of our faith, which lifts us to the heights. We know then that if we fall, we fall deeper into the arms of God. 'If my bark sink, 'tis but to another sea.' For as our hell is deep, so is our heaven deep; our hell is so deep because we were made for so deep a heaven"* (Forsyth 1971a).

There is a natural way to pray. True prayer is a cry from the heart, ungarnished by logic or philosophy or, even, theology. True prayer begins where we are, and erupts from our need—from our feelings which are pressuring us at the time. Prayer is a cry for help, as the psalmist does over and over. It is a false piety which keeps us from telling God what we cannot help thinking or feeling.

Usually such prayer leads to the discovery of a deeper need, the need for confession. We cry to God because we cannot handle the pressure of our conscience. From somewhere there come the suppressed images of our involvement in hurting or exploiting another. We are driven to set before God our deeper need—the need for mercy, the need for forgiveness. We confess that we have sinned and cannot handle that fact. Praying thus makes us naked before God.

If we listen we will hear the gospel. "You do not have to cope," says God. "That is the devil speaking. Just let go and let me help." His love moves us to confess, even as the need for love prompts all our praying. Love assures us that the "bottom line" with God is something bigger than our accountability. The bottom line is that he hears, and has already encircled us with his arms. The basis for everything in this life—everything—is his forgiving and healing love.

"Jesus, Lover of my soul, Let me to thy bosom fly" (*Service Book and Hymnal*, 393).

"Out of the depths I cry to thee, O Lord! Lord, hear my voice!" (Ps. 130:1-2).

Use Your Freedom

"The living God is the basis of the living church. We need a God as near to us as life is. We must have a searching and a shaping God. This we have in the son of the living God. The living God alone can make us living persons; the mighty God alone can make us mighty people; the loving God alone can make us consecrated human beings" (Forsyth 1971a).

Sometimes God seems so far away, so uninvolved that our prayers seem to hit the ceiling and bounce back into our hands. If God is not dead, as some theologians claimed a few years ago, he does seem to be so remote, so unattainable that we may as well forget about him.

When this happens, our religious life becomes a preoccupation with the "dead letter of the law" and is shaped by rules. The strange result of this is that we often feel we can redefine the rules to fit our needs, and thus the rules cease to be rules.

But Jesus was resurrected. He lives, and because he lives, we too shall live. When we pray we are dealing with a living God, and this places our lives in his hands, not in ours. Wherever we go, whatever we do, we discover that God was here first. As we seek for God, we find that he has been seeking us all along. Because he lives, nothing is predictable. He is everywhere, working in human hearts.

God lives—that is, he is a personality, not an idea.

God lives to reshape us into our initial glory—his image. Because God lives among us and in us through his Holy Spirit, anything can happen. The constant miracle is that we are being transformed to live as trusting children, not rebellious runaways.

Because he lives, we live—in the fullest sense of the word. We are empowered to make right choices. We are re-created to love the good and hate the bad. We are even given the ability to walk the second mile, to give our cloak, and to so limit our intoxicating freedom that we refrain from anything which may tempt another. We walk in his freedom all the way.

"You may know how one ought to behave in the household of God, which is the church of the living God, the pillar and bulwark of the truth" (1 Tim. 3:15).

Surprised by Love

DAY
13

"The true majesty of God is his mercy. His greatness is not in his loftiness, but in his nearness. He is great not because he is above feelings, but because he can feel as no human can. God's majesty is saturated through and through with his forgiving love, which comes out most of all in his treatment of sin" (Forsyth 1971a).

The prayer of the church for the seventeenth Sunday after Pentecost expresses Forsyth's words: "O God, you declare your almighty power chiefly in showing mercy and pity. Grant us the fullness of your grace, that, pursuing what you have promised, we may share your heavenly glory; through your son, Jesus Christ our Lord" (*LBW* p. 27).

Jewish theology insisted that only God could forgive sins. Jesus' contemporaries were therefore horrified when he forgave the sins of the paralytic. It seemed to them that Jesus was usurping the place of God and offering "cheap grace." "Sin is sin, after all," they said, and "God alone is the Holy Lord of all life."

Sin is rebellion, whether it expresses itself in dramatic ways or quietly. It is therefore beyond our poor ability to atone for our sin. God, who knows this even better than we, moves to convince us that we have one great hope. He is not a "hanging judge." He does not give moral lectures. He takes our rebellion to himself by dying on the cross and coming to us with his offer of mercy, which is simply forgiveness of sin.

The experience of forgiveness is always a surprise. Though we've heard many times that God is always available, the experience of his nearness, his mercy, his empathy, and above all his power, sends shock waves to our heart. All seems new—everything is changed, simply because the God of power expresses his power by showing love and mercy.

"And when he saw their faith he said, 'Man, your sins are forgiven you'" (Luke 5:20).

With Us All the Way

"The more Christ changes the more he is the same. Stability is not stiffness. Jesus, 'the same yesterday, today and forever,' is not a dead identity, a monument that we leave behind, but persistent personality that never ceases to open upon us. Our real and destined eternity goes round by Nazareth to reach us" (Forsyth 1957c).

P. T. Forsyth concludes with the words, "He is born again in each soul that is born anew." He has written elsewhere, "Each soul is the first to be." This is true because of the changeless nature of Jesus our Lord. Jesus speaks to each one of us by name. We are not interchangeable parts of a giant machine. The church is not a collection of robots. We are not evaluated by our sameness, but our authenticity. We are competing, in life's race, with ourselves, not with others. The mark of any true champion is that he/she says, "I can be and do better than I have done," not, "I am better than others."

So Jesus adjusts to our individual needs, one by one. To some he is stern: "Sin no more." To some he is tender: "Come to me for rest." To some he is didactic: "The kingdom of God is like this." Peter's big sin was that he violated his own God-given name—"The Rock"—not that he sinned more grievously than others.

How wonderful this is! Jesus is not a dictator, demanding uniform responses from all of us. Nor is he an anarchist, letting us all do as we please. He is a savior, reaching out for each of us in our uniqueness. He is a friend, who walks with us all the way. He is the same in the way he treats us. Each of us, regardless of what we have done or not done, is precious in his sight.

A mother understands this. She sees her children as individuals, and so is often surprised when someone says, "They are just alike." She knows better—she knows that one responds to pressure and one buckles under pressure, for instance, and treats them accordingly.

Our biggest sin just may be sinning against such mercy. Jesus breaks fresh upon us each day—with a renewed hope and a renewed vision.

"Hence we can confidently say, 'The Lord is my helper, I will not be afraid; what can man do to me? . . .' Jesus Christ is the same yesterday and today and for ever" (Heb. 13:6,8).

Roy Hammerling

JOHANNES TAULER

 EW parish preachers have received as much recognition as Johannes Tauler (ca. 1300–1361). After preaching a sermon, most pastors are fortunate if they receive a kind word from an elderly person of the congregation. However, the sermons of Tauler's were so popular that they were collected and circulated until they found a wide audience.

Tauler was born in Strasbourg which was considered a part of the Rhineland of Germany. His father, Nicholaus Tauler, was a wealthy property owner and magistrate of the area who, along with his wife, was devoutly religious. Johannes and his sister joined the Dominican order of the Roman Catholic Church. The Order of Preachers was the perfect place for Tauler, because he wanted nothing more in life than to preach and teach the word of God.

Only a little is known about Tauler's life. He probably became a novice in the Dominican order in Strasbourg around 1314–1315 and it was then that he started his training to become a preacher. Tauler's most famous teacher was Meister Eckhart, who lived and taught in Strasbourg from 1312–1320.

Eckhart and Tauler were both mystics. Central to their sermons was the mystical ideal of becoming one with God. Tauler's mysticism encouraged his listeners to enter into the "ground," or very depths of their souls. This "ground" of the soul is where God can be found. To enter the depth of the soul, through contemplation or by some mystical experience, means becoming one with God. This union with God is a mystical union, which can be explained only by experience.

Tauler became a Dominican priest around 1325, and preached primarily to the Strasbourg sisters of the Dominican Order, although his sermons also give evidence that lay people heard him preach on a number of occasions.

Basel, Switzerland became Tauler's home in exile in 1339 when a conflict broke out between Emperor Louis the Bavarian and Pope John XXII. The Dominicans in Strasbourg supported Pope John, while the city of Strasbourg rallied behind the Emperor. The Pope, in retaliation for Strasbourg's allegiance to Louis, would not allow the Sacraments to be celebrated in the city. The Dominicans, in order to remain loyal and still celebrate the sacraments, went to Basel. Tauler returned to Strasbourg after about seven years and lived there for the rest of his life.

The Heavenly Plow

"We have to set to work just as the farmer does in March, when he sees that the sunny days are beginning to draw near. He trims and prunes his trees, pulls up the weeds, turns over the ground, and digs it most industriously. We too should spare ourselves no trouble; dig ourselves over well, examine the ground and turn up the under soil; clip back the hedges . . . and tear out all the weeds. First to be lopped off are the seven deadly sins; do not spare them, root or branch. Do away with all pride, interior and exterior, all avarice, anger, hatred, and envy; all impure delights of body, heart, sense or mind" (Tauler 1961).

The spring brings with it an anxious air in North Dakota. The farmers emerge from their sheds with their tractors roaring like lions set free from their cages. Too long have they paced back and forth waiting for this day. The dirt, which has become mingled with their blood, tells them that the moment is right. Setting their hearts and minds to long hours of work, the ground is prepared. Rough fields are dealt with harshly and a fruitful harvest usually awaits the end of the farmer's labor.

Seldom are we so eager to deal with sin in our lives. Unlike the farmer, the desire to plow up what is evil is not a part of our blood.

Sin grows in our hearts like a weed. If we try to ignore this evil weed, it will spread out its roots until the whole field is overgrown. The key to controlling our sinful desires is not in fulfilling them, but in uprooting them and utterly destroying them.

But alone we cannot plow under our sin, for none of us knows how to prepare the ground of our soul. Only Christ can turn us in repentance to God. For when we repent, we plow under the sin which keeps us from God. Once repentance has done its harsh work in our lives, only then can we experience the harvest of forgiveness. Then we will know what Tauler means when he concludes the above quote by saying, *"So it is that our beloved and eternal God makes the soul grow rich, like green fields, and blossom, and produces the most wonderful fruits such as no tongue can describe and no heart can conceive, so great is the happiness which fills the soul"* (Tauler 1961).

"Thus it is written, that the Christ should suffer and on the third day rise from the dead, and that repentance and forgiveness of sins should be preached in his name to all nations" (Luke 24:46-47).

Thirst for God

" Just as the deer thirsts for the stream, so my soul thirsts for you, O Lord.' [Ps. 42:1] The deer is hunted across woods and hills, till the great heat of the chase causes an intense thirst, and he longs for water. . . . The harder and fiercer the chase the more intense our thirst for God ought to become. . . . God allows the soul to be hard pressed, till there is no other path open to it, but permits this, so that the drink which quenches our thirst may taste all the sweeter and more delicate, now and throughout eternity" (Tauler 1985).

The deer grazes calmly upon grass. The sun crests the hill and peace rules the valley, but unexpectedly a rifle shot rings out! Instinctively, the deer bounds high into the air and soon is at a dead run, flying through coulees and over hills. The hunter does not give up, setting loose the trained dogs who force the deer to strain its limbs to their limits. One dog sinks its teeth into the belly of the deer, but the deer dashes the dog against a tree and once again is free. The deer's desire for life makes it run, sparing no energy, until thirst itself almost overcomes it.

Every time the deer stops to rest or drink a sip of water another dog howls or another bullet splits the air. Finally, the hunter calls off the dogs, and the deer comes to a stream and it drinks a deep drink. As the deer laps up the water it forgets itself.

One of the great dilemmas of American society is that many us have become so wealthy we no longer hunger or thirst for anything. Can you remember the last time you were so thirsty that you would have gladly given all you had for a glass of cold water? Our money can buy for us whatever we want and so we have forgotten what it means to truly thirst for anything. What becomes of God then? If we have no thirst, have we also forgotten how to thirst for God?

God thirsts for all people to thirst for Him. Suffering and tribulations, trials and temptations create in us a thirst for the water of peace. Only those who have a thirst can have it quenched by God. Augustine, one of Tauler's favorite writers, once wrote, "My soul is restless, O Lord, until it rest in thee." Whether we are thirsty or not, only one thing can truly quench our thirst and that is the God who hunts to bring us to Himself.

"If any one thirst, let him come to me and drink" (John 7:37).

Knowing How to Die

"Children . . . our natures have to die many a death and we must travel along many a rough and unknown path, along which God draws us, teaching us to die. Dear children, what a noble, fruitful, wonderful, joyful life is born in this dying! What a noble, pure and immeasurably good thing it is to know how to die!" (Tauler 1961).

During World War II, a Lutheran bishop was thrown into a Nazi concentration camp because Hitler wanted the bishop to confess that he was a traitor. The SS tortured him relentlessly, but he refused to admit any crime. After the bishop had endured much suffering, the SS officer said, "Don't you know that I could kill you?" The bishop quietly replied, "Oh yes, I know that quite well. Do as you please. I belong to Christ. I have already died with him when I was baptized. There is nothing you can do to me." At that moment the SS officer could no longer torture the bishop. Torture only works when a person wants to hold onto his or her life. Because the bishop had already died with Christ in baptism, the threat of death by torture was no threat.

God teaches us to die when we deny ourselves, when we admit that we are sinful, and when we turn to Christ for forgiveness. Only in daily returning to our baptism by confessing and dying to our sins can there be life in Christ.

What we ought to fear in life is not that life will come to an end, but rather that in the end we never had any life. Once a child muddled her bedtime prayer by saying, "Now I lay me down to sleep, I pray the Lord my soul to keep, if I wake before I die. . . ." When we die to ourselves then we wake to true life in Christ.

Dying is something that we not only do to ourselves, but also for our neighbors. Henri Nouwen writes in *Way of the Heart*, "In order to be of service to others, we have to die to them. . . . To die to our neighbor means to stop judging them, to stop evaluating them, and thus become free to be compassionate."

Before we can be alive to God we must die to ourselves, and for our neighbor. Without death there is no life and without life we are already dead. Indeed, what a noble, pure, and immeasurably good thing it is to know how to die!

"Truly, truly, I say to you, unless a grain of wheat falls into the earth and dies, it remains alone; but if it dies, it bears much fruit" (John 12:24).

No Nails in the Cross

" 'Whoever will follow me,' [says Christ] 'let him take up his cross daily and follow me. . . .' But alas, we have come to this: nobody nowadays thinks that he can endure any pain at all. People are grown weak-spirited and delicate natured. . . . If we could find some new way of perfection involving no manner of suffering, we might preach and propagate it with success. In our day men love only themselves" (Tauler 1910).

Do you know what type of product is advertised more than any other on television today? Pain relievers! Whether it be a headache or back pain, minor arthritis or a major toothache, we are counseled to take a pill to get rid of our pain. But this phenomenon is not unique to our day. Over 600 years ago, Tauler spoke of how people of his day were constantly looking for a pain-free life.

But what happens if we carry this idea into the arena of our Christian faith? Tauler recognized the fact that if a preacher would preach a doctrine doing away with suffering, people would flock to it. Down through the ages, and especially today, this has always been true. Preachers tickle the ears of their listeners and tell their congregations that if they follow Christ, God will bless them and make them successful. Such false teaching is attractive because none of us wants to suffer. These modern day preachers of glory avoid the cross of Christ by saying that Jesus bore the cross so we wouldn't have to. They ignore the Scripture which calls us to a life of following Christ by taking up our cross. These popular preachers of no suffering have TV shows and large congregations, and they point to their success as evidence that God is with them. In reality, they have traded the cross for a soft bed of money and luxury. People do not change, only the times change. People, like you and I, have always wanted to avoid suffering. But in so doing we avoid our cross and ultimately God. A healthy caution is needed when it comes to religious teaching. If any teaching pulls the nails out of the cross or wipes away the wounds of Christ, then beware, for it is only quick temporary relief from true Christian pain.

"But rejoice in so far as you share Christ's sufferings, that you may also rejoice and be glad when his glory is revealed" (1 Pet. 4:13).

Deadly Sunshine

D A Y
5

"A life of ease and consolation would be a contradiction to the testimony of Jesus Christ; He is the serpent which Moses lifted up in the desert, at which all must look who wished to be healed. . . . In fact, if these troubles of ours should ever abate, we ought to invite them back and beg them to return, so that they may scour off the rust which they had caused in the bad old days; that they may now take away what once they brought to us" (Tauler 1961).

An ancient Arabic proverb reads, "If you only have sunshine in life, then the only land you can live in is the desert!"

Victor Frankl, the famous psychiatrist, as a young man was taken to Auschwitz concentration camp. When he arrived he overheard a man saying, "You must be strong. If you look too weak they will just take you off to the ovens to be burned." The man pointed at Frankl and said, "People who look like you will never survive here." But Frankl did survive. Frankl observed that the people who lived through the horror of the holocaust were not necessarily "strong" people. If a person lost hope, if a person had no purpose or meaning in life, that person would die no matter how strong he was. If a person, however, had a strong faith in God, or a family that gave her courage, then she lived no matter how weak she was. Said Frankl, "He who has a 'why' to live for can suffer any 'how' to live."

None of us can escape suffering. And yet, all of us would rather have a life of pure sunshine. Tauler points out that such a life would ultimately be a desert. We should not avoid suffering when it comes upon us, but rather know that in suffering God draws us unto Himself. Therefore, Tauler can even say that we should ask for our sufferings to return if they leave us. In suffering we learn that God is the "why" we live for. Christ with us in our afflictions helps us to suffer the "how" we are forced to live. Without Christ in our pain we are lost, like a ship in the ocean with no place to go. Clinging to Christ in our suffering is our only safe port of call.

"Three times I [Paul] besought the Lord about this [suffering], that it should leave me; but he said to me, 'My grace is sufficient for you, for my power is made perfect in weakness. . . .' For the sake of Christ, then, I am content with weaknesses, insults, hardships, persecutions, and calamities; for when I am weak, then I am strong" (2 Cor. 12:8-9, 10).

The Tremendous Mystery

<table>
<tr><td>D A Y
6</td><td>*"When we come to speak of the Most Blessed Trinity, we are at a loss for words, and yet words must be used to say something. . . . To express it [the Trinity] adequately is as impossible as touching the sky with one's head. For everything we can say or think can*</td></tr>
</table>

no more approach the reality than the smallest point of a needle can contain heaven and earth. . . . To experience the working of the Trinity is better than to talk about it. . . . It is for us to believe in simplicity" (Tauler 1985).

C. S. Lewis once was teaching a Bible study class for some soldiers. On one occasion he got a bit carried away and began discussing the faith in such an intellectual way that most of the soldiers were lost in the presentation. One old hard-bitten officer stood up and said, "I don't have much use for all this fancy faith stuff. But mind you, I'm a religious man. I believe in God. I've felt him with me when I was on patrol in the desert at night. There He was, the tremendous mystery! I've met the real thing and your words seem petty to me."

God is mystery! How can we understand that which cannot be understood? In the end, all our words about God are like a cigar box trying to contain the Pacific ocean. They contain only a very small part of who God really is.

And yet, even if God is a mystery to our minds, God is not a mystery to our hearts. Because even though God is beyond our understanding, God is not beyond our experience. God comes to us in Jesus Christ and is made known to us through grace. Blaise Pascal wrote, "The God of Abraham, Isaac, and Jacob is not the same God of the philosophers!" Abraham knew God and listened to God's voice when God called him to leave his country and go to the promised land. Isaac experienced God's grace when God stopped his father Abraham from sacrificing him on Mt. Moriah. And Jacob wrestled with God at the Jabbok River. God may be encountered, but never fully understood.

If we could know the mystery of God we would not need faith, but as it stands, faith begins where knowledge ends. Faith is the experience of the tremendous mystery and the touching of the unknown.

"This is how one should regard us, as servants of Christ and stewards of the mysteries of God" (1 Cor. 4:1).

Silent Rest

DAY 7

"You should observe silence, in that manner the Word can be uttered and heard within. For surely, if you choose to speak, God must fall silent. There is no better way of serving the Word than by silence and by listening" (Tauler 1985).

There once was a brother and sister who were both afraid of their shadows. The boy was so terrified that every time he went outside he would run as fast as he could to get away from his relentless pursuer. Constantly worrying that his shadow would catch him brought the boy to an early grave. Even though the sister had the same fear, she lived to a ripe old age. Every time she went outside she would rest in the shade of every tree she walked by. The longer she rested the longer the shadows stayed away. The sister had found the secret of quiet rest, while her brother ate nothing but the bread of hurry and worry.

Carl Jung once said that hurry is not of the devil, but hurry is the devil. Fast-food stands dot the countryside and are perhaps the best sign that we are afraid of our own shadows. We often will eat food which is an insult to our health simply to save time.

If we are always on the move, how can God ever find a time or a place to speak to us in our lives? Many of us are afraid of silence. We don't want long silences for prayer in our worship services because we want to get it over with and get home. When we are alone at home, we avoid any silence we might have by keeping the TV on. When we are alone in the car, the radio helps us wipe out the silence. Perhaps the main reason we avoid silence is because silence is where God can come and speak to us. To be in the presence of God is a frightening thing.

Albert Schweitzer once said, "It is not enough merely to exist. It is not enough to say, 'I'm earning enough to live and support my family. I do well. I am a good father. I go to church.' That's all very well. But there is more to life than this. There is time alone with God." Take time, slow down, and rest, and hear God's still small voice speak to you in the silence of your heart.

"For thus said the Lord God, the Holy One of Israel, 'In returning and rest you shall be saved; in quietness and in trust shall be your strength'" (Isa. 30:15).

The Archer's Target

DAY
8

*"Keep in mind these two little points. First, be truly humble, through-
out your whole being, not only in mind and in outward conduct;
think lowly of yourself, and see yourself honestly for what you are.
And secondly, let the love you bear God be a true one; not just
what is usually understood by the term, which refers only to emotions, but a
love that embraces God most ardently. Such love is a far cry from . . . religious
feeling . . . [but be] drawn by love, just as a runner is drawn, or an archer,
who has a single goal before his eyes"* (Tauler 1985).

One of the most God-fearing women I have ever known once asked
me to come visit her. As we talked she said, "Pastor, I know I am not the
person God wants me to be. I am a sinner and in spite of my desire to
be God's child, I fail Christ daily. Can God forgive me even in my continued
unfaithfulness?" I was humbled by her humility. Before me sat a woman
who knew she was nothing and that God was everything. "Oh yes!" I said,
"God saves the humble, and destroys the proud. Fear not, Christ has saved
you through the cross!"

Throughout the centuries, Christian writers are almost in complete
agreement. Pride is the first sin! Adam and Eve, out of pride, ate the fruit
of the tree in the hope that they would be like God. Pride is simply wanting
to be more than one really is. Through pride we put others down, even
God, in order to attempt to build ourselves up.

If pride is the first sin, then humility must be the first virtue. Humility
is a woman in a parish who knows her own unworthiness before God.
Humility is being honest and knowing that one is a sinner in need of God's
grace. The humble person refuses pride a place in the heart by filling the
heart with God. Thus Martin Luther could say, "If pride would cease there
would be no sin."

Humility moves the believer to a true love of God, love not merely
made up of feelings. People who base their love for God on emotions alone
will be faithful when they are happy and unfaithful when they are discouraged. A true love of God includes emotions, but goes far beyond them
to involve the whole person in faithful commitment to God. As an archer
concentrates upon the center of the target, so the Christian zeros in on
Christ as the sole focus of life.

"God opposes the proud, but gives grace to the humble" (James 4:6).

The Painful Embrace

D A Y	*"A certain sister of our [Dominican] order had often longed to behold*
9	*our Lord as a little child, and once during her devotions He appeared*
	to her in this form. But the Divine Child was wrapped in a thorny
	robe. That she might embrace Him, she had to brave the sharp

points of many thorns and to suffer bitter pain from them. Thus was she taught,
that if any one would enjoy our Lord in close embrace, that one must be willing
to suffer sharp, piercing pain" (Tauler 1910).

The snow fell as the missionary drove away from the small South Korean village. His visit with the single pregnant woman was short because he had Christmas Eve services to perform in his own village five miles away. In the middle of night her labor pains began. Being young and afraid, the mother decided to try to walk to the home of the missionary. As the light snowfall turned into a storm, she found shelter underneath an old bridge, where she gave birth to a son. The next morning the missionary rushed to see how the woman was, but his car broke down. As he continued his journey on foot he heard a faint cry as he crossed the bridge. Scrambling below he found a baby wrapped in his mother's clothes and the frozen, naked mother beside the child. The missionary adopted the little boy and every year on Christmas Day they would visit the grave of the brave mother. On the boy's 12th birthday, as they came upon the grave, the boy asked the missionary to remain at a distance. The missionary, in unbelief, watched as the boy took off all his clothes and sat in the snow of his mother's grave. The dear child cried out, "Mother, were you colder than this for me?"

To love Christ is to welcome Christ's suffering. As the Dominican sister learned in her vision and as the Korean boy learned in the snow, true love is always a painful embrace. If we would cling to Christ in our lives then we must embrace Christ's sufferings. Whether we hold to Christ's thorny cross or are wrapped in the rags of winter, we will only find eternal life in the suffering and death of Christ. Christ's great sacrifice inspires in us awe and we cry out in wonder, "Were you colder than this for us, O Lord?"

"When I [Paul] came to you, brethren, I did not come proclaiming to you the testimony of God in lofty words or wisdom. For I decided to know nothing among you except Jesus Christ and him crucified" (1 Cor. 2:1-2).

The Flood

"This precious Holy Spirit came down upon the disciples and upon all who were able to receive Him, with tremendous richness, abundance, and generosity, pouring Himself out in their hearts. Imagine the Rhine in flood, with all the dams and barriers cleared away. How it would come rushing down in full stream, overflowing its banks as if to drown and submerge everything, filling all the valleys and meadows in its way! That is just how the Holy Spirit came upon the disciples and all those whom He found ready to receive Him. And so He still does, unceasingly at every moment. He fills and overflows the depths of every heart and soul where He can find a place, and He fills them with richness, graces, love, and gifts past all telling. He fills the valleys and the depths that are kept for Him" (Tauler 1961).

As the disciples were sitting around in an upper room on Pentecost they heard a sound like the roar of a waterfall. The Holy Spirit was poured out upon the followers of Christ and they were flooded by the grace of God. Tongues like fire danced on their heads and the Holy Spirit rose up in the disciples. Running out into the streets, the Spirit poured forth from the disciples as they began to preach in different languages. This flood of God swept away 3,000 people that Pentecost day, as they were drowned in the water of baptism. Some others who saw this thought the disciples were drunk, but in reality they were never more sober. For when the Holy Spirit makes you alive, you are alive indeed.

Today, the Holy Spirit still flows down into our lives like a flood, in a sudden, dangerous, and life-threatening way. The Holy Spirit comes upon us unexpectedly and washes away all the old dead debris of sin out of our hearts. As in the days of Noah, the Spirit comes like rain to drown all that is wicked, lifting up what belongs to God in the ark, to give life out of death. In baptism, Christ, the living water, fills every valley and place of our being.

> "Joy to the earth, the Savior reigns!
> Let all their songs employ.
> While fields and floods, rocks, hills, and plains,
> repeat the sounding joy!"
>
> (LBW 39)

"We were buried therefore with [Christ] by baptism into death, so that as Christ was raised from the dead by the glory of the Father, we too might walk in newness of life" (Rom. 6:4).

Rain Clouds

"Everyone should do for his neighbor what his neighbor cannot do so well as he, and in this way, by his love for others, he thanks God for His graces. Be sure of this: if we are not useful, profitable and helpful to our neighbor, we shall have much to answer for before God. The Gospel says that everyone will have to give an account of his stewardship. Each one of us has an obligation to pay back as best he can what he has received from God, because God gave it to him for the benefit of others" (Tauler 1961).

When God created the cosmos, God blessed each angel with a talent to take care of a part of creation. One angel was blessed with the talent to make the stars shine brightly, another had the gift of making the ocean waves roll, and still another painted the sky blue. However, the angel in charge of the grass was not happy. "What kind of job is this?" thought the angel. "The grass is here today and gone tomorrow. Why should I worry about something so unimportant?" So the angel forgot all about the grass. After a month of leading a carefree life the angel noticed that the grass had all turned brown. The animals in every land were starving, the earth was eroding away from the rains, and the angels in charge of these things complained to God. Feeling ashamed the angel went and fell down before God begging for forgiveness. God said, "I give no meaningless gift in this world. Everyone has a talent to use for the good of creation. When one angel refuses to take care of what I have given, no matter how insignificant the task may seem, all of creation suffers."

You and I are created with a God-given talent that others need. If we refuse to share that gift with others, then the task is left undone and all of creation suffers. Our blessed talents are not ours to do with as we please, but they are bestowed upon us by God in order that we might share them. When we withhold these gifts from others, then we become thieves stealing from our neighbor.

"Like clouds and wind without rain is a man who boasts of a gift he does not give" (Prov. 25:14).

50 Plus

DAY 12 *"Unless a man has reached his fortieth year, he will never attain lasting peace, never be truly formed into God, try as he may. Up to that time he is occupied by so many things, driven this way and that by his own natural impulses; he is governed by them although he may imagine that he is governed by God. Before the proper time has arrived, he cannot achieve true and perfect peace. . . . After that he shall wait another ten years before the Holy Ghost, the Comforter, the Spirit who teaches all things, is truly his"* (Tauler 1985).

The prisons are full of people who want to find a short-cut to prosperity. State lotteries, gambling, and letters telling us we could win millions of dollars, all encourage us to take easy street. We want everything in an instant. From instant oatmeal to instant money to an instant bank, short-cuts have become our way of life.

Even as Christians, we are tempted to take short-cuts. Many believers in America go to church on Christmas and Easter because Christmas offers a cute baby and Easter offers a risen Lord. Christians attempt to take a short-cut around Good Friday in order to have a God who is more to our liking.

Tauler's words seem strange and unreasonable. Can he really mean that no one under 40 can have true peace? Is the Holy Spirit reserved for those over 50? Certainly Tauler overstates his case to make an important point. There are no short-cuts which can bring one to peace in Christ!

Peace is a gift and one that is not easily grasped. Tauler believes that most people under 40 are simply too caught up in the things of this world to have true peace. Youthful enthusiasm wants a short-cut to the blessings of old age. So with faith, we all would like to have a mature faith instantly, but such faith takes time. A mature faith and perfect peace comes only after we have walked with the Christ child through Calvary to the empty tomb. The sin of the short-cut tempts us all, but Christ calls us to the long road, at the end of which stands a cross.

"The Holy Spirit, whom the Father will send in my name, he will teach you all things. . . . Peace I leave with you; my peace I give to you; not as the world gives do I give to you. Let not your hearts be troubled, neither let them be afraid" (John 14:26-27).

Anchor in the Storm

"Cast all your anxiety on God! Be solidly anchored in Him. When sailors are in danger of running aground and all seems to be lost, they throw their anchor overboard and it sinks to the bottom of the Rhine; that is the way they defend themselves against danger. And it is the way we, too, should act: When we are assailed by grave temptations of mind and body, we should abandon all else and let the anchor sink deep into the ground which means perfect trust in God's fidelity. . . . If only we could seize the anchor at the time of our death and so die in perfect hope and trust, what a blessed death it would be!" (Tauler 1985).

The storm blew in, but it was expected. Three sailing ships with cargo from the East were returning together to Venice. As the tempest broke, all three ships had anticipated trouble. The first captain attempted to sail around the storm, not wanting to interrupt the voyage. The captain of the second ship, not fearing the winds, drove his ship straight into the storm. The captain of the third vessel ordered that the anchor be put down, for he trusted the anchor would hold their position. The tempest broke with a tremendous fury. The first ship was blown hundreds of miles off course, the second ship was pounded against the shore, and the third ship, though nearly destroyed, held firm to its place in the sea.

After two years of struggling with cancer, 30-year-old Melody died. Her family and friends had anticipated this day, but not the magnitude of the storm. Some sailed around Melody's terminal illness, denying that Melody would die, and continuing on as if nothing would happen. Some moved straight into the storm, but having nothing to secure them from its fury, were crushed without hope. Others set their anchor down trusting in God to keep them safe. In the end, these people found peace in her death. Melody seized the anchor when the end came, and in perfect hope and trust she died a blessed death. All who grounded their anchor in God found safety in Christ in spite of the storm.

"A great storm of wind arose, and the waves beat into the boat. . . . They woke [Jesus] and said to him, 'Teacher, do you not care if we perish?' And he . . . said to the sea, 'Peace, be still!' . . . And they were filled with awe, and said to one another, 'Who then is this, that even wind and sea obey him?' " (Mark 4:37-41).

The Splintery Coat

"Children, turn which way you will, you must carry your cross and hang upon it. To be a good man desirous of coming to God, always means suffering. . . . Now Christ suffered all this before us in the severest possible pain; and He has drawn after Him in this trial all those whom He most dearly loves. His cross is Elijah's fiery chariot, bearing our prophet upwards to heaven, and from it He casts forth his prophet's mantle on Elisha, his disciple. Our Lord does this for us from His cross" (Tauler 1910).

The fiery chariot burned across the sky. Elijah whipped the reigns and turned his face toward heaven. As the flaming chariot soared higher the wind blew off Elijah's coat. Or did Elijah take it off and throw it into the wind? There is no way of knowing, but the slightly scorched mantle floated down to the earth landing at Elisha's feet. In a puff of smoke and flames the fireworks ended. Elisha was left all alone staring up at the sky and at his feet was the coat. Elijah's coat! As Elisha picked up the mantle, the symbol of Elijah's power as a prophet, he felt a chill. He draped the smoldering mantle over his shoulders and Elisha was transformed into God's newly chosen prophet (2 Kings 2).

The cross cast a dark shadow upon the earth. Jesus cried out with a loud voice, his face went blank, his head went limp, and life left his scourged body. Suddenly the clouds blotted out every trace of the sun, and the windows of heaven opened, pouring out rain cold as ice. The wind blew as they took Christ's body down from the cross to bury it in the hand-hewn cave.

All that was left was the cross wavering in the wind and the words Jesus had spoken a few days before, "If any [one] would come after me, let [that one] deny [himself or herself], and take up [his or her] cross and follow me" (Matt. 16:24).

The cross, like a coat, is left at the feet of all who would come after Christ. A chill in the air forces us reluctantly to drape the splintery coat over our shoulders, and in so doing we are transformed into God's chosen prophets to proclaim his death until he comes again. There is no other way, no other path, and no other hope, but to wear the coat that will bear us with fire into the very presence of God.

"For to this you have been called, because Christ also suffered for you, leaving you an example, that you should follow in his steps" (1 Pet. 2:21).

Edna and Howard Hong

Søren Kierkegaard

E VERYONE, from theologians and philosophers, to graduate students and journalists, is dropping the name Søren Kierkegaard these days. Major journals of philosophy, religion, or psychology that do not contain his name are rare. One is tempted to ask: Are people merely name-dropping, or is this man actually that important?

To the country (Denmark) and century (1813–1855) in which Kierkegaard lived, he was decidedly unimportant, and outside of Scandinavia was practically unknown. In this century the whole world considers him to have had and to have as much influence on contemporary thought as any other thinker of either his century or ours.

A century and a half ago Kierkegaard was grappling with the very issues that plague the modern conscience. Indeed, he predicted very precisely in his writings the dehumanization that has happened and is happening in this secular, materialistic society. No physician has ever diagnosed a disease more perceptibly than Kierkegaard has diagnosed the human condition. No preacher of penitence has described more honestly and devastatingly than he the consequences of the loss of self in the denial of God.

"What does it mean to exist?" Kierkegaard asked, using the word in its original Latin meaning, to stand forth, to live a life that is more than we mean when we say, "merely existing." But then he loads the phrase "to exist" with his own meaning—namely, to exist in what one understands, to exist in the truth one understands. For Kierkegaard, truth is not a matter only of knowing but of being. It is a life.

Kierkegaard also wrote out of the old-fashioned, orthodox Christian faith. For him, Christ was the truth, and to exist in the truth meant to follow Christ, to deny oneself, and to walk the same way as Christ walked in the humble form of a servant. This poses a special problem for Lutherans. The Lutheran principle of grace alone, faith alone, and Christ as gift has often meant that following Christ, the imitation of Christ, and good works have fallen by the wayside. But it is demoralizing, maintains Kierkegaard, to receive Christ only as gift. Indeed, has one received the gift if there is no response?

Thus Kierkegaard saw himself as a missionary, not to pagans, but to Christians! He perceived his mission to be to reintroduce Christianity into Christendom.

My Highest Perfection

*"To need God is man's highest perfection. . . . Man's highest achieve-
ment is to let God be able to help him"* (Kierkegaard 1967).

To need, to be needy, to be in any kind of extremity is
not something desirable in this day and age. If it is at all avoidable, one
is expected to escape need by any and every possible route. Feel good
about yourself. If we do not "feel comfortable" with something, we shun
it. The primary aim of the burgeoning business of counseling is to create
a sense of well-being in those who come seeking advice. Even the church,
says Kierkegaard, has become trendy and presents Christianity *"in a certain
almost enervated form of coddling love. It is always love, love; spare yourself
and your flesh and blood; have pleasant days or delightful days without self-
made cares, for God is love, love—of strenuousness nothing must be heard . . ."*
(Kierkegaard 1962).

"The method now," wrote Kierkegaard in his journals, *"is to leave out
the existentially strenuous passages in the New Testament. We hush them up—
and then we arrange things on easier and cheaper terms. We probably think
that since we did not mention these passages God does not know that they are
in the New Testament"* (Kierkegaard 1967).

No Christian would recommend hushing up the good news of our
soul's salvation through Jesus Christ, but ought the church hush the bad
news of the human condition that makes us desperately need God? Furthermore, ought we not assume that the Father is like the Son and is most
accepting and welcoming to the person who is most in need and knows
it? Indeed, says Kierkegaard, more pleasing to God than hymn singing is
a human being who genuinely feels that he or she needs him. With such
a person God wants to and can communicate and help.

*"God in heaven, let me rightly feel my nothingness, not to despair over it, but
all the more intensely to feel the greatness of your goodness"* (Kierkegaard 1967).

'Tis I, I Who Need God!

"Christianity is not at all right to stress that all humankind needs Christianity and then to prove it and demonstrate it. The Christian stress is: I need Christianity" (Kierkegaard 1967).

It is not society, my generation, my community, my church, my friends—it is *I* who need the relationship to God that Christianity proclaims is available to me in Jesus Christ. By disobedience the human race fell into sin and out of relationship to God, but by Christ's obedience the human race was not restored en masse to relationship to God. That amazing grace is offered to and received not by they's or we's, but by individuals, by I's. God needs and wants to relate to and to communicate to I's, and the I most welcome to him is the I who needs him most. God's ear is open to the I who says to him, "I need you, oh, I need you! Every hour I need you!"

A relationship such as that is a firsthand relationship, not second- or thirdhand. "A secondhand relationship to God," says Kierkegaard, "is just as impossible and just as nonsensical as falling in love at second hand." If I forget the price that Christ paid so that I can have a firsthand relationship to God and believe the cost for me is too high, there is no place where I can buy, beg, or borrow a secondhand relationship. One can be brought to God through the intimate relationship to God of parents, of a spouse, of a friend, but one cannot ride tandem into that relationship with them. God requires of you and me an original, direct, firsthand relationship. Only as an I, an I who needs God and knows that I need God, can I truly relate to him.

My Father in heaven, I know very well that you know that I need you. You do not need to hear me say it, but you want to hear me say it and I need to say it. Thank you for being that concerned with me that you want to hear me tell you my need of you. Amen.

Baptism Is No Insurance Policy

 "If people absolutely insist on infant baptism, then they ought all the more vigorously see to it that rebirth becomes a decisive determinant in becoming a Christian" (Kierkegaard 1967).

By no means does Kierkegaard deny or minimize the effect or benefit of baptism. He believes with Luther that "in baptism God forgives sin, delivers from death and the devil, and gives everlasting salvation to all who believe what he has promised" (The Small Catechism). He also believes with Luther that "it is not water that does these things but God's Word with the water and our trust in this Word. Water by itself is only water, but with this Word it is a life-giving water which by grace gives the new birth through the Holy Spirit."

Neither does Kierkegaard question infant baptism, but he has serious concerns about any mistaken view that infant baptism takes care of everything. What Kierkegaard questions is making infant baptism an insurance policy, a guarantee of salvation. He challenges being so secure and unconcerned about infant baptism that it can become what he calls "an ungodly flippancy."

I was born a sinner, but I was not born 20 or 30 years old, an adult who is conscious of my sin. I was born a baby Adam or a baby Eve. In baptism I was reborn and received a new quality. I became a new Adam or a new Eve. I was not conscious of the total qualitative transformation that took place in me in my baptism—a change that is just as totally qualitative, says Kierkegaard, "as the change from not being to being, which is birth." That consciousness is an adult consciousness. Growing into what I was made in baptism is an adult task, my lifetime task.

"Do you not know that all of us who have been baptized into Christ Jesus were baptized into his death? We were buried therefore with him by baptism into death, so that as Christ was raised from the dead by the glory of the Father, we too might walk in newness of life" (Rom. 6:3-5).

I Need Daily Rebirth

"But when the goodness and loving kindness of God our Savior appeared, he saved us, not because of deeds done by us in righteousness, but in virtue of his own mercy, by the washing of regeneration and renewal in the Holy Spirit, which he poured out upon us richly through Jesus Christ our Savior, so that we might be justified by his grace and become heirs in hope of eternal life" (Titus 3:4-8).

"If Christianity could become naturalized in the world, then every child need not be baptized, since the child who is born of Christian parents would already be a Christian by birth. The consciousness of sin is and continues to be the conditio sine qua non *for all Christianity, and if one could somehow be released from this, he could not be a Christian. And this is the very proof of Christianity's being the highest religion, that none other has given such a profound and lofty expression of man's significance—that he is a sinner. It is this consciousness that paganism lacks"* (Kierkegaard 1967).

Father in heaven, I do not remember being born, but sex education and sex glorification certainly have informed me how it happened. I do not remember being baptized, but my baptismal certificate tells me that it happened, and the Christian education I received from my parents, pastors, and Sunday school teachers tells me that my baptism is a gift of God's grace, by which I received a new nature and became a new self. Ah, but the nature I was born with, the me-first, me-want nature, is still with me. My old self, my self-seeking, self-centered, self-indulgent, self-worshiping self, is still hanging around. I desperately need the help of your Holy Spirit every day in every way. Hold me in the new self and the second nature to which I was reborn through baptism. Lord God, it seems that even though I am baptized I need a daily rebirth. In Jesus' name, amen.

Teach Me to Thank You Rightly

| DAY 5 | *"Of course, the fact remains that in regard to man's salvation Christ is everything and man himself is not capable of achieving anything, but although this is true, or just because it is true, Christ says, as it were, to the single individual: If you want to thank me, then* |

become my imitator. Then being born again becomes something in earnest" (Kierkegaard 1967).

Many of the early converts from paganism regarded baptism so earnestly that, fearing the consequence of sinning seriously after they were baptized, they postponed baptism until they were near death. Constantine the Great, who in 325 A.D. called the First Council of Nicaea that broke the ground for the formulation of the Nicene Creed, was baptized on his death bed. St. Ambrose, whom Augustine acknowledged as his spiritual father, was baptized, confirmed, and ordained all within a week when he was elected Bishop of Milan by popular acclaim. Some pagan Vikings were said to hold the right arm above the water when they were immersed in baptism so that the unbaptized right arm could continue to wield the battle axe and embrace the girls without the risk of plunging the rest of the body into the fires of hell.

Kierkegaard is not asking for a return to that kind of "earnestness" about baptism and rebirth. Neither is he making the grace of rebirth into a new law: "Thou shalt be reborn again—and again—and again." Dismayed by how the forgiveness of sins in baptism is taken for granted and regarded as "once and for all," he points out that "tomorrow is another day, and the day after tomorrow, and perhaps one will live fifty years. Now comes the difficulty—does one lay hold of grace worthily at every moment from that moment on. Alas, no, therefore grace is needed again in relation to grace. . . ."

Grace comes first. The striving to lay hold of that grace in one's daily life is in gratitude to Christ, who is everything. But for that striving in gratitude one again needs grace—grace upon grace.

Father in heaven, let me not misuse the amazing grace of forgiveness of sins that is my baptismal gift from you through Christ. Christ, my Savior, teach me to thank you with the only kind of gratitude you desire—that I follow and imitate you in my daily life. Holy Spirit, make me earnest about striving in gratitude to be like Christ. Amen.

Grace First and Last

"What does Christ require? First and foremost, faith. Next, gratitude. In the disciple in the stricter sense this gratitude is 'imitation.' But even the weakest Christian has this in common with the strongest disciple: the relationship is one of gratitude. Imitation is not a requirement of the law, for then we have the system of law again. No, imitation is the stronger expression of gratitude in the stronger" (Kierkegaard 1967).

If Kierkegaard did nothing else, he set Christian concepts in their proper order. However acrid he at times makes being a Christian taste, he always comes back to grace—first, last, and always, faith in God's grace. Although he accuses Luther of easing up on imitation, he credits him with the right order, but adds his own corrective: *"Luther rightly orders it this way. Christ is the gift—to which faith corresponds. Then he is the pattern, the prototype to which imitation corresponds. Still more accurately one may say: (1) imitation in the direction of decisive action, whereby the situation for becoming a Christian comes into existence; (2) Christ as gift—faith; (3) imitation as the fruit of faith"* (Kierkegaard 1967).

Luther lived in a time when the order was reversed and Christ as pattern or prototype was placed above Christ as gift. Kierkegaard lived in a time when Christ as gift had been made into a divine privilege to forget all about obedience, following him and imitating him. If there is no requirement, there is no guilt. If there is no guilt, who needs grace? If there is no need for grace, grace is taken for granted and there is no gratitude.

If Kierkegaard was scandalized by the confusion and disorder and dilution of Christian categories in his day, what would he think today, in this day of "gratitude for what? Everything I've got, I have coming to me! They are my rights, and if I don't get my rights, I'll sue anyone and even you to get them!"

Decisive action—and then comes the new situation of guilt, for even the best I can do is still shabby in relation to that new life. So once again I must return and knock at the door of grace. *"O, infinite grace,, have mercy on me for being here again so soon and having to plead for grace, for now I understand that in order to have peace and rest, in order not to perish in hopeless despair, in order to be able to breathe, in order to be able to exist at all, I need grace not only for the past but grace for the future"* (Kierkegaard 1967).

The Dialectic of Faith

"It is clear that in my writings I have supplied a more radical characterization of the concept of 'faith' than there has been up until this time" (Kierkegaard 1967).

If Kierkegaard's characterization of faith is radical, it is because it is dialectical. *Dialectical* is a favorite word in intellectual circles but do not cringe before it for that reason. It only means that there is more than one side to most things. This makes possible movement back and forth, from one side to another—in other words, dialogue.

Faith, says Kierkegaard, is dialectical, and the tragedy of Christendom is that we have removed the dialectical element. We make faith one-sided by defining it as merely hoping against hope and believing against understanding. So it is, but if that is all it is, faith becomes static, cozy, secure, and then, says Kierkegaard, faith is in grave danger. He quotes Savanarola: "The power of faith is secure in dangers, but in danger when a person is secure."

Kierkegaard adds to the definition of faith the tension of will, of choice, of obedience, "of venturing out upon water 70,000 fathoms deep." I am not to insist on proofs of the existence of God and then believe. I move on from the understanding that faith cannot be understood to the understanding that faith *must not* be understood. I choose to believe, I make the leap of faith, I will to venture my whole life on Christ's *if:* "If you continue in my word, you are truly my disciples" (John 8:31). I venture out into the deep waters of obedience, where it becomes a question of floating in faith or drowning in despair.

The dialectical movement of faith is from believing to striving and back to faith. *"Luther is completely right in saying that if a man had to acquire his salvation by his own striving, it would end either in presumption or despair, and therefore it is faith that saves. But yet not in such a way that striving vanishes completely. Faith should make striving possible, because the fact that I am saved by faith and that nothing at all is demanded from me should in itself make it possible that I begin to strive, that I do not collapse under impossibility but am encouraged and refreshed, because it has been decided I am saved, I am God's child by virtue of faith* (Kierkegaard 1967).

"For by grace you have been saved through faith; and this is not your own doing, it is the gift of God—not because of works, lest any man should boast. For we are his workmanship, created in Jesus Christ for good works, which God prepared beforehand, that we should walk in them" (Eph. 2:8-10).

Kierkegaard Defines Christianity

D A Y
8

"Christianly, the emphasis does not fall so much upon to what extent or how far a person succeeds in meeting or fulfilling the requirement, if he actually is striving, as it is upon his getting an impression of the requirement in all its infinitude so that he rightly learns to be humbled and to rely upon grace. To pare down the requirement in order to fulfil it better . . . to this Christianity in its deepest essence is opposed. No, infinite humiliation and grace, and then a striving born of gratitude—this is Christianity" (Kierkegaard 1967).

About this time someone may well sputter in protest: "Listen! You can't talk out of two sides of your mouth—is that what you mean by being dialectical? You can't talk about being saved by faith, about nothing at all being demanded, and then start yammering about striving to fulfil a requirement!"

No, we are not making grace into a new law, and neither did Kierkegaard. The requirement is the "for what?" that follows as a matter of course after faith. I am saved by faith. For what? Why, of course, to express my faith in my daily life! Grace is God's gift to me, and he gave it to me with the intention of transforming me. His hope is that I will respond to his gift by choosing to strive to obey his Word and his will as revealed by his son Jesus Christ and by his apostles. I don't have to look long and hard to find his Word and will—it's on every page of the New Testament.

Kierkegaard speaks scathingly about paring down the Christian requirement or suppressing it in order to make following it easy. This, he says, is taking grace in vain. The purpose of the requirement is not to make us torment ourselves or to judge others for not expressing faith in their lives. It is to humble us before its infinite demand and send us to grace—and then in gratitude for grace return again to the striving to follow and obey.

Christ, my Redeemer, teach me to thank you in the only way you want, the way of following you and obeying you. And when I flub and fail and fall flat on my face, forgive me, pick me up, and set me to striving in gratitude again. Amen.

Christk as the Sign of Offense

"Since Holy Scripture says 'Woe to the men by whom the temptation comes,' we confidently say: Woe to him who first thought of preaching Christianity without the possibility of offense. Woe to the person who ingratiatingly, flirtatiously, commendingly, convincingly preached to mankind some effeminate something which was supposed to be Christianity! . . . Woe to the person who betrayed and broke the mystery of faith, distorted it into public wisdom, because he took away the possibility of offense! Woe to the person who could comprehend the mystery of atonement without detecting anything of the possibility of offense . . ." (Kierkegaard 1962).

How in the world, asked Kierkegaard 140 years ago, could anyone be offended by modern Christianity? Even then he could see the cultural accommodation that was taking place in the established Church and could see that it was no longer proclaiming Christ as the sign of contradiction, as the sign of offense. He could see that it no longer was preaching Christ as a scandal to the world and to our human nature. He could foresee that if Christ is not proclaimed so that one is either offended by him or believes in him, then Christianity is bound to decline, people will become bored with the church or drop out. Then Christianity is as good as abolished and the churches might as well be locked up.

Are you perhaps thinking "What outrageous thoughts! That Kierkegaard must be a fanatic!" So you are offended! Good! Then you are in the situation where you must bring Christ out of history into this very present moment, must make him contemporary with you here on the spot and reflect on what he is saying to you—not some 2000 years ago, but here and now.

Jesus said to John's disciples, "Blessed is he who takes no offense at me" (Matt. 11:6). Christ clearly sees the possibility of offense in himself, and just as clearly is offended by our not perceiving it. To perceive it—and then believe—ah, then Christ can be sure that he has an invincible follower!

Christ Jesus, your most potent missionary, Paul, was so offended by you that he threatened to slaughter your followers. You had to knock him down and give him a blinding vision of yourself before he could believe. Christ Jesus, if my faith is so insipid that it offends you, do not spew me out of your mouth but let your Holy Spirit shake salt into it! Amen.

Care and Concern in the Right Place

D A Y **10**	*"Luther makes an utterly masterful distinction in his sermon on the Gospel about the lily and the bird. Faith is indeed without concern. Why, then, do the Scriptures elsewhere commend being concerned?*

Luther replies: In Christianity everything revolves around faith— and love. In relation to faith, care and concern are sinful. In relation to love, however, care and concern are altogether in place.—Masterful! But the sad thing about us human beings is simply that we usually have care and concern in the wrong place (i.e. in relation to faith, then care and concern are doubt, disbelief, etc.) and so rarely in the right place. Ah, how rare is genuine love-concern, and how common is worrying-concern" (Kierkegaard 1967).

The words *care* and *concern* have double meanings that can create confusion. Both can mean solicitude, anxiety, worry. We say: "Be careful!" "I'm concerned about your cough." We say: "I care for you." "Your happiness is my concern." Both words can mean tender regards, thoughtful consideration, or devoted interest in someone. Kierkegaard used the Danish word *bekymrig*, however, which does not create this confusion, for it quite simply means "anxiety, worry, concern." Thus when Kierkegaard speaks about faith-concern and love-concern, he is speaking about being concerned about faith and being anxious and concerned about love. The former, he says, is wrongly placed; the latter is rightly placed. To doubt and be skeptical about one's faith is sinful, but to question and examine one's love is proper.

In Kierkegaard's book *Works of Love*, he dethrones love as a feeling and makes sharp distinctions between the profuse and difficult concepts of love. *"It is obvious that in Christendom we have completely forgotten what love is. We pander to erotic love and friendship, laud and praise it as love, consequently as a virtue. Nonsense. Erotic love and friendship are earthly happiness, a temporal good just like money, abilities, talents, etc., only better. They are to be desired for happiness but should not be made delusively important. Love is self-denial, and is rooted in the relationship to God"* (Kierkegaard 1967).

"How could love be rightly discussed if You were forgotten, O God of Love, source of all love in heaven and earth, You who spared nothing but gave all in love, You who are love, so that one who loves is what he is only by being in You!" (Kierkegaard 1962).

The Proof of Faith and Love

" 'He who sees his brother in need, yet shuts his heart' (1 John 3:17)—yes, at the same time he shuts God out. Love to God and love to neighbor are like two doors that open simultaneously, so that it is impossible to open one without opening the other, and impossible to shut one without shutting the other" (Kierkegaard 1967).

Faith is known by love, and, Christianly, love is not a feeling but works of love. The proof of faith, the proof of love, is not in the language of words but in the language of works of love, in the language of bread and a cup of cold water. "Christ's love was not intense feeling, a full heart, etc.; it was rather the works of love, which is his life" (Kierkegaard 1967).

So often we say, "It would have been so easy to show my faith and love if I had been contemporary with Christ." Ah, but we are contemporary with the sick, the poor, the despised, the suffering. As reported by Matthew, Christ made it clear that if we do works of love to the "least of these" we do them to him (Matt. 25:31-46).

The Great Commandment, the one Christ calls "the great and first commandment" (Matt. 22:37-38) says: "You shall love the Lord your God with all your heart, and with all your soul, and with all your mind." Kierkegaard points out that it does not say "You shall love God as you love yourself." Christ pinned that phrase to the Second Commandment: "You shall love your neighbor as yourself." That little phrase "as yourself" causes us to think and struggle with what it means to love ourselves; in the struggle we learn to love ourselves in the proper way so that we can love the neighbor as ourselves. Moreover, Christ makes love to the neighbor a divine command, a divine duty: you *shall* love your neighbor as yourself. If one *shall*, then it is forever decided!

We obey the Great Commandment by adoration and obedience. We strive to obey and be like him whom we adore, and that means works of love. The word "shall" and the phrase "as yourself" in the divine Second Commandment place God in the middle of every human relationship, hence love to neighbor opens the door to love to God.

Source of all love, first of all let me never forget that you loved me first. Second, let me never forget that you are in the middle of every one of my relationships, that it is not a relationship of me—neighbor, but me—God—neighbor. Amen.

Loving the Unlovely, the Unlovable

DAY
12

"Just as 'faith' is a dialectical qualification, so also is true Christian love. Therefore Christianity teaches specifically that one ought to love his enemy, that the pagan, too, loves his friend. . . . When a person loves his friend, it is by no means clear that he loves God, but when a person loves his enemy, it is clear that he fears and loves God, and only in this way can God be loved" (Kierkegaard 1967).

Whom does one as a rule choose as a friend? With whom does one as a rule fall in love? Whom does one choose to marry? Someone who is lovable, of course! Someone whom one's instinctive, inclinational, spontaneous love is able to love. It is easy, so easy, to love a lovely lovable person—until one falls out of love, until the two become incompatible and quarrel, until the object of one's instinctive, inclinational, spontaneous love becomes unlovable—indeed, becomes hateable! Suddenly the very same instinctive, inclinational, spontaneous feeling changes, and one becomes able to hate and is unable to love.

But it seems that the second of Christ's great commandments asks us to love the ugly, the unlovely, the unlovable! That must mean those human beings who are blemishes and blots on the humanscape: That nasty neighbor who chases the neighborhood kids if they step on his lawn to retrieve a ball. That bully kid who terrorizes the children on the way home from school. That wife who has turned into a nag and a crab. That lovable child who has suddenly been transformed into a vulgar, boorish, ungrateful teenager.

So I am supposed to love those people whom I find unacceptable. Sorry, I find that unacceptable! My whole nature cries, "No thanks! I have no inclination to love the ugly, to say nothing of loving my enemies!"

God, you ask me to love the ugly. You ask me to love my enemies. God, I am not able! I am *unable!* I can't do it! Help! I need the help of your Holy Spirit! Amen.

Back to Need Again!

DAY 13

"What does it mean to be a Christian? It means to walk under the eye of the Heavenly Father, therefore under the eye of the truly loving Father, led by Christ's hand, and strengthened by the witness of the Holy Spirit. O, blessed companionship . . . !" (Kierkegaard 1967).

Love the unlovely? Love the ugly? Do not ask yourself if you are able to do it, says Kierkegaard, for then you will not be able. No, ready or not, able or not, you and I must be obedient to Christ's two great commandments—and then the Spirit, "the only vitalizing, enabling power for the future" comes to our assistance. Here we come back to need again! "To need God is man's highest perfection." You and I desperately need the Holy Spirit in his double role of Comforter and Strengthener.

In gratitude to God for the gift of his boundless grace in Christ Jesus and full of holy resolve to begin the completely new life we have through him, we venture to begin. But in a very short time we discover that the very best we can do is shabby and imperfect. We are unable to do it! Then and only then do we call upon the Holy Enabler! Only when we begin trying to make the possibility of the new life in Christ into actuality do we come into the situation of need that makes us cry out: Help! Help! I am weak and powerless! Holy Spirit, be my power and my strength as well as my comforter in my weakness.

"We human beings carry the holy only in fragile jars, but You, O Holy Spirit, when You live in a person You live in what is infinitely inferior: You Spirit of Holiness, You live in our filth and impurity, You Spirit of Wisdom, you live in our foolishness, You Spirit of Truth, you live in our self-deception! O, stay here, and You, who do not conveniently look for a desirable residence, which You would seek in vain, You, who creating and giving new birth, make your new dwelling place, O, stay here that it may at some time come to be that you are delighted with the house You yourself prepared for yourself in my filthy and foolish and cheating heart. Amen" (Kierkegaard 1967).

Like a Child! Abba, Papa!

<table>
<tr><td>D A Y
14</td><td>*"A man rests in the forgiveness of sins when the thought of God does not remind him of the sin but that it is forgiven, when the past is not a memory of how much he trespassed but of how much he has been forgiven"* (Kierkegaard 1967).</td></tr>
</table>

The following prayers of Kierkegaard are collected in *Journals and Papers*. They express the confidence that he could pray like a child to his *"Abba"* or Father:

Loving Father, I am a total failure—and yet you are love. I even fail to cling to this, that you are love—and yet you are love. No matter how I turn, this is the one thing I cannot get away from or be free of—that you are love. This is why I believe that even when I fail to cling to this—that you are love— it is still out of love that you permit it to happen, O infinite love.

Father in heaven! When the thought of you awakens in our soul, let it not awaken like a terrified bird that flutters about in confusion, but like a child from its sleep, with a heavenly smile.

Father in heaven, awaken conscience within us, teach us to open our spiritual ears to your voice and to pay attention to what you say, so that your will may sound purely and clearly for us as it does in heaven, unadulterated by worldly shrewdness undeadened by the voice of passions. Keep us vigilant in fear and trembling to work out our salvation. But also—when the law speaks loudest, when its earnestness terrifies us, when it thunders from Sinai—let there be a soft voice which whispers to us that we are your children, so that we may cry out with joy: Abba, Father. Grant that in every hour like that there may be born anew in our hearts (youthfully, hopefully,) the Abba, the father-name you wish to be called.

Teach me, O God, so that I do not suffocate and torture myself in suffocating reflection, but that I may breathe healthfully in faith.

Was Kierkegaard being whimsical when he wrote in his journal: "Theme for an edifying discourse: The Art of Arriving at an Amen"? "It is not very easy," he said. "There always seems to be something to add." The time has come for us to say "Amen" to these meditations on Kierkegaard themes, but we hope and pray that you who read will not say "Amen" to reading Kierkegaard.

Hubert Nelson

DIETRICH BONHOEFFER

I T WAS in the early, gray dawn of April 9, 1945, that German theologian and pastor Dietrich Bonhoeffer was executed in the concentration camp at Flossenburg by special order of Heinrich Himmler. The charge against him was treason for his part in the attempted assassination of Adolf Hitler on July 20, 1944. For Bonhoeffer, his resistance to Nazism was an act of obedience to Jesus Christ.

"For innumerable Christians in Germany, on the Continent, in England, and in America, Dietrich Bonhoeffer's death has been a contemporary affirmation of Tertullian's dictum: the blood of the martyrs is the seed of the church; for his life and death and his writings throb with the simple, downright faith of one who has met Jesus Christ and accepted the ultimate consequences of that encounter in the world" (Bonhoeffer 1954).

Bonhoeffer was 16 when he chose to study theology and by the age of 21 he presented his doctor's thesis. In 1928-29 he was assistant pastor of a German-speaking congregation in Barcelona. The following year he was an exchange student at Union Theological Seminary in New York City, and returned in 1931 to teach systematic theology at the University of Berlin. Bonhoeffer came from a privileged background. The future was his. He was willing to sacrifice all of that for a higher call.

In 1933 Hitler and the National Socialist Party came to power. Young Bonhoeffer recognized that there was a subtle shift from respecting the office to worshiping the leader who held the office. He recognized and resisted the growing anti-Semitism. In 1935 he was appointed by the Confessing Church to organize and head an illegal, clandestine seminary in Finkenwald for the training of pastors in Pomerania. By 1938 Bonhoeffer was forbidden to teach or write or publish and was identified as an enemy of Nazi Germany. Although he had an opportunity to escape his impending fate in 1939 while in the U.S.A., he felt compelled to return and be a part of the struggle of his people. His part in the resistance movement which sought the life of the evil dictator resulted in his execution only weeks before the arrival of the Allies.

In the following selections from several of Bonhoeffer's books, a common motif is grace, which Bonhoeffer saw as the interpretive center of all of life. But, as we will see, grace was always both promise and demand, gift and response, free and costly, gospel and law.

Grace and Baptism

DAY 1 *"Where the Synoptic Gospels speak of Christ calling [people] and their following him, St. Paul speaks of Baptism. Baptism is not an offer made by [a person] to God, but an offer made by Christ to [that one]. It is grounded solely on the will of Jesus Christ, as expressed in his gracious call. Baptism is essentially passive, being baptized, suffering the call of Christ. In baptism [a person] becomes Christ's own possession. . . .*

"Having taken their life from them, he sought to confer on them a new life, a life so perfect and complete that he gave them the gift of his cross. That was the gift of baptism to the first disciples . . ." (Bonhoeffer 1966).

"Child of God, you are marked with the cross of Jesus Christ and sealed with the gift of the Holy Spirit." How often I have wondered as I hold a child and mark him or her with those words, *Will they ever realize the nature of the gift that they have been given? And, if so, will they be able to embrace it?*

Bonhoeffer describes this gift of grace as being akin to receiving Jesus' call to discipleship. It is God's gift to us who are baptized that we should share the ministry of his Son. We are made partners in the family business, the family-of-God business. We are given in the Holy Spirit all the resources and authority we will need. The only catch is that we are branded with the mark of death.

It takes a measure of faith to receive and embrace the gift of Baptism. For to be baptized is to be commissioned to discipleship, and discipleship is to share the cross of Jesus Christ. Paul describes this gift as daily dying and rising with Jesus. It is a gift that transforms even the most powerful and talented into servants. An interesting gift, this Baptism.

"Do you not know that all of us who have been baptized into Christ Jesus were baptized into his death? We were buried therefore with him by baptism into death, so that as Christ was raised from the dead by the glory of the Father, we too might walk in newness of life" (Rom. 6:3-4).

Grace and Old Testament

"In recent months I have been reading the Old Testament much more than the New. It is only when one knows the unutterability of the name of God that one can utter the name of Jesus Christ; it is only when one loves life and earth so much that without them everything seems to be over that one can believe in the resurrection and a new world; it is only when one submits to God's law that one can speak of grace; and it is only when God's wrath and vengeance are hanging as grim realities over the heads of one's enemies that something of what it means to love and forgive them can touch our hearts. In my opinion it is not Christian to want to take our thoughts and feelings too directly from the New Testament" (Bonhoeffer 1965b).

It was not until I was 17 years old that I began to see my life in context. I worked as an orderly in a nursing home, bathing and shaving some of the older men. There was time for many conversations. Mostly, I just listened to stories that happened long before I was born. One man was a railroad contractor who helped build railroads into the western frontiers. One had been a farmer who cleared a piece of virgin land in southwestern Minnesota. One had been a grocer, another an attorney. Some had families and some were all alone in their autumn years. But, that year, listening to their stories gave me a context in which to look at my life. A context for my dreams, my values, my youth, my successes, my failures, my schooling, and my occupation.

The Old Testament in some sense provides a context in which to understand the riches of grace in the New Testament. For two millenia the people of God had experienced God's gracious acts. The call of Abraham, the Exodus, the mercies shown to David, the promises of Isaiah to the exiles, to name only a few.

But there is also an earthiness and a frankness with which the story of the Old Testament is told that places the New Testament in the context of the real world. The Old Testament helps us understand the importance of the humanity of our Savior. It provides a context for the receiving of the Christ.

"In many and various ways God spoke of old to our fathers by the prophets; but in these last days he has spoken to us by a Son" (Heb. 1:1–2).

Grace and Community

"Christian [community] is not an ideal, but a divine reality. . . . Innumerable times a whole Christian community has broken down because it had sprung from a wish dream. The serious Christian, set down for the first time in a Christian community, is likely to bring with [one] a very definite idea of what Christian life together should be and try to realize it. But God's grace speedily shatters such dreams. Just as surely as God desires to lead us to a knowledge of genuine Christian fellowship, so surely must we be overwhelmed by a great disillusionment with others, with Christians in general, and if we are fortunate, with ourselves. . . .*

"Only that fellowship which faces such disillusionment, with all its unhappy and ugly aspects, begins to be what it should be in God's sight, begins to grasp in faith the promise that is given to it. . . . [The person] who loves [one's] dream of a community more than the Christian community itself becomes a destroyer of the latter, even though [one's] personal intentions may be ever so honest and earnest and sacrificial" (Bonhoeffer 1954).

I often ask new members why they chose to join our congregation. It is easy to be lifted to great heights by their responses. "This is such a warm and friendly congregation. The music is so inspiring. The preaching gives me something to take home each week. There isn't all that talk about money often heard in other churches. . . ." I usually bask in the warmth of such comments for a spell but later I think to myself, "Will they want to remain as members when they find out what we really are like?"

Every member of every congregation is bound to be shocked or disillusioned sooner or later when they discover not only the humanity but utter sinfulness of fellow members. Sometimes the shock is that there are others like you. Those who are able to stay in a congregation and commit themselves to its fellowship and even find lasting joy and satisfaction are those who have discovered that it is God who has brought them together and it is by God's grace that they are a community.

"Now as they were eating, Jesus took bread, and blessed, and broke it, and gave it to the disciples and said, 'Take, eat; this is my body.' And he took a cup, and when he had given thanks he gave it to them, saying, 'Drink of it, all of you; for this is my blood of the covenant, which is poured out for many for the forgiveness of sins'" (Matt. 26:26-28).

Grace, Confession, and Community

"The final break-through to fellowship (often) does not occur, because, though they have fellowship with one another as believers and as devout people, they do not have fellowship as the undevout, as sinners. The pious fellowship permits no one to be a sinner. So everybody must conceal one's sin from oneself and from the fellowship. We dare not be sinners. Many Christians are unthinkably horrified when a real sinner is suddenly discovered among the righteous. . . . But it is the grace of the Gospel, which is so hard for the pious to understand, that it confronts us with the truth and says: you are a sinner, a great desperate sinner; now come, as the sinner that you are, to God who loves you. He wants you as you are; He does not want anything from you, a sacrifice, a work; He wants you alone. . . . He wants to be gracious to you"* (Bonhoeffer 1954).

I once offered to bring communion to a devout Christian man who was no longer able to worship with us because of age and infirmities. He quickly put his hands up and said, "No, I am not ready for that yet." About a year later, as he approached death, he asked for the sacrament.

His widow shared with me that her husband had been taught from the old country that only the very best Christians went to the Lord's Table regularly. The ordinary Christians were too sinful to go except at the end of their life as a preparation for heaven. He understood the "communion of saints" as meaning "communion for saints" and he saw sainthood as a level of holiness beyond his ability to achieve.

Perhaps we should use Bonhoeffer's suggestion as an antidote to such barriers to our fellowship. For awhile we could say instead of "I believe in the communion of saints" that "I believe in the communion of sinners." Some may feel excluded in the communion of saints but none should feel left out of the "communion of sinners." A communion of sinners would not have to have its guard up or keep it masks of righteousness so intact. A communion of sinners would be forced to acknowledge that they were a communion only as a gift, a gift of God's grace.

"If we confess our sins, he is faithful and just, and will forgive our sins and cleanse us from all unrighteousness" (1 John 1:9).

317

Grace and Law I

<table>
<tr><td>D A Y
5</td><td>*"It is grace to know God's commands. They release us from self-made plans and conflicts. They make our steps certain and our way joyful. God gives his commands in order that we may fulfill them, and 'his commandments are not burdensome' (1 John 5:3) for*</td></tr>
</table>

[the one] who has found all salvation in Jesus Christ. Jesus has himself been under the law and has fulfilled it in total obedience to the Father. God's will becomes [one's] joy, his nourishment. So he gives thanks in us for the grace of the law and grants to us joy in its fulfillment" (Bonhoeffer 1970).

The prophet Amos once spoke of a famine that was worse than any famine of food (Amos 8:11). It was a famine of the word of God. Nothing could be more devastating than to seek a word from God and to be met only by silence.

Quentin, in Miller's play, "After the Fall," had a dream in which he stood before the bench to plead his case and the bench was empty. Even a word of judgment would have been better than no word at all. The most devastating judgment of all is no word, that it just doesn't matter one way or another. Despair is to discover that there is no other person or standard by which one's life is being evaluated.

It is an experience of grace, therefore, to discover that God cares enough to share his Word with us. What joy could be greater than to realize that the creator of this universe is so interested in you and me that he actually discloses his will and purposes to us. You and I make a difference to God. The way we live our lives makes a difference to him. No wonder that we say that the greatest expression of grace was the Word of God become flesh. So we too join with the psalmist and Bonhoeffer and give thanks for the grace of law.

"I am a sojourner on earth; hide not thy commandments from me! My soul is consumed with longing for thy ordinances at all times" (Ps. 119:19-20).

Grace and Law II

"No one understands the law of God who does not know about the deliverance which has happened and the promise of what is to come. The one who asks about the law is reminded about Jesus Christ and the deliverance of human beings from the bondage of sin and death which has been completed in him, reminded of the new beginnings which God has made for all people in Jesus Christ. . . .

"God's law cannot be separated from his act of deliverance. The God of the ten commandments is the God who led you out of the land of Egypt (Ex. 20:2). God gives his law to those whom he loves, those whom he has chosen and taken to himself (Deut. 7:7-11). To know God's law is grace and joy (Deut. 4:6-10). It is the way of life for those who accept God's grace (Lev. 18:5)" (Bonhoeffer 1986).

Ehme Osterbur, former Lutheran bishop, once shared that the law, no matter how tough or firmly spoken, never expressed anything but love when spoken by his mother. The same command expressed much more tamely and softly spoken would often make him bristle when spoken by someone else.

What was the difference? The difference was the context. When his mother spoke it was always in the context of love. Love that had proved itself again and again and again. He knew without reservation that his mother was for him, on his side. His mother had literally given herself, often at great sacrifice, that he might know joy and beauty and happiness.

God's law, when spoken by some, makes us bristle. For the context is not love. God's law must always be received in the context of God's love. It is the one who has delivered us, whose mercy is without limit, who was willing to give up the glories of heaven and even die for us, who also gives us his commands. In that context we see God's law as an expression of God's grace.

"This is my commandment . . . you are my friends . . ." (John 15:12, 14).

Grace and Obedience I

DAY 7 *"The New Testament lays down no law about infant baptism; it is a gift of grace bestowed on the Church, a gift that may be received and used in firm faith, and can thus be a striking testimony of faith for the community; but to force oneself to it without the compulsion of faith is not biblical. Regarded purely as a demonstration, infant baptism loses its justification. . . . As long as there is a justifiable hope that that day is not far off, I cannot believe that God is concerned about the exact date. So we can quite well wait a little and trust in God's kindly providence, and do later with a stronger faith what we should at the moment feel simply to be burdensome law . . ."* (Bonhoeffer 1965b).

My younger brother once commented to me while we were both in college that he was perplexed by the fact that he had more fun with non-Christians than with Christians. In fact, the better Christians they were, the less fun they were.

It was hard to argue with him for that had also been my experience. Those who claim the name Christian are often so compulsive in their righteousness. They are often motivated by fear and guilt rather than by a free and serendipitous response to love. Their intensity often makes them judgmental rather than affirming of others. The new is treated first with suspicion and the unusual one with fear.

Bonhoeffer understands God's command to baptize to include children of Christian parents. But he does not see such a command as a manifestation of God's crankiness or arbitrariness. It is a command flowing rather from a heart of love. Parents bring their child for Baptism because they want to claim God's promise of love rather than because they fear his wrath. It is a subtle difference in attitude, but all the difference in the world if they are people with whom you live or work.

"And if you had known what this means, 'I desire mercy, and not sacrifice,' you would not have condemned the guiltless" (Matt. 12:7).

Grace and Obedience II

" 'Only [one] who believes is obedient.' It is quite unbiblical to hold the first proposition without the second. . . . For faith is only real when there is obedience, never without it, and faith only becomes faith in the act of obedience. . . . Only the obedient believe. If we are to believe, we must obey a concrete command. Without this preliminary step of obedience, our faith will only be pious humbug, and lead us to grace which is not costly. . . . The first step of obedience makes Peter leave his nets, and later get out of the ship; it calls upon the young man to leave his riches. Only this new existence, created through obedience, can make faith possible" (Bonhoeffer 1966).

Is it possible to believe in Jesus Christ and trust him and yet be disobedient? If this were not true, then who of us could be called believers? And yet, if God's grace is received but does not change us in any way, then God has not really been able to give us anything.

Suppose that we were traveling by night in the land of the enemy. We have been told that we will be coming to a critical intersection shortly before dawn. At that intersection will be a woman. She has chosen to risk her own life so that she might direct travelers down the path that leads to life and safety.

When we arrive at the intersection, it is as we have been told. We meet the woman and she points to a fairly narrow path. The other roads look to be more traveled. The road pointed to even appears to be going in the wrong direction. What do you do first? Do you decide whether or not to believe her, or whether or not to obey her? It would seem to be a moot point, for in that concrete situation, the two would seem to be the same. If you obey her you believe her, and if you believe her you obey her. In the concrete situations of life, faith and obedience cannot be separated.

"But someone will say, 'You have faith and I have works.' Show me your faith apart from your works, and I by my works will show you my faith" (James 2:18).

Grace and Discipleship

DAY 9

"We Lutherans have gathered like eagles round the carcass of cheap grace, and there we have drunk of the poison which has killed the life of following Christ. . . .

"We gave away the word and sacrament wholesale, we baptized, confirmed, and absolved a whole nation unasked and without condition. Our humanitarian sentiment made us give that which was holy to the scornful and unbelieving. We poured forth unending streams of grace. But the call to follow Jesus in the narrow way was hardly ever heard. . . . What had happened to all those warnings of Luther's against preaching the gospel in such a manner as to make [people] rest secure in their ungodly living?" (Bonhoeffer 1966).

I remember a teacher coming into our classroom after the lunch hour, tears rolling down her cheeks. We all felt bad for she had always been very nice to us. "What's the matter?" someone asked. "A former student told me that he never learned a thing in my class, that I was the worst teacher he had ever had."

The class was suddenly silent. We loved her but we also knew that the former student was probably right. She did whatever we wanted. Homework could be forgiven. She would go over our tests with us, allowing us to change the answers and improve our grades. We had parties whenever anyone brought the food and drink. She liked us, but not enough to take the risk of disciplining us and demanding commitment to our studies.

Bonhoeffer felt that the church in his day dispensed grace much like that teacher dispensed education. It was benevolently doled out in generous quantities to whomever put their hands out, but it was essentially worthless. It could not resist the forces of evil, whether it be the Nazi party or in any other shape or form.

It is impossible to receive the full richness of God's grace apart from the costliness of discipleship. Grace and the discipline of Jesus Christ cannot be separated.

"And he called to him the multitude with his disciples, and said to them, "If any man would come after me, let him deny himself and take up his cross and follow me. For whoever would save his life will lose it; and whoever loses his life for my sake and the gospel's will save it" (Mark 8:34-35).

Grace and Suffering

O Lord God
great distress has come upon me;
my cares threaten to crush me,
and I do not know what to do.
O God, be gracious to me and help me.
Give me strength to bear what thou dost send,
and do not let fear rule over me;
Take a father's care of my wife and children.
O merciful God,
forgive me all the sins that I have committed
against thee and against [other people].
I trust in thy grace
and commit my life wholly into thy hands.
Do with me according to thy will
and as is best for me.
Whether I live or die, I am with thee,
and thou, my God, art with me.
Lord, I wait for thy salvation
and for thy kingdom.
Amen.
(Bonhoeffer 1965b)

There are times when I feel simply overwhelmed by the odds that I am facing. Sometimes it is a matter of my own doing. I have painted myself into a corner. Other times it seems that the experiences of life have ganged up against me and I am not strong enough to fight them. There are times when the mustering of all my resources is not enough to survive and my bargaining position with God is nil.

It is at those moments that God's grace in Jesus Christ is like a light shining in the darkness. To be able to let go and let God take over is literally our salvation. To trust that our Lord can meet all the odds gives a peace beyond understanding.

Bonhoeffer made it very clear elsewhere that it is not our job to create these gaps for God to fill. We need not try to make people feel lousy so that God can make them feel good. Jesus Christ comes to us at the very center of our existence in both good times and bad. His love creates also our need for his love. But never is God's grace more beautiful than when we are simply overwhelmed by the odds that we are facing.

"Father, if thou art willing, remove this cup from me; nevertheless not my will, but thine, be done" (Luke 22:42).

Grace and God's Will

D A Y
11

"The will of God is not a system of rules which is established from the outset; it is something new and different in each different situation in life, and for this reason a (person) must ever anew examine what the will of God may be. . . . Our knowledge of God's will is not something over which we ourselves dispose, but it depends solely upon the grace of God, and this grace is and requires to be new every morning. That is why this proving or examining the will of God is so serious a matter. The voice of the heart is not to be confused with the will of God, nor is any kind of inspiration or any general principle, for the will of God discloses itself ever anew only to [the one] who proves it ever anew. . . .

"For this reason there arises every day anew the question how here, today and in my present situation I am to remain and to be preserved in this new life with God, with Jesus Christ. And this is just the question which is invalued in proving what is the will of God" (Bonhoeffer, *Ethics*, 1965a).

For more than half of my years as a pastor I served as copastor with one of my best friends. Most people said that such a relationship would be impossible. Others asked for documentation and procedural policies that defined how we made it work. Basically our copastor style worked and worked well for 13 years for two reasons. First, we had a deep and real friendship, and second, we agreed that the mission of the church was to take precedence over our personal or professional ambitions. Both of these had to be worked at and nurtured, but they were a reality. Thus, we had neither chaos nor did we live under the bondage of a set of rules. It was a style of pastoring that we lived out in freedom day by day.

This is a kind of homely illustration of the way that you and I seek to live within the will of God. There is freedom granted to us but it is not chaotic or lawless. There is also a serious consideration and examination of decisions and actions, but not a bondage to a static body of rules.

We seek to know God's will in the context of two realities. We have been given the gift of God's deep and never ending friendship in Jesus Christ. And, second, we have been called through our Baptism to share the cross of our Lord. Thus, it is grace that defines even something so important as seeking God's will.

"Beloved, if God so loved us, we also ought to love one another" (1 John 4:11).

Grace and Worries

"Please don't ever get anxious or worried about me, but don't forget to pray for me—I'm sure you don't! I am so sure of God's guiding hand that I hope I shall always be kept in that certainty. You must never doubt that I am traveling with gratitude and cheerfulness along the road where I am being led. My past life is brimful of God's goodness, and my sins are covered by the forgiving love of Christ crucified. I am most thankful for the people I have met, and I only hope that they never have to grieve about me, but that they, too, will always be certain of, and thankful for, God's mercy and forgiveness. Forgive me for writing this" (Bonhoeffer 1965b).

I never seem to worry when I look back. As with Bonhoeffer, I see an orderly pattern to my former journeys. I recognize God's guiding hand and the many ways my life has been touched by his love and protected by his providence. And when I recall my failures and even willful disobedience, I recall how God's forgiveness covered them all. Looking back over my shoulder seldom activates any real worries.

Worries come when I look ahead. Especially when I look ahead beyond the shadow of my remembrance of God's past grace. It is at these moments that I need others to pray for me and minister to me. When my memory becomes too short to give me confidence for the future, it is the longer and clearer memory of others that assures me of the sufficiency of God's grace.

Bonhoeffer tried to share his worries in such a way that they would not ignite further the worries of his friends and family. He tried to be their priest assuring them of God's grace while at the same time asking that they would be his priest. We need each other if grace is to truly dispel our worries.

"I can do all things in him who strengthens me. Yet it was kind of you to share my trouble" (Phil. 4:13-14).

Grace and Mealtime

DAY 13 *"God must feed us. We cannot and dare not demand this food as our right, for we, poor sinners, have not merited it. Thus the sustenance that God provides becomes a consolation of the afflicted; for it is the token of the grace and faithfulness with which God supports and guides His children. True, the Scriptures say, 'If any will not work, neither let him eat' (2 Thess. 3:10), and thus make the receiving of bread strictly dependent upon working for it. But the Scriptures do not say anything about any claim that the working person has upon God for his bread. The work is commanded, indeed, but the bread is God's free and gracious gift. We cannot simply take it for granted that our work provides us with bread; this is rather God's order of grace"* (Bonhoeffer 1954).

There is a sense in which we always come to our tables as a people who have come from the Lord's Table. We have been asked to be a people who eat in remembrance. We remember our hunger and we remember the unmerited gift of God that satisfied and continues to satisfy that hunger.

When we come to our tables we are invited to remember not only God but all the people, who, on behalf of God, have served us that our hunger might be satisfied. The ones who planted and cultivated, the ones who fed and cared for the livestock and poultry or caught the fish, those who harvested and prepared food for consumption, the ones who distributed and marketed those things that fill our cupboards and refrigerators, and then the ones at home or in restaurants who cook and serve. We experience a continuation of the grace experienced at the Lord's Table at our own tables.

Finally we remember those who are calling us to share and to serve that they might receive the same table grace that we have enjoyed. And, when we have learned to give and to share with those whose stomachs are empty, we experience grace again. We have been allowed to feed our Lord at our table even as he has fed us at his table.

"For I was hungry and you gave me food" (Matt. 25:35).

Grace and Marriage

DAY
14
"Certainly you two, of all people, have every reason to look back with special thankfulness on your lives up to now. . . . So today, however much you rejoice that you have reached your goal, you will be just as thankful that God's will and God's way have brought you here; and however confidently you accept responsibilities for your action today, you may and will put it today with equal confidence into God's hands.

"As God today adds his 'Yes' to your 'Yes', as he confirms your will with his will, and as he allows you and approves of your triumph and rejoicing and pride, he makes you at the same time instruments of his will and purpose both for yourselves and for others.

"It is not your love that sustains the marriage, but from now on, the marriage that sustains your love" (Bonhoeffer 1965b).

There is a special privilege in being able to meet with couples preparing for marriage. The stories of how and where they met, the subtle and sometimes painful games that are often played during courtship, and the plans and dreams for the future often bring a surge of vitality to my study.

The challenge is to help the couple whose focus is so solidly set on the intensity of their own emotions, feelings and plans, to prepare a wedding that will be a worship service. For God is at the center of a service of worship. It requires them to experience in their embrace of each other the embrace of God. To praise God and to thank him indicates that he had a part in the events that brought them together.

How easy it is for all of the above to sound like just so much preaching or throwing a wet blanket of religion on an otherwise joyful occasion. Sometimes the preacher has forgotten how to be gracious and sometimes a couple cannot see anything but unwelcomed intrusions on their plans of celebration. But when those obstacles are removed there are few experiences of grace comparable to entrusting your love for each other to the God who is love.

"Let the peace of Christ rule in your hearts, to which indeed you were called in the one body. And be thankful" (Col. 3:15).

Carroll and Mary Hinderlie

O. HALLESBY

ESTERN civilization is shaped by Acts 9:11: "Behold, he is praying!" We are the prayer children of the apostle Paul who declared, "In Christ's name I declare to you the forgiveness of sins!" In prayer is born our continual energy of youthful renewal.

Small wonder then that in World War II Franklin D. Roosevelt, the man who led America through that crisis, kept a copy of *Prayer* by O. Hallesby nearby. The paperback and the hardback both belonged at his bedside with his initials on them.

Hallesby's theme that prayer is "helplessness, simply opening the door to Jesus!" may have led to the incident in which a comment was made that FDR had a simple faith. But simple faith is not simplistic. There is nothing simplistic in Hallesby's treatment of the topic of prayer.

Hallesby was one of Norway's most popular authors of devotional books. Studying under him in 1939-40 at the independent seminary in Oslo, we found also that he was one of its most beloved professors.

As a teacher, Hallesby loved dialogue. His classrooms were socratic, always beginning with "Herr _____ , can you tell me . . .?" His chuckle captured us with its familiarity. Classes began with the half hour he had spent with us on our knees before each lecture. He practiced what he prayed so that we felt we had a modern Hans Nielsen Hauge in his "transparency." Like Hauge, he remained a layman, refusing to be ordained.

What Prayer Is

DAY 1

"To pray is to let Jesus come into our hearts. This teaches us, in the first place, that it is not our prayer which moves the Lord Jesus. It is Jesus who moves us to pray. He knocks. Thereby He makes known His desire to come in to us. Our prayers are always a result of Jesus' knocking at our hearts' doors. This throws new light upon the old prophetic message: 'Before they call, I will answer; and while they are yet speaking, I will hear' (Isa. 65:24)" (Hallesby 1931).

Prayer is response to God's seeking. Usually we think of prayer as initiated by us. We are the ones who are generating the power to pray. It is not so. We pray first because we are lost—and found, dead—become alive, and all because of the four letter word *help*.

Most people who remember Edvard Munch's famous painting "The Shriek" would not see it as an illustration of prayer. I don't know that Dr. Hallesby would. But for one to whom the Spirit has revealed the thoughts of the soul, the cry for help can indeed be such a shriek. To sense something of what it means to live before God helps us to understand our lostness, our deadness. Our cry for help is the beginning of a life of prayer, of response to the searching passionate love of God.

The psalmist says it for us: "Thou hast said, 'Seek ye my face.' My heart says to thee, 'Thy face, LORD, I do seek'" (Ps. 27:8). This is the pulse of the heart in prayer. Only God can produce this longing for himself; only God can satisfy.

Prayer is a life lived in God's expectancy of our lives. The calling to be *you*, the calling to be *me*, is a lifetime of renewal in prayer as God calls forth the new in each of us every morning. Return and renewal happens daily. Daily we "crawl back to our baptism," Luther tells us, as we share his body and blood in Holy Communion. He renews our life of prayer and fellowship with him.

And not to us only, O Lord, but to all who love thy appearing. Amen.

Prayer and Faith

DAY 2 *"When an honest soul examines himself in the light of the Scriptures, he soon finds that faith is just what seems to be lacking in his prayers. It says that he should ask in faith, nothing doubting. He does just the opposite. . . . 'a double minded man, unstable in all his ways.' He is in distress, helpless; and he prays"* (Hallesby 1931).

Hallesby reminds us of the many times that Jesus says, "Your faith has saved you." And what did that faith look like? It was simply coming to Jesus and "pleading their distress before Him, whether it was physical or spiritual or both." It is given a clear image for our doubting hearts in those words that have echoed this cry of all of us in our tunnel of despair, "I do believe; help thou my unbelief!"

It is the paradox of our lives—believing and doubting. But only when we come to Jesus in our helplessness and hear His radical answer, "If thou canst! All things are possible to him that believeth"—only then do we give way and confess that Jesus must also create faith in us.

It is essential for us that we go to the words of Jesus to get the firsthand information about prayer and faith. Out of this springs all the wealth of Acts and the Epistles that are constant resources and strength for our lives in prayer. When we keep ourselves in the words of our Lord and the words of the apostles, we understand that the energy for the life of prayer comes from the love of the Savior. This energy produces a life of companionship in prayer.

Lord, we want to live in your love. Your love for us promises a life of prayer like yours, because it is yours alone to give. We cannot make it on our own. We can listen to your promises in Paul's letter to the Philippians: "Have no anxiety about anything, but in everything by prayer and supplication with thanksgiving let your requests be made known to God" (Phil. 4:6). Amen.

Difficulties in Prayer

DAY

3

"To pray, really to pray, is what is difficult for us. It feels like too much of an effort. . . . Prayer can become a burden for us, an effort. . . . The more of an effort prayer becomes, the more easily it is neglected. . . . Our minds become worldly, and we feel more and more alienated from God, and therefore less and less eager to speak with Him. Then we develop an unwilling spirit which always finds pretexts for not praying and excuses for having neglected prayer" (Hallesby 1931).

Sometimes our very helplessness freezes us into inaction and despair. "Our words fly up, our thoughts remain below." Often a good hymn can rescue us from that numbness.

Our life in a Japanese prison camp during World War II would have been bleak indeed if we had not had the treasure house of hymns that we had memorized as children and as young Christians. I had carried my small wedding hymnary into prison camp and it caused no problems with our captors. A month after we missionaries were imprisoned, I was sent into a hospital away from camp, away from our new baby, away from all who were dear to me. My little hymnary became my communion of saints, the voices from the clouds of witnesses who had sung the song of salvation in the tents of their pilgrimage, in persecution and peril and sword. I was not alone. Jesus spoke clearly and personally through those hymns, some of them centuries old . . . some were psalms from before Jesus' time on earth. They sang joy and a sturdy comfort into my frightened soul. They literally shouted at me as I looked out of the hospital ward with the window that opened only to a wall that would sometimes reflect a ray of sunlight.

It was the ringing chorus from Romans 14:8 "Whether we live therefore, or die, we are the Lord's" in the Epiphany hymn, "We Are the Lord's" that became my bulwark:

> We are the Lord's: His all sufficient merit,
> Sealed on the cross to us this grace accords;
> We are the Lord's, and all things shall inherit;
> Whether we live or die, we are the Lord's.
> (The Lutheran Hymnary, Augsburg)

Prayer strength returned in prison camp over and over again with the witness of the hymns and the psalms—the prayers of God's pilgrim people with whom we were privileged to be fellow travelers! Blessed be God. Amen.

Read as Slowly as You Can

 DAY 4

"As you kneel to speak with your Lord, it seems as though everything you have to do appears vividly before your mind's eye. You see especially how much there is to do, and how urgent it is that it be done, at least some of it. As these thoughts occur, you become more and more restless. You try to keep your thoughts collected and to speak with God, but you succeed only for a moment now and then. The time on your knees is just that much time wasted. Then you stop praying. The enemy has won a very neat victory!" (Hallesby 1931).

It was Roland Bainton who suggested the motto for the Meditation Library at the retreat center, Holden Village. The motto is "Read as slowly as you can." The sin of impatient haste breaks down our communication lines with one another, with ourselves, with the books we read, and certainly with the Scriptures and with God in prayer.

"As slowly as you can." Think about this when you take time for prayer. How incongruous to use such a phrase when we all know how organized and busy our lives are! We decide to take a specific hour in our day, or part of it, for prayer. What happens? Hallesby had experienced this and described it well.

How can we recapture our prayer post, so obviously under the enemy's attacks? We need to learn, little by little, to let every thought be captive to Christ; let it happen! In Philippians Paul has this strong conclusion to his advice on the attitude of prayer. Hallesby reminds us of this verse: "And the peace of God, which passes all understanding, will keep your hearts and your minds in Christ Jesus" (Phil. 4:7).

When we read Scripture as an entrance to prayer, communication begins again. It was the medieval bishop of Canterbury, Anselm, who alerted me to this. For Anselm, reading Scripture meant absorbing a text until it became a prayer. This meant for Anselm that prayer was simple in style for all believers, but "costing not less than everything."

For this old medieval saint, prayer happens when we know inwardly as well as objectively that we are helpless, needing God: "Come now, little man, turn aside for awhile from your daily employment, escape for a moment from the tumult of your thoughts. Put aside your weighty cares, let your burdensome distractions wait, free yourself awhile for God and rest awhile in him" (Anselm 1973).

Jesus says, "Come away . . . and rest awhile." Even so, Lord Jesus. Amen.

Cast All Your Cares on Him

<table>
<tr><td>D A Y

5</td><td>*"The work of praying is prerequisite to all other work in the Kingdom of God, for the simple reason that it is by prayer that we couple the powers of heaven to our helplessness, the powers that can turn water into wine . . . the powers that can capture strongholds and*</td></tr>
</table>

make the impossible possible" (Hallesby 1931).

The classic book for our generation of missionaries was *Hudson Taylor's Spiritual Secret.* Even in prison camp we could recall with a chuckle how that giant of the China Inland Mission would whistle in the midst of insurmountable odds. When his anxious and worried colleagues questioned him about his calm joy during the difficulties, he simply responded that he was just waiting and wondering how God would rescue them this time.

We think that we are not worthy of the care that Hudson Taylor knew, the care that all other great pioneers of the faith in danger spots throughout the world have known as a gift from God. But how can we consider ourselves unworthy of God's care? Think how often Jesus uses the creatures of the earth and sky as examples of the Father's care! "Are you not of more value than they?"

So to speak of faith in prayer is not to call down on ourselves our guilt, our lack of consecration and discipleship. It is rather to see the love of God which, as Luther says, sees much more clearly those contrite souls who are so far below him.

Hallesby used the account of Jesus at the Cana wedding as the key to the secret of prayer. Mary (as mothers will do) goes at once to the person whom she thinks can help the host and family out of an embarrassing situation. She does what we too can do. She tells Jesus about the lack, and we all remember the abrupt answer of Jesus. She is not daunted, nor should we be. She tells the servants to do whatever he tells them. There is certainly no record that Jesus had ever done anything like this before. But Mary did not live on past miracles. Jesus is always a surprise to our limited and traditional minds. The longer we know Jesus, the more we grow to realize that unless we are led directly into some different path that connects with our prayer, we simply can relax and expect a miracle. Like Mary the mother of Jesus, like Hudson Taylor whistling while he waited God's rescue, we can go about our daily tasks in calm expectancy.

Thanks be to God! Amen.

Praying in the Name of Jesus

DAY 6

"To pray in the name of Jesus is, in all likelihood, the deepest mystery in prayer. It is therefore exceedingly difficult for the Spirit of prayer to explain this to us. Furthermore, it is easier for us to forget this than anything else which the Spirit teaches us.

"The name of Jesus is the greatest mystery in heaven and on earth. In heaven, this mystery is known; on earth it is unknown to most people. No one can fathom it fully.

"The longer a sinner stands in the heavenly light which the Spirit of God has shed upon him . . . the more he feels that God cannot have anything to do with anyone who is as impure and dishonest as he is.

"To him the Spirit of prayer says, 'Come, in the name of Jesus.' That name gives unholy men access to a holy God" (Hallesby 1931).

Prayer in the name of Jesus is to pray in the strength and power of that name. In our business world, naming a name often gives entrance; it gives a recommendation. The power lies in the name, not in the person who repeats it. In a far more profound way, to pray, to enter in prayer in the name of Jesus is to come into a kingdom of a different nature, so different as to be frightening, certainly awe inspiring if we dared to take time to meditate on it. How can we approach God, the Promiser who never fails, with our lives strewn with fragments of broken promises crowding our memories? How can we expect to pray when we are such strangers to that kingdom of love and mercy and so ego-centered even in our prayers? Do we dare link ourselves with the Name of Jesus in the solitude of prayer?

We not only dare to pray in the Name; we are commanded to do so. That name embodies for us the grace to come in prayer, "to pour out our hearts like water" before God, thanking God that we know this grace. We know the love of God in the name of Jesus that overcomes all our fear, even the fear of not being heard.

Blessed be God! Amen.

Prayer in Community

"First of all, then, I urge that supplications, prayers, intercessions, and thanksgivings be made for all men" (1 Tim. 2:1).

Luther says in one of his sermons that we should *"bethink ourselves so that with genuine affection we pray because we feel all men's need and therefore pray to God . . . in sure trust and confidence."* And again, *"Would to God that some multitude might so pray that one common and genuine heart-cry of the whole people should soar to God!"* (*Day by Day We Magnify Thee*, Fortress Press, 1982).

This united heart-cry, this common prayer, is empty unless the individuals in that united prayer are praying. Hallesby's preoccupation with the individual person's prayer life may seem too "private," too intimate, too little concerned with the wide, wide world. Hallesby himself wrote that his concern was for the individual Christian life that each one might be "quiet, but steadily flowing streams of blessing, which through our prayers and intercessions should reach our whole environment" (Hallesby 1931).

Dr. Bernhard Christensen, former president of Augsburg College, was a beloved and prophetic leader of our particular student generation in the '30s. His intense spirit of discipleship to Jesus always centered on the social crises of the world. His comments on this book of Hallesby's are to the point here: "This type of 'lay Christianity' has often been despised by the worldly-wise, at times also in the church. And it does have its weaknesses, such as a certain narrowness of outlook and, frequently, a lack of stress upon the larger, world-wide Christian community. But granted such weaknesses, few spiritual lighthouses of Christendom are more dependable guides than lives of evangelical prayer" (*Inward Pilgrimage*, Augsburg Publishing House, 1976).

Make us responsible in prayer, dear Lord. Amen.

The Image of God and the Reality of Prayer

D A Y

8

"What we do in God's kingdom is entirely dependent upon what we are. And what we are depends again upon what we receive. And what we receive, depends again upon prayer. This applies not only to the work of God in us, but the work of God through us. . . . Every believer presents a daily influx into this world of eternity's powers of salvation . . . and helps to transform this world into God's kingdom. These believing prayers are unquestionably the means by which God, in the quickest way, would be able to give to the world these saving powers from the realm of eternity which are necessary before Christ's return" (Hallesby 1931).

Hallesby asks the question we ask: "Are our intercessions really necessary?" The answer is clear. Jesus says that it is God who must send forth the workers for the harvest, but also that He is dependent upon our prayer. It is impossible for God to bring the world forward to its goal without human beings. God has voluntarily bound himself to us in His governance of the world.

An image from the late Herbert Butterfield, an English philosopher of history, reinforces the words of Hallesby. Butterfield sees history as a great orchestration with all of us involved. Like Hallesby, Butterfield sees God as the symphony conductor, composing as he directs according to the way that each of us plays or does not play her or his part.

This image of God being dependent upon our prayers is like the question Kierkegaard asked, "How could an Almighty God create beings who were independent of their Creator?" Kierkegaard concludes, as we must, with another question, the final one, "Who else?"

"I appeal to you, brethren, by our Lord Jesus Christ and by the love of the Spirit, to strive together with me in your prayers to God on my behalf . . ." (Rom. 15:30).

Prayer as Work

DAY 9 *"Christians of our day are busy people. We do not live for nothing in the century of work. Never in the history of God's church have His people worked more than now. And never have we had so many workers . . . or been so well organized as it is today"* (Hallesby 1931).

But in all this machinery of activity, there is one job that cannot be done by computers or machines. The job is to pray. The actual work of praying has to be done by individual people; there is no shortcut, no substitute.

We look on prayer as our daily breath, our lifeline of the Spirit in a world of claustrophobic consumerism that draws us along into its vortex. We do get outside our own little group and pray for larger needs occasionally. Still, the easiest way is to stay in the old patterns. We are not energetic enough to venture out into the fields of God where the harvest waits.

The Spirit of prayer will lead us, if we ask. We hear our Lord saying, "Go ye into all the world. . . ." When did you put up a map of the world where you and your household could see it daily and be reminded that our beloved John 3:16 means just that: the world is peopled with human beings whom Jesus came to save. We so quickly adjust ourselves to the fact that there are so many needs, so many places and frightening situations, so much suffering and what are we, a small family group among so much? "And the disciples said to him, 'Where are we to get bread enough in the desert to feed so great a crowd?' And Jesus said to them, 'How many loaves have you?' They said, 'Seven, and a few small fish.'" (Matt. 15:33-34). That is the word for us. All we need to do is remember to whom we belong and re-read the Gospels and the Acts of the Apostles, and ask the Spirit of prayer to enlighten our imaginations to pray around this great planet, beloved and redeemed by its creator.

Now enter that "closet" that Kierkegaard said held the lever that could move the world, prayer! "Call to me and I will answer you, and will tell you great and hidden things which you have not known" (Jer. 33:3).

We believe you, O Lord, help our unbelief. Amen.

Pray to the Lord of the Harvest

DAY 10 The sentence is like a lightning bolt: "There came a man sent from God." The energy of the Almighty God is in those few words and in the man that they describe. Things happen when God sends a person out into the harvest field. Such people are sent out today when a person or persons follow the words of Jesus into the work of prayer. Sometimes they see the fruits of their prayers, sometimes not.

Here Hallesby uses as an example Great Aunt Bolette of the Hinderli family in Norway. Some people called her a witch, a crazy woman, because she walked the rocky shore and prayed for the sailors. She kept a prayer notebook with dates in it, and often the sailors would return and talk with her about the influence of the prayers on their lives. *"One night she had a vision, a prisoner in a prison cell. She saw plainly his face and his whole form. And a voice said to her, 'This man will share the same fate as other criminals if no one takes up the work of praying for him. Pray for him and I will send him out to proclaim my praises among the heathen.'*

"She was obedient unto the heavenly vision; she suffered and prayed and fought for this prisoner, although she did not know him. She waited longingly, too, to hear of a convict who had become converted and called to missionary work. Finally, during a visit to Stavanger, Norway, she heard that an ex-convict who had been converted was to preach in that city that evening. When Lars Olsen Skrefsrud stepped up to the speaker's stand, she recognized him immediately as the one she had seen in her vision" (Hallesby 1931).

This is one of the ways that we pray for the gifts of grace so that the right person is in the right place at the right time. No prayer task is more important than this. Only when this is an ongoing labor of prayer that each of us undertakes will we experience the kind of miracles told of in Acts. Then we will know the truth of that last word in the book of Acts, "Paul was preaching the kingdom of God and teaching about the Lord Jesus Christ quite openly and unhindered" (Acts 28:31).

Dear Lord of the church, begin that labor of prayer in me. Amen.

Prayer Is for Glorifying God

DAY 11

"Prayer is ordained for the purpose of glorifying the name of God. If we will make use of prayer, not to wrest from God advantages for ourselves or our dear ones, or to escape from tribulations and difficulties, but to call down upon ourselves and others those things which will glorify the name of God . . . then we shall see such answers to prayer as we had never thought were possible" (Hallesby 1931).

One woman I knew closed prayer with the phrase "And, God, we will give you all the glory." It sounded almost phoney to me, but I knew the person who was praying—she was real. It makes it sound as if God were greedily on the lookout as to who gets the credit. How totally anthropomorphic we are in our conception of such a phrase as "the glory of God." How could we possibly understand even a slight bit of it, except as we catch a glimpse of it in our Lord Jesus? And when he referred to the glory of God it had something to do with making people whole. To make people whole is to glorify God; to glorify God is to make people whole.

When this conviction takes root in us, we come to the Lord with a deep sense of need, asking for the true Spirit of prayer. And as our Lord prays with us and through us, the glory of God will be borne out in the lives of those for whom we pray. From icy mountains to tropical deserts, jungles of forests to jungles of asphalt, continents apart—but no farther apart in reality than each of us is from the grace of God. That is the geography of prayer. The planet shall be made whole to the glory of God in Christ Jesus.

Thine be the glory, forever. Amen.

Prayer in the Cross

DAY 12 Prayer is always centered in the cross. It is one activity of the disciple that allows for no ego satisfaction. It is not like the feeling one has while sharing a profound insight for the mutual benefit of the Bible class, or challenging and inspiring groups for greater sacrifice or more specific commitments. Even when one confesses one's own faults and sins, there creeps in the shadow of the ego again, even if one has suffered in the telling.

So, what is it with prayer that makes it unique in the life of the Christian? First, it is a solitary task, at least much of the time. We do not grow in intimate prayer life with our Lord if we are always in public. And the very solitude of the prayer time is an anxiety and at times becomes a burden. It is lifetime growth. Just as our lives have ups and downs, so does our prayer life.

Then it is difficult to let go and let Jesus speak out of the Word or out of silence. But sometimes situations and people to be prayed for come into one's line of vision. In the solitude of prayer, in our very anxious and weak spirits, God speaks, and in that speech there is the energy-giving power to do, to be, to act.

Hallesby suggests that this lifetime school of prayer was never promised as a crash course. There is something about this school of prayer which tries our patience sorely. Jesus himself alludes to it on several occasions, especially in Luke 18:1-8, where he says "that they ought always to pray and not lose heart."

Hallesby also says, *"We become faint very easily. How many times have we not earnestly resolved in our own minds to pray for certain people and for certain causes, only to find ourselves growing faint? We were not willing to expend the effort. And little by little we ceased to intercede for others"* (1931).

Prayer can never be a source of pride, so seldom do we see results. When we do see results we can never point to them as ours! So we live our prayer life, as all of our life, under the cross, putting all our faint-hearted efforts there where he "who writes straight with crooked lines" can also use us to further the kingdom.

Thy kingdom come, Thy will be done. Amen

Come and See

"In the school of prayer," Hallesby writes, *"there are not a variety of subjects . . . but purposely a few central things."* This is not, we might add, a school in meditation nor even of contemplation; this is a school of just plain prayer. Hallesby goes on: *"In the first place the Spirit must be given an opportunity to reveal Christ to us every day. This is absolutely essential. Christ is such that we need only see Him, and prayer will rise from our hearts. Intercessory prayer is like an ellipse, which rotates about two definite points: Christ and our need. The work of the Spirit in connection with prayer is to show us both, not merely theoretically, but practically, making them vital to us from day to day"* (1931).

It is Christ who gives us the vision of the world. I remember my first Student Volunteer Convention in Indianapolis back in 1935, the year in which Christ had literally made all things new for me. The Student Volunteer Movement had drawn some of the great servants of the kingdom in our generation. Toyohiko Kagawa was there from the slums of Tokyo. William Temple, the archbishop of Canterbury, was there; his concerns were for the needs of society, domestic and foreign. Indira Pak spoke for her Indian sisters and brothers. A young social worker took me out to lunch one day and asked me where I had picked up such radical ideas like voluntary poverty and working for the disenfranchised. "You are from St. Olaf College in a little town in Minnesota?" he said. "You sound as if you had lived in New York City or Indianapolis!" He was utterly amazed when I said that Christ, not social studies or city life, had opened my mind.

John Masefield's wonderful poem about his own conversion, "The Everlasting Mercy," says it far better than I could:

> O glory of the lighted mind,
> How deaf I'd been, how dumb, how blind.
> I knew that Christ had given me birth
> To brother every soul on earth.
> The station brook to my new eyes
> Was bubbling out of paradise.

Renew us, Jesus, to see you afresh. Amen.

Gospel and Law in Prayer

"My one desire has been to preach the gospel of prayer without setting aside the laws governing prayer life" (Hallesby 1931).

To be before God without forgiveness is an impossible life. That is the entrance to prayer. Without prayer's access to God our lives would wither up in unbelief, despair and eternal fear.

Hallesby's *Prayer* is most clear on the order of the life of prayer. It is not a series of steps that we master. The priority is our helplessness, our need which Jesus not only creates, but satisfies when we open the door to his knock. The climate of the book is grace, grace, grace as the ongoing sustenance of the prayer life.

The difficulties of prayer life, its problems, wrestlings, misuse, meaning, and varying styles of expression are all here. They are all, however, in the context of the one source and reason for this life, Jesus Christ, who never promised us a "rose garden." But he did promise us himself, and that makes all the difference.

Jesus is not only the "end" of the communication, Jesus is also the "means." The daily interweaving of our lives with his makes our prayer lives grow, even when we are unaware of it. The problem with writing about prayer is that because we are individuals we should not take the pattern of prayer from anyone else. We have to remember the one prayer our Lord taught the disciples, and let him teach each one of us from there.

The life of discipleship, the life of prayer—can they be separated? How well Jesus knows us! He is continually reminding the first disciples and the latest ones to "watch and pray," and that "the spirit is willing but the flesh is weak." Only the Lord can tighten the muscles, sharpen the vision, pour compassion into hearts of stone to motivate the life of the Christian to perseverance in prayer. When the great Hallelujahs are re-echoing through the universes, perhaps then we shall know that prayer is just beginning!

Come quickly, Lord Jesus. Amen.

Jeanette Strandjord

SIMONE WEIL

T HERE are many ways to describe Simone Weil (1909–1943). T. S. Eliot speaks of her as a great soul, a saint. Many would add that they see her as a genius, one who wrestled with and wrote profoundly about issues of truth and justice. She is also seen as a person of great integrity. She not only wrote but lived what she believed. She brought this same commitment to Jesus Christ after her conversion in 1938.

Finally, though her work is of great depth and seriousness, it is also penetrated by warmth, humor, and great passion. This saint, serious and blessed with genius, loved God, her neighbor, and the world.

In 1928 Weil began her studies at what was regarded the finest school in France. There her brilliance was recognized and she completed her degree in philosophy at the age of 22. She then turned her attention to teaching. She enjoyed this as well as being involved in local political concerns.

Weil's political interests led her into activities on behalf of local unemployed workers. In deep sympathy with their situation, she took leave of teaching and went to work at a car factory. This was not the last time Weil would voluntarily shed her position and comfort to join in the work and suffering of others. Later she would travel to Spain during its civil war, not to fight, but to support the anti-fascist forces. Then, after her faith conversion, she would take a job working with peasants in a French vineyard. The suffering she saw and personally experienced left a lasting mark on her.

Through her life Weil's health had not been good. She suffered attacks of pleurisy and severe headaches. It was while she was experiencing one of these headaches that she first felt the impact of Christ. While recuperating in France from burns received in Spain she was listening to a Gregorian chant. Through this the joy and bitterness of Christ's passion first impressed her. It was also at this time that a friend introduced her to the poetry of George Herbert, which became a way for her to begin to pray.

In 1943, when France was occupied by Nazi Germany, Weil was living in London. She yearned to rejoin her fellow French citizens but never could. In sympathy for her fellow French citizens she refused to eat any more than a prisoner of war was allowed. As a result of this and her weak constitution, she died in August 1943.

Gravity

D A Y 1 *"Men have the same carnal nature as animals. If a hen is hurt, the others rush upon it, attacking it with their beaks. This phenomenon is as automatic as gravitation"* (Weil 1973).

"I must not forget that at certain times when my headaches were raging I had an intense longing to make another human being suffer by hitting him in exactly the same part of his forehead. . . . When in this state, I have several times succumbed to the temptation at least to say words which cause pain. Obedience to the force of gravity. The greatest sin" (Weil 1987).

The key fact of our broken human condition is gravity. This is the metaphor Weil uses to describe how we are bound by our own sin and by the suffering in this world. We may make small attempts to escape, but gravity always pulls us back again. Weil compares this to a person jumping toward the sky. We jump and jump but never escape the force of gravity.

The power of gravity is most keenly felt in the midst of great suffering. As we are weighed down by pain, whether physical or spiritual, we feel God is very far away. If we are the one suffering we lash out. We want to cause the same sort of suffering, as Weil candidly says regarding her own raging headaches. We feel powerless in our own suffering and so we exert self-centered power by causing others pain.

The power of gravity is also at work when we see someone else suffering. The temptation is to rush in upon the sufferer like hens in a chicken yard. Weakness scares us. Gravity causes us to despise, exclude or blame the sufferer. This is our human condition. We cannot help ourselves any more than we can escape the earth's gravitational pull.

We human beings don't readily admit that we are so bound. We like to explain away our sinful nature and the problem of suffering by blaming others or addressing only particular sins. The convenient thing about this is that once the blame is shifted or one particular sin is overcome we can imagine ourselves free, unburdened, no longer weighed down. But our bondage goes on. We are bound by gravity. Only God can free us who are so utterly bound.

Grace

DAY 2 *"God created through love and for love. God did not create anything except love itself, and the means to love. . . . He created beings capable of love from all possible distances. Because no other could do it, he himself went to the greatest possible distance, the infinite distance. This infinite distance between God and God, this supreme tearing apart, this agony beyond all others, this marvel of love, is the crucifixion. Nothing can be further from God than that which has been made accursed"* (Weil 1987).

The grace of God is that God goes the greatest possible distance to join gravity-bound humanity. The distance is so great that it means a supreme tearing apart of God's own self. When Jesus Christ is crucified, "made accursed," he is as far from God as is possible. Jesus, bound by the gravity of human sin and suffering, is God going the ultimate distance out of love for creation.

Weil sheds new light on the familiar word *grace*. Grace is the supreme "tearing apart" of God. God, powerful creator of all that there is, is loving enough to lay down all that power and submit himself to the force of gravity. In Jesus the crucified God becomes the victim of gravity. Grace means God becomes the accursed and suffering servant, joining us where we are.

In the world of human affairs, being the victim, the weak one, seems so insignificant and ineffective. Weil knows this is not the way the world wants to operate. Similar to Jesus' parable of the yeast which leavens the whole lump, Weil compares God's grace to a catalyst which "operates by their mere presence in chemical reactions." God's "supreme tearing apart" means that the world will never be the same again. This act becomes the catalyst which creates our love of God and love of neighbor.

God is the only one who could submit to the force of gravity, take it upon himself in Jesus Christ and continue to love. God's love is stronger than the force of gravity. Because it is, we have the sure hope that gravity cannot keep us in bondage forever. God has bridged the distance, suffered and died, but continued to love. Grace is at work in our world.

Self-Denial

DAY 3

"A woman looking at herself in a mirror and adorning herself does not feel the shame of reducing the self, that infinite being which surveys all things, to a small space. In the same way every time that we raise the ego . . . as high as we raise it, we degrade ourselves to an infinite degree by confining ourselves to being no more than that. When the ego is abased . . . we know that we are not that.

"A very beautiful woman who looks at her reflection in the mirror can very well believe that she is that. An ugly woman knows that she is not that" (Weil 1987).

How do we know who we are? Weil's words tell us that we cannot leave our identity up to ourselves or other human beings. When we do, we end up limiting ourselves. We usually recognize this when we are seen in a bad light. Like the "ugly woman" we know that we are more than some negative surface view of ourselves. We resist being limited by the negative judgments some person or group has of us.

A greater danger to our identiy is when we *like* what we see. We raise our ego because of our own accomplishments, our group identity, or our material possessions. Ironically, when we base our identity on these superficial things we end up degrading ourselves. We have reduced ourselves to being only these things. We become like the "beautiful woman" who believes her reflection tells her everything there is to know about herself.

Weil shows us the way to discover our true identity and avoid all superficial limitations. This way is self-denial, submitting ourselves to God, confessing we are nothing apart from God. When we do this we refuse to be the authors of our own identity. God, our original creator, establishes who we are. Nothing else, not ourselves, not the group or the state, not our wealth tells us our identity.

Self-denial means we become what God has meant us to be. We are no longer apart from God, resisting God and God's way. We also do not see our neighbor as competition, someone we need to outdo or protect ourselves against. Humble self-denial means the restoration of our relationship with God and neighbor.

Waiting

D A Y | *"Notice that in the Gospels there is never, unless I am mistaken,*
4 | *question of a search for God by man. In all the parables it is the*
| *Christ who seeks men. . . . Or again, a man finds the Kingdom of*
| *God as if by chance, and then, but only then, he sells all"* (Weil
1976).

Weil believed that God in Christ was seeking her and all others. Therefore she waits for God, trusting that God will find her. Such waiting requires great humility. Waiting acknowledges that we are gravity-bound creatures and cannot leap up to God. It also acknowledges that it is God who establishes the relationship and not the actions of our own searching for God.

But, how hard it is for us human beings to wait! Waiting means giving up control of a situation or a relationship. It means trusting in another to act faithfully. We would be more comfortable with searching—at least then we are doing something and have the illusion of being somewhat in control. Weil counsels us, though, to be wary of our searching for God. We are gravity-bound human beings who always end up settling for less than God. We tend to settle for what is comfortable, self-serving and manageable. God is none of these. So, Weil says, practice waiting.

Yet waiting is not simply inactivity. Weil herself speaks of wrestling with God out of "pure regard for the truth." She dedicated her life to thinking about and wrestling with faith issues, especially regarding the injustice and suffering in the world. This was not a means by which to reach God. Instead it shows her trust in God to reach her. As she says with great faith, even if we turn aside from Christ to go toward the truth, "one will not go far before falling into his arms."

The Scriptures also call us to wait for God. But there too waiting (or as it is often translated, endurance) is not simply inactivity. It means continuing to live faithfully in the face of evil. We seek to understand and to serve out of faith in God. All this is done as God leads us, done in God's name, according to God's way of doing things.

We are called to be waiting people. Wait, let God establish your path by God's word, especially the Word-in-the-flesh, Jesus Christ. Wait courageously, asking the hard questions and wrestling for the truth. The Lord Jesus is already there for you.

Affliction

DAY 5

"Affliction hardens and discourages us because, like a red hot iron, it stamps the soul to its very depths with the scorn, the disgust, and even the self-hatred and sense of guilt and defilement that crime logically should produce but actually does not. Evil dwells in the heart of the criminal without being felt there. It is felt in the heart of the man who is afflicted and innocent.

"Men struck down by affliction are at the foot of the Cross, almost at the greatest possible distance from God" (Weil 1973).

For Weil, true affliction is distinguished by the depth to which it sears the soul. We feel abandoned by God, misunderstood and excluded by our neighbor and even disgusted with ourselves. We blame ourselves and feel guilty about our own suffering. True affliction is never sought by the one who suffers. Such seeking would make it a self-serving project in which we maintain control.

Weil struggled her whole life with her own personal affliction in the form of poor health which involved severe headaches. She was also very sensitive to the suffering of others whether it was physical or spiritual. She has no cure for affliction but does put it in the Christian context by relating it to the cross of Christ and to the Christian life.

Weil wrote that the greatness of Christianity "lies in the fact that it does not seek a supernatural remedy for suffering but a supernatural use for it." This happened most clearly on the cross. Jesus did not come to offer us some miraculous escape from physical and spiritual affliction. Rather he came to endure it. In Christ God joins us in our affliction, experiencing the same great distance from God and neighbor that we do. Still, in all of this suffering, Christ continues to love both God and neighbor. This is the supernatural use of affliction, to enter it and endure it in love. Such stubborn love breaks the seemingly crushing power of suffering.

In daily life, Christians are not exempt from affliction. It will come, spiritually and physically. There is no easy explanation for the why, where or when of it. It is a soul-tearing experience but, because Christ entered into it with us we have reason to hope and endure. Great suffering does not mean God has abandoned us or that we are being singled out for punishment. Christ was innocent but afflicted just the same. When Christians do find themselves in true suffering their highest calling is to refrain from ceasing to love. Pray for the strength to love in the face of affliction.

Prayer

"Prayer consists of attention. It is the orientation of all the attention of which the soul is capable toward God. The quality of the attention counts for much in the quality of the prayer. Warmth of heart cannot make up for it" (Weil 1973).

Directing all our attention to God through prayer is a prime way to submit ourselves to God. The prayer does not have to be long, outstanding in warmth or eloquence. Rather, humble submission in prayer means "suspending our thought, leaving it detached, empty, and ready to be penetrated. . . ." We do not focus on what we have to say but come waiting for God.

To focus all our atttention on God is humility. And such humility is a victory over evil in ourselves. Weil understood that part of every human being resists focusing on God. Our own concerns, our own schedules, our own goals keep ourselves at the center of our attention. To focus our attention on God, especially through prayer, is to begin to destroy this evil self-centeredness. This is why the attention we pay to God is far more important than the particular prayer we pray or the amount of time we spend praying.

Weil often prayed the Lord's Prayer with great attention. She prayed as she worked in the vineyards of France as well as during times of solitude. She wrote that she had to limit herself to two recitations a day of the Lord's Prayer because its effect was so overpowering. Prayer became especially important to Weil during her times of intense physical suffering. Focusing beyond her own pain to God, praying kept Weil's suffering from overwhelming her and cutting her off from God.

We must be careful, though, not to see prayer as some magical way to coerce God into doing what we want. Weil saw it as a means by which God draws near to us. When this happens God's own purity touches us. To be touched by God keeps us in a right relationship with God. Our own suffering, our own problems and projects no longer overwhelm us.

Respect

<table>
<tr><td>D A Y
7</td><td>*"We owe a cornfield respect, not because of itself, but because it is food for mankind. . . . In the same way, we owe our respect to a collectivity, of whatever kind—country, family or any other—not for itself, but because it is food for a certain number of human*</td></tr>
</table>

souls" (Weil 1979).

In 1943 the Nazis occupied Weil's homeland of France. Many French citizens fled to London in order to continue to work against this occupation. They knew of Weil and her work. Anticipating the end of the war they asked her to write a report on how to bring about the regeneration of France once World War II ended. Weil's book, *The Need for Roots*, was her response outlining a way for her fellow citizens to recover their spiritual roots. She holds up respect as one basic need of any society. The need for respect applies to a cornfield, an individual, or any kind of group. Respect is never for the thing in itself because that would be idolatry. We are to respect each person or group because they are a means to life.

Though it may seem tame in comparison to love, faith, and hope, respect, too, deserves the attention of Christians. Our promotion of respect can be a means by which our society is renewed and recovers its sense of purpose. We would be calling for the protection and nourishment of whatever gives life and dignity in this world. We will find ourselves promoting many of the same things Weil does—cornfields, the land, families, country. This can happen in our workplaces, school board meetings and city council hearings as well as at the national level of government. Our goal is to protect life. We follow the one who created it and nourishes it still today.

Justice

"The supernatural virtue of justice consists of behaving exactly as though there were equality when one is the stronger in an unequal relationship. Exactly, in every respect, including the slightest details of accent and attitude, for a detail may be enough to place the weaker party in the condition of matter, which on this occasion naturally belongs to him, just as the slightest shock causes water that has remained liquid below freezing to solidify" (Weil 1973).

Weil realized that our living in equality does not happen naturally; that is why she calls it a "supernatural virtue." Justice and equality become possible by the grace of God. When we act justly by refusing to act or speak in a superior manner we are mirroring God's original generosity in creation. Just as God consented to give life to us, so we are called to give life to others. This happens when we treat each other as equals.

Treating another as an equal means refusing to use our position of strength over one not so strong. Weil saw that special privileges upset the balance of justice by creating distinctions of worth among people and robbing individuals of their God-given dignity. In response to this she developed the notion of counterbalancing.

Counterbalancing means that wherever there is unequal balance God's people must be ready to add weight to the lighter side to achieve balance or equality. Therefore we cannot identify ourselves with any one group or state permanently. Our vocation is to seek a balance, not to promote one group for all time.

Such balancing happens on the cross. God in Christ comes down in order to raise us up, we who are so weighed down by the suffering and evil in the world. Only God could lift the world in the face of all evil. God alone is humble and loving enough to shed all power to come and join us where we are. We are not called to raise the entire world up as God has done, but we are called to act as a balance in order to lift up individuals or groups.

Who is denied justice and equality? Where can I help restore the balance so that those who are hurting or weaker may be lifted up? Pray for the humility to meet others as equals so that there may be justice in our workplaces, our homes, our world.

Uprootedness

D A Y 9 *"Money destroys human roots wherever it is able to penetrate, by turning desire for gain into the sole motive. It easily manages to outweigh all other motives, because the effort it demands of the mind is so very much less. Nothing is so clear and so simple as a row of figures"* (Weil 1979).

As the world became increasingly mechanized and industrialized, Weil saw how this was destroying people's ties to the land, their work, their families and communities. All these things were being made subservient to money or material possessions. Weil saw the world as being "submerged in materialism" (1973).

In today's materialistic society we tend to define someone's importance by how much they earn. Many people make huge sacrifices in order to earn larger and larger salaries to buy more and more things. In our scramble for money and the comfort and prestige it brings, we've sacrificed a certain quality of life. We end up shortchanging our families and communities the time and involvement they deserve.

Not only have our roots to our homes and communities been damaged but also our roots to our environment. As we debate the care and protection of our land and air, we drag our feet when we learn it will cost us money to care and preserve it. So often the outcome of the argument is determined by the answer to: "How much will this cost?" As Weil says, "Nothing is so clear *and so* simple as a row of figures."

It is true that it is simpler to measure everything in terms of dollars and cents. To make money the top priority saves us from having to wrestle with the questions of justice, balance, of God's will in this world. But the price we pay is a great one. We cut (uproot) ourselves from the blessings God would give us through the land, through family and community.

The human soul needs to be rooted. We belong to this good earth, to family and community and finally, above all, to God. These roots tell us who we are, where we've come from and where we are going. A simple row of figures can never give us so much.

Jesus warns us of the dangers love of money poses to our faith and our relationships with others. His encounter with Zacchaeus, the rich and hated tax-collector, shows us how one person was rerooted in God and his community. The simplicity and the concrete power of money is beguiling. Pray, so not to fall for such deceptive and empty simplicity.

Beauty and Nature

"It is true that there is little mention of the beauty of the world in the Gospel. But in so short a text, which as Saint John says, is very far from containing all that Christ taught, the disciples no doubt thought it unnecessary to put in anything so generally accepted. . . . It does, however, come up on two occasions. Once Christ tells us to contemplate and imitate the lilies of the field and the birds of the air, in their indifference as to the future and their docile acceptance of destiny; and another time he invites us to contemplate and imitate the indiscriminate distribution of rain and sunlight" (Weil 1973).

Weil sees God secretly present in the beauty of the world. She says of this beauty that it is "Christ's tender smile for us coming through matter" (1973). Christ himself also speaks of the beauty of the lilies and the birds to help us understand the workings of God. We are to follow Christ's lead.

To contemplate the beauty of creation requires self-denial. That is, we need to come to the beauty of creation with humility, refusing to exert power and control. When we do this, Weil says that we mirror God's own attitude toward the beauty of this world. God created it, but consents not to arbitrarily command it, even though God has the power to do so. When we come to beauty in humility, then we can be touched by God's presence in it. We have come to receive and not dominate.

In our present day, many have experienced Christ's tender smile through the beauty of the world. Weil recognizes that this beauty is the only way many allow God to touch them today. We are often more willing to see God in the beauty of nature than we are to meet God in worship or our neighbor. This does not mean we stop with nature but it does say that it may be an appropriate place to start for anyone who has trouble seeing God anywhere.

Christ bids us to consider the beauty of the lilies and birds in order to understand the love of God. Where and when can you do this? Time and humility are required but in the splendor of the wild flowers you will find an image of the extravagance of grace; in the vastness of the sky you will find an image of the great love of God.

Religious Things

DAY 11

"Religious things are special tangible things, existing here below and yet perfectly pure. This is not on account of their own particular character. The church may be ugly, the singing out of tune, the priest corrupt, and the faithful inattentive. In a sense that is of no importance. It is as with a geometrician who draws a figure to illustrate a proof. If the lines are not straight and the circles are not round it is of no importance. Religious things are pure by right, theoretically, hypothetically, by convention . . . the convention by which religious things are pure is ratified by God himself. This purity is unconditioned and perfect, and at the same time real" (Weil 1973).

Weil believes that religious rites are a way God's own purity touches us. We see such purity in the beauty of the liturgy, the Lord's Prayer and even in the architecture of the church building. All of these are important in the life of the believer. As we practice them we are touched by God.

We may not always experience worship as beautiful but that does not mean God is not present for us. Weil's call for us to approach beauty with humility seems to apply to worship also. Like Weil's geometrician, our illustration (our worshiping) is imperfect but it still witnesses to the truth. Our actions, our artistic accomplishments do not give worship its purity. God does. We are not the center of worship. God is.

God is most clearly at the center of worship in the Lord's Supper. Here God meets us in all purity. God knows we need tangible things and so consents to meet us in ordinary bread and wine. When God meets us in the purity of Christ's body and blood, we are not only touched but changed. As Christ on the cross took upon himself the sin and evil of the world, so in the Supper he continues to take our own sin upon himself.

Come and worship. The "church may be ugly, the singing out of tune . . ." but to worship is to be touched by God. To receive the Lord's Supper is to be cleansed by God's perfect purity. We leave the Lord's table rejoicing; the heavy weight of sin and evil has been taken from us.

Joy

"We know then that joy is the sweetness of contact with the love of God. . . . Joy and suffering are two equally precious gifts both of which must be savored to the full, each one in its purity, without trying to mix them. Through joy, the beauty of the world penetrates our soul. Through suffering it penetrates our body. We could no more become friends of God through joy alone than one becomes a ship's captain by studying books on navigation" (Weil 1973).

Joy is not a word Weil uses frequently. When she does, it is connected with contact with God. One of the ways she talks about this happening is through the beauty of the world. Another way this happens is in our contact with God's love through worship and especially the Lord's Supper. As with beauty, the earthly points beyond itself to God. As God meets us in the bread and wine, we have joy.

Joy never fully describes the Christian experience. Weil speaks of joy and suffering as "two equally precious gifts." We cannot know one without knowing the other. In other writings she puts it this way: "Suffering is still to joy what hunger is to food" (Weil 1987). Suffering creates our appetite or longing for contact with God which brings us joy. But neither of these is to be actively sought. This would be especially true of suffering. True suffering is never our own project, it simply comes. If it is our own project then it is a self-serving one which only leads us to focus on ourselves and not God. The focus must be on God in order to experience true joy.

Weil would counsel us not to settle for counterfeit joy in the form of earthly pleasures or comfort. Our joy is found only in the love of God which comes to us. We are most hungry for such love in the midst of suffering. It is as we suffer that our gaze rests upon a suffering God who also comes to save us.

Pray for this sturdy joy.

Neighbor

DAY 13 *"Christ taught us that the supernatural love of our neighbor is the exchange of compassion and gratitude which happens in a flash between two beings, one possessing and the other deprived of human personality. One of the two is only a little piece of flesh, naked, inert, and bleeding beside a ditch; he is nameless. . . . Those who pass by this thing scarcely notice it, and a few minutes afterward do not even know that they saw it. Only one stops and turns his attention toward it. . . . The attention is creative. But at the moment when it is engaged it is a renunciation. . . . The man accepts to be diminished by concentrating on an expenditure of energy, which will not extend his own power but will give existence to a being other than himself. . ."* (Weil 1973).

Weil writes of the parable of the Good Samaritan. In it Jesus teaches us what it means to love our neighbor—attention and renunciation. This is how Christ first loved us. Out of love he renounced his power and glory to undergo the sin and evil of this world. Because of Christ this same love now flows through us to our neighbor, anyone who is deprived of full human personality, anyone whose suffering goes unnoticed and is not treated as a full and equal human being. The naked, bleeding man in the ditch is all of these.

To love our neighbor is to pay attention to anyone who is in a weaker position than we are. That sounds so simple! But attention is more than just looking at something or someone. Attention is creative. It restores the full humanity, full equality of the sufferer. This takes time, concentration, and energy away from us. To pay attention is to deny ourselves, diminish ourselves in order to restore another human being.

In this way attention goes beyond charity. Charity is easy. We give leftovers and fleeting moments of notice and time. When we do this we are like those who walk by the bleeding man in the ditch. We received more than charity from God and we are called to give more than that to our neighbor.

Friendship

DAY 14 *"The greatest blessing you have brought me is of another order. In gaining my friendship by your charity . . . you have provided me with a source of the most compelling and pure inspiration that is to be found among human things. For nothing among human things has such power to keep our gaze fixed ever more intensely upon God, than friendship for the friends of God. . . . You bore with me for so long and with such gentleness . . . I feel that your patience with me can only spring from a supernatural generosity"* (Weil 1973).

Weil was not known as an easy person to befriend. She was extremely independent in life-style and thought. Her words above are directed to Father Perrin who became her spiritual mentor as she visited and corresponded with him. These words penned to him reveal what friendship meant to Weil. Friendship comes from God's "supernatural generosity." It is because God first comes to us with patience, without coercion, that we can treat others in the same way. As friends we do not try to dominate or restrain the other. We are patient with each other and respect one another's individuality (as did Perrin).

Weil's words not only help define friendship; they also show us how true friendship can keep another's attention on God. Not every Christian of her day would have taken time to meet and discuss matters of faith with her. Father Perrin did not let her questions and her novel thoughts and language become a barrier to their friendship, nor did he coerce her into his way of thinking. Weil's writing reveals how much that meant to her, especially as it fostered her love of God.

All too often disagreement and diversity frighten us Christians. In our efforts to avoid a divisive argument (we do this rightly) we also avoid dealing with diversity. When we run from diversity we can end up dominating or excluding people who have questions and perspectives different from our own. Christian friendship means that we do not fear such diversity but instead bear it with patience and respect. We can do this because we follow one who promises to draw all to him.

Pray for the patience and respect to be a Christian friend so that faith in God may grow.

Mark Gravrock

JOHN BAILLIE

M Y GENERATION was not reared on John Baillie (1886–1960) nor, as I recall, was his name ever mentioned in the family or church of my upbringing. My first contact with Baillie was in a tract containing one of Baillie's prayers. The prayer remains a favorite: *"O Holy Spirit of God, visit now this soul of mine, and tarry within it until eventide. Inspire all my thoughts. Pervade all my imaginations. Suggest all my decisions. Lodge in my will's most inward citadel and order all my doings. Be with me in my silence and in my speech, in my haste and in my leisure, in company and in solitude, in the freshness of the morning and in the weariness of the evening; and give me grace at all times to rejoice in Thy mysterious companionship."*

Baillie was born in Gairloch, Scotland, the eldest son of a Calvinist preacher. His father died when John was five, so he and his brothers were raised by their mother who, though rather poor, saw to it that her boys would get a good education. Baillie attended Inverness Academy, then went on to Edinburgh University, where he was a medalist in philosophy. At New College in Edinburgh he prepared for ministry in the United Free Church.

In 1914 war broke out in Europe, and Baillie did educational work for five years for the troops in France under YMCA auspices. There he met Jewel Fowler, and they married in 1919.

Baillie's professional life began after the war. He taught Systematic Theology at Auburn Theological Seminary in New York state, Emmanuel College in Toronto, and Union Theological Seminary in New York. In 1934 the Baillies returned to Scotland, where he served over 20 years as Professor of Divinity at Edinburgh University. While in the U.S. Baillie had challenged an overly simple liberalism; now in Scotland he found himself challenging an overly worshipful Barthianism, though he himself was influenced by Barth. It was in the early years of this period that Baillie wrote his *Diary of Private Prayer*, which has now been translated into a dozen languages.

Retirement brought Baillie a chance to involve himself more deeply in a long-standing concern, the ecumenical movement. He had participated in the famous 1910 Edinburgh conference, in the Faith and Order movement of the 1930s, and later in the British Council of Churches. Now at the first assembly of the new World Council of Churches he was elected a member of the Central Committee, and at the second assembly one of the organization's six world presidents.

Prayer Is Trust at Work

<table>
<tr><td>

D A Y
1

</td><td>

"And he spake a parable unto them to this end, that men ought always to pray, and not to faint" (Luke 18:1 King James Version).

</td></tr>
</table>

"St. Luke tells us that the moral of this parable is that men ought always to pray and not to faint. The word faint will, however, come to many people today as a surprise. We are so apt to interpret the meaning of prayer as if Jesus had said that men ought always to pray and not to work. That, I believe, is precisely the mistake that most of us make in our thinking about prayer: we think of it as an alternative to effort. We often speak as if there were two contrasted ways of facing the evils of our mortal lot—we may either fold our hands and pray about them, or we may pull ourselves together and do what we can to mend them. . . . But it is quite plain that our Lord's way of looking at prayer is as different from this as the day is from the night. What He said was that men ought always to pray and not to faint, or, as the modern versions have it, not to lose heart. That is to say, He regarded prayer, not as an alternative to effort, but as an accompaniment of effort and an alternative to despairing acquiescence and inaction" (Baillie 1962).

Prayer is not an escape! It is not a warm cocoon that shields us from the harsh realities outside. When struggles arise and threaten to overwhelm, it is no sign of weakness or failure of nerve to turn to our God in prayer. On the contrary, our Lord invites us, entices us, encourages us, even commands us to pray.

Prayer rejects two false paths. One is self-trust. The one who prays refuses to believe that "it all depends on me and my own effort," but clings instead to the God of resurrection who is alive and at work. The other false path is hopelessness. Prayer rejects despair, and does not give up or give in to "fate." Because Jesus teaches us to pray, "Your kingdom come, your will be done on earth as in heaven," prayer in his name rejects both self-trust and hopelessness, opting instead for bold partnership with the One who spoke and worlds were made, who speaks and the dead arise.

Our Lord invites us to come to him in prayer. Let us come!

"Have no anxiety about anything, but in everything by prayer and supplication with thanksgiving let your requests be made known to God" (Phil. 4:6).

Access to the Star-Mover

"I bless Thee, O most holy God, for the unfathomable love whereby Thou hast ordained that spirit with spirit can meet and that I, a weak and erring mortal, should have this ready access to the heart of Him who moves the stars" (Baillie 1949).

A *National Geographic* chart, *"Journey into the Universe,"* shows a mind-boggling sequence of maps within maps. Our own solar system appears as a mere speck within the Milky Way galaxy, which stretches 100,000 light-years across. The Milky Way itself shows up as one small spot within the "local group" of galaxies, which occupies in space a sphere 4,000,000 light-years in diameter. That local group, in turn, is only one little piece of our local supercluster, 150,000,000 light-years across. Even the local supercluster is dwarfed, finally, by the dimensions of the known universe stretching 20,000,000,000 light-years in every direction.

In the context of such incomprehensible reaches of space and time, our faith and God's Word make a claim that is either preposterously arrogant or amazingly gracious. The God who created all this wonder and still holds it in his hands is not only aware of our tiny existence on this speck in space, but makes himself personally available to each one of us! Even more: This Power that flings galaxies and superclusters took flesh on our tiny mote-of-a-planet and bore abuse, scorn, rejection, and death because he decided to love us!

This is the mighty One who wills to hold us like a mother suckling her child (Ps. 131). This is the one who invites us into prayer and promises to give us his full attention. This Star-Mover who in love became our teacher, "gentle and lowly in heart," and who poured himself out for us on a cross—this is the one who hears our prayers.

"Therefore, since we are justified by faith, we have peace with God through our Lord Jesus Christ. Through him we have obtained access to this grace in which we stand" (Rom. 5:1-2a).

Reflecting Jesus' Walk

 "Grant that the remembrance of the blessed Life that once was lived out on this common earth under these ordinary skies may remain with me in all the tasks and duties of this day. Let me remember—

His eagerness, not to be ministered unto, but to minister:
His sympathy with suffering of every kind:
His bravery in the face of His own suffering:
His meekness of bearing, so that, when reviled, He reviled not again:
His simplicity:
His self-discipline:
His serenity of spirit:
His complete reliance upon Thee, His Father in Heaven.
And in each of these ways give me grace to follow in His footsteps" (Baillie 1949).

It is a common observation that, over the course of many years together, husbands and wives begin to talk and act and even look alike. Groups of teenagers tend to adopt a common dress and languagae. For that matter, so do coworkers and business associates in later years. Some even claim that pets and their owners look alike. Through long-time association with one another we inevitably begin to reflect each other.

The same happens in our association with Jesus Christ. No imitation or performance on our part counts for anything before God. Our standing is granted to us only by the grace of Christ. At the same time, though, God calls us to watch and to walk with his Son, who himself says, "Take my yoke upon you and learn from me." Jesus walks the way of the devoted child of God, reflecting his father's ways, and so models true humanity for us. Paul calls us to help one another to grow to maturity, "to the measure of the stature of the fullness of Christ," that together as Christ's body we may "grow up in every way into him who is the head" (Eph. 4:13,15). How will that happen? As Christ's forgiveness frees us, he bids us walk with him, to watch where he steps in the Scriptures, to observe his gracious and compassionate dealings with people, and then to do as he does. Sinful though we are throughout our lives, God's Spirit is at work refashioning us and transforming us (beyond all our broken efforts and longings!) into a reflection of Christ's image.

"Therefore be imitators of God, as beloved children. And walk in love, as Christ loved us and gave himself up for us" (Eph. 5:1-2a).

Sharing Suffering with Christ

D A Y
4

"O Thou whose eternal love for our weak and struggling race was most perfectly shown forth in the blessed life and death of Jesus Christ our Lord, enable me now so to meditate upon my Lord's passion that, having fellowship with him in his sorrow, I may also learn the secret of his strength and peace.

I remember Gethsemane:
I remember how Judas betrayed Him:
I remember how Peter denied Him:
I remember how 'they all forsook Him and fled':
I remember the scourging:
I remember the crown of thorns:
I remember how they spat upon Him:
I remember how they smote Him on the head with a reed:
I remember His pierced hands and feet:
I remember His agony on the Cross:
I remember His thirst:
I remember how He cried, 'My God, my God, why hast Thou forsaken me?'" (Baillie 1949).

The cross of Christ is the very center of our faith.

At the cross God's love for us is demonstrated most fully. There Jesus reveals the heart of God for broken humanity most clearly. So deeply is this true that John's gospel calls the cross Jesus' "glorification."

The cross is the heart of our salvation. There the Son of God bears upon his own shoulders all the sin and grief and pain of a bleeding world. There we find our reconciliation. Earth's children are welcomed home for the sake of the one forsaken Son. By his wounds we are healed.

At the cross God invites us to die with Christ and to shoulder with him the burdens of the weary and bloodied world around us. "Unless a grain of wheat falls into the earth and dies," says Jesus, "it remains alone; but if it dies, it bears much fruit. . . . If any one serves me, he must follow me; and where I am, there shall my servant be also" (John 12:24, 26). There we see the path our Lord lays before us.

"That I may know him and the power of his resurrection, and may share his sufferings, becoming like him in his death" (Phil. 3:10).

Christian Worldliness . . . and More

DAY 5

"O omnipresent One, beneath whose all-seeing eye our mortal lives are passed, grant that in all my deeds and purposes today I may behave with true courtesy and honor. Let me be just and true in all my dealings. Let no mean or low thought have a moment's place in my mind. Let my motives be transparent to all. Let my word be my bond. Let me take no unchivalrous advantage of anybody. Let me be generous in my judgment of others. Let me be disinterested in my opinions. Let me be loyal to my friends and magnanimous to my opponents. Let me face adversity with courage. Let me not ask or expect too much for myself" (Baillie 1949).

In this prayer Baillie shows himself to be a worldly Christian, that is, a Christian who affirms the world (in the positive sense of the word). Here he lifts up virtues and values which are common to humanity and prays for them in his own life. There is nothing specifically Christian about courtesy, honor, justice, honesty, generosity, loyalty, or courage. Our faith affirms goodness and human excellence wherever we find it. We can praise God for it without feeling the need to make it Christian or to confuse it with matters of salvation.

But there's more. Baillie's prayer continues: *"Yet, O Lord God, let me not rest content with such an ideal of manhood as men have known apart from Christ. Rather let such a mind be in me as was in Him. Let me not rest till I come to the stature of His own fulness. Let me listen to Christ's question: 'What do ye more than others?' . . . O Thou whose love to man was proven in the passion and death of Jesus Christ our Lord, let the power of His Cross be with me today. Let me love as He loved. Let my obedience be unto death. In leaning upon His Cross, let me not refuse my own; yet in bearing mine, let me bear it by the strength of His"* (1949).

Solid human integrity is much to be valued. Let us appreciate it wherever we find it, and thank God for it wherever he causes it to blossom. Let us seek it and uphold it, and strive to live it ourselves. And in the grace of Jesus Christ let us live the self-giving love which surpasses every human excellence.

"Finally, brethren, whatever is true, whatever is honorable, whatever is just, whatever is pure, whatever is lovely, whatever is gracious, if there is any excellence, if there is anything worthy of praise, think about these things. What you have learned and received and heard and seen in me, do; and the God of peace will be with you" (Phil. 4:8-9).

Burdens

<table>
<tr><td>D A Y

6</td><td>*"O Lord my God, who dwellest in pure and blessed serenity beyond the reach of mortal pain, yet lookest down in unspeakable love and tenderness upon the sorrows of earth, give me grace, I beseech Thee, to understand the meaning of such afflictions and disappointments*</td></tr>
</table>

as I myself am called upon to endure. . . . Give me a stout heart to bear my own burdens. Give me a willing heart to bear the burdens of others. Give me a believing heart to cast all burdens upon Thee" (Baillie 1949).

"Humility is the obverse side of confidence in God, whereas pride is the obverse side of confidence in self. The very essence of the Christian pattern of life is that we rely for our salvation wholly upon God and not at all upon ourselves. Christ's yoke falls easily upon our shoulders, because He Himself has borne it for us" (Baillie 1962).

Our Lord calls us to carry much, and yet he carries it all himself! Our faith is one that lays upon us incredibly difficult demands, demands which cost us our whole lives, and yet the whole thing is free, easy, and light.

The central word of the gospel is "gift." "By grace you have been saved through faith; and this is not your own doing, it is the gift of God" (Eph. 2:8). Then, as soon as our Lord has spoken the word of gift, he calls us to pick up and carry the cross, to die to our selfish desires and give ourselves wholly in obedience to him and in compassionate service to the bruised around us. He calls us to radical allegiance and to a laying behind of every other priority. And *then* he says, "My yoke is easy, my burden is light"!

Every part of this compounded paradox resolves itself on one truth: Our God is utterly trustworthy. Our own selves and our resources are not dependable, but Jesus Christ is. We can throw ourselves upon him for salvation, because he is trustworthy. We can begin to spend ourselves and bear one another's burdens, because our lives, now and eternally, are grounded in Christ who is trustworthy, and his reliability enables us to risk ourselves. His yoke, finally, is easy because he promises to bear it himself, and he is trustworthy.

"Bear one another's burdens, and so fulfil the law of Christ" (Gal. 6:2). "Take my yoke upon you, and learn from me; for I am gentle and lowly in heart, and you will find rest for your souls. For my yoke is easy, and my burden is light" (Matt. 11:29-30).

Contentment

DAY 7 *"I am content, O Father, to leave my life in Thy hands, believing that the very hairs upon my head are numbered by Thee. I am content to give over my will to Thy control, believing that I can find in Thee a righteousness that I could never have won for myself. I am content to leave all my dear ones to Thy care, believing that Thy love for them is greater than my own. I am content to leave in Thy hands the causes of truth and of justice, and the coming of Thy Kingdom into the hearts of men, believing that my ardour for them is but a feeble shadow of thy purpose. To Thee, O God, be glory for ever. Amen"* (Baillie 1949).

During the first months of the infancy of each of our children, I was held in the grip of an irrational but very real fear. It was irrational because I had no reason to suspect it might come true. It was real because the thing I feared really does strike homes with tragedy. My fear was Sudden Infant Death Syndrome. Finally, the only rest I could find from my fear was the difficult prayer of returning my child to her Lord, for life or death, at the end of each day.

As a teacher of college-age youth, I often find myself a listener to anguished wrestlings over crucial life decisions: What career shall I pursue? Shall I marry? What sort of life-style and what level of consumption is right for me? Where does God want me? Why don't the answers come more easily?

The fears and questions that come with each stage of our lives can leave us restless and struggling. But the call of our Lord is not to quit caring or quit searching or quit acting. Rather it is to entrust all into his hands, even as we continue to do whatever he lays before us to do, and to trust that his concern for the situation and his love for the people involved are far greater than our own concern and love.

"Unless the LORD watches over the city, the watchman stays awake in vain" (Ps. 127:1b). "Cast all your anxieties on him, for he cares about you" (1 Peter 5:7).

Pilgrim of Eternity

DAY
8

"O eternal God, though Thou art not such as I can see with my eyes or touch with my hands, yet grant me this day a clear conviction of thy reality and power. Let me not go forth to my work believing only in the world of sense and time, but give me grace to understand that the world I cannot see or touch is the most real world of all. My life today will be lived in time, but eternal issues will be concerned in it. . . .

"I, a pilgrim of eternity, stand before Thee, O eternal One. Let me not seek to deaden or destroy the desire for Thee that disturbs my heart. Let me rather yield myself to its constraint and go where it leads me. Make me wise to see all things today under the form of eternity, and make me brave to face all the changes in my life which such a vision may entail: through the grace of Christ my Saviour. Amen" (Baillie 1949).

God stepped back from the work of creation and declared, "It is very good!" Even in its fallen, rebellious, God-denying state, this world and its inhabitants are precious to our Lord, who "so loved the world that he gave his only Son."

At the same time, in our brokenness we are all too apt to look no further than the surface of things, to foreshorten the depth of the life which God intends for us, and to make idols of what is at hand. Although biblical religion is truly "materialistic," world-embracing, we only rightly embrace things which we see when we embrace and are embraced by the One who is unseen. And we embrace that One only when we embrace him hidden in visible flesh, in his Son Jesus.

Throughout this much-loved world God has placed pointers to remind us of who undergirds it all. The clearest pointers, of course, are in the Word, in the tangible gospel of water, bread and wine, and in the presence of a faithful sister or brother. But even beyond those obvious signs, God sets up pointers everywhere: in the beauties and terrors of the creation, in the joy and tenderness of true friendship, in the devoted love of a mother or father, in the beauty of art and poetry and music, in the cries of need, in the voice of conscience, and in the longing of the heart in the depths of night.

"But seek first his kingdom and his righteousness" (Matt. 6:33a). "These all died in faith, . . . having acknowledged that they were strangers and exiles on the earth. . . . Therefore God is not ashamed to be called their God, for he has prepared for them a city" (Heb. 11:13,16).

Lord of All Life

To embrace the Creator, and to rejoice in the Creator's embrace, means, among other things, that we embrace his creation, that we rejoice in God's handiwork. The created world around us constantly beckons us out of our selves, and out of the tiny spheres of labor and diversion to which we so often limit ourselves. Only the cross of Christ can show us the heart of God, but the natural world, bursting with life, constantly entices us to enjoy our Lord's world and to consider again our extravagant God who delights in life. This Creator promises that the creation itself will also share in his grand plans for the future (Rom. 8:19-21).

"Creator Spirit, who broodest everlastingly over the lands and waters of earth, enduing them with forms and colors which no human skill can copy, give me today, I beseech Thee, the mind and heart to rejoice in Thy creation.

Forbid that I should walk through Thy beautiful world with unseeing eyes:

Forbid that the lure of the market-place should ever entirely steal my heart away from the love of the open acres and the green trees:

Forbid that under the low roof of workshop or office or study I should ever forget Thy great overarching sky:

Forbid that when all Thy creatures are greeting the morning with shouts of joy, I alone should wear a dull and sullen face:

Let the energy and vigour which in Thy wisdom Thou hast infused into every living thing stir today within my being, that I may not be among Thy creatures as a sluggard and a drone:

And above all give me grace to use these beauties of earth without me and this eager stirring of life within me as means whereby my soul may rise from creature to Creator, and from nature to nature's God.

O Thou whose divine tenderness doth ever outsoar the narrow loves and charities of earth, grant me today a kind and gentle heart towards all things that live. Let me not ruthlessly hurt any creature of Thine. Let me take thought also for the welfare of little children, and of those who are sick, and of the poor; remembering that what I do unto the least of these His brethren I do unto Jesus Christ my Lord. Amen" (Baillie 1949).

You Have Known Me

D A Y 10 *"O Thou who seest and knowest all things, give me grace, I pray Thee, so to know Thee and so to see Thee that in knowing Thee I may know myself even as I am most perfectly known of Thee, and in seeing Thee may see myself as I verily am before Thee. Give me today some clear vision of my life as it appears to Thine eternity. Show me my own smallness and Thine infinite greatness. Show me my own sin and Thy perfect righteousness. Show me my own lovelessness and Thine exceeding love. Yet in Thy mercy show me also how, small as I am, I can take refuge in Thy greatness; how, sinful as I am, I may lean upon Thy righteousness; and how, loveless as I am, I may hide myself in Thy forgiving love. Cause my thoughts to dwell much today on the life and death of Jesus Christ my Lord, so that I may see all things in the light of the redemption which Thou hast granted to me in His name. Amen"* (Baillie 1949).

Our Lord knows us through and through. And, even knowing us as he does, he loves us through and through. That is grace!

We spend a great deal of time and energy either missing or hiding from the truth about ourselves. Often I may overrate myself. I can do that by refusing to face seriously my sin and my twisted selfishness, but the word of the cross silences that opinion. I can overrate myself simply by pouring the lion's share of my energy and attention on myself instead of on those around me. Again, the cross shows me up. I can do it by avoiding thinking about my own mortality, but God's word tells me that I am an insubstantial vapor (James 4:14).

Or instead I may sell myself short. I can do that by wallowing in my sinfulness, refusing to take to heart the word of forgiveness that flows from the cross of Jesus Christ. I can sell myself short by focusing on my warts and forgetting that I am created in the image of God. I can do it by refusing to accept the grace of love and acceptance that flows warmly from people who care for me, and flows completely and eternally from a God who embraces me forever.

Often, in fact, my view of myself is a warped one which combines the overrating and the selling-short, a view that is simply stuck on myself and cannot see the truth.

Our God sees us truly. Our Savior sees both the darkness of sin in us and the beloved, valued children we are created to be. His response is the cross! The cross takes seriously our sin in all its horror and at the same time claims us as people worth dying for!

"See what love the Father has given us, that we should be called children of God; and so we are!" (1 John 3:1a).

In God's Hands

DAY 11 *"Now, O Lord, when the day's work is done, I turn once more to Thee. From Thee all comes, in Thee all lives, in Thee all ends. In the morning I set out with Thy blessing, all day Thou hast upheld me by Thy grace, and now I pray that Thou wouldst grant me rest and peace. I would cast all my cares upon Thee and leave to Thee the issue of my labour. Prosper, I beseech Thee, all that has been done today in accordance with Thy will, and forgive all that has been done amiss. What good I have done today, graciously own and further; and if I have done any harm, annul and overrule it by Thine almighty power"* (Baillie 1949).

How often do we tumble late into bed with the mind so full of plans or of regrets that we cannot sleep? And how often, when something is beyond our control or influence, do we hang onto it and wrestle with it nonetheless?

You're deeply concerned about someone you know who's going through difficult times. Perhaps you've spoken to that person, expressing your care. Perhaps you've written or phoned. You've prayed. Maybe you've even linked that person up with someone else who can help. Now you've done all you can, but the mind can't seem to shut off. What better thing to do than to lay the one you're concerned for in the hands of the One who can make a difference?

A barrier has arisen between you and someone else. You've done what you can do to reconcile, but you fear that a hurt or even a wall still remains. What better thing can you do than to lay yourself and the other in the hands of the Prince of Peace, from whom forgiveness and healing flow?

You've been called upon to serve your Lord in some concrete way, and you have responded, faithfully giving it your best. It all feels so inadequate though. Your efforts seem inconsequential. What better thing to do than to lay those efforts in the hands of the One who took five loaves and two fish and fed a multitude?

Our Lord takes our efforts seriously and uses them in his work, but is not limited to our powers and our doings. What comfort to know that the universe and the kingdom and each child are all in his hands!

"Therefore, my beloved brethren, be steadfast, immovable, always abounding in the work of the Lord, knowing that in the Lord your labor is not in vain" (1 Cor. 15:58).

A God of Surprise

DAY 12

"Almighty God, who of Thine infinite wisdom hast ordained that I should live my life within these narrow bounds of time and circumstance, let me now go forth into the world with a brave and trustful heart. . . .

Let me face what Thou dost send with the strength Thou dost supply:

When Thou prosperest my undertakings, let me give heed that Thy word may prosper in my heart:

When Thou callest me to go through the dark valley, let me not persuade myself that I know a way round:

Let me not refuse any opportunity of service which may offer itself today, nor fall prey to any temptation that may lie in wait for me:

Let not the sins of yesterday be repeated in the life of today, nor the life of today set any evil example to the life of tomorrow" (Baillie 1949).

Our God is a God of surprise. On any given day, we may set out our agenda, but how many apparently chance encounters intervene, how many unforeseen circumstances arise, how many "interferences" to our plans come along! God is not necessarily the author of those surprises, but the possibility is always there that behind any particular surprise stands our God. In hindsight it's often easier to discern the pathways of God's leading. Looking back over many years, what unpredictable twists and turns the road has taken, and what surprising and grace-filled avenues have led off from unexpected intersections! Our God is a God of surprise.

Let us plan our personal agendas, yet submit them to our Lord's scrutiny and interference. The agenda of Christ will inevitably be more on target and gracious than our own. The same for our life-plans: let us plan, yet let us submit them to the Spirit for creative reworking. And the same applies to our corporate lives, in our households and in our congregations. Our God is a God of surprise, and knows best where to lead us, both for our own sake and for the growth of the kingdom.

The Scriptures clearly warn us that the path of discipleship has many such dark places along the way. But even there, "let us not persuade ourselves that we know a way round," but rather let us walk on with courage, because our God is a God of surprise, even of resurrection surprise.

"Lord God, you have called your servants to ventures of which we cannot see the ending, by paths as yet untrodden, through perils unknown. Give us faith to go out with good courage, not knowing where we go, but only that your hand is leading us and your love supporting us; through Jesus Christ our Lord. Amen" (*LBW*, p. 153).

When the Way Seems Dark

"When the way seems dark before me, give me grace to walk trustingly:
When much is obscure to me, let me be all the more faithful to the little that I can clearly see:
When the distant scene is clouded, let me rejoice that at least the next step is plain:
When what Thou art is most hidden from my eyes, let me still hold fast to what Thou dost command:
When insight falters, let obedience stand firm:
What I lack in faith let me repay in love."

(Baillie 1949)

God does faithfully lead us, yet sometimes we get lost. Sometimes anxiety or pain clouds our sense of direction. Sometimes tragedy or grief arises and overwhelms us and we lose our bearings. Sometimes we've simply not been paying attention, and need to have God's word refocus our sights. Sometimes the enemy of our Lord throws a smokescreen in our way to distract or confuse.

Sometimes the darkness comes from God. Some time back, a dark shadow came over me, stripping me of emotion, of drive, and of sense of purpose for some months. During that time, my pastor, the late Bishop Cliff Lunde, urged me to be open to the possibility that this was God's doing. He was right, and the result, finally, was blessing and new direction. Sometimes the darkness is to be embraced as the womb of new creation.

In all these circumstances, God calls us simply to cling to his Word, his command, his gospel, and to take the next step, and then the next, until clarity returns. Baillie continues his prayer: *"O infinite God, the brightness of whose face is often shrouded from my mortal gaze, I thank Thee that Thou didst send Thy Son Jesus Christ to be a light in a dark world. O Christ, Thou Light of Light, I thank Thee that in Thy most holy life Thou didst pierce the eternal mystery as with a great shaft of heavenly light, so that in seeing Thee we see Him whom no man hath seen at any time.*

"And if still I cannot find Thee, O God, then let me search my heart and know whether it is not rather I who am blind than Thou who art obscure, and I who am fleeing from Thee rather than Thou from me; and let me confess these my sins before Thee and seek Thy pardon in Jesus Christ my Lord. Amen" (1949).

"The LORD is my light and my salvation; whom shall I fear?" (Ps. 27:1a). "The LORD is near to the brokenhearted, and saves the crushed in spirit" (Ps. 34:18).

Faithful

DAY 14

"Gracious God, I seek Thy presence at the close of another day, beseeching Thee to create a little pool of heavenly peace within my heart ere I lie down to sleep. Let all the day's excitement and anxieties now give place to a time of inward recollection, as I wait upon Thee and meditate upon Thy love.

"Give me tonight, dear Father, a deeper sense of gratitude to Thee for all Thy mercies. Thy goodness to me has been wonderful. At no moment of the day have I lacked Thy gracious care. At no moment have I been called upon to stand in my own strength alone. When I was too busy with my petty concerns to remember Thee, Thou with a universe to govern wert not too busy to remember me" (Baillie 1949).

God is faithful! Throughout this day God has graciously kept us in mind. He has brought joys our way. He has steered us clear of some dangers and troubles. He has led us or allowed us to come into other trials, but never without taking us by the hand. He has rebuked us when we needed rebuke. He has brought us comfort when we needed comfort. He has given us companions within his fellowship to share the walk with us. He has taken seriously our sin and our deepest wants. He has set his peace around us as a garrison and a defense. And in all things, in good and evil circumstances, God has been at work to build good for those who are called according to his purpose.

God is faithful! His faithfulness stretches from eternity to eternity. "Those whom he foreknew he also predestined to be conformed to the image of his Son. . . . And those whom he predestined he also called . . . and justified . . . and glorified" (Rom. 8:29-30). From eternity beforehand to eternity afterward God has been and will be faithful to his people. His grand master plan enfolds us in grace. And at the very center of the ages stands the supreme emblem of God's faithfulness: the cross of Jesus Christ, where God's utter faithfulness pours itself out for us at an incomprehensible price.

And today, as individually we thank God for his faithfulness, or as we gather in groups to praise him in the midst of shadows and uncertainties, we look forward to the day when all will gather around his throne, acclaiming God and his Lamb and singing, "Lord, you are faithful!"

"The LORD passed before [Moses] and proclaimed, 'The LORD, the LORD, a God merciful and gracious, slow to anger, and abounding in steadfast love and faithfulness'" (Exod. 34:6).

GEORGE HERBERT

EORGE HERBERT (1593–1632), public orator at Cambridge University and later a minister in the Church of England, was born in Wales. Early in his life he sent his mother two sonnets avowing his dedication to sacred poetry. From this early resolve he was never to retreat. He, perhaps more than any other poet, was a "religious" lyricist, revealing in all his work a profound understanding of basic Christian doctrine. His indebtedness to both Luther and Calvin is apparent in his use of the great themes of the Protestant Reformation: Word alone; faith alone, grace alone.

Herbert's faith was grounded in Scripture and his piety flowed from that source. He lived in the time of Shakespeare when precision and beauty in language was very much cultivated, but one feels even in the most elegant expressions of his literary work that Herbert speaks simple convictions regarding the sinful estate of humankind and the love and forgiveness of God. His delicate health no doubt made him especially receptive to the love and comfort which he found in the Word and in the service of the Church. While he lived a relatively short life, scarcely 40 years, his work has had significant influence. Poets continue to study his carefully crafted writing, and hymn writers such as John Wesley have used many of his verses in hymnody.

Herbert's work enjoyed greater acclaim after his death than during his lifetime, perhaps because he lived in the shadow of the more famous poet, John Donne, whom he knew and admired. His legacy includes both poetry and prose works, of which the best known are a collection of poems under the general title, *The Temple: Sacred Poems and Private Ejaculations,* and the prose work, *A Priest to the Temple,* or, *The Country Parson.* The latter work, "A Prayer After Sermon" gives one a feel for the vibrant faith that is evident in all of Herbert's writing.

"... O Lord! thy blessings hang in clusters, they come trooping upon us! they break forth like many waters on every side ... thou hast fed us with the bread of life ... O Lord, make it health and strength to us. ..."

God Gave Thy Soul Brave Wings

Flie idlenesse, which yet thou canst not flie
By dressing, mistressing, and complement.
If those take up thy day, the sunne will crie
Against thee: for his light was onely lent.
  God gave thy soul brave wings: put not those
feathers
    Into a bed, to sleep out all ill weathers.

                                        (Herbert 1941)

George Herbert never enjoyed what we would call "strong health." He knew frequent illness. An early biographer, Izaak Walton, writes that Herbert "had a body apt to a Consumption, and to Fevers, and other infirmities which he judg'd were increas'd by his studies."

In spite of all this, Herbert accepted major positions of responsibility at Cambridge University and later as a parish pastor. During this time he composed both poetry and prose works in praise to God for the blessings of life. With brave wings he would fly!

Many circumstances stood as obstacles in his path. At one point, Herbert was forced by his delicate health to retire to a friend's home for two years to rest. He had hoped for an appointment to government service, but with a change in rulers, that appointment fell through. When ordained to ministry as a clergyman of the Church of England, he was called to serve a very small parish where a great deal of his time was spent mending the stone work of the tumble-down churches. Although his income was small, he and his wife invited three young nieces who had been left homeless to live with them.

Here was a person who by the ever-present grace of God could rise above illness and ill-fortune to write poetry of beauty and praise, to preach sermons about God's great love in Christ, and to reach out with kindness and compassion to those less fortunate. He refused to fold his wings in self-pity, but spread them wide to soar where the Spirit led him.

"My grace is sufficient for you, for my power is made perfect in weakness" (2 Cor. 12:9).

Almighty God, preserve us from self-pity and morbidness when illness, misfortune or adversity comes our way. Help us, by your Spirit to bear burdens cheerfully and to use the brave wings you have given us to bring blessings to others, in Jesus' name. Amen.

The Cream of All My Heart

King of Glorie, King of Peace,
*   I will love thee:*
And that love may never cease,
*   I will move thee.*

Thou hast granted my request,
*   Thou hast heard me:*
Thou didst note my working breast,
*   Thou hast spar'd me.*

Wherefore with my utmost art
*   I will sing thee,*
And the cream of all my heart
*   I will bring thee.*
             (Herbert 1941)

    Biographers point out that George Herbert would write and rewrite his poems so they best expressed the riches he found in Scripture. He sought to do his very finest work in tribute to God.

    I regularly brought the Word and sacraments to Grandma Ehrie, an elderly widow who lived by herself in a very tidy upstairs apartment.

    Often we talked about the local congregation and the people she knew. On one visit I told her about progress on the new church that we were hoping to build soon. I knew she had no money so I was careful not to dwell on finances.

    Once as I was preparing to leave, Grandma Ehrie excused herself, stepping into the back bedroom. She returned with a knotted handkerchief that she was slowly untying. When the knots were undone, there in her hand lay two shiny 20 dollar gold pieces. "These were given to me on my wedding day by my husband," she said. "I want you to have them for the new church."

    I backed away, hesitant to take this greatest treasure she had. However, looking into her eyes, I quickly discerned this was a gift of love, "the cream of her heart," and I took the gold pieces with much thanks and some tears.

Dear Lord, you have blessed me with many gifts. Help me to respond gratefully with "utmost art" and the "cream of all my heart!" Amen.

A Life of Praise

Though my sinnes against me cried,
Thou didst cleare me;
And alone, when they replied,
Thou didst heare me.

Sev'n whole dayes, not one in seven,
I will praise thee.
In my heart, though not in heaven,
I can raise thee.

Thou grew'st soft and moist with tears,
Thou relentedst.
And when Justice call'd for fears,
Thou dissentedst.

Small it is, in this poore sort
To enroll thee:
Ev'n eternitie is too short
To extoll thee.

(Herbert 1941)

The mercy of God as seen in Jesus' sacrifice on our behalf is a frequent theme in Herbert's poetry. He was very much influenced by Luther's emphasis on justificatiion by faith alone, and here, as in other poems, he praises God for his unmerited favor. In fact, his verses can scarcely contain his praise.

Life, for the Christian, is a life of praise. Not because we are always joyful, or because things are turning out well for us, or because we have been successful at our endeavors; but because God has blessed us with a great gift, a gift we are unable to secure for ourselves. We have been granted a reprieve. No, more than that, we have been granted full pardon. The Bible tells us we have been forgiven. It is just-as-though-we-had-not-sinned.

Before dinner was served we held hands around the table and sang "Oh the Lord is good to me . . . ," words and music that young and old enjoy. When we sang the chorus of "Amens," our young grandson looked with delight from one person to the other and said, "Encore, Encore!" So be it. Life can be a life of praise, a joyful repetition of wonder and thanks.

"I will bless the LORD at all times; his praise shall continually be in my mouth" (Ps. 34:1).

On Worship

When once thy foot enters the church, be bare,
God is more there, then thou; for thou art there
Onely by his permission. Then beware,
And make thy self all reverence and fear.
　　Kneeling ne're spoil'd silk stocking; quit thy state.
　　All equall are within the churches gate.

(Herbert 1941)

When we worship God comes to us with gifts for mind and soul. In many religions, worship is thought of more in terms of what people do in approaching a divinity, but Christianity stresses the action of God on our behalf. The poet says we come "bare, God is more there, than thou. . . ."

We come to worship recognizing that we are sinners and God is holy. We kneel, in spirit if not in fact, not worrying about silk stockings or creaking knees. All pride and pretensions common to humankind are put away. The Lord of Hosts is with us and sends us out to do God's will in the world.

How do we come to church for worship?

We come humbly. *Bare,* in Herbert's poem, pictures our state. As we sing in "Rock of Ages," "Nothing in my hand I bring; Simply to thy cross I cling."

We come often. We are faithful and regular worshipers because we cannot survive without the nurture of God's Word and sacraments and the encouragement of the communion of saints.

We come joyfully. Christ has made it possible for us to come in confidence, knowing that God will hear our prayers and help us.

We come thankfully. We do not merit God's favor, but we are given it nonetheless. We have sinned, but God forgives. We grow weary, but God empowers us. For a lifetime we shall thank and praise God!

"One thing have I asked of the LORD, that will I seek after; that I may dwell in the house of the LORD all the days of my life, to behold the beauty of the LORD, and to inquire in his temple" (Ps. 27:4).

Bless us, O God, with a reverent sense of your presence, that we may be at peace and may worship you with all our mind and spirit through Jesus Christ our Lord. Amen (*Lutheran Book of Worship,* p. 47).

Listening to God's Word

<table>
<tr><td>D A Y
5</td><td>*In time of service seal up both thine eies,*
And send them to thine heart; that spying sinne,
They may weep out the stains by them did rise:
Those doores being shut, all by the eare comes in.</td></tr>
</table>

In time of service seal up both thine eies,
And send them to thine heart; that spying sinne,
They may weep out the stains by them did rise:
Those doores being shut, all by the eare comes in.
  Who marks in church-time others symmetrie,
  Makes all their beautie his deformitie.

Let vain or busie thoughts have there no part:
Bring not thy plough, thy plots, thy pleasures thither.
Christ purg'd his temple; so must thou thy heart.
All worldly thoughts are but theeves met together
  to couzin thee. Look to thy actions well:
  For churches are either our heavn'n or hell.

(Herbert 1941)

How easy it is to be distracted in worship! One begins to think about work and plans and pleasures. Herbert urges us to let our eyes turn inward to the need of forgiveness and listen for the voice of God speaking to us through the Word, hymns, and prayers—"all by the eare comes in." In this way, the most wonderful messages come to us: "I am with you always"; "The King of love my shepherd is"; "Thy kingdom come."

One winter Sunday, when not a car could travel on the streets because of an all-night storm, Dad challenged us to bundle up and trudge through a mile and a half of heavy snowdrifts to attend church. My brothers and I did, with Dad in the lead. When we got to church, we found only about 20 others who had made their way through the drifts.

It was really a very different service! The organist was snowbound so we sang the hymns without accompaniment. The custodian was not there either, so the furnace was not producing the usual amount of heat. The few worshipers who came looked like arctic travelers, all bundled up in an odd assortment of mittens, scarves, jackets, and heavy boots. The pastor seemed to have an extra measure of God's grace and comfort for us that day and we sang the simple hymns with full voice and thankful hearts. We felt heaven very close.

Now, after all these years, that morning is one that I remember well. Our hearts were somehow purged, as Herbert writes; nothing distracted us from the worship of God.

"Faith comes from what is heard, and what is heard comes by the preaching of Christ" (Rom. 10:17).

Judgment

Almightie Judge, how shall poore wretches brook
Thy dreadfull look,
Able a heart of iron to appall,
When thou shalt call
For ev'ry mans peculiar book?

What others mean to do, I know not well;
Yet I heare tell,
That some will turn thee to some leaves therein
So void of sinne,
That they in merit shall excell.

But I resolve, when thou shalt call for mine,
That to decline,
And thrust a Testament into thy hand:
Let that be scann'd.
There thou shalt finde my faults are thine.
(Herbert 1941)

In God's good time, the world as we know it will come to an end, and there will be a judgment. This is clearly taught in the Scriptures. The Lord has not spelled out for us all the details that have to do with these final times, but we are told enough to know that there is salvation for those who claim the Savior's sacrifice on their behalf.

The Bible calls all baptized believers *saints*. St. Paul uses the term often. He addresses his letters to those "sanctified in Christ Jesus, called to be saints together with all those who in every place call on the name of our Lord Jesus Christ . . ." or "to God's beloved . . . called to be saints." One can sense that the biblical term is not limited to those who are sinless or who have earned particular distinction because their lives have been marked with exceptionally good deeds. We are saints, holy ones, because of Christ and his life and death on our behalf. We are called saints, not because we are inherently good but because God loves us and is gracious to us.

While the thought of judgment is awesome, the fear of it is taken away in Christ. We are the saints of God now. We await the glories of the future life with Christ in great expectation and longing.

"And, when our last hour shall come, support us by your power and receive us into your everlasting kingdom, where, with your Son our Lord Jesus Christ and the Holy Spirit, you live and reign, God forever." Amen (*Lutheran Book of Worship*, 129-30).

A Thankful Heart

DAY

7

Thou that hast giv'n so much to me,
Give one thing more, a gratefull heart . . . .

Not thankfull, when it pleaseth me,
As if thy blessings had spare dayes:
But such a heart, whose pulse may be
                    Thy praise.
                (Herbert 1941)

In the poem, "Gratefulnesse," from which the above verses are taken, the poet describes the human tendency always to want more of everything. God showers us with blessings and "thy gifts occasion more," the poet writes. We make "perpetual knockings at thy doore," . . . "Gift upon gift, much would have more. . . ."

We ask God for much in this life, and God is good and grants what is best for us. Oftentimes, we take God and our blessings for granted, forgetting to be grateful. The poet's words are a reminder that what we need most of all is a grateful heart.

In my early ministry I called on an elderly woman in a nursing home. She had lost her power of speech except for one word, the Norwegian word "Takk," or "thanks." After we had devotions together she would take my hand in hers, look up at me with shining eyes, and say, "Takk, takk, takk." Her heart was the heart of which Herbert spoke, "whose pulse may be Thy praise." It was like a benediction to visit her and receive her thanks, and I would leave feeling richly blessed.

But she was not only thanking me for my visit. Her word to me was a reflection of her love for God and her gratitude for all the blessings God had poured into her life. She had come, in the wisdom of her years, to turn from the self-centeredness that plagues us all, and give herself away in praise and thankfulness.

"Be filled with the Spirit . . . singing and making melody to the Lord with all your heart, always and for everything giving thanks in the name of our Lord Jesus Christ to God the Father" (Eph. 5:18b-20).

Extravagant Grace

I Struck the board, and cry'd, No more.
I will abroad.
What? shall I ever sigh and pine?
My lines and life are free; free as the rode,
Loose as the winde, as large as store. . . .
Away; take heed:
I will abroad. . . .
But as I rav'd and grew more fierce and wilde
At every word,
Me thought I heard one calling, Child!
And I reply'd, My Lord.

(Herbert 1941)

What makes a person run away, to squander life and substance and inheritance so rebelliously? What makes a person go to "a far country," as far away from home as possible? What makes a person rave and grow "more fierce and wilde at every word" to get one's way?

The story of the wayward son is one of three stories in Luke 15, each about losing and finding: the lost sheep found by the shepherd; the lost coin searched for diligently by the woman sweeping her floor; the lost son welcomed home by the forgiving father. Each story ends with joy and celebration. The lost is found! The stories are not so much about a sheep, a coin, and a son, as about God who seeks us, cares for us and forgives us who are lost through ignorance and wilfulness.

The last story has been called "the parable of the prodigal son." It is interesting to note that *both* the son and the father are prodigal. A prodigal is one who is recklessly wasteful, given to extravagance. The son's behavior is certainly that, in the most negative sense. He thinks of no one but himself, abandoning his responsibilities at home, and wasting his inheritance in high living. The father, on the other hand, is recklessly extravagant in the most positive sense. He has no doubt been deeply hurt by the rejection of his ne'er-do-well son, yet he welcomes him home with unrestrained compassion and forgiveness.

Herbert, in his poem describes this scene. Selfish and flagrant free-spiritedness is met by the extravagant grace of God.

O God, you have called me to be your child. Humbly I call you Lord. Amen.

The Love That Holds Us

I Threatned to observe the strict decree
Of my deare God with all my power & might.
But I was told by one, it could not be;
Yet I must trust in God to be my light.
Then will I trust, said I, in him alone.
Nay, ev'n to trust in him, was also his:
We must confesse that nothing is our own.
Then I confesse that he my succour is:
But to have nought is ours, not to confesse
That we have nought. I stood amaz'd at this,
Much troubled, till I heard a friend expresse,
That all things were more ours by being his.
What Adam had, and forfeited for all,
Christ keepeth now, who cannot fail or fall.

(Herbert 1941)

A good friend who was an alcoholic used to call me in the middle of the night to talk, usually seeking pity, but confident he could handle all his troubles. After several efforts to help him, I realized that neither my efforts nor those of his family were accomplishing anything. Tears, pleadings, sleepless nights, and many prayers seemed of no avail.

Then, when things seemed hopeless, and when family, business, and personal health were threatening complete collapse, my friend finally "hit bottom" and in his total collapse turned to Alcoholics Anonymous for help. Wise counselors directed him to God's never-failing love and others supported him until he was safely back on his feet. He lost all his egotistical sense of self-righteousness and he discovered Christ's strength and forgiveness.

We often feel weak and helpless when overwhelmed with our failures; but we seek refuge in Christ and his forgiveness. Love, righteousness, and peace are ours because they are first his. He shares them freely. These gifts are "more ours by being his."

Dear Lord, rescue us from ourselves. Grant that we may surrender our proud hearts to the gracious working of the Spirit within us and lay claim to Christ's love and righteousness as our very own. Amen.

I Believe in the Resurrection of the Body

DAY

10

What though my bodie runne to dust?
Faith cleaves unto it, counting evr'y grain
With an exact and most particular trust,
Reserving all for flesh again.

(Herbert 1941)

Years ago I stood in the cemetery by the side of a forlorn widow. We watched as dirt was shovelled onto the casket containing the body of her husband. It was a gray, forboding winter day. An icy wind whipped through our coats and left us numb with cold. I put out my arm to support her. Her body was shaking with grief and tiredness and cold.

The first frozen clods of dirt hit the casket like rifle shots and we reacted instinctively to each shovelfull. Custom required that we stay until the grave was filled. Then at last we returned to the warmth of the church. There, in the company of family and friends, was comfort and understanding. In our conversation we spoke of the man who had died and we recalled his life of faith. In fact, faith was at the heart of all we said to one another. People expressed their sympathy in ways that revealed their faith in the providence and promises of God. Faith is the theme of the longer poem which concludes with the above lines. The poet writes:

And where sinne placeth me in Adams fall,
Faith sets me higher in his glorie.
If I go lower in the book,
What can be lower then the common manger?
Faith puts me there with him, who sweetly took
Our flesh and frailtie, death and danger.

(Herbert 1941)

This is the comfort we have, in life and in death. We are united with Christ by faith. He took upon himself our flesh and weaknesses, our death and danger. He died and rose again and promised that our bodies will be raised from the grave. This is the Christian hope; the Christian faith.

Lord Jesus, by your death you took away the sting of death. Grant to us, your servants, so to follow in faith where you have led the way, that we may at length fall asleep peacefully in you and wake in your likeness; to you, the author and giver of life, be all honor and glory, now and forever. Amen (*LBW*, p. 213).

The Gift of Peace

Sweet Peace, where dost thou dwell? I humbly crave,
Let me once know...
(Herbert 1941)

George Herbert never ceased to long for peace. He saw the need for it at the university where schools of thought clashed and threatened calm and reflective study. He saw the need for it in the church of his day which was torn with tension between the Puritans, the Church of England, and the Roman Catholic church. He at one time hoped to become Secretary of State where he could promote peace between nations. None of these dreams of peace-making were fulfilled; but in one search he found a sense of victory. He found peace within.

The road to peace within was not an easy one. Herbert had a full share of pride, ambition, and self-will. There was an ongoing conflict between the claims of religion and worldliness before he finally subjected his stubborn will to the will of God.

In the beautiful poem entitled "Peace," Herbert describes one who searches in many places, without success, for the precious gift of peace. Finally, the searcher is told of a Prince of Salem (Jerusalem) who "sweetly lived" and at last died at the hand of foes. From his grave grew twelve stalks of wheat; their seeds were planted "through all the earth." Those who ate the bread made from this seed knew "peace and mirth."

> *Take of this grain, which in my garden grows,*
> *And grows for you;*
> *Make bread of it: and that repose*
> *And peace which ev'ry where*
> *With so much earnestnesse you do pursue,*
> *is onely there.*
> (Herbert 1941)

The poet points to the Bread of Life, Christ our Lord, as the only source of lasting peace. There is a reference here, as in many of his poems, to the Lord's Supper as the source of forgiveness and a right relationship with God. From Christ's agony on the cross, his death, and victory over sin, springs the "sweet peace" we seek.

God of love, we come to you with praise and thanksgiving for the victory over conflict and turmoil that Jesus, the Bread of Life, makes possible. Grant that we, knowing his healing within, may be messengers of peace throughout the world. Amen.

Welcome Love

Love bade me welcome: yet my soul drew back,
*   Guiltie of dust and sinne.*
But quick-ey'd Love, observing me grow slack
*   From my first entrance in,*
Drew nearer to me, sweetly questioning,
*   If I lack'd any thing.*

A guest, I answer'd, worthy to be here:
*   Love said, You shall be he.*
I the unkinde, ungratefull? Ah my deare,
*   I cannot look on thee.*
Love took my hand, and smiling did reply,
*   Who made the eyes but I?*

Truth Lord, but I have marr'd them: let my shame
*   Go where it doth deserve.*
And know you not, sayes Love, who bore the blame?
*   My deare, then I will serve.*
You must sit down, sayes Love, and taste my meat:
*   So I did sit and eat.*

                 (Herbert 1941)

The poet, in a most elegant way, describes our inability to comprehend the grace of God. With the poet we protest, "I am unkind, ungrateful, unworthy to look on you." But the God who is Love pursues us, "I bore your blame and I will serve you. You are my guest."

God had a special plan for the disciple Peter. Peter often seems confused about his assignment and slow to catch on to Jesus and his message. Peter's instability is obvious. At one point he confesses Jesus as Christ, and in the next scene he rebukes him for teaching that the Messiah is to suffer. He promises to be faithful to Jesus but later denies his Lord three times. Peter and other disciples are unable to stay awake while Jesus struggles in Gethsemane. By now the reader begins to think that surely Jesus will give up on Peter.

"Love bade me welcome." God does not give up on Peter, who, in spite of himself, is overwhelmed by God's grace. He did nothing to deserve it, yet Love invites him to "sit and eat."

Dear Lord, your love has brought us to your table, thankful and expectant. Let us taste of your forgiveness. Amen.

Blessed Weariness

When God at first made man,
Having a glasse of blessings standing by;
Let us (said he) poure on him all we can:
Let the worlds riches, which dispersed lie,
Contract into a span.

So strength first made a way;
Then beautie flow'd, then wisdome, honour, pleasure:
When almost all was out, God made a stay,
Perceiving that alone of all his treasure
Rest in the bottome lay.

For if I should (said he)
Bestow this jewell also on my creature,
He would adore my gifts in stead of me,
And rest in Nature, not the God of Nature:
So both should losers be.

Yet let him keep the rest,
But keep them with repining restlesnesse
Let him be rich and wearie, that at least,
If goodnesse leade him not, yet wearinesse
May tosse him to my breast.

(Herbert 1941)

We often think of tiredness as an inconvenience, a kind of curse with which we are doomed to live. The poet, who was frail and required periods of rest, came to see weariness in quite another light.

He writes of the Creator God giving gifts in lavish fashion—a whole "glasse of blessings"—but in such a way as to save us from adoring the gifts and not the Giver. Only the gift of rest is withheld so that in our weariness we would turn to God—"weariness may tosse him to my breast."

I remember her well. At 82 she lay in the nursing home waiting to die. Life had been good but now she was ill and death was imminent. One day, overcome with restlessness, she said, "It takes so long to die." After reading some favorite Bible verses, I sang the words from the oratorio, *Elijah*, "O rest in the Lord, wait patiently for him, and he shall give thee thy heart's desire." She sang along with me and then repeated, "Rest . . . rest . . . rest . . ." as she dozed off to sleep.

"Come to me, all who labor and are heavy laden, and I will give you rest" (Matt. 11:28).

Life in Christ

Come, my Way, my Truth, my Life:
Such a Way, as gives us breath:
Such a Truth, as ends all strife:
Such a life, as killeth death.

Come, my Light, my Feast, my Strength:
Such a Light, as shows a feast:
Such a Feast, as mends in length:
Such a Strength, as makes his guest.

Come my Joy, my Love, my Heart:
Such a Joy, as none can move:
Such a Love, as none can part:
Such a Heart, as joyes in love.

(Herbert 1941)

Prayer has many themes. Two of the most important are reflected in this poem of Herbert's which many of us know as the hymn set to music by R. Vaughn Williams. Here the prayer is one of invitation and confession. "Come . . ." we pray as we invite the Lord into our hearts and lives. As little children we learned to pray before meals, "Come Lord Jesus, Be our guest . . ." and sometimes we sang, "Come into my heart, come into my heart, come into my heart, Lord Jesus."

Prayer, above everything else, is receptivity to God. It is an eagerness to allow God to come into our hearts, minds, and lives to direct us day by day. When we pray, we live consciously in the presence of God and know the transformation God's Spirit brings about. This poem is about those changes. Each line, though short, is rich with allusions.

The opening line of each stanza speaks *to* God in nine familiar scriptural metaphors, such as, "Way, Truth and Life." The succeeding lines speak *about* God, confessing who God is and what God does. God is a Truth that ends all strife. God is a Life that kills death.

We know that it is Christ who declared himself to be "The way, the truth, and the life," and that all the metaphors of this hymn point to Christ. He is our Life, his body and blood our Feast, and his Joy can never be taken from us.

Amen. Come Lord Jesus.

Paul Ofstedal

GERHARD EMANUEL FROST

T O introduce Gerhard Frost we offer portions of a letter written to him four days before his death by Alvin N. Rogness, for many years Frost's colleague at Luther Theological Seminary, St. Paul, Minnesota. Frost never read the letter, but at the family's request, Rogness read it at the funeral.

"You once expressed doubt that you should be teaching education when you were no expert in pedagogy. You may remember that I told you then that you were singularly the person to translate the concepts of the faith into the concrete language of the pulpit. I could say 'the poetry of the pulpit,' because that's preaching at its best. You were a teacher. You made students see the beauty of truth and the wonder of grace.

"I wonder to how many thousands who read and reread your books you have been their silent pastor. You have an uncanny ability to make the commonplaces charged with great truths. We turn page after page to be surprised by the truths hidden in the ordinary. I have fallen asleep many nights ushered into your world of truth, beauty, and humor."

These words of Rogness about Frost bring to mind lines by Edwin Markham: "The poet is a dweller between two worlds, the Seen and the Unseen; he beholds objects and events in their larger outline and deeper mystery. . . . He frees us from the tyranny of the moment. . . . Poetry is the revelation of the strange in the familiar, of the eternal in the transitory. It is the impassioned cry of the heart in the presence of the wonder of life" (Cynthia Pearl Maus, *Christ and the Fine Arts,* Harper & Brothers, 1938).

Gerhard Frost was born January 17, 1909, in Sheyenne, N.D. He grad-uated from Luther College in Decorah, Iowa, in 1931, from Luther Theological Seminary in St. Paul in 1934, and in 1950 received his M. Th. from Princeton Seminary. He served parishes in Montana and North Dakota, became campus pastor and a faculty member at Luther College and then a faculty member at Luther Seminary. Following his retirement he was in wide demand as a retreat leader and speaker. Frost died after a brief illness on May 23, 1987.

Think about These Things

D A Y 1 "Finally, brethren, whatever is true, whatever is honorable, whatever is just, whatever is pure, whatever is lovely, whatever is gracious, if there is any excellence, if there is anything worthy of praise, think about these things" (Phil. 4:8).

I have a friend who is admired by all who know him for his wisdom and creativity. Throughout his life he has been a voracious reader, but now his sight is failing.

Recently, he served as a resource person at a study workshop. After the workshop, I met a student who had attended, and asked, "Was he in his usual excellent form?"

"Yes," he answered, "I especially remember his opening remark. He was standing at the front of the room, looking out at us. We all knew that his eyesight was getting poorer. He waited for the room to become quiet, and said, 'I can't read much any more, so I don't think about as many things as I once did,' and then he paused and added, 'But I think more!'"

I think more. We seek breadth naturally. We frequently need no urging to be interested in many different things. We like to take pride in the fact that we're always learning something new. But when our options are suddenly narrowed through illness, or accident, or some other circumstance, we find ourselves with time we never had before. Although we wouldn't choose it, our sudden deprivation can be an act of grace. Without it, we might miss the chance to examine ourselves and reach new understanding. A crisis can help us stop, think, and absorb more fully the depths of God's will and purpose for us. This process can move us from being simply informed to being truly wise.

Paul the apostle urges us to think selectively and with discrimination. He advises us to be less concerned about details, and to concentrate on what is true, honorable, just, pure, gracious, excellent. Our wisdom can flourish if we take the time to think about these things. (This devotion is from Frost 1978.)

389

Behold, the Lamb

DAY 2

"...And he looked at Jesus as he walked, and said 'Behold, the Lamb of God!'" (John 1:36).

I was teaching a confirmation class of 16 young Navajo Christians, and we were discussing the subject of time as God's gift of opportunity. We talked about our own mortality, and then discussed why we measure time. I stepped to the blackboard and wrote May 2, 1977 A.D.

I stood there for a few moments as we considered how we have divided the centuries into B.C. and A.D. Then I asked the class, "What's so special about Jesus that we measure our time from the years when he lived as a man on earth?"

During the thoughtful pause that followed, 16 pairs of dark eyes looked inquiringly at me and then at one another. Finally, one boy spoke. He formed his answer as a question: "No more lambs killed?"

The Navajo people are shepherds. All of the youths in my class had early recollections of tending sheep and goats with their mothers and older brothers and sisters. The death of a lamb held deep meaning for them, and this young boy had beheld the Lamb of God from his shepherd's perspective.

No more lambs killed. Jesus is the Lamb. To behold him and his mercy is to see universality and intimacy at once. It is to see the red trail of thousands of sheep and goats slain in sacrifice, with no power to atone, leading up to the cross—the saving event.

Jesus was the last lamb; there will be no more sacrifices, no more lambs killed. I am grateful for that shepherd's eye as I seek anew to "behold the Lamb of God." (This devotion is from Frost 1978.)

I Love a Tree

I have a love affair,
a very private thing,
with one familiar oak.
It grows ten paces from our door,
massive and strong and tall.

This tree comforts and encourages,
calls to me as I leave for my next class:
"If I can grow from a buried acorn,
forgotten by one absentminded squirrel,
perhaps you, too, an absentminded professor,
may say something today, and then forget,
something that may plant an oak
in the forests of humanity."

So, I believe in acorns;
this is a part of my teacher's creed.

Unique among our trees,
this oak speaks.
It speaks of power and age,
and deep, deep roots;
but, most of all, it tells of suffering,
in its most stark and visible feature:
no major branch grows toward the east!

In some harsh moment of a long and testing past
my tree has felt disaster,
such force of tragedy that it must live its years
without the slightest symmetry.

Distorted, bent, unyielding in every wind
it wrenches at its roots,
but holds and stands to greet the dying winds
that mark the end of the storm.
This special tree,
I name it Job.

(Frost 1980)

Satan's Slander

DAY 4

"Then Satan answered the LORD, 'Does Job fear God for naught? Hast thou not put a hedge about him and his house and all that he has, on every side? Thou hast blessed the work of his hands, and his possessions have increased in the land. But put forth thy hand now, and touch all that he has, and he will curse thee to thy face.' And the LORD said to Satan, 'Behold, all that he has is in your power; only upon himself do not put forth your hand.' So Satan went forth from the presence of the Lord" (Job 1:9-12).

The adversary, Satan, now appears as a roving spirit, ceaselessly active in aggressive assault on all who, like Job, are in the company of God's servants. His question "Does Job fear God for naught?" exposes the very nerve of the book. Everything hinges on the answer.

Is there true worship on earth? In the case of Job, the Lord issues a challenge in the words "my servant." Are these words true? Does the Lord create faith and establish relationship? Is he able to elicit sincere worship, or is all so-called devotion nothing more than fear-motivated expediency? Is all service and obedience only a kind of slave morality? Is there such a thing as human freedom, or are we, as the behaviorists maintain, conditioned by reward and punishment?

"Does Job fear God for naught?" This is the permanent front line of the Book of Job, the focal conflict and ultimate slander. It slanders the Lord before it touches Job. God is the main character in this story. In New Testament terms, the question becomes: Is the Christian community sustained by love? Is there reality in the body of Christ as faith affirms it? Is the Holy Spirit truly at work in the creation of new beings, reclaiming persons for God? In short, does God have integrity?

The adversary appears as more than a tester of people. He has a quarrel with God, and it is not a lover's quarrel. His question is a sniper's bullet, intended to undermine and destroy. His strategy is to blend truth with falsehood by insinuation and innuendo.

There is truth in the assertion that the Lord has "put a hedge about" Job and "blessed the work of his hands." It is true, too, that the Lord has many false friends and that there is much hypocrisy in us all. But this is not the whole truth about Job or about us. All of God's servants aren't cheap opportunists whose faith is mere superstition and whose religion is all in the purse. God does continue to create and sustain his family in our very midst. This is the continued story. (This devotion is from Frost 1977.)

Why?

"Why did I not die at birth? Why did the knees receive me? Or why the breasts, that I should suck? Or why was I not as a hidden untimely birth, as infants that never see the light? Why is light given to him that is in misery, and life to the bitter in soul? Why is light given to a man whose way is hid, whom God has hedged in?" (Job 3:11-23).

Six *whys*, arrows from the quiver of darkness, have pierced the heart of Job, and now he lets his anger erupt in that aching, hollow word.

With the turbulence of a volcano, Job's hot *whys* tumble over each other. "Why was I not stillborn? Why did my father and mother pledge to care for me when this is the terrifying outcome? Why was I brought this far when the road leads to a dead end?" Job sees himself as God's tragic blunder. He asks to be blotted out.

Our first impulse may be to say, "How melodramatic, how untrue to my life!" But don't we, too, know moments when we hurl our No! into the face of God? Aren't there times of "too much," when we feel trapped by the sheer weight of circumstance? If we don't literally damn the day of our birth, don't our complaints against God and our arguments with him become loud and angry within us? "I wish I'd never been born!" Or, if we don't reject life outright, we may reject our own: "Why wasn't I someone else?"

Surely no one of mature years is a stranger to Job's wilderness of despair. One of the deadliest and most constant temptations is to live by negation rather than by affirmation, to withdraw from courageous participation and turn one's face to the wall.

Job loses his head because he has given his heart. The intensity of his struggle is evidence of the depth of his commitment. Perhaps God takes more pleasure in the child who shakes a fist at heaven than in one who sulks and never looks up. I am reminded of a recent conversation with one whose faith I deeply respect. Frustrated, this person said about God, "But lately I've mostly been yelling at him!" Job yells at God because he cares.

For us, there are still those reassuring words, "my servant," which Job couldn't hear. There is the open road, blazed not by the courage of human heroes, but by the faithfulness of a loving God. To follow this road is to know that the heart's adventure is not in human quest but in encounter with the divine. (This devotion is from Frost 1977.)

Why Such Mystery?

DAY 6

"Why is light given to a man whose way is hid, whom God hedges in?" (Job 3:23).

The spearpoint of Job's many questions is this: Why so much mystery? Why must I travel blind?

This is one of the most profound levels of pain. Job's outcry is more than protest against the anguish of isolation and the loss of his supporting community. It is the supreme agony that comes from trying to make sense of that which lies beyond the reach of logic. It is a crisis in meaning. Job feels himself to be in the grip of ultimate nonsense. His cry is qualitatively above the *whys* of intellectual inquiry. It is a religious outcry, a protest against life's unyielding absurdity, against the incoherence of his situation.

We are meant for this reflective warfare. This is our dignity. We are exploring, probing, searching, and reaching creatures. We are God's hurting ones. Amid the magnificence of Who? What? How? Where? and When? is the ennobling Why? It must never cease to be asked.

We must raise our *whys*. And we will, whether we wish to or not. The mind can no more contain its whys than the body can hold its breath. But there are many ways of asking why. It can be whined or cursed or snarled or pouted. But it can also be prayed.

A why can be a child's empty cup, held up to the love and wisdom of our gracious God. Our Lord doesn't fill it to the brim, but he satisfies each person's need. He is too kind to drown us in all the knowledge we crave. He doesn't give more than we can hold; sometimes we must wait to be made larger cups. Our present questions may be the wrong ones. Then he helps us outgrow them and prompts us to move on to better ones.

God knows that the road we must travel would overwhelm us if we could, in a single moment, see around every bend. He gives us a candle rather than a floodlight—and he promises to be there. He asks us to remember that mystery is one form of his mercy. His aim is not to keep things from us, but to keep things—the best things—for us! (This devotion is from Frost 1977.)

God Has Hated Me

DAY 7 "Surely now God has worn me out; he has made desolate all my company. And he has shriveled me up. He has torn me in his wrath, and hated me; he has gnashed his teeth at me; my adversary sharpens his eyes against me. God gives me up to the ungodly, and casts me into the hands of the wicked. I was at ease and he broke me asunder; he seized me by the neck and dashed me to pieces; he sets me up as his target, his archers surround me. He slashes open my kidneys and does not spare; he pours out my gall on the ground. He breaks me with breach upon breach; he runs upon me like a warrior" (Job 16:7-14).

This is perhaps the lowest point in the mountainous terrain of the book of Job. Here the suffering one bluntly accuses God of being an active enemy. In dramatic detail he pictures the Lord's attack.

I lived with this book for many years, believing that this picture of the Enemy God was overdrawn and untrue to the believer's experience. "It can't be as bad as that!" I thought. The change came, for me, when my own 11-year-old led me into the deep valley of her pain.

She had post-polio surgery involving muscle transplants, radical incisions in the foot and leg. Pain was intense, especially throughout the night following surgery.

I remember her mother and I standing at her bedside that morning, saddened by her drawn face and fevered lips—evidence of the anguish she had endured. My wife spoke to her comfortingly, "But you did pray, though, didn't you?" Looking almost defiantly at us, the child exclaimed, "Yes. But mother, last night, for a while it seemed like God was my enemy!"

Since then I have reflected that if a child can be required to endure such a fearful sense of abandonment, this experience cannot be far from any of us. And I must add that in the intervening years I, too, have looked into such an abyss of spiritual desolation.

It is best to be realistic about the blackouts and eclipses which can come without warning, even to those who have lived with God through the high places and low places of many years. We are indebted to all believers of every age who have survived the wild and lonely heights and valleys of desolation, and reported back to us that God is there. (This devotion is from Frost 1977.)

God's Longing for Us

We are the questing ones, we say,
searching, groping for our God.
But would that we could know ourselves as he
knows us—
fugitives, escapees, rebels,
the wanted ones, the longed-for ones.

God is the questing one, the gaunt and tireless one;
he calls and sends us to one another
to speak the wooing Word, the Name,
to break each habit of ingenious evasion,
and gently block all exits
from chastening love,
to listen for each footfall of those strong feet
that even now follow, follow after.

(Frost 1985)

Any consideration of human longings—the hungers of the heart—must begin with God's expressed longing for us, the people, and his created world. The only safe place in which to think about our complex, elusive moods and feelings is in the love of God. We are mysteries to ourselves and others. Therefore, any attempt to sort out our longings and deal with them wisely can only begin with God's great act of rescue in the sending of the Son.

We do not distort God's truth when we say that God so longed for his world that he gave his only Son, that whoever believes in him should not perish but have eternal life (John 3:16). Whenever we spurn or neglect this loving act, we find ourselves becoming heavy on our hands. Therefore, it is not too bold a claim to say that the first step in dealing with the hungers of our hearts is to relate them to God's eternal purpose which sustains and upholds the world (Frost 1986a).

The Hunger for Righteousness

DAY 9

Deeper than any other need is our need for oneness and rightness with God. This is the longing with many names, the longing for rest, for peace, for home! Deep as it is, sometimes it hardly finds words. I've found myself voicing it in words like these:

Dear God,
I'm sorry!
I really am.
That's all I have to say today;
You understand.
Thank you. Amen.
(Frost 1985)

"Blessed are those who hunger and thirst for righteousness, for they shall be satisfied" (Matt. 5:6). The only righteousness within our reach is that we are in God's reach. The highest use of his power is in the forgiving of our sins. This righteousness is an alien gift, alien in the sense that it can only come from outside us and beyond. Only God can declare it. Nothing we do can bind up our broken relationship with God. Christ is our righteousness. This is grace. And this is always gift! But it can be ours, whoever and wherever we are.

Where forgiveness and salvation are at stake I must not consult my fluctuating feelings. When I say this I'm reminded of my childhood days along the banks of a little local stream, the Riceford Creek. It was a tame little waterflow under normal circumstances, but following a heavy rain it could be quite a challenge for a child to cross it. I learned early, however, that when I stepped from one flat rock to another I was safe as long as I looked at the rocks; but dizziness would surely set in if I failed to concentrate on the unmoving rocks and looked away at the foaming stream. Today I know that spiritual dizziness sets in whenever I seek stability in my moods and feelings—all that foam and spray. I am at peace only when my heart is stayed on Christ, for he is the sole ground of my joy and hope (Frost 1986a).

Certainty

DAY
10

Sermon time in the little chapel
of the local retirement home,
the sermon carefully prepared
and well conceived.

The young preacher
    holding a globe in his hands
praised the goodness
    and the greatness of God,
proclaiming that "he's got
    the whole world in his hands."

Suddenly, from the white-haired
    sage in the second row,
like a blast from a torpedo
came the harsh ejaculation:
"But *you sure would*
    never know it sometimes!"

Enough to sabotage any sermon,
but true to the human situation:
one can't know; one is called to trust;
one can never explain one's faith.
If it can be explained, it isn't faith.
Our certainty is sustained in heaven.

   The old man was right. The mystery of suffering can't be solved in this broken world. No matter how hard I try, I can't satisfactorily prove either the love or the omnipotence of God. I would like to be able to meet the puzzling experiences of life with nothing more than simple logic, but at its center, life calls for humility and trust.
   The word *humility* comes from the Latin word *humus*, which means rich and fertile soil. Humility is the fertile soil of faith. Like soil it receives all that God gives.
   If we insist on immediate proof we oversimplify and falsify our lives. We waste ourselves in anger and hostility toward God. If we surrender to his purposes and follow where we can't see, affirming ultimate meaning without demanding immediate clarity, he will lead us toward the light. And one day we will see. (This devotion is from Frost 1986b.)

What Shall I Say?

What shall I say when they come,
my sister, my brother in distress,
I who am mortal, and so fallible, too?

Shall I say
"Take a trip to the Grand Tetons,
stop by their snow-fed streams,
drink like a breast-fed babe
and try to taste God?"

Or,
"Hold a puppy in your lap
and stroke its silken ears?"

No, not these footnotes,
grace-filled as they may be.
I'll invite them to the
headline—the Name:
"Jesus-Emmanuel (God with us)!
Whisper it, shout it, pray it.
Yes, cry it, cry out against it,
you must, but test it,
taste it, experience how true it is,
how tough and how tender.
Yes, come to him!"
That's what I'll say.

There are times when we must comfort one another even though we, ourselves, are anxious and afraid. And often we can't think of what to say.

When I most want to speak, I find it most difficult to communicate, and when I most need to pray, I am least able to command the thoughts and words. Then I turn to God's many names. They are inexhaustible sources of strength and consolation, and they aren't too much to say, even for a tired heart and mind. I love the name, "Emmanuel," my own middle name. It means *God with us.*

We can find no answers to our most tormenting questions. We know so little about life or death. But we have refuge in Emmanuel. And we can share this haven with our friends.

We walk as children in a dark and strange room. We can't see our way around the corners or the obstacles, but we sense a presence. God's hand holds ours, and he has confided in us. He has told us his intimate, everyday name—Emmanuel. (This devotion is from Frost 1986b.)

God's Way for Me

The profoundest thing
one can say of a river
is that it is on its way to the sea.

The deepest thought
one can think of persons
is that they are citizens of eternity.

Moments and years,
years and moments,
pass like sea-bent streams.
And I? I'm carried on the current
of an all-possessing love.
I'm on my way, God's way for me,
so let it be.

(Frost 1980)

As God's journeying people, we find that sometimes we are driven by changing circumstances, and at other times we are drawn by our own yearnings.

There are journeys of the heart. These are concerned with my loves and loyalties. Only God can free me to forsake the trivial and devote myself to the best. Only God can draw me into a deepening relationship and a greater commitment to God's dream for me.

There are journeys of the mind. These are often threatening to me. Great courage is required when I am asked to let go of old prejudices or faulty judgments. It is difficult to change my patterns of thinking and responding. They seem to be a part of my very bone marrow and blood stream.

Finally, there are the journeys of the feet, the geographical journeys in which I must leave the familiar for the unfamiliar. Most painful among them is the moment when I must leave one home for another. Then I may find that God is helping me to discover that place is not as important as person and presence. In fact, my real and permanent home is in God!

Psalm 90, one of the most ancient of the psalms, movingly affirms this: "Lord, thou hast been our dwelling place in all generations. Before the mountains were brought forth, or even thou hadst formed the earth and the world, from everlasting to everlasting thou art God" (Frost 1986c).

Look Again

"I'm of the old school,
and I'm against it!"

She said it with a toss
of her proud gray head,
and I knew the discussion was over.

I wanted to say,
"But, friend, you forget.
School isn't out yet.
Living is learning,
and learning is living.
It's sad to see you hunker down
and burrow in like that.
Our world is in trouble;
the good old days weren't
good enough, so now we must
re-think what we've accepted as true.
Please look again at all you've looked
at; there's more to be and to become."

(Frost 1985)

As we live in the midst of constant change, fear is our greatest enemy. The only thing that can conquer this is faith.

Fear makes me brittle, and everything brittle or rigid is weak. Faith makes a person pliable and strong. When I travel on the road I ride on rubber, not on cast iron or even tempered steel. Why? Because rubber "accepts" the road. It doesn't fight the hardness of the road. Its very softness is its strength. It yields under the pounding, and in its yielding saves itself from being torn or broken. Metal would not only rob me of my comfortable ride; it would break itself in a few short miles.

It is possible to travel life's highway, fighting everything that happens. I can spend myself in brittle fear, suspicious of every new thing, refusing to move forward, and trying to remain as I am. This makes me a harried settler rather than a free traveler because when I resist change, I miss the rhythm and flow of living. I fight myself and God (Frost 1986c).

My Bush Burned

My bush burned this morning,
burned and was not consumed,
as I gathered with sisters and
brothers in the faith
for the ultimate act of defiance,
a Christian burial service.

My heart soared and sang
as I joined in the demonstration
and hurled the name of Jesus
into the face of the enemy,
Death.

Never have I sensed so deeply
the heaven-sent boldness
of comforting one another
"with the comfort with which
we ourselves are comforted by God"
and taking to the streets again
with other comforted ones
under the defiant benediction.

The bush still burns.

(Frost 1985)

I found my burning bush one day in church, at the funeral of a friend. It happened that he was not only my classmate, but he shared my birthday, too. Because of this coincidence the service was one of high drama for me. I thought of the fact that our journey had begun on the same day, and now his earthly stay had ended, but I was going on!

Never before or since have I felt so dramatically the significance of the Christian burial service. I saw it as a beautiful act of defiance in the face of the enemy, death, the boldest act of all. I drank in the meaning of each promise, line for line, as the Scriptures were read. I rejoiced in every stanza of each hymn. I received what God was giving with bread-hungry eagerness, and faced the future with faith renewed.

When we rose to receive God's benediction I asked myself, "Why do we stand?" Then answered my own question: "Because there is more traveling to do." We face the world again, with changed horizons. Our march continues. "He is risen, indeed, and *it had better be true!*" Praise God, it is (Frost 1986d).

BIBLIOGRAPHY

Anselm
1973   *Prayers and Meditations.* Translated by Benedicta Ward. New York: Penguin Books.

Augustine
1886   *Corpus Christianorum.* Series Latina. Turnholt, Belgium: Brepols.
1954   *Nicene and Post Nicene Fathers.* Augustine Series, Vols. 1-3. Buffalo, New York: Christian Literature Company.
1965-71   *Patrologiae Cursus Completus.* Edited by J. P. Migne. Series Latina, Vols. 34-37. Evanston, Ill.: Adlers Foreign Books.

Baillie, John
1949   *A Diary of Private Prayer.* New York: Scribners.
1962   *Christian Devotion.* New York: Scribners.

Bodo, Murray
1972   *The Journey and the Dream.* Cincinnati: St. Anthony Messenger Press.
1984   *The Way of St. Francis.* New York: Image Books.

Bonhoeffer, Dietrich
1954   *Life Together.* Translated by John W. Doberstein. New York and Evanston: Harper & Row.
1965a   *Ethics.* Translated by Neville Horton Smith; edited by Eberhard Bethge. New York: Macmillan.
1965b   *Letters and Papers from Prison,* ed. 4. Translated by R. H. Fuller; revised by Irmgard Booth. New York: Macmillan.
1966   *The Cost of Discipleship.* Translated by R. H. Fuller; revised by Irmgard Booth. New York: Macmillan.
1970   *Psalms: The Prayer Book of the Bible.* Translated by James Burtness. Minneapolis: Augsburg.
1986   *Meditating on the Word.* Edited and translated by David McI. Gracie. Cambridge, Mass.: Cowley Publications.

Brother Lawrence
1941   *The Practice of the Presence of God.* Translated by G. Symons. Cincinnati: Forward Movement Publications.
1977   *The Practice of the Presence of God.* Translated by John J. Delaney. Garden City, N.Y.: Image Books.

Bunyan, John
1952   *The Spiritual Riches of John Bunyan*. Edited by Thomas Kepler
                        Cleveland: World Publishing.

Cailliet, Emile
1945   *Pascal (The Emergence of Genius)*. New York: Harper and Broth-
                        ers.

Cornelia, Jessey
1985   *The Prayer of Cosa*. Minneapolis: Winston Press.

Donne, John
1953–63   *The Sermons of John Donne*, 10 vols. Edited by George R. Potter
                        and Evelyn M. Simpson. Berkeley: University of California
                        Press.
1978   *The Divine Poems*, ed. 2. Oxford: Clarendon Press.

Doyle, Brendan
1983   *Meditations with Julian of Norwich*. Santa Fe: Bear and Company.

Farrell, Edward J.
1974   *Disciples and Other Strangers*. Denville, NJ: Dimension Books.

Forsyth, P. T.
1953   *This Life and the Next*. London: Independent Press, Ltd.
1954   *Soul of Prayer*. London: Independent Press, Ltd.
1957a   *The Cruciality of Christ*. London: Independent Press, Ltd.
1957b   *God the Holy Father*. London: Independent Press, Ltd.
1957c   *Positive Preaching and the Modern Mind*. London: Independent
                        Press, Ltd.
1971a   *Address to Students*. Grand Rapids, Mich.: Eerdmans.
1971b   *Message to Students: An Anthology*. Grand Rapids, Mich.: Eerd-
                        mans.

Fox, Matthew
1983   *Meditations with Meister Eckhart*. Santa Fe: Bear and Company.

Frost, Gerhard
1977   *The Color of the Night*. Minneapolis: Augsburg.
1978   *Homing in the Presence*. Minneapolis: Winston Press.
1980   *Blessed Is the Ordinary*. Minneapolis: Winston Press.
1985   *A Second Look*. Winston Press.
1986a   *Hungers of the Heart*. Minneapolis: Logos Productions.
1986b   *Silent Spaces*. Minneapolis: Logos Productions.
1986c   *God's Way for Me*. Minneapolis: Logos Productions.
1986d   *It Had Better Be True*. Minneapolis: Logos Productions.

Hallesby, O.
1931   *Prayer*. Translated by C. J. Carlsen. Minneapolis: Augsburg.

Herbert, George
1941   *The Works of George Herbert*. Edited by F. E. Hutchinson. Oxford:
                        Clarendon Books.

Hopkins, Gerard Manley
1953   *Poems & Prose of Gerard Manley Hopkins.* Edited by W. H. Gardner. New York: Penguin Books.

Julian of Norwich
1966   *Revelations of Divine Love.* New York: Viking Penguin.

Kierkegaard, Søren
1962   *Works of Love.* New York: Harper.
1967-78   *Søren Kierkegaard's Journal and Papers.* Vols. I–VII. Bloomington, Ind.: Indiana University Press.

Langer, Jiri
1961   *Nine Gates to the Chassidic Mysteries.* New York: David McKay.

Lewis, C. S.
1947   *Miracles: A Preliminary Study.* New York: Macmillan.
1950   *The Lion, The Witch, and The Wardrobe.* Great Britain: Penguin Books.
1955a   *The Magician's Nephew.* Great Britain: Penguin Books.
1955b   *Surprised by Joy: The Shape of My Early Life.* New York: Harcourt Brace Jovanovich.
1956   *The Last Battle.* Great Britain: Penguin Books.
1958   *The Pilgrim's Regress: An Allegorical Apology for Christianity, Reason, and Romanticism.* Grand Rapids, Mich.: Eerdmans.
1965a   *Perelandra.* New York: Collier Books.
1965b   "The Apologist's Evening Prayer" in *Poems.* New York: Harcourt Brace & World.
1971a   *Mere Christianity.* New York: Macmillan.
1971b   *The Four Loves.* New York: Harcourt Brace Jovanovich.
1973a   *The Great Divorce.* New York: Macmillan.
1973b   *Letters to Malcolm: Chiefly on Prayer.* New York: Harcourt Brace Jovanovich.
1977   "The Weight of Glory" as quoted in *The Joyful Christian.* New York: Macmillan.
1982   *The Screwtape Letters.* New York: Collier Books.

Luther, Martin
1906   *D. Martin Luthers Werke, Kritische Gesamtausgabe*, vol. 32. Weimar: Hermann Böhlaus Nachfolger. Author's translation.
1911   *Luthers Werke*, vol. 45.
1913   *Luthers Werke*, vol. 49.
1914   *Luthers Werke*, vol. 51.
1941   *Luthers Werke*, vol. 9.
1951   *Luther Discovers the Gospel.* Translated by Uuras Saarnivaara. St. Louis: Concordia; reprinted in *The Reformation: A Narrative History Related by Contemporary Observers and Participants.* Edited by Hans J. Hillerbrand. Grand Rapids, Mich.: Baker Book House, 1978

1953, 1956	*A Commentary on St. Paul's Epistle to the Galatians.* Revised and edited by Philip S. Watson. London: James Clarke and Co., Ltd.; reprinted in *Martin Luther: Selections from His Writings.* Edited by John Dillenberger. Garden City, N.Y.: Anchor Books, 1961.
1957	*Luther's Works,* Vol. 31. Edited and revised by Harold J. Grimm. Translated by W. A. Lambert. Philadelphia: Fortress Press; reprinted in Dillenberger's *Martin Luther: Selections from His Writings.*
1959a	*Luther's Works,* vol. 51. Edited and Translated by John W. Doberstein. Philadelphia: Fortress Press.
1959b	*Luther's Works,* vol. 51.; reprinted in Dillenberger's *Martin Luther: Selections from His Writings.*
1974	*Luther's Works,* vol. 52. Edited by Hans J. Hillerbrand. Philadelphia: Fortress Press.

Macdonald, George

1956	*George Macdonald: An Anthology.* Edited by C. S. Lewis. New York: Macmillan.
1965	*Diary of an Old Soul.* Minneapolis: Augsburg.

Merton, Thomas

1956	*Thoughts in Solitude.* New York: New Directions.
1961a	*Emblems of a Season of Fury.* New York: New Directions.
1961b	*New Seeds of Contemplation.* New York: New Directions.
1966	*Raids on the Unspeakable.* New York: New Directions.
1968	*Conjectures of a Guilty Bystander.* New York: Image Books.
1971	*Contemplative Prayer.* New York: Image Books.
1975	*The Silent Life.* New York: Farrar, Straus and Giroux.
1978	*Sojourners* magazine.

O'Connor, Flannery

1979	*The Habit of Being.* New York: Farrar, Straus and Giroux.

Pascal, Blaise

1958	*Pensees.* New York: E. P. Dutton & Co.

Tauler, Johannes

1910	*The Sermons and Conferences of Johannes Tauler.* Translated by Walter Elliot. Washington, D.C.: Apostolic Mission House.
1961	*Spiritual Conferences.* Translated and edited by Eric Colledge and Sr. M. Jane. Cross and Crown Series of Spirituality. Rockford, Ill.: TAN Books.
1985	*Johannes Tauler: Sermons.* Translated by Maria Shrady. New York: Paulist Press.

Thomas à Kempis

1986	*The Imitation of Christ.* New York: Hippocrene Books.

Trueblood, Elton
1948   *Alternative to Futility.* New York: Harper.
1952   *Your Other Vocation.* New York: Harper.
1953   *Recovery of Family Life.* New York: Harper.
1961   *The Company of the Committed.* New York: Harper.
1967a   *The Incendiary Fellowship.* New York: Harper.
1967b   *The Predicament of Modern Man.* New York: Harper.
1968-69   *A Place to Stand.* New York: Harper & Row.
1970   *The New Man for Our Time.* New York: Harper & Row.
1975a   *The Humor of Christ.* New York: Harper & Row.
1975b   *The Essence of Spiritual Religion.* New York: Harper & Row.

Weil, Simone
1973   *Waiting for God.* New York: Harper Colophone Books.
1976   *Intimations of Christianity Among the Ancient Greeks.* London:
                Routledge & Kegan Paul, Ltd.

1979   *The Need for Roots.* New York: Hippocrene Books.
1987   *Gravity and Grace.* New York: Ark Paperbacks.

Wiesel, Elie
1967   *The Gates of the Forest.* New York: Avon.
1972   *One Generation After.* New York: Avon.